D1271082

Katharine and R. J. Reynolds

Katharine and R. J. Reynolds

Partners of Fortune in the Making of the New South

Michele Gillespie

The University of Georgia Press
ATHENS AND LONDON

Athens, Georgia 30602
www.ugapress.org

Set in Minion by Graphic Composition, Inc., Bogart, Georgia
Manufactured by Sheridan Books

The paper in this book meets the guidelines for permanence and durability of the Committee on Production Guidelines for Book Longevity of the Council on Library Resources.

Printed in the United States of America

16 15 14 13 12 C 5 4 3 2 1

Library of Congress Cataloging-in-Publication Data

Gillespie, Michele.
Katharine and R.J. Reynolds : partners of fortune in the making of the new south / Michele Gillespie.
pages cm
Includes bibliographical references and index.
ISBN 978-0-8203-3226-0 (hardcover : alk. paper) —
ISBN 0-8203-3226-7 (hardcover : alk. paper)
1. R.J. Reynolds Tobacco Company—Biography.
2. Reynolds, R.J. (Richard Joshua), 1850–1918.
3. Reynolds, Katharine Smith, 1880–1924.
4. Businessmen—United States—Biography.
5. Businesswomen—United States—Biography. I. Title.
HD9139.R4G55 2012
338.7'63371092273—dc23
[B] 2012010004

British Library Cataloging-in-Publication Data available

For Kevin

Contents

Acknowledgments

I am indebted to many wonderful people in the researching and writing of this book. Let me begin with all the archivists whose knowledge of their respective repositories and whose support for my work has helped me enormously. I would like to thank especially the interlibrary loan staff at the Z. Smith Reynolds Library at Wake Forest University; Max Moeller, archivist at the Hagley Library and Archives; Amy Snyder, curator of the Mount Airy Museum of Regional History; Carter Cue, former archivist, and Tom Flynn, archivist, at Winston-Salem State University; Suzanne Durham, former special collections manager at the Biltmore Estate; Barry Miller, director of communications and external relations, Hermann J. Trojanowski, special projects archivist, and former director of the archives Betty Carter, all at the University of North Carolina–Greensboro Library; Molly Rawls, Fam Brownlee, and the staff of the North Carolina Room at the Forsyth County Public Library; and Robert G. Anthony of the North Carolina Collection at the University of North Carolina–Chapel Hill. I am also most appreciative of the North Caroliniana Society for granting me an Archie K. Davis Fellowship. Mount Airy attorney David Hite, though not an archivist by profession, took time out from his own work to assist me in my research in the Deeds Room of the Surry County Courthouse.

I am especially grateful to the staff of the Reynolda House Museum of American Art, where the Reynolds family papers, along with many family objects and photographs, are housed. Museum director Allison Perkins has been a constant champion of this project. I have benefited greatly from the collegial support of the Reynolda History group: Phil Archer, director of public programs; Camilla Willcox, Reynolda Gardens curator of education; Sherry Hollingsworth, special assistant to Barbara Millhouse; and Todd Crumley, archivist. Their kind invitation to join them for their monthly lunches led to pleasurable discussions about our latest discoveries over the past few years. Sherry Hollingsworth and Todd Crumley have been exceptionally generous with their time and their knowledge of the Reynolds family and available sources beyond those lunch engagements. Sherry has dedicated many years to documenting the lives of the first two generations of Reynolds family, friends, and staff, and I cannot thank her enough for her willingness to share that work with me. Todd put up with my many archival visits, never-ending requests, and incessant questions with the best of cheer over some seven years. I also received valuable advice and support from Richard Murdoch, former archivist, Elizabeth Clymer-Williams, assistant director of collections management, and Kathleen Hutton, director of education. Former chairman of the board J. D. Wilson helped me untangle Roaring Gap connections to the Reynolds family. I am also grateful to Barbara Millhouse, Katharine and R. J. Reynolds's granddaughter and the president of Reynolda House from 1965 to 2004, whose own research into her family history and relating of family memories have enlivened this book immeasurably. Noah Reynolds shared with me important documents in his private collection that greatly enhanced my understanding of Katharine Reynolds's relationship with her oldest son, Dick, at the end of her life. Although I have benefited greatly from all the support of the many people affiliated with Reynolda House and the Reynolds family, let me note that the conclusions and interpretations conveyed herein remain completely my own.

My friends and colleagues in the history profession have supported this book throughout its development and provided me with multiple opportunities to share and hone my ideas. At an early stage, Jonathan Berkey, Vivien Dietz, and Sally McMillen invited me to present my research to their fine students at Davidson College. John Boles brought me to Rice University, where graduate students and faculty in the Houston Area Southern Historians group gave me a great critique of an early paper. Cindy Kierner provided me with the welcome opportunity to present my work in the form of an annual address before the Southern Association for Women Historians at the Southern Historical Association meeting in Richmond. Melissa Walker invited me to present my work to her terrific students at Converse College, and Catherine Clinton and Mary O'Donnell brought me to Queen's University in Belfast to give a paper at their women's history seminar. Bill Link at the University of Florida had me share my work at his Milbauer Seminar, where I received especially valuable feedback from his colleagues and students.

Four special people who were very generous with their time and information have unfortunately passed away since I began this project. Earline King, a well-known local sculptor, shared her memories of first- and second-generation Reynolds family members. So did the ever-gracious Zach Smith, Katharine and R. J. Reynolds's nephew, who spent many hours with me relating stories about his family's past. In a great piece of good luck, I was able to locate Ed Johnston Jr., Katharine's fifth and only surviving child, in Baltimore, and spent several amazing days interviewing him about his family memories. My colleague Jing Wei, who helped me with one technical problem after another for nearly a decade, passed away unexpectedly and much too soon as this project neared its completion. I am so sorry that she and these other kind and supportive people are not here to see the completed book, which bears the fruits of their labor.

I am thankful to Betsy Taylor and Anna Smith for their advice and encouragement early on, and similarly to Joyce Schiller, former curator at Reynolda House. Nick Bragg, former director of Reynolda House, and close friend of the late Nancy Reynolds, has not only shared his extensive knowledge of the Reynolds family with me on multiple occasions but gave me a fabulous tour of Mount Airy and the Reynolds Homestead in Critz, Virginia, too. Beth A. Ford at Reynolds Homestead has been most helpful. Reverend Allen Wright at Reynolda Presbyterian provided insight into the evolution of Katharine Reynolds's and his church. Historian Becca Sharpless gave me great suggestions on researching household relationships across the color line while her important book was in the production pipeline. Likewise Louis Kyriakoudes encouraged me to make good use of the online Tobacco Legacy documents. One fine day I received a thick packet in the mail from historian Lu Ann Jones. Early in her career, Reynolda House had hired her to conduct a series of oral histories with surviving family and staff members. Those oral histories, now over thirty years old, have been an invaluable set of sources for this project. In preparation for the interviews, she had also taken notes on family papers and correspondence now no longer extant, and after coming upon them many years later, thought to send them to me, a kindness for which I will always be grateful. Walter Beeker, southern studies scholar extraordinaire, has provided me with invaluable information and sources as well as his friendship.

I am grateful to my students in my History of the South since 1865 and my America at Work courses who crunched census data with me to get at the key demographic changes taking place in Winston between 1890 and 1920. Many thanks to my former student assistants and summer research fellows: Andrew Canady, Eleanor Davidson, Kyle Erickson, Kate Kammerer, Mary Elizabeth Crawley King, and Elizabeth Lundeen. Their intelligence, hard work, and good cheer have always reminded me how fortunate I am to teach such gifted students, many of whom have since become outstanding graduate students and young scholars.

My sincere gratitude goes to Ken Badgett, independent researcher and an expert on the history of the Piedmont region and the Boy Scouts of America. Ken's deep knowledge of local and state North Carolina history is unparalleled. He is the most meticulous of scholars, and his willingness to share his findings with me and point me in the right direction time and again has made this book far better than it might otherwise have been. I am most appreciative of all my terrific colleagues in the history department at Wake Forest but want to single out Paul Escott, Simone Caron, Tony Parent, Sarah Watts, and Ed Hendricks for their advice and help. I also wish to thank the Kahle family for their generous fellowship; Jacque Fetrow, dean of the college; Jill Tiefenthaler, former provost and current president of Colorado College; Mark Welker, interim provost; and Nathan O. Hatch, Wake Forest president, for their support, and my terrific former colleagues in the provost's office who championed this project too: Deb Alty, Velvet Bryant, Debbie Hallstead, Kline Harrison, Beth Hoagland, Anita Hughes, Rick Matthews, Matt Triplett, and Parul Patel.

I have had the great benefit of an exceptional writing group during the early years of this project and a fantastic reading group at a later stage. Bio Brio members Emily Herring Wilson, Peggy Smith, and Anna Rubino, all inspiring writers and biographers in their own right, not only encouraged me in my earliest fumbling attempts at defining this project but gave me constructive criticism that sharpened my thinking and writing considerably along the way. I will always be beholden to each of them. Likewise, my two years in my Landscape, Place, and Identity reading group with my Wake Forest colleagues Judith Irwin Medera, Gillian Overing, Emily Wakild, and Ulrike Wiethaus encouraged me to incorporate new theoretical constructs and more interdisciplinarity into my analysis.

Several people have been exceptionally generous in reading my manuscript and giving me outstanding feedback. Robert Whaples read an important chapter at a crucial point in the manuscript's development, and I am grateful to him for his evaluation. Catherine Clinton, Paul Escott, Randal Hall, and Bill Link read the manuscript in its entirety and made it far better for their insights, helpful remarks, corrections, and questions. University of Georgia Press senior editor Nancy Grayson has been a writer's dream to work with. She has been unwavering in her support for this project. It has been an extraordinary experience to work with such a talented and lovely person who is such a nuanced reader and gifted editor. The quality of the prose and the arguments herein have been made all the better for her care and attention. The staff at the University of Georgia Press has been exemplary, especially Barbara Wojhoski, who is a truly gifted copy editor; John Joerschke, for his commitment to this project and his ability to keep it marching forward smartly; John McLeod, for his enthusiasm for this book and his marketing savvy; and Beth Snead. As always dear friends have sustained me: Louise Gossett, Peggy Thompson, Jim Barefield, Sue Rupp, Mike Dowd, Leslie Bergman, and all my Tanglewood friends, Linda Dunlap, and Joe and Martha Allman, as have my wonderful family: my parents, Mike and Arlene Gillespie; my aunt and uncle, Ron and Patricia Ekins; my sisters, Heather and Colleen Gillespie, and their families; my sons, Michael and Matt Pittard, and my husband, Kevin Pittard, to whom this book is dedicated.

Katharine and R. J. Reynolds

Introduction

Richard Joshua Reynolds lived the proverbial American success story on a big southern stage. Contemporary narratives extolled his modest origins in the Virginia backcountry and his rags-to-riches scramble to fame and fortune. A rugged individualist with deeply engrained habits of hard work and thrift, R.J.R. used his all-American virtues to build a nationally renowned company in the heart of North Carolina's bright-leaf tobacco country. As a southern-born business hero, he embodied the South's version of the everyman-made-good story. "His career reads like [a] romance," observed a close friend.[1] "He made his many millions," enjoined the *Winston-Salem Twin City Sentinel*, "but he started in a small way . . . with nothing but the best practical common sense, and built a little at a time."[2] Remarked the *Raleigh News and Observer*, "Starting life in modest circumstances he became a multi-millionaire [through] habits of industry and application . . . uncommonly fine business judgment . . . [and] imagination and daring."[3] Self-made men have always stood out in our national imagination as proof positive of America's especially elastic social system. R.J.R.'s archetypal transformation from alleged bumpkin to national business leader made the perennial myth of American meritocracy more convincing to southerners hoping to escape the region's tenacious poverty and benefit at long last from modernization's impact.[4]

R.J.R. turned fifty years old in 1900. He had come to look and act the part of a southern captain of industry. A big man with a graying mustache and beard outlining his mouth, he had boundless energy and stood "well-proportioned and erect as an Indian." Reynolds was uncannily able to motivate all kinds of people, building a national business based on a long-time southern staple crop and a homegrown manufacturing process, and balancing the competing interests of labor, management, farmers, fellow industrialists, financiers, and politicians all along the way. The largest producer of chewing tobacco in the nation by 1900, he had been one among many minor-league tobacco manufacturers at the outset of his career. But the consolidation of the tobacco industry under American Tobacco in the 1890s, the popularity of his Prince Albert Tobacco first marketed in 1907, and the 1911 U.S. Supreme Court decision to break up Buck Duke's American Tobacco monopoly catapulted R.J.R. into the major leagues, cementing his reputation not just as a poor southern boy made good but as a sharp-witted industrialist and down-home paternalist committed to the welfare of his fellow North Carolinians.[5]

Adroit at incorporating new technologies, launching new products, recognizing the value of clever advertising, building distant markets, and maneuvering his competition, he transformed the makeshift market town of Winston into the consolidated industrial city of Winston-Salem. His intelligence was as legendary as his success: "The wonderful grasp of his mind, his power over details, the all but instant solution that came of every problem which presented itself to him; his [was an] understanding of propositions, accompanied by a bold and capable initiative."[6] Yet it was more than his good mind, business acumen, and homegrown fortune that made him such a respected public figure. His reputation as a quintessential southern man committed to kin and community stood out too. His easy familiarity with all kinds of people from all walks of life and his interest in their well-being and success made him a beloved father figure in all communities. "Big Dad Is Dead," ran the headline of tribute from the African American Reynolds Temple congregation when news of his passing reached the city.[7]

The son of the largest slaveholder in Patrick County, Virginia, R.J.R. grew up in an antebellum world where white manhood was defined by honor and mastery. The Confederacy's loss shattered that ideal, leaving in its place increasingly contested notions of southern manliness. The image of the civilized, pious southern gentleman, embodied in the memorialization of Robert E. Lee, competed with a martial manliness that celebrated violence and honor in the name of family and region. These archetypes were crafted not only in response to great loss—the loss of the Confederacy, the loss of slavery, the loss of economic opportunity—but as an implicit critique of the North. Northern men had "domesticated" themselves in southern eyes by embracing an urbanizing, industrializing, and ultimately a "civilizing" world. R.J.R. balanced those two southern ideals of manhood throughout his life. On one hand, he acted out the role of the rough backwoodsman with consummate ease—a listener, not a conversationalist; a hands-on fixer of things, not an abstractionist; a man who preferred horse racing and hunting possum to New York City. On the other hand, R.J.R. was more responsible than any other single person for creating a brand-new urban world in Winston-Salem and ushering in all the attendant social problems, political machinations, and economic ills that characterized northern metropolises. By 1920, the R. J. Reynolds Tobacco Company was the 120th largest corporation in the country and Winston-Salem the largest city in the state of North Carolina.[8]

Despite the modernizing changes his enormous success unleashed in the southern Piedmont, R.J.R. never truly succumbed to the prevailing urban business ideal. His actions conveyed his tacit agreement with the old-style southern boosters, postwar men like journalist Henry Grady and textile manufacturer Daniel Tompkins, who swore by the progressive and civilizing benefits of following the North's economic example. But Reynolds rejected the social and cultural expectations that accompanied that booster role, preferring to be seen as an erstwhile captain of industry rooted in his rural origins, an identity he employed alongside his penchant for paternalism and entrepreneurial savvy. He had no interest in the Victorian posturings that prevailed throughout American culture at that time. While he cut deals and made plans with many of the nation's biggest business elite, he had little time for their social maneuverings or consumer trappings. As long-time family friend Rev. D. Clay Lilly observed, "He was one of the most unaffected, unspoiled men that ever lived in spite of his great wealth and success."[9]

Stories and myths about R.J.R. abound, and previous generations of historians have not been immune to their charms. Scholars have touted the rise of R.J.R. as compelling evidence of a South undergoing fundamental transformation in the first few generations after the Civil War. They point to him as testament to a new kind of southern leader. This perspective has reached across several generations since the publication of C. Vann Woodward's monumental book *The Origins of the New South* (1951). Woodward contended that R.J.R., and many other new men in the New South like him, represented the vanguard of a middle-class revolution. "The passing of leadership from Virginia to North Carolina [was due] . . . to the superior aggressiveness and the bold tactics of a group of young southern entrepreneurs rising with the raw towns of Durham, Winston, and Reidsville," wrote Woodward about the tobacco profiteers. "[These were] new men, uninhibited by the traditions and complacency of the Old Order, William T. Blackwell, James R. Day, Julian S. Carr, R.J.R., the Dukes, and their kind." Southern manufacturers of cotton, lumber, steel, and coal shared the new tobacco czars' outlook and energy. All were bursting with a fresh set of values and ideologies that had won out over the planter elite of the past. The force of their industry making, argued Woodward and a large coterie of historians following him, thrust the American South into a national economy even as it spread new opportunity across the region.[10]

To make this argument, Woodward had turned his back on journalist W. J. Cash's pronouncements a decade earlier in his contentious book, *The Mind of the South*. The Charlotte journalist challenged the iconic story of R.J.R. as a plucky undereducated lad fleeing the Appalachian Mountains to make his fortune in a rough new town.[11] "It was true, wasn't it," Cash wrote in jest, "that Reynolds had come to his destined fief, Winston, in true Dick Whittington style, perched atop a tobacco wagon, and barefoot in his turn, that he had not learned to read and write until he was already a rich man?" Cash argued that the Horatio Alger escapades of R.J.R. and other brash young southern men like him did not so much signal a class revolution as convey the big reach across time of parvenu planters-made-good. "The widening of opportunity was indubitable. The Dukes and the Reynoldses and the Cannons were real," Cash allowed. But in the end these "New Men of the New South" were really not so new. Reynolds and most of his ilk were in point of fact the sons of powerful men who had dominated their local worlds in the Old South. These New South sons had expanded their fathers' commercialized agricultural slaveholdings into urban industrialized ones, and it was this generation (and their progeny) who supplied most of the members of the ruling elite in the new order, just as their elders had done in the old one.[12]

Looking closely at the life of R.J.R. suggests that neither W. J. Cash nor C. Vann Woodward got it quite right. Context means everything in the shaping of opportunity. Reynolds, the master of nicotine, was never the master of slaves, though he wound up controlling the lives of thousands of unskilled urban wage-workers, some white, the majority black. Because he was the son of a successful planter-manufacturer-entrepreneur, he benefited greatly from his father's gifts of education, experience, and money. But the end of the Civil War necessitated he turn away from the plantation and the home manufacture of chewing tobacco toward new forms of economic development that extended well beyond the local economy. He transformed himself, like so many other entrepreneurial men of his time and generation, into a rising member of the urbanizing southern middle class. While Reynolds retained a deeply personal approach in all his human dealings—one far more characteristic of the plantation world, where elite men threaded friendship with business across their entire social sphere—his willingness to embrace innovation in all aspects of his business, deliberately going after national markets and building a competitive urban infrastructure to bolster his ambitions, distinguished him from his father's generation.[13]

R.J.R. began his postwar tobacco business in the very heart of the brand-new bright-leaf tobacco district of North Carolina. His country origins made him so knowledgeable about purchasing, manufacturing, and selling tobacco that he needed no outside expertise or support beyond plentiful capital during his first several decades of business. Once he elected to engage in national advertising, following the lead of W. T. Blackwell and Company, the maker of Bull Durham tobacco, and then Washington and James Buchanan Duke, he became "the leading innovator of his community in technology, product development and marketing."[14] Unlike virtually all other goods manufactured in the South during this period, tobacco products were essentially new to the market. As a result, no other chewing-tobacco manufacturer could outpace him on his home turf.

To create his mammoth enterprise, R.J.R. relied on personal relationships steeped in paternalism to help secure him the relative loyalty of black workers and white managers as well as rural tobacco farmers and middle-class townspeople. He mixed that personalism with a cagey understanding of how to build a national business in a modernizing era. Reynolds played his leadership hand with a real knack for finding the middle ground, and this was reflected in his social outlook too. He never challenged the reactionary greed for power and money evinced by the elite white Democrats in power, those makers and enforcers of a horrific set of repressive racial and political policies, and indeed he moved in their circles. But he also committed to a color-blind philanthropy unusual for a southern industrialist of that era, bestowing frequent gifts on white and black social institutions in equal measure within the scaffolding of white supremacy, which he accepted. His actions taken as a whole suggest not so much an implicit social critique as a tacit acknowledgment of the problematic social worlds split by a deep-rooted racism he helped perpetuate. As a prominent North Carolina manufacturer, he benefited greatly and helped sustain a racist world where blacks were paid less than whites for equal work, if they could get it, since most jobs were color coded, and the most menial relegated to black men and women simply by virtue of their skin color. This racism was hardened by the imposition of a Jim Crow system that denied African Americans their civil and political rights. Reynolds then, like so many other men and women of his generation, embodied an amalgam of Old South and New. Descended from Cash's arriviste planters made good, he embraced business progressivism as a natural extension of his heritage. He did not see himself turning his back on his rural origins in doing so. Reynolds's famous company secured him great wealth. It promoted broad economic development that helped build a New South city almost from scratch and augured rampant change across the region. But under his powerful hand his company also helped preserve a social and political conservatism that he condoned, one that ensured broad social stability by a small moneyed elite and his own prosperity.

Throughout the five decades during which he built his tobacco empire, R.J.R. was neither a polished southern urbanite nor a charming cavalier. Friends and acquaintances alike considered him a shrewd but likable man of the people who was more comfortable checking on his livestock at his Skyland Farm than making Wall Street deals. He was the beneficiary of a particularly southern system of economic and social capital characteristic of the last decades of the nineteenth century and the first decades of the twentieth that turned on four critical hallmarks. The first was place. The southern Virginia and northwestern North Carolina Piedmont region, while long settled, remained relatively underdeveloped after the Civil War. The region lacked a mature infrastructure and an established elite, leaving room for homegrown young Turks and brash outsiders to make their way. The discovery that this unassuming piedmont soil could produce a particularly prized and profitable golden-leafed tobacco encouraged hundreds upon hundreds of would-be entrepreneurs to leave their farms and carve out new professions in this nascent local market. Unfortunately economic hardships pummeled the region long after Reconstruction offset real opportunity for any but the luckiest and best capitalized. R.J. R., on whom fate almost always seemed to smile, had the double good fortune of great timing and significant family financial support. Those factors made all the difference.

The second hallmark of this system was racism. This was a world where those in power committed themselves to re-creating a racialized social hierarchy that bore many of the characteristics of slavery. The rapid postwar adoption of tenant farming and sharecropping as substitute sources of cheap farm labor kept poor farm families indebted to exploitative landlords and merchants in near perpetuity. Opportunity proved so nonexistent in the countryside that many rural blacks understandably preferred seasonal wage-paying jobs in unhealthy and often dangerous factories, even if their wages never equaled those of whites. R.J.R. benefited from this racialized reality, for he was able to hire the majority of his wage-labor force—African American men, women, and children—at bargain-basement prices. The formation of a Jim Crow political and legal system not only denied African Americans basic rights but left them even more vulnerable within and outside the law.

The third hallmark of this system centered on a developing national market and a concomitant change in consumer habits, a reality R.J.R. grasped (and ultimately manipulated) more quickly than most. As demand for tobacco products increased exponentially, he used his central location in bright-leaf tobacco country, long-standing knowledge of tobacco production, familiarity with the latest modes of transportation and their politics, and his inherent savvy to serve a broadening marketplace with a national obsession for chewing and smoking tobacco. These critical particularities of place, race, and market in late nineteenth-century North Carolina all contributed in fundamental ways to the making of R.J.R., but a fourth important factor remains.

Although Reynolds had plenty of brains and talent and was in the right place at the right time to make his mark as a tobacco magnate, he was also the beneficiary of a powerful system of social capital. His extensive kinship network provided him with an important safety net of family members committed to his welfare. That support system was integral in the making of his success and in the making of the larger world in which he ran his business and lived his life. Despite the folklore, Reynolds was never a solitary poor-boy privateer. His identity and his values were rooted in his notion of himself as an integral member of a tightly bound multigenerational family. These thick strands of kinship, tightly roped across place and time, cradled his boldest dreams. So strong was this blood network that when he finally married at the age of fifty-four, he wedded his first cousin's daughter, Mary Katharine Smith (1880–1924), thirty years his junior. In fact, family legend holds that he had already singled her out as his future betrothed while she was still a girl. This pretty, smart, energetic first cousin once removed proved his ideal partner in many ways. Ambitious in all things, she was as committed to his twin passions of family and business as he was, socially permissible pursuits for a talented and driven elite southern woman in the early twentieth century.

There is no question that R.J.R. was the architect of his own considerable success long before he married Katharine. He remained paterfamilias throughout the next thirteen years of their marriage in what proved to be the last years of his life. But during those years, the R. J. Reynolds Tobacco Company moved into the mainstream of American business and secured its greatest commercial successes and growth. Katharine played an important and hitherto ignored role in that development. Together, R.J.R. and Katharine Smith Reynolds constructed a complex American success story with a southern twist. Two relatively ordinary people, born a generation apart in the rural nineteenth-century South, one before the Civil War and one well afterward, built a national tobacco company and shaped a New South city. In doing so, they contributed in critical ways to the shaping of a new southern order. That Katharine Reynolds's role has been omitted in the telling of R. J. Reynolds's alleged climb from rags to riches should not surprise us. After all, there has been little room for powerful women in virtually any of the iconic self-made man stories that have long fired the national imagination.

This book examines the complex lives of Richard Joshua Reynolds and Katharine Smith Reynolds. Both were leaders, R.J.R. in industry and Katharine in social reform, in a state that northerners and southerners alike held up as an exemplar of economic development and southern progressivism. A daring man from the Virginia backcountry who turned homegrown bright-leaf tobacco into pure consumer gold for a full five decades, R.J.R. stood head and shoulders above the dozens of spanking-new captains of commerce in the New South. His wife, Katharine, defined a new kind of southern woman, gracious, self-sacrificing, and ladylike, but modern too, insistent on putting her own ideas into action, whether in her household, in her husband's tobacco company, in her community, or in her state. Their lives, together and apart, tell a larger story about ambition and privilege. Their vaunted social positions as wealthy whites afforded them new opportunities for authority and power. They benefited from the racial ideology of white supremacy and the political system of Jim Crow that denied African American men and women equality. Arguably Katharine, because she understood that the cultivation of men of means gave her a ticket to social and economic influence, gained the most from their marriage. But R.J.R.'s willingness to take on new business risks late in his career and the phenomenal successes that resulted must be attributed in no small way to Katharine, his most trusted advisor.

In many respects their marriage was not unique. Powerful men and women have used the institution of marriage to build their fortunes and extend their commands since the beginnings of civilization, but the mutuality of R.J.R. and Katharine's partnership was exceptional. R.J.R. expected Katharine to take on the conventional responsibilities of their children and their extensive household as his wife and helpmate. But he shared with her the responsibilities of building strong business networks and social relationships. He taught her how to work the stock market and build her own fortune independent of his, gave her carte blanche to build a complex one-thousand-acre estate and model farm, consistently relied on her business counsel, and supported her leadership in multiple social reforms. Although at first glance both seemed bound by traditional expectations about southern men's and women's roles, this was not the case. R.J.R. had forged a new identity as a self-made man rooted in his business acumen and proletarian presentation. That identity, far removed from traditional notions of southern manhood steeped in honor, valor, and the protection of frail womanhood, freed him to respect Katharine as his near equal.

Katharine in her own right was a forceful presence in all her undertakings. In her own way, she was a feminist. She fully supported organized clubwomen in their search for a political voice to solve social problems but refused to wholly commit herself to their ethos of maternal service. While she understood that she could use social expectations about femininity to great advantage as "the gracious mistress of the manor," she did not believe men's and women's most important talents and skills were uniquely different. She had no compunction about pressing forward a number of important social reforms across her community and took credit for doing so. While Katharine masked almost all her actions in ladylike, feminine trappings, she was a shrewd businesswoman at heart, more capable than most men of managing a hundred employees and making a killing on Wall Street. Katharine spent her adulthood extending her freedom and authority as a woman, and R.J.R. supported her in that quest. As much as R.J.R. and Katharine challenged traditional gender conventions by creating a more modern model for marriage, however, they did not question the fundamental inequalities of the new order that they themselves generated and benefited from. While both took action to improve the quality of the lives of many people, white and black, throughout the city and the state as benevolent paternalists, they never questioned the myriad racial injustices imposed on African Americans by white supremacy and the Jim Crow system. Nor were they troubled enough by structural inequities experienced across the whole working class, white and black, male and female, to propose substantive change.

Over the thirteen years of their marriage, Katharine gave birth to four children, two daughters and two sons. She claimed a succession of new social roles, as a leader in numerous local and state benevolent associations; as an advocate for poor, uneducated rural men and women; as a champion for Christian missionary efforts in the Appalachian Mountains and Africa; and as a patron of education and the arts. She worked to ameliorate unhealthy living and working conditions for the poor and had a special interest in the welfare of women and children. Because she lived in a narrow society that afforded few opportunities for women to evince public leadership, Katharine Reynolds ultimately elected to build a model world of her own. She used her estate not only to display her status and power but to support Christian fellowship for family, friends, and neighbors, to educate local children in the three Rs, and to train their parents in progressive farming. Even as she supervised the building and management of the Reynolda Estate, however, she remained a full partner in her husband's business. She also embraced her hostess/socialite role, holding and attending balls and parties and vacationing at resorts up and down the Atlantic coast outfitted in the latest New York fashions. The life of Katharine Smith Reynolds demonstrates how elite white women contributed to maintaining multiple social boundaries even as they stretched gendered ones within marriage, family, and the home and in politics and the public sphere.

It is fortunate that R.J.R. and Katharine lived out so much of their adult lives in the public eye because Reynolds American, the institutional descendant of R. J. Reynolds Tobacco Company, does not make its archives available to researchers. Today it is the second-largest tobacco company in the United States and the maker of such cigarette brands as Camel, Pall Mall, Winston, Misty, Salem, and Kool. Reynolds American remains headquartered in Winston-Salem, North Carolina, where it was founded by R.J.R.

Like the other leading U.S. cigarette companies, Reynolds American fought hard during the U.S. tobacco battles of the 1990s and was a principal defendant in the 1998 Tobacco Master Settlement Agreement. The largest civil settlement in U.S. history, the agreement recouped billions of dollars in expenses from tobacco companies to treat smoking-related illnesses in forty-six states.

Though he was the founder of this important and controversial company, R.J.R. has never been the subject of a biography. Nannie Tilley does dedicate the first chapter of her mammoth business history of R. J. Reynolds Tobacco Company to R.J.R. and his family and their beginnings in Critz, Virginia. Katharine Reynolds's life has been researched and interpreted by the staff of the Reynolda House Museum of American Art, and she is the subject of a 2006 biography by landscape architect Catherine Howett, but her life has not been treated in a fuller biography, one that integrates her public and private lives, and her relationship with R.J.R., Reynolds Tobacco, the city of Winston-Salem, and North Carolina.

Margaret Supplee Smith's outstanding 1989 article examined the Reynolds family home, known as the Reynolda Estate, as part of a national country-home movement. That essay persuaded me that Katharine Reynolds was worth deeper examination, and as I began exploring her life, I became convinced that her life story reflected critical historical change in the period: the impact of industrialization, the rise of new social classes, the remaking of gender roles, and the institutionalizing of racism in the early twentieth-century South, to name the most predominant themes. But midstream into the research, I realized that I could not truly understand Katharine or tell her story without more fully understanding R.J.R. and the company that he created. Although I lacked access to the early company archives, I have had plentiful public documents, including newspapers and trade journals to review. I have also followed Nannie Tilley's source trail religiously and have yet to "catch" her in a factual error. Alas, I could not track down all her sources, some of which came from company files, others of which appear to be no longer extant, making the available printed sources all the more invaluable. I have also used the enormous cache of documents created by the Tobacco Legacy project. Finally, I have been the beneficiary of plentiful private family documents housed in the archives at the Reynolda House Museum of American Art, where I have received exemplary help from the generous and knowledgeable staff there. These terrific resources notwithstanding, it is important to note that neither R.J.R. nor Katharine was an inveterate chronicler. They did not leave dozens of rich letters detailing their emotional lives. Nor did they discuss their political outlook and social ideologies in their limited writings. R.J.R. and Katharine worked hard and played hard. They had little interest in documenting their ideas or their actions, however much we might wish otherwise.

What can a historical study of the lives of Richard Joshua Reynolds and Katharine Smith Reynolds help us better understand? R.J.R. came of age in a post–Civil War society where old models of plantation elites as southern success stories had become defunct. Forced to create his own blueprint for success, Reynolds wielded his deep knowledge of tobacco culture and southern social relations, along with his prescient appreciation for innovation and technology, to build a modern corporation with a national mass-market reach. The story of R.J.R. centers on the ability of this nineteenth-century man, born a slaveholder's son, to live out the quintessential twentieth-century American dream. Examining his life can tell us how and why he was able to achieve this transformation, and in what ways the economy, politics, culture, and society of the South shaped this decidedly American outcome. It can also show us how the changing social and economic order of the nineteenth-century South, caught in the throes of large-scale industrialization, gave way to a modernizing one, as well as illuminate how many vestiges of that old order continued to frame the new one. Ultimately, it highlights the relative malleability of southern social and political constructions within economic transformation—with the stark exception of race.

Katharine came of age a full generation later, the daughter of a middle-class tobacco merchant, with access to hitherto unheard-of freedoms, not the least of which were a college education and paid work. Marriage to R.J.R. created plentiful new opportunities for Katharine to stretch the South's traditional expectations for women. Why she chose some new directions and not others over the course of her relatively short life deserves explanation and reminds us that, while structural change was rampant in this era, political and cultural change (especially as it applied to gender, but also to race and class) still anchored the South to its past.

How Katharine and R.J.R. balanced their embrace of economic change and possibility through the R. J. Reynolds Tobacco Company with political and cultural expectations that molded their behaviors and actions is the last theme of this biographical exploration. The Reynoldses together could accomplish more for each other, for the company, for their community, and for their society than they could individually. In this sense, their complementarities despite their differences in age and sex, and especially their shared temperaments and talents, had a particularly telling impact on the world around them. The two were highly interdependent. R.J.R. benefited greatly from Katharine's understanding of mass consumer culture as he positioned his company to escape James B. Duke's grasp. Katharine thrived on the company challenges that R.J.R. shared with her.

It was not until I had written many chapters of this book that I recognized how deeply personal this project had become. I told my friends and colleagues that I took on this project out of a fascination with two people who pursued two interdependent but essentially American notions of how to live their lives—one as a tobacco industrialist selling the leading national cigarette and commanding world markets by the time of his death, the other building a private estate to raise a family, pursue a series of cultural and social experiments, and secure privacy from the public demands of the family business and the business of social reform. I also liked this project because it was in my own backyard—literally. Yet the lives of these two people, although largely confined to the small city of Winston-Salem, had broader implications for understanding American economic history, the politics of race and class in the American South, and transformations in gender from one century to the next in the United States. The bulk of the documents that let me piece their lives together, as well as the people who remembered Katharine and R.J.R. best, were largely congregated some one hundred years later in this same city where I have made my own home. Local is global, I have always told my students. I was able to act out that belief with this project.

But its personal nature proved deeper than this accident of proximity. It also tapped into my coming of age in the second half of the twentieth century in a culture profoundly shaped by cigarettes. As I looked at the R. J. Reynolds Tobacco Company's campaign for the Camel cigarette launch in 1913 and its role in the origins of mass-market advertising, I thought about my grandmother, who began smoking Camels in the 1920s as a college girl and who as an old woman always had her pack of Camels and cigarette lighter close at hand. I remembered sneaking out behind my house at the age of five with my mother's pack of Salems and a book of matches, striking match after match until I finally lit one. Alas, my inhalations brought me none of the pleasurable associations promised in all those alluring magazine ads and billboards that have since been outlawed. I must also state for the record that this project may represent my need to come to some sort of uneasy peace with my community and my university, for there is no denying that both were built on the backs of tobacco, R. J. Reynolds's tobacco to be precise. The former CEO of Reynolds American recently served on the board of trustees at Wake Forest University and performed her corporate noblesse oblige community role well, heading up local nonprofit campaigns like the United Way with plentiful energy and enthusiasm.

As American society has at long last recognized the devastating impact of smoking not only on individual lives but also on our health-care system, our policies and politics have changed dramatically from the days when smoking was such an appealing cultural pursuit. Corporate tobacco in the wake of the extraordinary Master Settlement Agreement remains tenacious and adaptive though, looking not to American youths for its newest markets but instead to the entire globe. One billion people are projected to die of tobacco-related illnesses before this current century is over.[15] For all their energy and vision, it is hard to believe that R. J. and Katharine Reynolds could have ever imagined the prominence of the tobacco industry in American business, politics, and culture across the twentieth century, nor its lethal reach around the globe across the twenty-first.

1 Making a Business of It

Born in 1850 in Patrick County, Virginia, where the rolling hills of the Piedmont lap the Blue Ridge Mountains just above the North Carolina border, Richard Joshua Reynolds was a child of the slaveholding South who came of age in the tumultuous years of Reconstruction. The third of twelve children and the second surviving son, R.J.R. was descended from two generations of tobacco farmers who valued discipline and thrift but had no aversion to risk. It had certainly taken a streak of the gambler to make good in this part of the world. This southside country was landlocked. Despite the promise suggested by abundant streams and rivers, none flowed into the Chesapeake, and where the waters finally emptied into Albemarle Sound in North Carolina, the shoals were too dangerous for merchant ships to risk. This geographic challenge discouraged settlement in that part of the Virginia Piedmont south of the James River. The migrants who did make their way to Pittsylvania, Henry, Franklin, and Patrick Counties had either gravitated west from the tidewater or east off the Great Wagon Road that pitched north-south along the Virginia valley linking Pennsylvania all the way to Georgia. Promises of tax exemptions lured bold Scotch-Irish and German settlers to the area first despite the French and Indian War. Their arrival pleased the elites. A buffer of "marginal" people now protected the more-established Virginia coast.[1]

These plucky migrants, immigrants and native-born alike, found rich bottom land nourished by clear creeks and streams but just as many rock-strewn hillsides nearly impossible to plow. Once they had finished driving the remaining Native Americans westward, these eager settlers began cultivating the golden leaf on these cheap lands, rolling the precious weed a long way to market in Petersburg or Lynchburg in hogsheads pulled by oxen. By the early republic, several generations of white farmers and their slaves claimed Patrick County as their home, including prominent planter families like the Hairstons who had arrived well before the American Revolution.[2] But new folks were still coming.

R.J.R.'s grandfather, Abraham Reynolds (1771–1838), was one of them. Descended from a Scottish family, he had left Pennsylvania, like so many other pioneers, drawn south by stories of fine harvests, ample game, and plentiful land in the valleys and hilly piedmont along the Appalachians.[3] Although he purchased only fifty acres in 1814, on a fork of the North Mayo River, he amassed some one thousand more over the next three decades. He married Mary Harbour (1784–1853), and the couple raised two boys: R.J.R.'s father, Hardin (1810–82), and Hardin's younger brother, David (1811–36). In a world where formal learning was uncommon, Abraham provided both sons with a modicum of education. Both could read and keep accounts.[4]

Learning to cultivate tobacco, speculate on land, and loan cash were probably more valuable skills than book learning in this particular backcountry, however, and here R.J.R.'s grandfather taught his sons especially well. A believer in the value of practical experience to inculcate self-sufficiency and bring on manhood, Abraham sent his son Hardin, at the age of eighteen, on a five-day trip to Lynchburg with a family slave, hauling a hogshead of tobacco to market over rough Indian trails and across difficult waterways, including the Staunton River. Young Hardin, intent on proving himself, was disappointed when his arduous journey netted him nothing but a ridiculously low price for the leaf. On returning home, he promptly chiseled a hole in a chestnut tree and put a beam through it. He used his new homemade device as a makeshift tobacco press to manufacture tobacco on his own. No longer would he be dependent on the fickleness of tobacco buyers. He used his press to squeeze the moisture from his father's cured leaf, before he spun it and rolled it into tightly bound ropelike strands for smoking and chewing.

Like so many other fledgling manufacturers in southside Virginia, Hardin was soon traveling to South Carolina to peddle his homemade product. Younger brother David followed in his footsteps, exchanging manufactured tobacco for bacon, molasses, wine, tin, and dry goods as far south as Savannah in a mercantile partnership with two other investors. David, who never married, died young in 1836. Hardin's father passed away only eighteen months later. Bereft of male kin and responsible for his widowed mother, R.J.R.'s father was now heir to two considerable estates, including his own birthplace, Rock Spring Plantation.[5]

Realizing that tobacco manufacturing was more lucrative than growing leaf alone and now blessed with abundant land, Hardin Reynolds set two of his slaves at cultivating one of his new properties, Rich Hollow, where they produced six thousand pounds in a season. Meanwhile, Hardin cultivated double that amount at his home place with the help of his other slaves and then bought "much more from the Negroes." He turned his bumper crop into twist and sold it in the Palmetto State.[6] He may not have been producing for a national market, but his clientele was decidedly regional in scope. His contacts and clients soon stretched as far northeast as Baltimore and as far southwest as Alabama. He bought more land and more slaves continuously, working as both a tobacco planter and a tobacco manufacturer, thereby eliminating his dependence on wholesalers and their roller-coaster prices. The more risks he took over the course of his career and the more complex his pursuits became, the more profits he earned.[7]

R.J.R.'s father had no trouble embracing a capitalist ethos in a slave world. Tumbling tobacco prices had pushed the pragmatic Hardin down the road toward capitalist farming and manufacturing early in his adulthood. By 1850, he had quadrupled the number of slaves he owned to thirty-seven and owned thousands of acres of land.[8] His innate curiosity and his willingness to take chances by trying out new enterprises, coupled with his sheer good fortune, allowed him to rebound despite tough times throughout his career, even over the course of the Civil War and Reconstruction, when he lost his enslaved workers and the capital he had invested in them.[9] Hardin Reynolds was no self-satisfied planter aristocrat. His wealth, measured in human property, land, goods, and cash, was never plentiful enough to make him complacent. His was a fluid society where downward mobility was just as likely as a fast climb to financial success. He witnessed and in many cases benefited from the numbers of farmers who had grown increasingly dependent on their cash crops just when prices plummeted. He understood that the market revolution was changing the terms of their economic possibilities.[10] Hardin Reynolds prevailed because he grasped the significance of the capitalist order, with its new opportunities for profit and growth, and balanced it with his agrarian roots. It would be the next generation of Reynolds men, including his second son, R.J.R., who would eschew that balance to fully embrace capitalist economic development in an urban industrializing world.[11]

Hardin Reynolds's economic wherewithal made him influential in his community. As an independent, property-holding white man of considerable means, he was vested with authority over his wife, children, chattel, and in many instances his neighbors too. The local community respected him and was often beholden to him. Known to all by the honorific title "Captain Reynolds," he undergirded his hegemonic power with the letter of the law. Litigious to a fault, he consistently invoked the supremacy of the courts to settle disputes with neighbors over questionable property lines and debt payments. These public records reveal a new breed of planter-cum-petty industrialist, one who ruled his rural empire with an iron fist.[12]

Hardin Reynolds in more ways than one resembled the opportunistic planter enshrined in Cash's *Mind of the South.* Indeed, his 1842 marriage to Nancy Jane Cox (1825–1903), fifteen years his junior, suggested that he entertained some class aspiration and in return ceded his new wife a measure of power and control in the household. The descendant of a local legend—the fiery six-and-a-half-feet-tall Captain Joshua Cox, who had escaped the French and the Indians by swimming miles down the Susquehanna before settling in Stokes County—Nancy had grown up in Quaker Gap, North Carolina, just across the Virginia state line. Her father was a large landholder who could well afford his daughter's penchant for music and culture. Her meticulous handwriting and spelling, far superior to her future husband's, underscored her good education.[13] Hardin built a lovely brick home for his bride and enlarged it in the 1850s as the family mushroomed in size.[14] Originally constructed of red brick (probably made by Reynolds's slaves) laid in a Flemish bond pattern, which signaled superior craftsmanship, the two-story home was adorned with two sets of white plaster columns supporting a single-story portico. A Patrick County landmark because of its location on the well-traveled Norfolk–Bristol road, it was roomy inside by the standards of the time, with a fireplace, windows, and wainscoting in every room and transomed doors on the first and second floors.[15] The furniture and decor were of fine quality for a rural Virginia household. Nearby stood a milk house, also brick, an icehouse, and a smokehouse, with a good spring a quarter mile down the hill. More barns, the factory, and the slave cabins lay scattered beyond the house. Tobacco fields and a cemetery for the slaves stretched beyond the east–west highway that crossed the property a mere hundred yards from the front door.[16]

In a world where women, even elite women, had little social autonomy and no political independence, Hardin's wife and R.J.R.'s mother, Nancy Cox

Reynolds, held her own. She showed a fondness for (and had the means to partake of) bourgeois consumption, rare in this rural part of the world. She owned a pewter tea set, plenty of crystal, and a piano. Upon her marriage to Hardin, according to family tradition, Nancy brought her young personal servant to the Reynolds homestead. The slave proved so unhappy in her new residence that she ran away often, only to be captured and returned to her mistress. Though Hardin eventually insisted the slave be sold, Nancy refused until he agreed to buy her a rosewood and mahogany grand piano.[17] She understood the relationship between property holding and power in this society, challenged a world where a wife's assets could be legally claimed by her husband, and wielded enough clout to advance her own values early in the marriage. She was nonetheless also willing when pressed to sell a human being with whom she had been long intimate.[18]

Hardin and Nancy Reynolds made a formidable partnership. R.J.R. must have learned his respect for strong women by observing his mother and her role in his parent's marriage. A hard-working, resilient couple blessed with good health, Hardin and Nancy were ambitious for themselves and for their children. Those attributes nevertheless did not protect them from heartache. Nancy Jane gave birth to sixteen children over the course of their thirty-nine-year marriage. While enduring that many pregnancies and births stands as testament to her physical strength at a place and time when female mortality during childbearing years was high, only half of her children lived to adulthood. These premature deaths meant Nancy, Hardin, and their surviving children, especially the oldest five (Mary Joyce, Abraham David, Richard Joshua, Hardin Harbor, and Lucy Burrough, all born between 1844 and 1858) had to endure considerable sadness. Twin infant boys died five days after their birth in 1849. Another set of twin boys was born dead in 1865. But the loss of those newborns paled beside the death of sixteen-year-old Agnes Catherine, who was enrolled at Danville Female Academy when she died in 1861. Then, just a year later, after Hardin insisted on vaccinating each of his children with the cowpox virus to protect them from smallpox, John Gilmore, five years old; Nancy Bill, three years old; and Earnest C., nineteen months old, died within five days of each other after receiving the inoculations.[19] Nancy bore three more children after this tragedy, all of whom lived to adulthood: William Neal (1863); Robert Walter (1866); and Nannie Kate (1870).

The Reynolds family and their slaves did not live in isolation. The highway brought them the latest news from Bristol, Roanoke, Norfolk, and beyond. The Reynoldses were active in their church and community. The family traveled to nearby towns, including Mount Airy, Lynchburg, and especially Danville to shop and trade. But their relationships with their kin came first and foremost. Nancy Reynolds remained close to her older sister, Catherine; Catherine's husband, Madison Smith; and their four children. The two families spent time together and shared similar expectations for their offspring. Not surprisingly given their ages, R.J.R. and Zachary Smith (1847–1938), Catherine and Madison's youngest child, shared a special friendship that lasted a lifetime. It was Zachary's oldest daughter, Katharine, whom R.J.R. would wed in 1905.[20]

By 1860, when R.J.R. turned ten years old, Hardin Reynolds had accrued substantial holdings. He held title to nearly two dozen properties, including some eight thousand acres in Patrick County and some three thousand acres in Stokes County worth $40,000. His Rock Spring home alone was valued at $11,000, and his personal estate added up to a hefty $10,500. He had increased his slaveholdings sixfold in twenty years' time, with fifty-nine slaves to his name on the eve of the Civil War, making him one of the larger slaveholders in Virginia, a state where the average holding was nineteen. He was certainly the largest slaveholder in his county.[21] Hardin operated a tobacco manufactory. He also ran a thriving country store that sold corn, rye, and oats, as well as coffee, sugar, salt, flour, bacon, molasses, cloth, thread, pins, needles, peaches, rope, suspenders, boots, clothes, spoons, and even manure. His account books after the war document exchanges with dozens of white and black men and women in cash, goods, crops, and services (e.g., butter, woven cloth, six days of work, tobacco). They include formal accounts with his own family members (son R.J.R. owed six dollars for rent, for example, while grown daughter Mary owed for jeans, thread, shoes, cabbage seed, blacking, and a boy's hat).[22] Ever the entrepreneur, Hardin Reynolds built a strong business model based on meeting local needs and maintained it even in a challenging postwar economy. While he continued selling his own home-produced chewing tobacco, he also sold leaf to larger concerns as far away as Baltimore, increasingly taking advantage of the Richmond and Danville Railroad line completed in 1848. He traveled to Danville, only about fifty miles away, not only to sell his crop but to acquire a broadening array of goods for his store.[23] In addition to growing foodstuffs and tobacco, manufacturing the tobacco, and running a store, Hardin studied the transformative power of the railroads and was purchasing their stock by 1869.[24]

Like other men of his generation, Hardin had benefited from the long marriage between world demand for tobacco and the relative ease with which it could be grown in his Piedmont surrounds. That he and other farmer-manufacturers had secured new markets for twist and plug to the south and west had heralded a new chapter in the history of Virginia tobacco, slavery, and the Atlantic market.[25] Slavery was critical to Reynolds's success and a requisite for his Rock Spring business plan. Hardin's investment in the peculiar institution was not motivated by paternalism or benevolence. He valued hard-working bondspeople because they helped him make more money. He bought "Big Jack," a young boy, in 1849 from M. T. Smith because the youth's size and strength prefigured a tremendous capacity for work. In 1858, he paid a fifty-cent tax on Jack for a legal permit allowing him to perform a skilled trade, probably blacksmithing, wagoneering, or distilling. Hardin made more profit from Jack's artisanal output than by working him in the fields. Reynolds willingly exchanged his slaves and their families to secure debts.[26] Yet he also expected his slaves to be loyal, even during the chaos of the Civil War. Such was his confidence that he sent two slave drivers with his oldest son, Abraham David, over mountain routes crisscrossed by Union soldiers to procure salt in 1862.[27]

Hardin was dumbfounded by the departure of many of his slaves at war's end. Yet he was not the most generous of landlords to his newly freed tenant farmers during Reconstruction. It took the commitment of his two oldest sons, A.D. and R.J.R., as well as his son-in-law, Andrew M. Lybrook, who had married Hardin's oldest daughter, Mary, to get him back on his feet in a world newly devoid of slave labor. In these latter years, Hardin may have turned his racist pragmatism into white paternalism. Well into the twentieth century, Patrick County residents loved to tell the story of Aunt Kitty Reynolds, a Rock Spring slave, who coming upon her master being gored by an angry bull beat off the animal with a stick. At emancipation, Hardin Reynolds assumed care of Aunt Kitty for the remainder of her life, allegedly as payback for her bravery. Lybrook, a lawyer and judge, even defended her offspring against murder charges in a legal case that eventually wound its way to the U.S. Supreme Court in 1881.[28] Although relatively scant, the evidence about Hardin Reynolds's relationships with his slaves and later his former slaves-turned-free-people suggests an antebellum insistence on their value first and foremost as workers and investments, not as people, perhaps tempered in the wake of the war by emancipation and long-term personal relationships.

By 1882, the year Hardin Reynolds died at the respectable age of seventy-two, three generations of Reynolds men had relied on African American labor, slave and free, to grow tobacco on the family homestead and run a home manufactory, a common enough practice in the Piedmont up-country. "Nearly every planter who raises tobacco to any extent is a manufacturer" who uses slave labor, observed Joseph Martin about Patrick County. Still, as Martin pointed out, only a few could "make a business of it."[29] Trained by his father before him, Hardin Reynolds made an especially successful business of it, and he trained his sons to do likewise.

By the 1850s, when R.J.R. was just a small child, Hardin had turned his tobacco factory into his principal income, supported by his general-merchandise store. Throughout Patrick County and all those parts of Virginia and North Carolina served by the Staunton, Mayo, and Dan Rivers, farmers had begun buying up the local leaf in the 1830s, manufacturing it into plug for chewing and snuff, and selling it in the southern and western backcountry, rather than taking it straight to market, where they faced weakening prices.[30] But most could not sustain a profit from home manufacture over the long term. Business historians have identified the Jacksonian era as a time when family businesses and entrepreneurial fever changed the contours of economic development in the United States. Patrick County was no exception. By the late antebellum era, only a handful of home enterprises in this locale, including Hardin Reynolds's, had survived. The switch from family businesses to a corporate capitalist order with the establishment of more heavily capitalized and more complex manufacturing centers, especially in growing towns like Richmond, Petersburg, and Lynchburg, had increasingly choked off country efforts.[31] This was a rural world in transformation despite its rootedness in a plantation economy based on slave labor. Important commercial and trade centers were developing almost overnight, connecting the Piedmont to a new social and economic system that was decidedly modernizing and capitalistic.[32] Although Hardin Reynolds and the owners of the remaining five or six other successful ventures in Patrick County had to vie with new factories in nearby Danville to buy leaf, they managed to stalemate their town competitors, ultimately preventing them from attaining the size and scale of urban tobacco factories elsewhere in

Virginia.[33] But these planters needed more than a plentiful supply of local tobacco and ample slave labor to keep town manufacturers at bay. They needed a good manufactory of their own to produce plug and twist.

By 1860, urban tobacco manufacturing had experienced significant technological change. Transformation in the countryside was much slower. Although most rural manufacturers had eventually exchanged their wooden screws for iron ones to press their tobacco as tightly as possible, none had purchased the new state-of-the-art hydraulic presses quickly adopted in urban factories. Home factories remained fairly traditional. They contained twisting benches, where workers sat to roll and snake the leaf. Stoves, boilers to add flavorings, cutting knives, and scales and balances were also requisite for these operations. With the spread of home manufacturing in the 1830s and 1840s, the use of special flavorings began to occur in the countryside. Druggists bragged to home manufacturers about their oils, spices, and licorice available for purchase to enhance taste. Meanwhile, mechanics and machinists advertised the virtues of their various presses and screws, as well as their services. R.J.R. and his brothers learned the mechanics of the press early in their youth, the relative value of one flavoring over another, the factors that led to fluctuations in tobacco prices, and the chief criteria for selecting the choicest leaf.[34]

At Rock Spring, Hardin Reynolds used as much as twenty-five thousand pounds of tobacco each year to make twist, at least three times his own crop. Falling tobacco prices had actually benefited him over the course of the 1850s, for he could now buy tobacco as cheaply as he could grow it. While declining tobacco prices had not helped those tobacco farmers forced to give up manufacturing thanks to the competition from town factories, he was in fine shape. The panic of 1857, a bumper crop in 1859, and national political debates over the winter of 1859–60 had reduced local tobacco prices all the more, and to Hardin's great advantage, for the demand for his plug never declined.[35] He also benefited from a broad network of commission merchants in Danville, Richmond, Baltimore, and New York who sold his plug on commission.[36] Hardin's embrace of industrialization was no maverick pursuit. Slaveholders and nonslaveholders across the region actively sought out market development and fought hard for the economic advantages it secured them. Hardin was just especially good at it.[37]

Hardin had understood that his successes to date had rested on his ability to recognize the technological and market innovations that would advance his business. He expected each of his sons to do likewise as he trained them, one by one, in the family business.[38] As a grown man, R.J.R. frequently boasted that he had learned the tobacco trade by working as a hand in his father's factory, an embellished story that undoubtedly ingratiated him with his hundreds of workers and furthered his reputation of rags-to-riches success.[39] In reality, although he had in fact worked in the little plug factory on his father's farm, young R.J.R. had done so as the slave owner's son, with the requisite privileges that went along with that status and with the stipulation that he learn this part of tobacco production along with all the other ones. Hardin understood what scholars today confirm. Children involved in family work while growing up usually develop into entrepreneurial thinkers and problem solvers.[40] This imposing head of the family expected all his sons to acquire a strong work ethic, pay attention to detail, cultivate people skills, grasp the fast-changing contours of the market, and make sound decisions about money. Each of these skills was attributed to R.J. R. many years later. His exceptional business acumen, cultivated in its earliest form at the Rock Spring plantation, would turn him into a twentieth-century southern legend.[41]

By the time R.J.R. reached eighteen, he was a physically imposing young man at six feet two inches and 215 pounds.[42] A friend described him as "active, strong and vigorous."[43] Each day he set out to work in the family tobacco business eager to meet his father's approval and expectant in the knowledge that he and his brothers must fill Hardin Reynolds's shoes one day. The air around the factory shed was redolent with the smell of cured tobacco and the sweet concoction that flavored it. Factory hands took leaves of tobacco from hogsheads, sprinkled them with water to soften them, and then de-stemmed and dried them. Big pots of flavoring, usually a licorice and sugar mixture, needed constant stirring to prevent burning. Slave workers, eight men in 1850, and seven men and seven women in 1860, a sign of the manufactory's growth (as well as Hardin's lack of interest in respecting sex differences among his slaves), poured the tar into vats. The leaves were thoroughly saturated with the thick syrup, left to dry, sprinkled with more flavorings, and finally molded into lumps.[44]

The makeshift factory was not a particularly safe place to work. The grown slaves kept all children, free and slave, away from the boiling kettles and the loose knives. The hands used the latter to trim the newly wrapped plugs down to the right weight and shape, varying from pocket-size pieces to full-pound chunks. The lumps were put into heavy pans and then into the screw press. The strongest slave men lugged on the press lever to eliminate all the moisture in the cured tobacco. After three presses, the hands boxed the plugs, gave them a final prizing, and declared them ready for delivery.

R.J.R. learned the business of growing tobacco as well as manufacturing it, of course. This education too was critical. The particularities of soil and climate in this region necessitated the acquisition of knowledge from experienced growers to succeed at it.[45] Tobacco cultivation, even in good soil, was labor intensive and tricky. The best tobacco farmers devoted loving attention to the money crop. During the winter, farmers prepared new plant beds, burned off the weeds and brush, then sowed the seed, before finally hoeing the little hills to protect the fragile seedlings over the spring. Then the plantlets had to be moved from the beds to the fields at just the right time, after the last frost but before the killing heat of a premature summer. They needed to be fertilized once they had established themselves. During the hottest months, the now fast growing plants had to be "topped," their flowers removed to encourage more leaf growth, and the bottom leaves removed as well. Corpulent caterpillars, their color camouflaging them as new growth, had to be handpicked from the waist-high plants. The weather could be the farmer's best friend or his worst enemy. Too much rain proved crueler than drought. Sudden storms could produce hail that flattened the entire crop. Even a light rain could spell trouble. Tiny droplets magnified the sun's rays, leaving burned spots on the golden leaves that lowered their value. In September the leaves were cut and set on sticks, then cured, initially with charcoal fires but increasingly with flues by the late nineteenth century.[46] Once cured, the leaves were stripped of their stems, tied by hand, and packed into hogsheads weighing 750 to 1,000 pounds for storage. The rhythms of the long tobacco season and its many kinds of demands were realities all members of the Reynolds household, white and black, slave and free, knew by heart. Every year was different, making the very act of growing tobacco suspenseful.[47]

Theirs was a growing market. The Napoleonic wars had unleashed a European craze for smoking tobacco and a return to the eighteenth-century habit of using snuff. By midcentury, Cubans had turned from sugar to tobacco as their main export and were producing Spanish cigars that were the delight of the Old World. Americans soon grew as addicted to nicotine as their European counterparts, but most preferred their "chaw" over the Continental fondness for pipe tobacco, cigars, and, increasingly, cigarettes. Much to the disgust of European visitors, including Charles Dickens, American men and many women, too, openly cut off a wad of tobacco from the plug they kept in their pocket, then chewed the wad repeatedly like gum, producing copious amounts of mud-colored saliva that necessitated frequent expectoration. Spittoons abounded in nineteenth-century American society, as did public signs demanding the emission of said secretions into the vessels provided. The chewing habit would not be discouraged by public health authorities in the United States until the 1880s. By 1886, the journal *Tobacco* was extolling the virtues of pipe smoking for men. Not only was it much less messy than chewing tobacco and "a great safeguard against infectious diseases," but pipe smoking fit neatly into the Victorian lifestyle. Outdoors, pipe smoke kept the flies away at picnics and while fly-fishing. Indoors, it cultivated relaxation over a book, the admiration of women, and an excuse to stay home. Meanwhile, the cigarette, even less messy than pipe tobacco and much easier to transport, consume, and extinguish, had just begun its American ascendancy. R.J.R., who learned tobacco making at his daddy's knee, remained the master of plug long after most other U.S. manufacturers had switched to more socially acceptable tobacco products—pipe tobacco and cigarettes. Eventually, however, even he would commit to cigarettes and in doing so propel his company to the top of the industry, first with Prince Albert pipe tobacco and then with the Camel cigarette during World War I.[48]

But in rural nineteenth-century southern Virginia, plug remained the name of the game. The dwindling numbers of home manufacturers who had survived the market challenges of the 1850s relied for their sales on an expanding rural market that stretched down the spine of the Appalachian Mountains and across the shoulders of the southern Piedmont. Like Hardin Reynolds's factory, virtually all rural proto-industrialist ventures were vertically integrated. Farmers and planters-turned-home manufacturers grew tobacco, produced plug from their own supply and that of others, and sold their product themselves. Although most of the tobacco in the mid-nineteenth-century United States was distributed by northern factors, hundreds of men from across the south Atlantic, including Hardin Reynolds, loaded two-horse wagons with several dozen boxes of "chaw" to sell each fall and winter beyond their own locale. These peddling farmers traveled throughout the backcountry of the Carolinas, Georgia, Tennessee, Alabama, and sometimes farther. They preferred selling their plug for cash but bartered for produce and goods when specie was scarce. These sales treks brought them romance and adventure as well as profits. It was not uncommon for these men to find wives along the way. Nor was it uncommon to be robbed by highwaymen.[49]

Because Hardin was knowledgeable about all stages of tobacco cultivation, production, and marketing and because he was a prominent property holder in the region, he remained a respected businessman and citizen over the course of his long life.[50] He kept abreast of the world by subscribing to several newspapers and magazines and collected news from the draymen who hauled goods back and forth on the Bristol–Norfolk highway just beyond his front door.[51] A merchant, trader, planter, manufacturer, and even informal community banker, he was in addition a devout Methodist and a charitable man, known to provide for poor whites during Reconstruction years.[52] He cashed pensions for Confederate widows and provided grain to indigent female-headed households.[53] He expressed his commitment to his faith by regularly leading his family in prayer, not only at the closing of each day like many families but also at dawn, testament to his great piety according to his neighbors.

Hardin Reynolds's godliness did not hamper his profit making, even during the Civil War. The Reynolds family suffered much less than most Patrick County residents between 1861 and 1865. On the eve of national strife, Patrick County was inhabited by 9,300 people. Slaves comprised a fifth of the population and were owned by about 5 percent of the white inhabitants. Despite the small number of slaveholders, 80 percent of Patrick County voters had favored secession, not anticipating the long-term suffering that the creation of the Confederate States of America would generate in their lives. Over four long years, Patrick County's white families withstood inflation; labor shortages; confiscation of slaves, livestock, and foodstuffs; growing numbers of indigent soldiers and their families; rampant disease; and the deaths of their men on the battlefields. Black families bore the same conditions but had more opportunities for resistance and even escape and toward the war's end could anticipate their freedom. Patrick County, although removed from the scene of battle, was a tumultuous place during wartime. Pacifist Quakers and Moravians sought sanctuary here, as did armed Confederate deserters and Union sympathizers.[54] Nonetheless, Confederate loyalty remained high among the native-born community, where wartime deprivation was considered a sign of patriotism in sharp contrast to the disaffection of nearby North Carolinians.[55]

The Reynolds family was affected by wartime hardship and peril, though less so than many other Patrick County families. At the outbreak of war, Hardin was too old at fifty-one to be conscripted and his oldest sons too young (A.D. turned fifteen and R.J.R. eleven in 1861). They were expected to supply troops with foodstuffs, however. Hardin donated twenty-seven pounds of bacon, for example, to Lieutenant Page's detachment of cavalry.[56] But by the spring of 1862, the Reynolds family like so many others had begun to suffer some critical shortages, especially of salt. Over the winter of 1861, Union forces had gained control of the salt mines in western Virginia, leaving thousands of inhabitants in nearby Confederate states with no means to preserve their beef, fish, and pork. Hardin, knowing that Confederate troops were pressing ahead to retake the mines, sent A.D. and a slave hand over the mountains and across enemy lines to Charleston, Virginia, to secure this white gold. The trip was far more dangerous than his own rite of passage to Lynchburg some thirty years earlier, but his fifteen-year-old son not only managed to sell along the way the half load of plug he carried but found shelled corn to feed his four-horse team. When A.D. entered Raleigh County, "whare Evry thing was distroyed" by the fighting, his sleek team of horses surprised the other wagoners, who had secured only half loads from the salt mines to spare their starving teams, some of which were dropping dead in their traces. By contrast, A.D. brought back four thousand pounds of salt, so much that the family was able to meet its own needs and sell the excess for the remainder of the war.[57] One wonders how the wider community responded to the Reynolds family's wartime profiteering.[58]

A.D.'s astonishing success prompted Hardin to send the teenage boy on a second expedition with two slaves the following year. This time A.D. traveled south to the cotton mills in Randolph County, North Carolina, to purchase cotton yarn to make cloth to replace worn-out clothing. Hardin planned to sell the scarce commodity at the family store. So intent was A.D. on fulfilling his duty that he defied the smallpox quarantine he encountered upon his arrival in Deep River and purchased the cotton goods anyway. He returned home not to triumph this time, however, but to his father's wrath. Hardin ordered A.D. and the slaves who accompanied him to unload the cotton into a barn basement and then told A.D. to be prepared for quarantine in a cabin on the hill, tended only by slaves. A.D. was aghast, recalling,

“[My father] centured me very Sevierly for being So reckless [and] Said we would bring death to my Brothers and Sisters,” a prophecy that proved true. Hardin so feared the disease that he immediately had his whole family inoculated but lost his three youngest children anyway, whether due to bad vaccine or the ravages of the disease A.D. had brought back with him we do not know. Although the Reynolds family was not alone in such heartrending losses, for hundreds of Patrick County children died of smallpox, diphtheria, and fevers over the course of the war, few other families could blame their oldest son for such sadness.[59]

Those terrible deaths left father and oldest son burdened with an awful guilt. The tension between the two must have been unbearable. Hardin and his wife wrote Virginia Military Institute (VMI) within two months after the death of their youngest children to request a place for A.D. The young man enrolled in the summer of 1863, but after five forced marches to keep the Yankees at bay and less than a year of classes, he returned home in March 1864 to report that he had been dismissed and was now old enough at seventeen to enlist in the Confederate army (thanks to expanded age qualifications). A.D. departed for Taylorsville, where he made a compelling speech; fifty years later he related that it had proved so rousing he had been elected company captain, despite his older opponent's attempt to secure votes with liberal amounts of apple brandy. A.D. went on to command sixty-six men in Company I, Fifth Battalion Virginia Reserves, and was promoted to major within a year.[60]

Once A.D. had departed for VMI, R.J.R began to fill his older brother's shoes.[61] The heir apparent after A.D.'s tragic error in judgment, R.J.R. took over his brother's farm responsibilities, working more than double time to make up for the loss of seven bondsmen and all the wheat and corn confiscated by the Confederacy.[62] Fortunately, although Patrick County suffered from home-front scarcities throughout the war as well as the unease caused by delinquent soldiers on the move, the Reynolds farm did not experience physical threat from military action until the early spring of 1865, when Union raiders swooped in from eastern Tennessee across the mountains into southwestern Virginia and then dipped into the North Carolina Piedmont. Led by Maj. Gen. George Stoneman (1822–94), the troops marched through Patrick County in March and April, burning mills and wagons, destroying bridges and rail lines, capturing munitions, and stealing horses and supplies. Upon reaching Mount Airy, North Carolina, just across the

Patrick County border, in early April, the troops found the town nearly deserted. "I don't know how many there was but it was the most men I ever saw and some say ten thousand," wrote one young woman to another. "They commenced coming about dark Sunday night and kept coming all night. Most all the men in town left and run to the woods," she reported. Rock Spring did not escape Stoneman's raiders, but fifteen-year-old R.J.R. and his brothers managed to keep the family's horses and other livestock safe by hiding them high up on No Business Mountain.[63] When R.J.R. returned to the homestead after their departure, he was relieved to see no buildings had been burned, although the family's provisions had been pilfered. More shocking to the family than the loss of foodstuffs was the departure of their male hands, who like so many other Patrick County slaves, had fled their masters to follow behind Stoneman's cavalry to gain their freedom.[64]

Meanwhile, Maj. A. D. Reynolds and his Company I, mostly old men and young boys, saw no action until late in the war. After Union troops occupied Richmond on April 3, 1865, A.D. stopped at Rock Spring to visit his family on his way west to the trans-Mississippi theater. He recalled about that fateful visit, "My father was a fine disciplinarian and always Kept me at a distance and I never Knew he loved me until then[.] [W]hen he saw me he ran to meet me and threw his arms around me." Hardin told him, "[M]y Son the Yankees have been here and torn up Evry thing and my Negro men have all gone with them but Since you have Come back alive and well it is all right[.] [W]e Can rebuild our lost fortune." Hardin's joy at his eldest's return and the degree to which he wanted to depend on A.D. meant everything to this prodigal son. "I was glad my father made this demonstration[.] [I]t made a better man of me—Love is the greatest gift that was bestowed on man—it has brought many wayward Children[.] [P]arents Should never give up a wayward child[.]"[65] We do not know what R. J. Reynolds made of this homecoming, but it augured a new period in which A.D. reentered his father's good graces. At war's end, after helping his father recover from his post-emancipation woes, A.D. attended school in Baltimore and then taught for two years, only to return to Rock Spring following "a pathetic appeal from [his] old father . . . to go into business with him."[66]

Filial duty was requisite in the Reynolds family. No matter how estranged A.D. felt from his father after the death of his siblings, no matter how hard he had worked to establish his own life after the war, he let himself be pulled back into the family fold. He became a partner with his father for a time, and his parents remained committed to his success and happiness, evidenced, in one instance, by their sending out invitations to his wedding to Sarah Hage in 1873.[67] Although his younger brothers did not struggle between responsibility and freedom to this extent, they too accepted their father's expectation that they learn the family business. Like A.D., they benefited from doing so. Hardin was a smart man. He had long ago learned to capitalize on his own labor, even in a slave economy. His continued purchase of land, along with his rotating business partnerships with his sons, showed his commitment to capitalizing on their labor too. But this mind-set also revealed Hardin's limitations. For his sons to advance economically, they would have to move on. Patrick County and its surrounds had proffered significant opportunity for two generations of Reynolds men, but the third generation had to strike out for new places and apply new approaches to continue making money.

The story of the rise of the Reynolds men personalizes the history of economic development in modernizing America. With few exceptions, American entrepreneurs have descended not from wealthy but from middle-class families who valued hard work and new ideas and were willing to take risks. Hardin Reynolds used his inheritance along with his own sweat equity and that of his slaves to build a business model that survived and even thrived after the Civil War, despite the loss of his biggest capital investment, the more than four dozen human beings he had once owned. His continued success and the incorporation of his sons into that business model secured each of them, and especially A.D. and R.J.R., enough money to finance their own ventures, but necessitated their moving elsewhere to do so, like so many other young men on the make in late nineteenth-century America.[68]

As committed as Hardin was to teaching his sons how to be entrepreneurs, he and Nancy also invested in their education.[69] They believed, like their Critz neighbors, that "with a good solid education, you can always have your way in every position in which you are placed no matter if you have not a dollar you can make it."[70] R.J.R. learned reading, writing, and mathematics, but whether from his mother, a hired tutor, or a teacher in a neighborhood country school is unclear. Family records contain receipts for country school costs and salaries for tutors for several of the Reynolds children before and after the Civil War, but there is no specific bill designated for R.J.R.'s primary schooling.[71] R.J.R. later bragged that in his youth he "studied little and learned less," despite an aptitude for numbers. He told a close friend that his parents encouraged him to become a tobacco businessman because of his poor eyesight.[72] R.J.R. disliked formal learning and suffered from what was probably mild dyslexia. He tended to transpose letters and could not spell particularly well. His parents may have wanted to blame these struggles on bad vision. A.D. later recounted that R.J.R.'s academic difficulties were due to "an ocular defect, which made it impossible for him to see more than one letter at a time," but there appears to be no basis for this statement. R.J.R. had no trouble registering numbers, and his few extant letters are vast improvements on those of his father in respect to handwriting, spelling, grammar, and style. Whatever the cause, R.J.R. did not embrace his schooling, despite his parents' best efforts.[73]

Hardin and Mary sent both their sons and their daughters to good regional schools. Their girls attended Danville Female Academy and Salem Academy and then Sullins College.[74] Their sons enrolled at Trinity College, VMI, Randolph-Macon College, Kings College, Emory and Henry College, Virginia Agricultural and Mechanical College, and Bryant and Stratton, a business school in Baltimore.[75] Unlike the more prestigious state universities in the South, regional schools not only cost less but did not demand training in classical languages as a prerequisite for admission. Although Hardin and Nancy Reynolds lived in a rural world and did not provide their children with the most privileged of primary or higher schooling, they clearly valued learning. Their children, and particularly their sons, especially benefited from the network building and associations that higher education encouraged.[76]

Hardin Reynolds may have been a stern taskmaster, but he was also an influential mentor. When A.D. returned to Rock Spring after business school in Baltimore, he ran the family business with his father for five years, along with his brother-in-law Maj. Andrew Lybrook. A.D. eventually sold out his part of the company to R.J.R., who sold out to younger brother Hardin Harbour (known as H.H., following the family penchant for using initials as nicknames) after three years, who then sold out to his younger brother Walter and brother-in-law Robert Critz several years later.[77] Hardin was deliberately training his own sons (and sons-in-law) to run a homegrown industry, while at the same time benefiting from their labor, their education, and their own newly acquired social and business networks.

Although the Reynolds family had survived the war years better than most, the years immediately afterward were not easy ones. Hardin had to reinvent production on the farm and in the factory in the absence of the slave system. Taxes were high, labor limited, and cash resources minimal.[78] His investments in slave capital had dissipated with freedom, the value of his land had plummeted, and the cash he had speculated on wartime cotton had been lost to a corrupt merchant, despite his extensive legal efforts to recoup it.[79] A.D. recalled those times as challenging for both brothers. Both had hoped that their father's lawsuit over his wartime cotton investments would secure them welcome cash. "If we had got this money," A.D. later rationalized, "RJ and my self might have felt Rich and bought bay horses and [a] top buggy and Splurged and done no good as Some of our neighbor boys did."[80] They had been forced to work hard instead. In later years, both men would raise and race some of the finest horses in the South, making up for their unmet youthful ambitions.

The absence of cash was only one of a bucketful of postwar worries in the Reynolds family. A more immediate concern was the absence of black labor, upon which three generations of Reynolds men had relied for some fifty years. Hardin Reynolds had despaired at this turn of events at war's end, compelling A.D. to return from the Confederate army to help him. "Now my second ambition was formed to help my father rebuild his lost fortune—," A.D. wrote. "He would say Evry now and then what will we do for bread Negroes all gone Corn planted and no one to work it." A.D. assured Hardin, "[F]ather R.J.R. and I Can Save your Corn Crop as soon as we Can brake up the Scott Camp[.] [H]e will take our horses if we don't Keep them hid out[.]"[81] Hardin's oldest son was courageous, for upon assessing his father's situation, he immediately organized a raid that permanently disbanded this large group of marauding former soldiers, not only allowing R.J.R. and A.D. to get to work on the crops but returning some stability to Patrick County as a whole.

With the Scott group ousted, the two oldest Reynolds sons turned to the fields. Though slavery as an institution had been eliminated, and the Reynolds slaves were now free, Rock Spring rebuilt its reliance on black labor with tenant farming. The new Reynolds labor-management system did not differ all that much from prewar days.[82] As late as 1860, Virginia still boasted the largest slave population in the South, and the tobacco belt held almost half of those slaves, who produced nearly three-fourths of the state's cash crop. To most whites, hiring freedmen and freedwomen to work the fields seemed the only way to jump-start the postwar economy. The transition to a free-labor system was problematic for all parties. While postwar tobacco prices were initially high, labor was extremely scarce. At the same time, new consumer tastes necessitated more careful cultivation of the tobacco leaf, which in turn, required 50 percent more man hours to bring an acre of crop to market. Meanwhile, slavery, the traditional source of tobacco labor, was defunct. Newly freed men and women, who tobacco farmers assumed would work their fields as wage laborers, wanted rights, respect, and opportunities, and the federal government promised to back them up.[83]

Receipts and lists provide a glimpse of these developing postwar employer-employee relationships at Rock Spring. Qualitative evidence suggests that many of Hardin's former male slaves had departed for parts unknown. Legal contracts with several freedmen who remained behind indicate he continued to rule with an iron hand despite so few laborers. In a contract dated January 15, 1866, Hardin Reynolds spelled out expectation after expectation for his former slave and current sharecropper Abe Reynolds. Over the next year, Abe was to tend and clear the land on the branch, "n tend it good," put up "a good fence," plant tobacco, wheat, rye, and oats, help collect firewood for the white Reynolds family, feed and curry the mules, find two mules to plow and enough tools to make the crops, plow a truck garden for himself, and was cautioned "not to have idolers about him." In return he could live in "the old Store" and keep half of the crops harvested from his efforts.[84]

Hardin made nearly three dozen sharecropping and tenant-farming contractual agreements with freed people, most of whom were illiterate, after the war. They included specific improvements he expected to be made on his property as well as the percentage of crops he expected to receive. He was not generous in his terms, especially at the end of the war. He gave Amory Freed and a family member a paltry $7.25 and clothes for their services in 1865. In another instance, the Freedmen's Bureau accused Hardin of driving off a former slave woman named Cely, although he was legally required to provide her a home and support until Christmas.[85]

Although the transition from slave labor to free labor and the loss of capital invested in slaves, along with the ruined tobacco economy, spelled long-term hardship for most white farmers and home manufacturers in Patrick County, Hardin defied the norm. With the help of able-bodied sons, along with his tenant farmers and sharecroppers and the white and black laborers he hired, he continued farming, manufacturing, and storekeeping.[86] He sold some land to pay his taxes, and he invested in stocks and bonds.[87] He still kept meticulous books and held all his customers accountable, even his adult children.[88] Upon his death in 1882, he was owed thousands of dollars by dozens of people.[89]

Hardin's business credentials remained spotless in the seventeen years he lived after the war. Correspondents for R. G. Dun and Company, the first commercial reporting agency in America, prepared twenty-two credit reports on his home manufacturing company between 1868 and 1879. His reputation was sterling from the beginning of these assessments. "Reynolds very good for $100,000 owes nothing of account and as good for his liabilities as any man in Virginia," detailed the assessor. Successive reports repeatedly documented Hardin's business as "clear of debt and perfectly solvent," "perfectly good and safe," "credit where ever known," and "entirely reliable and prompt."[90] He remained as litigious as ever, still frequenting courtrooms to settle disputes over property boundaries and claim more land.[91]

It was during these postwar years that R.J.R. grew into manhood and became intimate with his father's business. He had entered adolescence during the Civil War, in the most precarious of nineteenth-century times. He had watched his older brother go to battle for the Confederacy, and he himself had hidden from Stoneman and his troops when they raided the family homestead. But he had reached his majority in the disordered era of Reconstruction. Although he was a relatively young man during the war and did not serve in the Confederate army, he seems to have embraced many of the ideologies and values of those who had. R.J.R. looked up to A.D., despite his older brother's earlier fall from grace over his siblings' deaths. The two brothers were closer in age than the others. They slept together and worked alongside each other well into adulthood.[92] R.J.R. also admired his sister Mary's husband, Maj. Andrew Lybrook. Both A.D. and Lybrook represented that "last generation" of Virginians who had come of age as privileged youths in a slave society. As masters' sons, they had embraced secession and then fought in the Confederate army as junior officers. But during Reconstruction, these youthful former Confederates remade themselves into northern reconcilers and free-labor capitalists. They embraced political and economic transformation in the hope of remaking Virginia (whose fortunes had suffered mightily since the revolutionary generation) into a revitalized state characterized by rapid economic progress and national political importance.[93]

R.J.R., though he was too young to be a member of this Last Generation and so never fully internalized the same set of disappointments, aspirations, and ideologies, let alone actual military experiences, caught their contagious spirit of economic improvement and innovation, along with the taste for risk taking and courage needed to act on those beliefs. He fervently welcomed the future, rather than worrying about the past as so many other southern men of his generation would do, including Thomas Dixon in his blockbuster best sellers about "the dark days" of Reconstruction.[94] In some respects then, R.J.R. was a new man in a new world, one where the old rules of the game no longer worked. Many well-born southern men would use this explanation as self-justification for their financial failure in the post-war world, and with good reason.[95] After the war, Reynolds's neighbor Peter Critz, for example, left his home near No Business Mountain and relocated in Augusta, Georgia, but was unable to make a decent living. He counseled his kinsman Billy back home about the challenges young men faced in 1867. He railed against the Republican Party and the ways it emboldened "Blacks and soldiers" there. He urged Billy to consider relocating to West Virginia given the slow economy of Patrick County and its surrounds and his own disappointing experiences back home and further south.[96] Peter and Billy's precarious place mirrored that of thousands of other young white men in the region who lacked any prospects in this new era.

But unlike the Peter Critzes of the postwar South, the Reynolds sons and sons-in-law could rely on their privilege to help them make their way in this new society. First and foremost, they had Hardin Reynolds, a tough task-master but also a well-off entrepreneur and property holder. Although initially taken aback by the end of slavery and the scale of loss he experienced at war's end, Hardin had weathered the worst of these times with their help while encouraging each of them to work all the harder. They also benefited from Hardin's broad social network, built over a lifetime, which included local and regional farmers, politicians, lawyers, businessmen, bankers, merchants, and manufacturers. Now that that they were coming of age themselves, his sons and sons-in-law were developing their own networks too, from their school and college experiences, Baltimore exposure, and wartime service.

For three generations, manhood in the Reynolds household at Rock Spring had turned on habits of character that facilitated economic success: self-denial, hard work, sobriety, thrift. Like many men of this time and place, grandfather, father, and sons shared more character traits associated with northern commercial men in the Victorian era than those traditionally attributed to southern men, often crudely depicted in nineteenth-century popular culture as loutish, lazy, and brutal or as myopic and sometimes even effete.[97] Hardin Reynolds measured the success of his young male kin with the national yardstick of a rising middle class, actively cultivating their manly individualism and competitive ethos. Although his daughters are shadowy figures in the historical record, Hardin wished for them, in contrast to his sons, long lives as cherished and dependent wives "treated like queens."[98]

Like his father and brother before him, R.J.R. came of age by journeying through the backcountry. He hit the road selling tobacco at age seventeen or eighteen. Early vignettes describe him as a strapping young man learning the rough ways of the world from the buck seat of his two-horse wagon. "In the days when there were no jobbers and few railroads, he sold the family product from a wagon in the wilds of Virginia, Kentucky and Tennessee. In this primitive school, dealing with the shrewdest of speculators, he learned the lessons of life."[99] Tradition holds that Hardin feared his second son lacked the wherewithal to be a salesman and decided to put him to a test. He hitched two spavined horses to a light wagon loaded with Rock Spring plug, armed R.J.R. with nothing but two dollars cash, and sent him to the toll road. Unfortunately for R.J.R., the story goes, no matter how hard he tried to persuade farmers to buy his product, they refused. The thrifty farmers had learned they could buy cheaper "blockade tobacco" on the sly from men who avoided the government revenue tax. The Reynolds family paid their taxes, so R.J.R. could not afford to meet the blockaders' bargain basement prices. He had little choice but to keep traveling down the toll road through Carroll, Wythe, and Smyth Counties, until his last cent was gone and a tollgate barred his progress. Because his horses were starving, he picketed them alongside the road, then headed off through the fields with a load of tobacco in his arms. Eventually he figured out how to sell enough of the plug to pay his toll, feed himself and his horses, and head west. By the time he reached Morristown, Tennessee, he had mastered the selling game. He managed to sell or barter all his plug, developing a winning personality along the way and returning home safely.[100]

R.J.R. confronted an often violent world in the backcountry as a tobacco peddler, and his closest friends believed he acquired his canny understanding of humankind from these experiences.[101] Years later, R.J.R. liked to tell his children a scary story about thwarting his own murder while on the road. At the end of a long day of trading, he had spied an isolated farmstead and drove up to the cabin to request a place to sleep. A farmer and his three grown sons met him at the door and begrudgingly offered him their corncrib for the night. The sun had almost dropped when R.J.R. climbed into the makeshift shelter. He noticed, despite the fading light, that the rough-hewn crib floor was caked in dried blood. The weather was bitterly cold, the ground frozen solid, but he fled quickly to avoid what he feared would have been another bloody affair—his own demise.[102] This story hints at the courage it took to travel this backcountry, as well as the opportunity it afforded to cultivate independence, quick judgment, people skills, and brokering abilities. It was on these back roads that R.J.R. allegedly first applied what his father always preached: honesty was more important than being a good salesman. "One of the things that has remained with me most clearly is the day my father saw me start on the road," he recalled as an adult. "Knowing that some of the boys accounted as the best salesman the fellow who could tell the best lies and 'get away with them,' he impressed on me that 'the man who would lie for a dollar will steal a dollar,' and that asking more than a fair profit was clean-cut lying." Hardin's most famous son contended that he looked straight into his father's eyes and swore his commitment to honesty for the remainder of his life as he embarked on his first sales journey.[103]

By the time R.J.R. enrolled at Emory and Henry College in nearby Emory, Virginia, in 1868, he had helped his family escape from Stoneman's raiders, assisted his older brother and father at farming and manufacturing at Rock Spring with minimal black labor, and sold plug up and down the Appalachian Mountains. College courses must have seemed tame given R.J.R.s youthful adventures.[104] Although Emory and Henry was a good school offering a bachelor of arts degree, its curriculum covered less ground and moved more slowly than the more prestigious University of Virginia up the road. The school did have a heavy mathematics requirement, which was to R.J.R.'s liking, and commencement included a public examination before a committee of respected and learned men.[105] R.J.R. did not graduate from Emory and Henry, however; he left after less than two years.[106] He had struggled in all his classes except mathematics, where he had been recognized for his genius with numbers. Apparently, he had either been so enamored with arithmetic or so desperate to escape the rest of his courses that he had been allowed to construct a second-year curriculum composed solely of algebra, geometry, and trigonometry.[107] That year he even worked out a mathematical system that enabled him to make amazingly rapid calculations. It was reported he relied on that system for the rest of his life.[108]

No one ever labeled R.J.R. a cultured and erudite man later in life. But people did identify him with a particular kind of genius, honed from common sense, an astute sensibility about people, and an agility with numbers. The training grounds for most of this genius, folks concluded, had come from his many years as a backwoods peddler, which afforded him ample time "for thinking and studying human nature, and working out problems with intelligence and originality." Implicit in these conclusions was a celebration of the value of the common man's experiences and a critique of higher education.[109] R.J.R.'s earliest biographers, newspaper journalists writing at the height of his success in the first two decades of the twentieth century, liked to describe the New South industrialist as a down-to-earth frontiersman made good, the living embodiment of the American success story. Selling plug in the backcountry was a formative experience, but it was not R.J.R.'s only one by a long shot. After leaving Emory and Henry, R.J.R. returned home and worked under the supervision of his father, his brother A.D., and his brother-in-law Andrew Lybrook. He once again drove a wagon loaded with plug through the Blue Ridge and Smoky Mountains. But after several years at this work, he followed his older brother's lead and headed north to Baltimore. He later explained that he "felt the need of a more thorough business education and gave up [his] work to take a course in a business college," Bryant and Stratton, at his own expense in 1873. While taking classes, he solicited orders for his father's plug tobacco and came to know all the city merchants and wholesale dealers, relationships that would serve him well in later years.[110] That summer he returned home to No Business Mountain, entered into a formal partnership with his father, and employed his newly acquired business methods at the Rock Spring manufactory.[111]

Although all the early published portraits of R.J.R. imply he was a smarter man, a more independent man because he did not dally too long in the world of higher learning, he had in fact attended not one but two colleges. Still, his biographers insisted, his education occurred outside schools. "His mind was too active, the spirit too restless, to be content with the student life, the plodding, digging, confining study that makes what is known as a scholar," wrote William Blair. "His very nature craved activity and, measured by his knowledge of men and the practical affairs of life."[112] There is some truth in that statement. During his time in Baltimore, R.J.R. discovered that opportunities for manufacturing plug tobacco were burgeoning. He had come to understand how something as finicky as taste could dictate demand and price. He knew that the new flue-cured tobacco, which grew to the southeast of Patrick County, was increasingly more desirable than the local burley. He also understood, after witnessing the great railroad hub in Baltimore, that cheap, reliable transportation facilitated market spread in a way that traipsing the mountains in horse-drawn wagons never could. While he knew his father's business well and was a good partner in that concern, he had greater ambitions. His father, moreover, felt some obligation to make room in their partnership for his younger, less experienced sons.[113] But the third-generation Reynolds men had to confront an even more pressing change.

During the war and in the years that immediately followed, country factories had competed relatively successfully with city factories in Virginia. But by 1870 they began to disappear, the victims of errant labor, cash, and credit.[114] In response, many would-be farmers and home manufacturers moved to other states in search of more opportunity.[115] Like these other young men, R.J.R. and his brothers recognized that tobacco production in southern Virginia could no longer sustain the local economy. Despite the individual accomplishments of large-scale Virginia manufacturers like Lewis Ginter, the Mayo family, and the Dill brothers in Richmond, John W. Carroll in Lynchburg, and the Cameron family in Petersburg, and despite Virginia's continued supremacy as a tobacco producer, the state would never recover its prewar command of manufactured tobacco. As late as 1890, when the state's economy should have recuperated from its postwar challenges, the value of manufactured tobacco had yet to match its 1860 numbers. National competition had grown too intense. New northern enterprises took advantage of cheap immigrant labor, while to the west stellar burley-leaf crops attracted new manufacturers. The lightning-speed spread of bright-leaf tobacco cultivation along the border and especially in the North Carolina Piedmont drew more new men away from Virginia.[116] The soil and climate of Patrick County and its surrounds could no longer match its newest competitors. Nor did it lend itself to the development of any other kind of market sustenance. The final blow to country production was the arrival of the railroads. The steam engine favored towns over countryside and hastened the abandonment of rural manufactories. All told, the Reynolds sons had little choice but to leave their father's plantation and Patrick County.[117]

At the same time that R.J.R. was evaluating these economic realities and thinking through his next steps, the tall, handsome young man with long brown hair and an ever-present chaw of tobacco in his mouth was also grappling with Reconstruction politics. A lifelong moderate Democrat, R.J.R. seems to have been heavily influenced by his brother-in-law Andrew Lybrook. The Giles County native had attended Emory and Henry College (along with J. E. B. Stuart, who was born in Patrick County) and encouraged R.J.R. to attend his alma mater some years later. Lybrook graduated in 1852 and was practicing law in Patrick County by 1858, where he came to know Hardin Reynolds quite well. A wide reader with a philosophical, even scientific bent, he had little to his name on the eve of the war and boarded with a local tailor and his family.[118] On May 31, 1861, he organized Company I at the Patrick County Courthouse, apparently with the help of Hardin Reynolds, who bankrolled the company on at least one occasion.[119] The unit joined Col. Jubal Anderson Early's Twenty-Fourth Virginia Infantry Regiment at Lynchburg and subsequently participated in the battles of First and Second Manassas, Antietam, and Gettysburg. Captain Lybrook returned to Patrick County at war's end, entered into a partnership with Hardin, and married his oldest daughter in 1867.[120] A graduate of Salem Academy and Danville Female College and a capable portrait painter, Mary had eight children with Andrew. Her devoted husband mourned her premature death in 1888 and then died himself in 1899. R.J.R. supported their orphaned children years later and remained quite close to each of them throughout his life.[121]

During Reconstruction, Lybrook became a judge and then a politician. Elected state senator from the Twenty-Third District, comprised of Patrick and Henry Counties, he was one of the founding members of the Virginia political coalition known as the Readjusters, who were committed to breaking the political control of the state's wealthy and privileged. Lybrook's leadership had swung three out of four Patrick County voters to elect the Readjusters in 1879. Hurt by conservative legislation that demanded astronomically high state taxes at a time when cash was scarce, many voters in majority-white counties in southern and western Virginia forged tenuous alliances with black Republicans in the eastern part of the state under the Readjuster coalition. As a state senator, Lybrook fought for reduced state debt to ease tax burdens on the state's citizens. But when a well-known Readjuster, the former Confederate general and railroad entrepreneur William Mahone, was elected to the U.S. Senate in 1881, declaring himself a Republican and calling on all Readjusters to do likewise, Lybrook backed away from the coalition, publicly decrying Mahone in a well-circulated pamphlet titled *Mahoneism Unveiled! The Plot against the People Exposed, Judge Lybrook, the Readjuster Senator from Patrick County Tears the Mask from Mahone.*[122]

The temporary rise of the Readjusters had given new political and civil rights to black men and confounded long-held notions about blacks' "place."[123] Judge Lybrook had been an early leader in this movement, seeking support for white "plain people" in the form of reduced taxes and increased appropriations for schools, but the Confederate veteran shunned his Readjuster identity once the party formally committed itself to the Republicans and black political rights. Still, Lybrook's willingness to forge early alliances with the black electorate, when linked with his famous legal battle on behalf of two young Patrick County black men, suggests a tentative commitment to new forms of black equity.[124]

In 1877, two young African American men, Lee and Burwell Reynolds, were accused of murdering a white man in Patrick County. The mother of the defendants was Kitty Reynolds, the former slave woman who had rescued Hardin Reynolds from a charging bull decades earlier. Her sons, ages nineteen and seventeen, had entered into a violent brawl with two white brothers, allegedly because the latter defamed a local school for former slaves. One of the white boys was killed, and murder charges against the Reynolds youths were filed. Judge Lybrook, in an unusual move, stepped down from the bench to defend the young men. Burwell was convicted of murder, despite Lybrook's best efforts. Lybrook petitioned the Virginia Supreme Court for a retrial for Burwell and a trial for Lee on the basis that both men had been denied their equal rights since their cases were tried by all-white juries. His appeal was denied, so he took the case to federal court. In a writ issued by Federal District Court judge Alexander Rives, the two brothers were ordered to be released from the Patrick County authorities and held in the Pittsylvania County jail to await trial in federal court. Judge Rives agreed that the Reynolds brothers' rights had been denied, resulting in state and regional newspaper headlines like "Judge Rives Attempts to Force Negro Jurors upon the State Court." By January 1879, a federal grand jury was charged with determining whether black men were excluded on petit and grand juries in six southside counties and soon concluded that five of the judges in these counties in fact had not included black men on their lists for juror selection. Eventually this decision led to Judge Rives issuing warrants for the arrests of fourteen judges in the state of Virginia, which created a regional conflagration over federal usurpation of states' rights that was resolved in a series of Supreme Court cases in 1880 (*Virginia v. Rives*, *Ex parte Virginia*, and *Neal v. Delaware*). Much to the white South's delight, the court ruled that the absence of African Americans from juries did not in and of itself violate the Fourteenth Amendment.

In short, Lybrook had initiated a critical civil rights question when he argued that the young black men had been denied their civil rights in the course of the trial. Undoubtedly he never imagined that the case would become a cause célèbre and would be argued all the way to the Supreme Court (*Ex parte Virginia*, 1880). Although the Supreme Court overturned the case, the Reynolds brothers were initially acquitted. The court ruled that they had not received equal protection under the law because African Americans had been excluded from their jury selection, thereby violating the Civil Rights Act of 1875 and the Fourteenth Amendment. Indeed, as the Supreme Court case established, no African American had ever served on a jury in Patrick County. Lybrook's position, not popular among white southern Virginians, nevertheless demonstrated a substantial commitment to civil equity for freed people. His motivation for this stance is unclear. Was he acting out of family loyalty to the black Reynolds boys? Was he committed to equal protection under the law? His actions did not harm his political popularity, for after being elected to the state legislature in 1879, he was reelected in 1881.[125]

The Reynolds-Lybrook families remained close throughout Lybrook's public career. Lybrook consistently went to court on behalf of many other Reynolds family civil issues.[126] Andrew and R.J.R. worked together on behalf of Hardin's manufactory, and Mary and Andrew loaned R.J.R. money to start his tobacco business. R.J.R. had attended Emory and Henry College, Lybrook's alma mater, the only Reynolds son to do so. R.J.R. cared for Mary and Andrew's children after their deaths.[127] It is hard not to imagine that Judge Lybrook had a significant impact on R.J.R.'s public outlook on business, race, law, and politics. Lybrook had publicly defended two young men most likely born on the Reynolds plantation during slavery and championed the Readjuster position in its earlier phases of racial alliance. A staunch but not uncritical Democrat for virtually all his life, R.J.R. may very well have acquired his penchant for political moderation from his brother-in-law.

By the end of Reconstruction, family patriarch Hardin Reynolds was an old man. He had trained five of his sons and two of his sons-in-law in the tobacco business, and he remained successful at this work despite high taxes, changing markets, the rise of commercial manufactories, and the transition from slave labor to free.[128] True to their genes and their tutelage, the Reynolds sons had matured into tobacco men through and through. A.D. eventually left his father's employ to start a commercial tobacco-processing company in Bristol, Virginia, on the Tennessee border. Although it was not the first such venture in Bristol, he would turn it into the top one in short order.[129] Hardin and R.J.R. formed a partnership on July 1, 1873, subsequently producing forty thousand pounds of plug, but R.J.R. sold out his share to his father and brothers within the year.[130] Like A.D., R.J.R. soon departed Rock Spring and journeyed south into North Carolina, a day's ride from his birthplace. Hardin remained involved in his second son's business affairs, those that continued near Rock Spring as well as those in Danville.[131] Walter and Will later followed their older brothers into the business world and eventually spent the rest of their careers working for R.J.R.'s company.

Tobacco plantations like Hardin's, especially those incorporating bright-leaf tobacco, which grew miraculously in the worst of soils, were not sustainable. Although bright leaf breathed new life into one of the poorest regions of the South as the crops sold at record highs and as a whole host of new tobacco manufactories were launched, its long-term impact on rural land and rural people was devastating. While farmers had hoped for financial stability and improved agriculture by embracing the crop, it ironically created generational dependencies and poverty and helped shore up white notions of racial supremacy and justifications for segregation.[132]

R.J.R. did not understand these ramifications in the early 1870s, but he did recognize that his future was no longer on his father's land or in his businesses. Some claim R.J.R. had a very small venture of his own that he pursued in Stokes County, North Carolina, briefly before his arrival in Winston in 1874. Here in a community once known as Lash, he allegedly began manufacturing tobacco in a small log cabin with $2,700 in capital.[133] The winter of 1873–74 would not have been a propitious time to start a new business, for it marked the beginning of a protracted depression that afflicted all world markets.[134] Moreover, R.J.R. had left Baltimore in 1873 and would have seen the signs of a pending economic decline there. Meanwhile, 1873 marked the completion of a railroad spur to Winston that finally linked this rawboned town to bigger markets, and R.J.R. certainly understood the value of railroad networks. All we know is that R.J.R. told reporters years later,

"The first year in business I manufactured 40,000 pounds, the next year 80,000 pounds and then sold my brands and trade-marks to my partners, and moved to Winston-Salem for the benefit of the railroad facilities, and on account of this town being located in the center of the belt in which the finest tobacco in the world is grown."[135]

Winston, little more than a raw village, sat a half mile north of Salem. By the time of R.J.R.'s arrival in 1874 or 1875, this established Moravian community was a well-known enclave for religious piety as well as trade, textiles, and education. R.J.R. was familiar with Salem. His close friend and first cousin Zachary Smith had attended the Salem Boys' School before the Civil War, and his parents had enrolled his three sisters in the highly touted Salem Academy for Girls. His younger sister Lucy Burrough had graduated just two short years before R.J.R. made Winston his new home.[136] R.J.R. had about $7,500 in cash from his short partnership with his father and a formal agreement with Andrew Lybrook as his silent partner when he arrived in town. The arrangement with Lybrook lasted a year while R.J.R. got on his feet. Lybrook reportedly earned 25 percent on his investment, before selling out to Reynolds.[137]

R.J.R.'s choice of locale was an important one. Salem was the seat of the bishopric of the Southern Province of the Moravian Church in America and had a distinguished one-hundred-year history of communitarian pietism, cultural accomplishment, economic prosperity, and a measure of racial toleration. Many considered Salem the most literate town in the Carolinas thanks to the highly educated German Moravians who founded the Wachovia Settlement there in 1753. Requisite for the Moravians had been first-rate academies to educate their own boys and girls, and over time also the children of the well-off from across the Atlantic South, including the daughters of the Cherokee elite. A strong tradition of training talented musicians to play European compositions to accompany religious rites and festivals also remained rooted in Salem society, along with an Old World love and respect for literature, writing, music, painting, and craftsmanship.[138] By the middle of the nineteenth century, Salem's Moravians could also brag about their embrace of industrialization, if not their movement away from their eighteenth-century pietistic roots and the authority of the church. The small community claimed a score of successful enterprises, including Salem's woolen and cotton mills owned by the Fries family; the Salem Manufacturing Company, owned by the Banners; the iron foundry and oil mill owned by the Belos; and the cigar factory, gristmill, tanyard, and bank owned by Edward Lash.[139] By the 1870s, Salem was known nationally for processing and shipping big bales of dried blackberries to New York and Chicago, earning Salem residents nearly half a million dollars a year.[140] The community held on to its European traditions, with its early modern German architecture and red-tiled roofs, its Easter sunrise services and Christmas eve "lovefeasts." Nearby Winston made quite a contrast.[141]

It was this brash upstart town of Winston, nothing like its cultivated neighbor, that attracted the young entrepreneur. Its rough-and-tumble eight hundred residents had tobacco on the brain. Several years before R. J. Reynolds's arrival, Thomas J. Brown had opened the first tobacco warehouse and Hamilton Scales the first tobacco factory. Both had been inspired by the Piedmont's infatuation with bright leaf, which in turn was fueled by growing international demand for a sweeter tobacco.[142] Although served by a small spur of the North Western North Carolina (later the Southern) Railway that connected Winston to Greensboro, the little town was far from navigable rivers, lacked most other industrial and cultural advantages, and seemed an unlikely candidate for what it would become in fifty years: the biggest, wealthiest city in the state thanks largely to R.J.R., who recognized the opportunities inherent in this place and pursued them.[143]

2 A Hardworking, Painstaking Student

R.J.R. had already settled in Winston a full five years before his future wife was born, so great was their age difference of thirty years. R.J.R. grew up during slavery and the Civil War. Katharine grew up in a late nineteenth-century South racing to catch up with the industrializing North. R.J.R. came of age on a rural plantation. Katharine did so in a town. R.J.R. received a patchy formal education, and although he attended two colleges, his enrollments were brief, and he graduated from neither. Katharine's education was far better than his; not only did she attend two colleges, but she accumulated all kinds of honors along the way and graduated from the last one. Yet these first cousins once removed shared many attributes, including their strong family ties, their deep-rooted values of industry and thrift, and their ambitious temperaments. Moreover, their age difference proved an asset. The beneficiary of a southern society in transformation, Katharine grew up with access to a whole slew of new opportunities denied southern women of R.J.R's earlier generation. She took advantage of those opportunities, better enabling her to complement R.J.R. as his respected partner as well as his beloved wife.

Born in 1880, Mary Katharine Smith, the first of seven children, was named for her paternal grandmother.[1] Psychologists claim firstborns are far more inclined to internalize the hopes and dreams of their parents and to feel a deep responsibility to carry them out than their siblings. This was decidedly true in Kate's case. She shared important character traits with both her parents, and not only met their hopes and dreams for their oldest daughter but exceeded them beyond their wildest imaginings.

By the late nineteenth century, Katharine's father, Zachary T. Smith (1847–1938), was a successful tobacco businessman and real-estate speculator in the market town of Mount Airy, North Carolina, at the foot of the Blue Ridge Mountains.[2] Katharine's mother, Mary Susan Jackson Smith (1855–1924), a devout Methodist and an avid housekeeper, supported her husband in many of his business dealings.[3] The couple was part of the city's new commercial elite. They lived in a big Victorian house, ran a farm, bought and sold commercial properties, and provided college educations for their daughters as well as their sons. Members of an emergent southern middle class, they sought financial success and the social status that accompanied new wealth in new places.

Psychologists also contend that girls' personality development takes significant shape from the father-daughter relationship. Successful women in business and government consistently attribute their desire for public achievement to supportive, caring fathers, and rigorous studies back them up.[4] At the same time, self-reliant young women have almost always been influenced by at least one strong, independent woman during their childhood. Kate and her father were two peas in a pod; their shared ambition for moneymaking was obvious. But Kate's mother, adept at balancing new business pursuits with the moral order of the household, exerted considerable influence on her oldest daughter too.[5] Together, this determined couple raised an intelligent, independent, and forceful young woman intent on shaping the world around her.

Kate's family origins were local and rural. She was born in her great-grandfather's house in Stokes County, North Carolina.[6] Land grants had brought her great-grandfather Joshua Cox and his brother to Brown Mountain after the revolution.[7] He had two daughters who wedded promising young men who lived a half day's ride away. Catherine Cox (1818–93), Kate's grandmother, married Madison Tyler Smith (1808–96) in 1837. Nancy Jane married Hardin Reynolds in 1843. Catherine and Madison Smith had four children. They named the youngest child, Katharine's father and R.J.R.'s first cousin, Zachary Taylor Smith, after Zachary Taylor, the hero of the Mexican-American War (and later twelfth U.S. president).

Kate's mother, Mary Susan Jackson, was raised in nearby Surry County. The Jackson family had farmed land just north of Mount Airy since before the Civil War. Surry County had been frontier in the eighteenth century. The Great Wagon Road from Pennsylvania had spilled band after band of German Moravians, Lutherans, and Scotch-Irish settlers into its borderlands, thickening the countryside with hamlets and farms by the mid-nineteenth century. This was humorist H. E. Taliaferro's country.[8]

The town of Mount Airy would not emerge as the most important of these quiet little communities in the foothills until the end of the century. Agriculture dominated this northwest section of the North Carolina Piedmont for much of the 1800s. All farmers, no matter how big or small their properties, grew corn to ensure their self-sufficiency.[9] They also harvested fodder crops, oats, wheat, and rye, for their cows, hogs, and mules, and cultivated plentiful vegetables, especially cabbages and sweet potatoes.[10] They pursued cash crops too, mainly tobacco and fruit (grapes, apples, cherries, and peaches), which they increasingly sold in Mount Airy by the late nineteenth century. The arrival of the Cape Fear and Yadkin Valley Railroad in 1886, which linked the town to Greensboro to the southeast, ensured its development as a market town. A whole new generation of opportunists subsequently embraced commerce and manufacturing so quickly that Mount Airy seemed to transform itself overnight.

Katharine's parents welcomed this change despite their rural roots. The couple differed little from many other ambitious post–Civil War southern families, including the Reynoldses, in their quest for financial success in a changing economy. Both Mary Susan and Zachary Smith, like R. J. Reynolds, had grown up on a slaveholding farm.[11] They too valued hard work and discipline and were not averse to risk taking. More so than R.J.R, they respected book learning and higher education.

Zachary's family had been quite comfortable before the war. They had farmed their land in Reeds Shore with twenty-six slaves.[12] They sent Zachary's older brother, Joshua Cox Smith (1841–64), to Trinity College in Randolph County, North Carolina, and enrolled Zachary as a boarder at the Salem Boys School.[13] The Civil War turned their world upside down. Joshua went to Texas to join the Confederate army as a sergeant under General Hood and was killed at the battle of Franklin, Tennessee.[14] Zachary volunteered for service in the Seventy-Second North Carolina regiment in 1864, was captured with other soldiers while performing scout duty at Fort Fischer on the North Carolina coast, and spent the remainder of the war imprisoned at Point Lookout near Baltimore. He was released on June 20, 1865, when he took an oath of allegiance to the United States.[15]

Returning home at war's end, Zachary helped his father make meager ends meet. Like millions of other southerners, Zachary's father, Madison Smith, had suffered enough economic hardships between 1860 and 1870 to put him in deep debt. He owed money to many creditors and lost much of his land because he could not pay his taxes. By 1870 his personal estate had dropped to a paltry $750. His real estate had shrunk in value to $3,700.[16] At some point, Zachary left his struggling parents behind to head west. He wound up in Nebraska, probably to homestead, at a time when Indians and pioneers were still battling over the land.[17]

Whatever experiences Zachary encountered in the West have been lost to posterity. He returned after some years to North Carolina and renewed his friendship with his cousins at the Reynolds family home. Lucy Reynolds Critz, R.J.R.'s married sister, introduced him to her former schoolmate and friend Mary Susan Jackson, and a courtship between the two ensued, followed by their wedding in 1879. Mary Susan's family was well off. Her father owned substantial property and had sent his daughter to Salem Academy.[18] Zachary, who had not had the benefit of much formal education because of the Civil War, and whose family had lost its financial footing long ago, was "marrying up." The two moved to Mount Airy, where Katharine was born a year after their marriage.

By 1886, Zachary and Mary, with five-year-old firstborn Kate and her little brother, Joshua (named for Zachary's older brother), in tow, had acquired a big wooden farmhouse with ample land just northeast of Mount Airy on what is now known as Old Sulphur Springs Road. Mary's brother and sister-in-law, bent on homesteading in Indiana, had sold the couple their seventy-acre homestead for $1,520.[19] Mary gave birth to five more children on this farm, the last in 1898. The eldest son, Joshua Franklin, died in 1887 when he was only four. The remaining six children, four daughters and two sons, lived well into adulthood. The farm guaranteed that the growing family had plenty of fresh fruits, vegetables, milk, butter, and eggs. Grandchildren recalled the table always laden with heaps of potatoes and tomatoes as well as delicious pumpkin pies.[20]

The town of Mount Airy lay in a fertile valley nearly encircled by the Blue Ridge foothills. Three mountain-fed streams and rich farmland marked its borders. Its fortuitous location in the tobacco belt turned it into one of the largest tobacco markets in North Carolina in the late nineteenth century.[21] Commercial enterprises, including furniture and textile manufacturing and the largest granite quarry operation in the United States, also contributed to Mount Airy's growing status as a trade center.

It was a place of extremes. Breezes off the mountains and a reputation for a healthy climate made the town a desirable summer destination, drawing the wealthy from up and down the Atlantic coast to its local resorts and hotels.[22] At the same time, Mount Airy's proximity to the Appalachians attracted hundreds of mountain families eager to market homegrown goods and find wage work. By the 1890s, the dusty main street had grown wide enough to accommodate wagons passing in both directions. Investors and contractors began replacing the ragged line of frame stores with imposing brick and granite storefronts and three-story hotels.

Tobacco had thrived here for many years. Plug manufactured in Mount Airy had been hauled to markets as far away as Mississippi in huge wagons drawn by four horses. But the panic of 1893, followed by the establishment of the Tobacco Trust under James B. Duke, put the smaller operators out of work and limited the local tobacco business to the buying and selling of leaf. A North Carolinian, Duke had introduced an automated cigarette machine in 1885, captured almost half of the U.S. cigarette market by 1890, and purchased his four largest competitors to create a giant monopoly, the American Tobacco Trust, that crippled tobacco manufacturers, large and small, across the country. This frightening transformation pressed bright commercial men in whole new directions and literally reshaped the landscape. Downtown mountain views were soon obstructed by the erection of iron foundries, kilns, wagon factories, tanneries, and dozens of textile and sawmills.[23] Boasting only two thousand inhabitants at its incorporation in 1885, Mount Airy saw its prospects soar three years later with the completion of the railroad.[24] Electricity arrived in town following the formation of the Mount Airy Power and Light Company in 1891.[25]

The economically schizophrenic community that developed in the aftermath of these changes and was served by this variety of communities resembled many of the other new towns taking shape in the Piedmont. Rough folks gambled, drank, and frequented prostitutes.[26] The new middle class pressed for local laws to curb those social vices, while wealthy socialites passed through town to take the healing waters at the nearby resorts. A visitor to Mount Airy in 1897, sick to his stomach after traversing the winding train route from Greensboro, marveled at the mule-and-oxen-drawn wagons barreling down Main Street and the colliding worlds they represented. "Everything comes from the mountains, apples, chestnuts, cabbage, men, women, children, horses, mules, dogs, cows, oxen, rain, hail, snow, wind and everything else except sunshine," he opined. "For . . . clever people, stirring people, working people, prosperous people, crooked streets, hilly streets and a general good time," he concluded, "go to Mt. Airy."[27]

The Civil War had left a deep imprint on this place. The citizens of the town and its surrounds were known for not only their economic self-sufficiency but also their political independence. Unlike Virginians, who had witnessed Federal and Confederate troops alike decimating their homes and farms, Surry County residents observed only the Confederacy wreaking ruin upon the foothills inhabitants before 1865. Although early on many local men had volunteered to serve in the state's militia, the imposition of the Conscription Acts requiring service in the Confederate army sent many into hiding and initiated substantial disaffection across the hills. Everyone's morale worsened as wives and children suffered increasing hardships and deprivations, and Confederate troops hunted down deserters and commandeered provisions.[28] The final blow came near the war's end when Federal troops marched across the land, plundering supplies and livestock, burning factories, decimating rail lines, and enticing hundreds of slaves to leave their owners and seek Union protection. "The brigade . . . raided the houses, cellars, barns, and fields," recalled one eyewitness. "What they couldn't carry away, they destroyed, burning the wheat in the fields."[29] Still, Union general George Stoneman's cavalry did not harm the inhabitants, just their livelihoods.[30]

After Appomattox, many local residents remained angrier about the suffering they had endured at the hands of the Confederate troops than at Stoneman's raiders. Less than two years later, a series of Union Leagues formed in support of the Republican Party. The Hamburg Lodge in Mount Airy was the largest and most active of these efforts. It not only gathered local backing for its candidate for the Constitutional Convention but counted 106 African American men among its members.[31] This local legacy of interracial cooperation and political independence from Confederate traditions and ideals was not insignificant. It undermined the resurgence of the planter elite into political and economic power and made room for a new generation of commercial men, including Zachary Smith.

Smith, his wife, and his children all thrived in this rawboned town on the move. By the turn of the century, Zachary not only farmed just northeast of the downtown but owned a tobacco warehouse, significant shares in a prominent hotel, and dozens of properties in and around Mount Airy.[32] He bought and sold land to the Mount Airy Granite Company, the Mount

Airy Construction and Manufacturing Company, the First National Bank, and dozens of private citizens. Between 1886 and 1910, he traded almost exclusively in larger business and land tracts. Like most speculators, he had no aversion to real-estate transactions that took advantage of others' misfortune. In 1888, for example, he acquired a half-acre lot "sold to [him to] satisfy the mortgage debt of Joseph Nelson (colored)."[33] Like most people, Smith was color-blind when it came to making money, selling land to establish a "colored" public school though many protested the growing presence of blacks in the city.[34] Many Mount Airy whites, threatened by growing black political and economic power, consistently expounded upon black abuse of imagined boundaries of behavior and space in the local newspapers. Zachary was not one of them.[35] When commercial lots available for speculation grew scarce, Smith began buying up small town lots with modest dwellings on them instead. He rented these properties across town in white and black neighborhoods alike, on Arch Street, where white textile workers lived, and in "colored town" around Needmore.[36]

Zachary and Mary Susan were friends with everyone around Mount Airy. Mary Susan's gracious hospitality, a trait Katharine would inherit, was so keenly honed that she provided Eng and Chang Bunker, the world-famous Siamese twins who had retired in Surry County, a specially made chair that allowed them to sit comfortably when they visited.[37] Zachary was known around town as a raconteur with a keen sense of humor. In his later years, when it became increasingly difficult for him to walk around town to collect his many rents, the proprietors of Midkiff Hardware and the First National Bank provided the well-known Civil War veteran with a rocking chair outside their storefronts, where he collected his payments, keeping tabs in a little notebook he kept in his shirt pocket, and talked politics.

Katharine's father was an imposing man.[38] He looked like a stern Saint Nicholas with his white hair and beard, but he loved a good laugh.[39] He adhered to a telling regime throughout his life. Each morning his servant awakened him by handing him two ounces of twenty-five-year-old whiskey. He immediately drank it, without leaving his bed, a practice he claimed he began as a teenager in the Confederate army. He drank no alcohol besides this morning pick-me-up. Nor did he smoke.[40] Remembered as a man who "would not let misfortune or failure halt him in his march to success," he remained proud of his Confederate war experience to the end of his days.[41] Because he was a well-known local Democrat, candidates for state office always sought out his support.[42] Zachary was a respected Mount Airy citizen throughout his lifetime, and his reputation was only enhanced by his eldest daughter's marriage to R.J.R.[43] His grandson related a story that cannot be verified but suggests his local fame. When Zachary was quite elderly, and long after both R.J.R. and Katharine had died, word passed throughout the community that he was nearing death. Dozens of people held a vigil outside his home. Although he ultimately rallied to live several more years, Zachary Smith was already a legend.[44]

Kate was the light of his life as his first child, even if she was as strong willed as he himself. Father and daughter shared other passions too. Both were detailed and precise, and both liked to make money. Katharine meticulously toiling away at the ledgers she eventually kept for R. J. Reynolds differed little from her father bent over his little notebook of carefully penciled-in accounts. Although Kate was heavily influenced by her father, one key difference between the two of them later manifested itself. Zachary Smith, who witnessed his cash-poor father burned by postwar taxes and bad debt, hated borrowing money. Although one of his sons would grow up to work for a bank, so affecting were Zachary Smith's lessons to his other children about penury that at least one son avoided borrowing money as an adult, and daughter Maxie was a cautious stockholder throughout her lifetime. In that respect Kate proved the exception to the family rule.[45]

Katharine learned how to be entrepreneurial not only from her father but from her mother too. In fact, Katharine's younger sister Ruth later told interviewers, "Mama was rather ambitious."[46] She learned from both parents that women not only could have roles as business partners with their husbands but also could pursue trade transactions on their own. Although Mary Smith may have been raised to conduct herself as a gentlewoman, she was quite active in her husband's commercial ventures during the 1890s. While the listing of her name alongside his in most of their property transactions was not unusual at this time, in several cases she bought and sold property under her own name alone, a rare legal act for married women in North Carolina—even today.[47] In 1898, Smith assumed the debt of the Blue Ridge Inn in exchange for the property.[48] Mary Susan secured legal recognition as a feme-sole trader that same year and was an active stockholder (she actually owned stock in her own name) in the Blue Ridge Inn Company. Three years later, she was elected vice president of the company (and her husband was elected secretary).[49]

The post-Reconstruction drive for a strong regional economy, the dynamism of town building, and the emergence of a new middle class spawned multiple opportunities for entrepreneurial women with some family capital in hand to participate in the making of a modernizing southern business world, and Mary Susan was no exception. This foothills region had long harbored independent women. Tabitha Anne Holton, the first woman to sit for the bar in North Carolina, after Albion W. Tourgee argued her case before the North Carolina Supreme Court in 1878, settled in Dobson to practice law with her brother. She had prevailed against the presumption that a southern lady should not be "permitted to sully her sweetness by breathing the pestiferous air of the courtroom." The *Greensborough Patriot* praised her bravery and damned her detractors. "Blast the prejudice that puts women down as only fit to be men's slaves or playthings!"[50] Less than a generation later, Lottie M. Robertson, in addition to marrying and then raising seven children, served as a well-known and much-beloved Quaker preacher throughout the region.[51] In these changing times, this society seemed more willing to forgo prescribed gender roles than historians have previously recognized. In fact, in 1935 a local historian observed that Surry County had undergone a sea change in its attitudes about women working by 1910. "A decided change had taken place in the popular mind for women working in the stores and mills," he observed. "So pronounced was this change that the daughters of the rich actively sought employment in the stores and mills in competition with the girl from the factory district. Such conditions freed the women from home drudgery and at the same time opened up a new phase of social democracy."[52]

The nature of wealth in town households, as opposed to rural ones, enhanced these new possibilities for women's commercial involvement. The diminished role of white women's housework, especially in homes with hired black domestic help, made it easier for women to work with their husbands.[53] The Smith family employed a young African American woman, Frances Pateat, as a live-in servant, sparing the Smith women from most of the household chores.[54] Though chronic illness would reduce Mary Susan to a frail patient by the early twentieth century, she was an important role model for a smart girl eager to influence the world around her during the 1880s and 1890s.[55] That Katharine as a young adult developed an avid interest in moneymaking and became a critical advisor to her husband in his business dealings does not seem surprising in light of her family background.

But Katharine learned more than business acumen from both her parents. She also learned moral responsibility. Although both her mother and father had been raised in the Protestant church, Mary Susan was particularly devout.[56] Though neither mother nor daughter left any written testaments of their faith, both made church work integral in their lives.

Her parents also inculcated in Katharine a sense of responsibility for her younger brothers and sisters. She was closest to sister Maxie, four years her junior. Reserved, a great reader, and an accomplished bridge player as an adult, Maxie had a fine sense of humor and a wonderful imagination. Madison, six years younger, loved to play tennis, grew up drinking and smoking too much, and died early. Eugene, eight years younger, was steady in his pursuits, working for a bank as an adult, and was good friends with his oldest sister until she pressed him to move to Winston, take a top job at Reynolds Tobacco, and buy the lot across the street. Gene turned down the offer, telling Katharine that he did not want to go into debt or try to keep up with rich people. Plus, he knew others would assume he got the job because of her. After he explained his decision, she refused to speak to him for a year. Irene, eleven years younger than Katharine, was also a great reader like her older sister Maxie. Irene never married and cared for her aging father after her mother died. Ruth, eighteen years younger, born while Kate was away at college, was attractive, funny, and an expert horsewoman, as was Katharine. Katharine was dedicated to her family, just as her future husband would be. As the oldest child and later as an adult, she assumed a surrogate parental role with each of her siblings, especially her youngest sisters.[57]

Katharine's unique circumstances, particularly the nature of her family members' interactions with one another and their larger ambitions as they played out in this booming little community, often defied traditional gendered conventions. Her father taught Katharine as well as his two sons to shoot, for example. One day, Katharine was told to catch a chicken and kill it for supper by wringing its neck. According to family tradition, she refused. An excellent markswoman thanks to her father's tutelage, she allegedly mounted her horse, pulled out her gun, and shot the chicken right through the neck instead.[58]

Though something of a tomboy, Katharine understood and increasingly practiced social conventions thanks to her mother's training.[59] Mary Susan was locally renowned as "a gentlewoman of the old school, modest and refined, a home lover and a Christian," and had trained Katharine well.[60] She was also a talented seamstress and a gifted gardener. She passed on her knowledge about the rules of southern ladyhood as well as her love for sewing and plants to her oldest daughter, who stitched her own clothes well into her affluent adulthood and created a spectacular series of gardens on her future estate. A perfectionist whose domestic standards were tightly knitted into her moral values, Katharine's mother passed these traits on to her oldest daughter as well, along with her ability to balance her gentility with her business acumen.[61] These traits, coupled with Zachary's support for his wife's dual identity, provided Katharine with an exceptional model for a companionate marriage.

Kate's penchant for being independent and seeking out opportunities was nurtured not only by her parents but also by her education. She benefited from a good private girl's school followed by a coed public school. Even her most privileged extended family, all of whom had grown up in the countryside, had been haphazardly educated by parents, tutors, or itinerant teachers before heading off to local academies and colleges. Her experience was quite different. By the 1890s, New South reformers across the state believed that their burgeoning towns and cities, with their nascent commercial and manufacturing activity, promised a brighter future for the entire population. All the more reason, the reformers argued, to institute a system of public schools "as a staging ground for the great race of life" to educate future citizens for this new world.[62] Town children, boys and girls, black and white, proved the first beneficiaries.[63] Like so many other local leaders across North Carolina, Mount Airy progressives embraced this vision for regional development.[64]

The introduction of graded schools meant casual attitudes toward education were quickly wiped away by newer and stricter expectations. Graded schools were noteworthy for their imposition of order, from their insistence on tidy rows of desks to numerical rather than letter scores for tests. Educators believed in fostering more "active" minds by facilitating not the tried-and-true acquisition of foundational learning but the application of experience.[65] Katharine, who established two schools of her own as an adult, was attending a private girls' academy just as these new ideas began to percolate in her hometown.[66] Although primary schools of every size, shape, and kind proliferated in and around Mount Airy in the late 1880s and 1890s, many run by young single women in their rural communities, only two—Miss E. A. Gilmer's and Miss Belle Graves's—were considered suitable "for the training of [Mount Airy] girls for college." While Miss Gilmer was recognized as one of the best teachers in the state, Miss Belle Graves's school, where Katharine was enrolled, was heralded as the most select in town.[67]

Miss Graves had graduated from the well-regarded Saint Mary's School for Girls in Raleigh. She offered her female charges instruction in all branches of literature, languages, elocution, and music, as well as drawing and painting, to ensure that her pupils would "be prepared for entering college, or here fitted for performing all the duties of life."[68] The students also received instruction in Latin, French, and German (the latter unavailable at Miss Lizzie's School). Although Miss Graves emphasized the arts in her advertisements and employed a vocal and instrumental teacher as well as a painting, drawing, and elocution instructor, the academic curriculum was rigorous and no different from the education young men received. Her curriculum included rhetoric, literature, botany, natural history, physiology, history, philosophy, chemistry, algebra, and higher mathematics.[69]

Katharine received the best education available to her in the northwest corner of North Carolina. Not only was she exposed to a strong curriculum, but she was well nurtured in this setting. She was heralded for playing piano and reciting verse at school performances, and like all Miss Graves's students, she was the beneficiary "of careful cultivated training" in an environment "where each pupil was made to feel that she contributed."[70] But while Kate was receiving a classic education for privileged girls, the world around her was calling all the louder for the imposition of graded schools for all children, with the expectation that boys and girls attend these schools together.[71]

In January 1896, R. C. Craven from Elloree, South Carolina, was installed as the new principal of Mount Airy Male Academy. He received rave reviews and even secured the impressive Charles D. McIver, president of the brand-new State Normal and Industrial School for women, as the Male Academy's first commencement speaker. "No town in the State," the local paper boasted, "except those cities where they have graded schools, has better educational facilities than Mount Airy."[72] Two months later, Principal Craven announced that the academy would be accepting "girls and young ladies" for the upcoming fall term in preparation for becoming a graded school.[73]

That autumn the academy welcomed thirty-six boys and ten girls, Kate Smith and her younger sister Maxie among them.[74] Katharine, fifteen years old at the time, quickly distinguished herself in this coed environment where outgoing and competitive students received the greatest rewards. Craven, who gave his best students military titles and published their names and designations in the local paper, appointed Kate the lieutenant of Company D almost immediately. She quickly ascended to captain.[75] She was among the top students to be recognized in the local paper for her high grades week after week throughout the year.[76]

At graduation time, Principal Craven judged Kate's work habits and her scholastic aptitude outstanding. In this new environment, girls could and did outperform boys. By adopting the methods of the new graded school system, despite its limits on imagination and intellect, Craven served his female students particularly well. In a society where well-heeled southern women's roles continued to be circumscribed, Kate and her female peers were rewarded for their intelligence.

While Katharine's experiences in the classroom were important to the development of her intellect and her sense of self, the fact that she was a middle-class, town-dwelling girl cultivated new opportunities to develop her independence. Attending school in town, whether it was single sex or coed, freed Katharine from the bonds of domesticity that had entangled so many earlier southern daughters into Victorian lives of adult dependency. By contrast, Katharine could explore her world with a new peer culture that existed beyond the immediate reach of her family, her church, and her traditional community.[77] In the classroom, girls were not expected to subordinate their own needs to be obliging and dutiful daughters. In the graded school, outstanding academic performance actually made girls equal and in some cases superior to boys. In town, access to commercial activities and new spaces created even more freedoms for young, middle-class women.

Girls now had access to public spaces—sidewalks, streets, factories, and shops—en route to and from their schooling, just like the boys. They could stop by the plug factories on the side streets to taste the licorice that made the air smell so sweet. They could indulge themselves in penny candy and a soda at the drugstores and grocery stores that had begun to line Main Street, and at the very least window-shop in front of the jewelry and clothing stores. Their time spent together in these activities built a new peer culture for them, away from the prying eyes of parents. They found whole new outlets for personal growth and for outright play and fun, all taking place in new public spaces traditionally off limits to white girls of their social class.[78]

Mount Airy was a small town, with all its commercial activity centered on the north-south axis of Main Street and all other schools and businesses no more than a block or two away. Katharine Smith and her friends learned every inch of this place and encountered all manner of people, from hired hands and wage workers to local politicians and dignitaries. Kate had traveled into town with her father by horse and buggy at an early age and explored the Smith warehouse, a beehive of activity, where she learned the seasonal rhythms of the tobacco-buying business. She met her father's customers, who drove their one-horse wagons to town loaded with tobacco, then often spent the night in the warehouse, awaiting the sales the next day. It was a place where young boys fell asleep on their daddy's wagon listening to the strains of country music played by the other farmers around them.

Once she reached school age, Katharine spent as much time in Mount Airy as on the farm. Most children walked to school, even when they lived a few miles away like Kate. During the lunch hour, town children ran home for a hot meal, but kids from the edges of the town gobbled down a cold biscuit, which left them plenty of time to play games or venture out of the school yard.[79] Class distinctions, on top of racial segregation, manifested themselves immediately to these youngsters. White children who lived in the North Main section of Mount Airy (known as the "uptown") fraternized at their own risk with white children from the working-class families of South Main, and vice versa. Boys fought over the right to walk on the sidewalk. Country boys in particular, with their "tacky clothes," were favorite fodder for the townies whatever their class origins. These social distinctions and their ramifications were not lost on Katharine, who would take a special interest in the plight of farm families as an adult but would also advocate a number of modern social reforms in her adopted city of Winston-Salem.[80]

Growing up in Mount Airy also gave Katharine a special education in one other area of life that would be important to her as an adult. Because of its location next to the Blue Ridge Mountains, with its clear streams and cool air, Mount Airy had developed a reputation as an especially healthy locale by the late nineteenth century. A number of hotels and resorts in the town and the surrounding countryside offered healthy air, pure water, and beautiful mountain scenery.[81] The Mount Airy White Sulphur Springs Resort, just to the north of town, had been offering "health and pleasure" to wealthy travelers from up and down the East Coast since the 1880s.[82] The Blue Ridge Inn had sheltered travelers even longer. It had opened in the 1820s, only to burn to the ground in a spectacular fire on New Year's Day 1892, taking six other buildings with it.[83] In the wake of this disaster, nine "public spirited" men, "our most progressive citizens," formed the Blue Ridge Inn Development Company. They hired Tennessee contractors to turn the charred ruins into the most modern and attractive hotel in western North Carolina.[84] Kate's father was one of these "progressive" entrepreneurial men.[85]

Zachary Smith's involvement in the Blue Ridge enterprise ensured that Kate also received an education in the world of hotels and resorts, in offering hospitality and comfort, shaping her own ideas about keeping house and gracious living.[86] Katharine came of age in a town of contrasts in the late nineteenth century. Farm families drove wagons in from the countryside laden with apples, corn, and wheat. Mountaineers herded hogs and turkeys down the muddy roads of Mount Airy. Migrants frequented the town's plentiful saloons and liquor joints, along with wage workers from local textile mills and tobacco manufactories, despite the local Women's Christian Temperance Union's chagrin. But at the same time, area resorts and hotels drew well-heeled summer tourists from around the country to what was considered a prime Blue Ridge resort destination. Undine Spragg, Edith Wharton's midwestern counterheroine in *The Custom of the Country* learned about Atlantic coast society in just such a fashionable Blue Ridge hotel. Mount Airy took pride in its Galloway Opera House, gathering place for political debates, temperance lectures, operettas, band concerts, Scotsmen concerts that paid tribute to poet Robert Burns, and performances by Blind Tom, the eighth wonder of the world. Dr. Potter, pastor of the Baptist Tabernacle of New York City, gave his "celebrated lectures on the Great World's Fair" to eager audiences on three consecutive nights there in 1894.[87]

While no one claimed Mount Airy to be cosmopolitan, it was not a remote outpost either. Even Max Weber, the father of sociology and author of *The Protestant Ethic and the Spirit of Capitalism*, visited Mount Airy during his tour of the United States.[88] Between the rural folks who relied on Katharine's father and other local merchants for trade and goods, the social engineering that new merchant families pursued through philanthropy and benevolence, and the visitors with their lectures, performances, dances, and parties that accompanied the summer resort season, Kate Smith's hometown introduced her to a far bigger world than one might have imagined.

The Blue Ridge Inn, with its great views of the burgeoning town below as well as the blue mountains in the distance, had special meaning for Katharine.[89] In its postfire reincarnated state, with its combination Queen Anne and Old Colonial architecture, the Blue Ridge boasted large, airy, well-ventilated rooms; spacious parlors; electric bells; hot and cold running water; the finest mountain views; first-class cuisine; and "polite and careful attention." The hotel's first-class service and extravagant meals were guaranteed "to woo back the bloom to the faded cheek and give the lusterless eye its old-time sparkle."[90]

Katharine proved a consummate hostess in her adult years. Her guests were constantly amazed at her beautiful table, sumptuous meals, and the warm atmosphere she created. She learned more than the rudiments of making guests feel welcome and pampered by observing life at the Blue Ridge. The ownership and management of the Blue Ridge changed hands frequently over the course of the 1890s, but Kate's father never strayed far from its development, and both her parents were stockholders once again by the early 1900s.[91] Given the sustained Smith family financial interest in the Blue Ridge Inn, as well as its centrality in the social and political life of the town, Kate would have known the place and the staff well, able to roam the hallways, watch the street life from the balconies, and stay abreast of visits by famous people.[92] Society dances and balls, replete with ladies "robed in rich and handsome gowns" and Italian bands were frequent, attended by guests from as far away as Baltimore and Charleston.[93] Kate and her siblings probably heard their first gramophone recording at the Blue Ridge in 1896 and witnessed "the wonders of Edison's Kinetophone" there too.[94] They even learned the unwritten rules of racial hierarchy by watching their father get his hair cut by Jesse Redd, the African American barber at the Blue Ridge, "a prominent man among the colored people here and . . . well liked by the white people."[95] Blue Ridge was not the only local resort in the vicinity. The lovely White Sulphur Springs Inn on the outskirts of town drew well-heeled clientele to its doors, boasting live music, a bowling alley, a billiard room, a horse-racing track, and fishing and rowing on the Ararat River, as well as electricity and private baths.[96]

Katharine's youthful experiences in Mount Airy belie traditional notions about the kind of education needed to become a southern lady. Her world was sufficiently expansive and her parents supportive enough to allow her to stake her own claim for self-determination. By the time she was sixteen, she did just that by pursuing more education. Katharine's quest was right in line with new developments in the Progressive Era. Young southern women who attended women's schools and colleges, public and private, assumed that the purpose of their education was to shape them into a special group of female citizen-leaders.[97] Alumnae from southern women's colleges, noted one college president, had led all the great women's movements of the era, including the Women's Christian Temperance Union, the Young Women's Christian Association, the Federation of Women's Clubs, and most charities, philanthropies, and Christian pursuits in general.[98]

Not all southerners were enamored of this idea of southern white women's public leadership. Women's colleges, fearful of public censure, in response to such critics often changed their tune and advocated more traditional female roles for their students instead. Within this larger backlash culture, women college graduates increasingly used their experiences and educations to establish separate women's communities from which to shape social policy and reform.[99] Even amid this changing landscape, the vast majority of parents did not consider educating their daughters particularly important business. As a result, only a tiny handful of women in the South were able to pursue higher education.[100] As one southern women's college president noted, "Parents would plan to send their daughters away for a year to *finish* [their] education. The serious, thorough education of girls was comparatively new. The movement for the college education of women had not begun, or if at all, had made very little progress in the South."[101] Katharine's parents were exceptions in that they were as committed to college educations for their daughters as for their sons.[102]

Katharine applied to and was accepted at State Normal and Industrial School, the first state school in North Carolina for white women that drew matriculates from across all socioeconomic strata. Normal promised all graduates a paid career as public school teachers upon graduation.[103] Many young southern women had gravitated into teaching careers out of economic necessity since the Reconstruction era. Normal signaled significant social change. The newest generation of young women could now secure professional training in a state-funded institution of higher education for a socially sanctioned wage-earning position. Unlike most Normal applicants, however, who needed the free tuition, Katharine had not decided to attend Normal out of necessity. Her parents could well afford the expense of tuition and board.[104]

Normal had been established as a result of the intensive lobbying efforts of renowned education leader Charles D. McIver. He had used the legislature's recent support for black public schools to leverage demand for an institution for white women. McIver argued that white women needed an education as much as black men and women. The state would benefit greatly if significant new numbers of young white women educators could train the state's largely ignorant and illiterate population.[105] As early as 1885, McIver was telling audiences that the greatest problem in the South was not the "negro problem" but the great mass of uneducated North Carolinians, white and black, male and female. But securing enough competent teachers to set up such a system was daunting. Although large numbers of young white women were available, McIver had pointed out, they lacked the necessary education themselves, making a public school dedicated to higher education for white women a must. The state's white citizens proved receptive to McIver's solution and enacted a universal public education system headed by young women teachers. They would later recognize that "grandfather" and "understanding" clauses intended to disfranchise African Americans would disfranchise illiterate whites too, making McIver's original argument all the more compelling in later years.[106]

McIver was an outstanding public speaker, so he aided his mission on behalf of women's education and the fight against illiteracy by speaking about his school all across the state. Katharine may very well have first heard McIver when he addressed the Male Academy in Mount Airy in 1896. McIver was well known for mesmerizing his audiences with passionate appeals for the betterment of North Carolina, and his powerful oratory and compelling vision may very well have persuaded Katharine that she had a special role to play in North Carolina's future. Older girls may have also inspired her interest in Normal. Family friend Carrie Sparburger, for example, had enrolled at Normal several years earlier.[107]

By 1897, Normal had been in operation for several years and was heralded across the state. Katharine's high school principal, R. C. Craven, deeply committed to public school education himself, supported Kate's decision to apply to Normal that year. In his letter of recommendation to President McIver, he described her as "a hardworking, painstaking student, who never sought to evade any duty or task." But it was her good mind that most impressed him: "Possessing a splendid intellect, she does everything that she undertakes with credit to herself and a great satisfaction to her teachers. . . . She is further advanced and more thorough than any student heretofore sent from Surry Co. to your institution."[108] Craven had captured in his assessment those attributes that best described her later in life: intelligent, tenacious, and ambitious.

But entrance to Normal was not assured. McIver received double the applications he could accept even though his school did not award baccalaureate degrees until 1902. Because he was committed to enrolling students from all walks of life and guaranteed a place at Normal for at least one student from every North Carolina county, McIver required each applicant to write a brief letter requesting admission in order to test her literacy.[109] Kate certainly must have been one of the strongest applicants from Surry County. McIver accepted Kate, as he did the other accepted students from all social classes and all parts of the state, with the understanding that her tuition, room, and board would be paid by the state provided she taught school for at least two years upon her graduation. She would be supplied a dormitory room on campus, and she was expected to arrive in September 1897.

Although expanding access to higher education created a host of new opportunities for white women during the Progressive Era in North Carolina, reformers still used traditional notions of southern womanhood, framed by popular ideas about the limitations of race and class, to make this possible. White women's education could be part of the broader southern social reform movement as long as it did not challenge existing social hierarchies.[110]

The South was not alone in seeking a safe middle ground for women's expanding roles. A national backlash had resulted from a widespread fear that "radical" women had been attempting to reshape the body politic for decades now, through their college educations and their organizations and associations and most recently through their quest for political equality and the right to vote. At the same time, economic opportunities for middle-class white women had expanded dramatically over the last decade or so. Young single women in urban locales could pursue a number of occupations newly available to them, from department-store clerks to office secretaries to public school teachers. These opportunities helped diminish the idea of marriage as the requisite next step marking a young woman's transition into adulthood. At the same time, young women's newfound independence fueled critics' fears about a disordered and uncivilized society, one where society's best daughters pursued their own needs and ambitions. In a worst-case scenario, they might not even marry, contributing to a kind of race suicide in the eyes of the most rabid naysayers.

If women's attitudes and behaviors needed to be tempered, then secondary school represented the ideal place in which to "restore" women's traditional role. High schools could be made into ideal grounds for "retraining" girls to be "domesticated citizens." Women must still take on sex-specific social roles, these critics argued, despite or even because of the massive social and economic shifts created by industrialization and urbanization and the rising numbers of immigrants across the nation. Social progress and the future of humanity, they argued, depended on their ability to do so.[111]

By the 1870s, high school educators across the United States had already begun to press for more "practical" studies for both boys and girls as greater numbers of youths less likely to attend college enrolled in high school. Girls, who were the majority of high school students in this era, began to lose academic status at the same moment women were ascending into public affairs. A new curriculum emphasized educational training through vocational guidance, rather than a classic education in the liberal arts, as the "ideal" preparation for girls well into the Progressive Era.[112]

It should be no surprise then that women's public colleges in the South followed suit. Even McIver promoted women's self-improvement and acquisition of a female vocation over intellectual development.[113] Normal's curriculum reflected this sensibility. Its courses indicated a stronger commitment to career preparation than to study in the traditional liberal arts and the conferring of a bachelor's degree. In point of fact, only a handful of select private liberal arts schools for women in the South offered a traditional curriculum and a BA. To be fair, most students enrolled at Normal had received woefully inadequate secondary educations and were not ready for college-level instruction.[114]

Thus, a Normal education promised young women of Katharine's generation both the requisite skills and the social sanction to be a schoolteacher in North Carolina. Theirs was a career path increasingly sanctioned for young white women by the larger culture. But there was a radical edge to this experience that bears discussion. While educating young white women of a certain class served the greater needs of the state, it also gave them a new measure of independence in a traditional culture. Normal offered young women like Katharine entry into a separate women's culture with its own female sphere of influence. Young women educated in this special community were often transformed by it, and that change was reflected in their actions and ideas throughout their entire lives, even if they ultimately pursued the more conventional path of marriage and motherhood.[115] This reality went largely unacknowledged during this era. McIver himself, like most men and women of the period, saw no contradiction between the inherent independence his students secured through their single-sex educations and teaching careers and the inevitable goal of marriage and family.[116]

This mind-set made Normal an oasis for progressives, rather than radicals, from across the county who loved to visit Normal to share their own progressive visions while applauding Normal's mission. The Honorable J. L. M. Curry, director of the New York–based Peabody and Slater Funds, for example, toured Normal's classrooms and labs and attended chapel in 1897, before traveling to Winston to visit Simon G. Atkins's Slater School for African American education.[117] This linking of white women's and African American men's social uplift through education was a common conception in this period.

That same year, Normal had made a big political splash at its commencement exercises. A series of dignitaries had given rousing addresses on the importance of a whole set of progressive reforms. Walter Hines Page, editor of the *Atlantic Monthly* and former North Carolina journalist, had made his famous "Forgotten Man" speech, vividly describing the common people of North Carolina who had been left behind in ignorance in their isolated villages and backcountry farms. Page railed at the reformers who had stranded rural women in their poverty and made them haggard in their youth, worn down by ceaseless toil and childbearing, enslaved by ignorant, filthy husbands and children. But these forgotten women, he argued, who contributed so mightily to the high illiteracy rates in the South Atlantic states (30 percent compared to 13 percent nationally), could become the foundation on which southern social change with the help of President McIver and the Normal graduates could be built.[118] Just a few months after Page delivered this speech, Katharine wrote McIver in her letter of application, "I have come to the conclusion that there is no better school in the State for girls."[119]

Traveling from home to attend a new school a half day's train ride away was quite an adventure for a young girl from Mount Airy. Greensboro, a transportation and industrial hub, with a decidedly heterogeneous population in the heart of the North Carolina Piedmont was a larger and more complex community than Mount Airy. The campus was at the edge of town and comprised only six buildings, including a brick dormitory that housed 150 students and the three-story Romanesque Revival Main Building. The entire campus sat in a former cornfield of red dirt.[120] Despite the novelty of this experience, the new students embraced their new home, and their parents received plentiful assurances from President and Mrs. McIver that they would look after their youthful charges like their own children, and they did. Kate certainly accepted the McIvers as in loco parentis, and she quickly embraced the professors, almost all women, in this role too.

Kate's newfound community shared a sense of mission that, however unconsciously, reshaped gendered norms.[121] President McIver constantly reminded his faculty and students that theirs was a shared commitment to transform the people of the state. He energized them with his faith in their capabilities as future teachers.[122] The necessity of women's leadership in this mission was implicit in all his speeches. The faculty, nearly all of whom were single women with degrees from top universities, including Wellesley and MIT, reinforced McIver's notions, and not just in the classroom. These women not only taught their students but lived in the dormitories and ate in their dining halls. Many had traveled extensively, and all had read widely, factors that served to connect their charges with a far more cosmopolitan world. Katharine relished these new role models and kept in touch with this special community for the rest of her life. She was not alone. Fellow students claimed again and again that the education they received at Normal was transformative. Faculty pressed their students to see themselves as independent thinkers and responsible participants in the sustaining of democracy.[123]

Kate initially enrolled in Course I, the standard curriculum for teacher preparation. She took courses in algebra, English, Latin, French, physical geography and botany, history, drawing, vocal music, and physical culture.[124] Although stricken with measles her first semester, which prompted her worried father to correspond with President McIver, she recovered and had an otherwise uneventful year. During her sophomore year, Katharine requested and was granted permission to switch from the Course I curriculum to the languages track. She had already placed out of introductory courses in English and French, subjects in which she excelled, and now added Spanish to her studies. Her curriculum change was a significant one, indicating that she had decided to jettison the teacher preparation path after only one year; expertise in multiple European languages and literatures had limited usefulness in the public school classrooms of North Carolina at that time. Katharine was a strong student throughout her Normal career. A college friend reminded her years later, "You always did everything better than anybody else—even [in] Spanish."[125]

McIver told all his students that the state had invested in each of them and expected a return on its investment. He urged civic responsibility upon all his pupils, insisting that it was their duty to give back to the world by recognizing real needs and doing something to remedy them after completing school. He framed this charge as a calling, using the language of evangelical Protestantism. "He could do more to convince and inspire his students than anyone I have ever come in contact with," noted former student Ida Wharton.[126] Professor Philander Priestley Claxton, who taught psychology and pedagogy, so movingly conveyed the plight of the illiterate in the mountains that Katharine's roommate, Emma Speight, "wanted to go to Buncombe County and teach the moonshiners," and upon graduation from Normal she did just that.[127]

Most State Normal and Industrial School students came from modest homes and relied on county scholarships to pay their tuition. Two-thirds of the students would not have been able to attend Normal without this support. Despite the free tuition, many students still had to work for wages to earn their room and board.[128] President McIver told Mattie Sessons that he could give her work in the dining room if she was "strong physically."[129] Some students enrolled for short periods of time because they lacked the needed financial resources. Marjorie Ratliffe Craig used money her mother had bequeathed her at her death, enabling Marjorie "at last, [to realize her] desire to go to the school the great McIver had established at Greensboro." Unfortunately, she ran out of funds after her first year and had to drop out.[130] Katharine's exposure to these ambitious but impoverished young women made an impact. Years later she provided the funds to send new generations of young women to Normal, and many of her reform efforts reflected her interest in the plight of poor women.

The State Normal and Industrial School drove home its mission not only through its curriculum but through its extracurricular activities and organizations too. Here faculty members also participated alongside their students. Each girl was invited to join one of two literary societies and was at least a nominal member of the Young Women's Christian Association club. On the surface, Normal's literary society events, including teas, parlor games, and concerts, tended to reinforce traditional gendered expectations, as did the YWCA programs, with their emphasis on salvation of self, salvation of heathens, and Christian motherhood. But in this all-female environment, these groups gave these new women opportunities for important leadership roles that served them well in their future civic lives.[131]

The literary societies met at least twice a month to read essays, hold debates on current topics, and act out plays. They held parties too, including an annual full-scale initiation banquet replete with costumes and carefully written toasts. The societies even aided McIver in establishing discipline by censuring undesirable behavior.[132] Katharine quickly emerged as a strong student leader in this environment. She was elected an officer in the Adelphian Society her freshman and sophomore years and then was elected president her junior year, mastering the organizational and social skills needed to run the club with ease.[133] She would put those abilities to good use for the remainder of her life.

Katharine's change of heart on teaching makes it less clear that she embraced McIver's ambition that his students see themselves as female soldiers in the army of social reform. The president certainly impressed on most of his charges the enormous needs of the state's population, "its resources and possibilities as yet undeveloped, the low state of literacy of her people," as Ida Wharton Grimes recalled McIver intoning. "And the way to remedy this was by trained mothers and teachers," McIver explained. "[He] challenged us by our loyalty and pride to accept the task of development and improvement."[134] Although being a foot soldier promised a certain kind of autonomy new to young southern white women, for running a classroom and determining a curriculum symbolized a new kind of public authority, Katharine chose a different route by which to make a difference.

Katharine may already have grasped that McIver's notion of women's new role remained prescribed within a certain social architecture. It was a fundamentally democratic, even a leveling one for newly educated women. In the end, she balked at this calling, despite her many successes at Normal. Self-determination and public distinction were her true calling cards, not a maternal ethos in which she was one of many women selflessly doing their part. Katharine's decision may also have been influenced by a series of health crises in her family and her school that gave her time to reflect on her abilities and desires. Unfortunately for Katharine and many other Normal students, communicable diseases, which had yet to be controlled by childhood inoculations, frequently impinged on their educations, sometimes with tragic results. Kate had been ill within weeks of arriving at Normal her freshman year. Then, over the winter break of her sophomore year, she had come down with such a bad case of chicken pox that she requested a late return to school. That summer, keenly aware of the dangers of living in close quarters, she had even made a special request for a well-ventilated dorm room for the ensuing year to protect her against illness.

Then in early November 1899, a typhoid epidemic struck the entire campus, killing at least a dozen people. Katharine had already withdrawn from school when the disease hit. That October she had allegedly suffered from malaria and returned home to recuperate. Officials later stated that they had incorrectly diagnosed the first spate of student illnesses as malaria, so Katharine may very well have had typhoid after all. Meanwhile, the students still at Normal that autumn grew sicker and sicker. "It was a most common occurrence and most depressing one to see the hearse driving by my window as it passed the brick dormitory," recalled one student about that sad time.[135]

Although McIver closed the school after some fifty students had been diagnosed with the disease and instituted new health policies to ensure future safety, about a quarter of the students failed to return for the second semester.[136] Katharine, however, did return. As president of the Adelphian Society that spring, she found herself in an important position from which to rebuild student spirit in the wake of the typhoid catastrophe. Kate was well known at Normal. Her parents sent her big boxes of goodies that she always shared with the other students. She always dressed beautifully, standing out in a community where many were too poor to own more than two outfits. She even had "a unique, precise way of speaking." She also pressed people to pursue their own self-improvement projects, albeit with some nudging on her part. In one such instance, Katharine urged her roommate, Emma, to forego her pillow to prevent round shoulders. Every time Emma failed to take Katharine's advice, she woke up in the morning without her pillow. Eventually like most people Katharine encountered, Emma surrendered to Katharine's will, giving up use of a pillow until she married seven years later.[137]

Despite her many successes and her prominence, Katharine did not return to Normal for her final year. She had run into a little academic trouble at the end of the year, failing to show up for her end-of-course physics exam, which she blamed on illness and oversleeping, but the repercussions were too few to bring about this change of heart. More likely was Katharine's own sensibility that she had outgrown Normal and needed a new set of challenges. She no longer wanted to be a public school teacher. She had mastered the leadership skills necessary for civic pursuits and social reform work. Though she wrote President McIver that she was accepting reappointment to Normal, days later she sent a second letter stating that she needed to attend to her sick mother and must return to school late. She eventually returned in the spring semester of 1901 but then departed immediately to care for her parents, both of whom were now ill. Katharine wrote McIver that her mother's declining health prevented her return for that semester, and shortly thereafter her name was crossed out in the Adelphian Society minutes book. That May she settled her expenses for medicines and lost texts.

Katharine requested reappointment one last time late in the summer of 1901, indicating she would rather pay tuition for a dorm room than board off campus and receive free tuition. She was polite but forceful in laying out her expectations. We do not know how President McIver responded to this request, but she did not return to Normal. Later that fall she enrolled at Sullins College in Bristol, an elite women's school in southwestern Virginia tucked against the border of Tennessee. Her younger sister Maxie joined her.[138] Lucy Reynolds Critz, their older cousin, had attended Sullins, although she had graduated many years earlier, in 1872.[139] But the sisters had relatives in Bristol, including R.J.R.'s older brother, A. D. Reynolds, and his family.[140]

At sixteen, Katharine had left Mount Airy to navigate the wider river of female meritocratic democracy at Normal.[141] Three years later, she had mastered this special white women's world of social-reform training and discarded the notion of pursuing a progressive career in female public service. It was time to test herself in new ways, and Sullins gave her a new set of opportunities to do so. This time she set out to master the conservative world of white southern ladyhood and begin the task of finding a husband and preparing for marriage.

Sullins College was a private finishing school for the upper-crust daughters of Kentucky, Virginia, and Tennessee. The Sullins yearbook explained, "The students . . . are purely of a Southern type in manner, deportment and bearing, and coming from the best families of our Southland, whose ancestors belong to the old cavalier family of England, they bring into their college life that congeniality, vivacity, and gaiety so characteristic of the Southern people."[142] The Sullins mission could not have contrasted more sharply with that of Normal.

The Sullins campus differed from Normal in appearance as much as it did in mission. Solid Victorian brick buildings with gleaming white porches, porticoes, and columns sat atop a hill in a parklike setting overlooking Bristol. The students were literally above the urban fray, protected and honored for their status as southern belles. "Like their native land, with its birds, flowers, and sunshine, [the students] are nature's children," claimed Sullins in its literature. "And being never depressed or melancholy, they see the bright side of things, and have the tact of infusing their happiness into the lives of all who come within the radius of their friendship." Moreover, Sullins girls always looked their best: "Their appearance on the streets and in social circles is always in civil dress of the latest and best fashion."[143]

The Sullins curriculum reinforced these values. This was a world where painting and deportment took precedence over studies. "[The students] are fond of the arts of music, painting, singing, and perhaps dancing. . . . Their College home is a scene of contentment, serenity, and pleasure, [where] no haggard and care-worn faces are seen."[144] In contrast to Normal, the Sullins task was to aid its students in their matchmaking. Its receptions and parties, "the grandest events of the session," marked the pinnacle of the Sullins College experience. The betterment of society and the alleviation of illiteracy were not topics of discourse here. In long halls decorated with flowers, flags, and bunting, Sullins girls met their gentleman guests and "soon humbled [them] to the ground" and turned them into "most faithful and obedient followers."[145]

Though she attended Sullins for her senior year only, Katharine was as successful in this environment as she had been at Normal. Her yearbook photograph shows an expensive studio portrait of a beautifully dressed and perfectly coifed Katharine. She headed multiple student organizations and emerged the school darling, a leader among her peers and a favorite among her teachers. She was secretary of the Class of 1902, editor in chief of the yearbook, a guard on the basketball team, and had the fifth-highest grade point average. She was voted "faculty favorite" and "most college-spirited girl."[146] President of the Fairesonian Literary Society and the Young Women's Missionary Society, she was a debater too; her team argued against the resolution "that choice is free" and won.[147] Young men reportedly lost their hearts to her.[148]

Normal and Sullins were worlds apart in expectations for their graduates. If Normal suggested the possibilities open to bright young women from all social classes eager to make their mark in the world as public-spirited educators, Sullins embraced an increasingly anachronistic past when young women were valued for their family's wealth and their suitability as marital partners. Katharine flung herself into her new social world at Sullins and made a tremendous success of it. She never completely detached herself from Normal, however. In the spring of 1902, she wrote President McIver that she had enrolled at Sullins College and would soon be graduating with a degree in English literature. She reported that she planned to study art in New York City and therefore wanted to redeem her pledge to teach for two years in North Carolina schools by paying Normal back for all her expended tuition. This rather remarkable letter, however short, reveals a great deal about Katharine. She was confessing to far more ambitious and decidedly selfish dreams for herself as a young woman artist than Normal would have ever allowed her. If she was serious about wanting to be an artist in New York City, she was also turning her back on the conservative social training she had just mastered at Sullins. No elite southern man would have wanted for his future wife a southern girl who had lived on her own in Manhattan as a struggling artist. Had she recognized as she neared the end of her college career and a busy year of fetes and parties and eligible beaux that this world was too limited for her? She was too smart, too capable, too ambitious to settle into the closed world of a limited southern elite that expected her to perform a narrowed role as wife and mother. New York, rich with excitement and possibilities, drew Katharine's interest like a magnet.

That Katharine wrote McIver to tell him her plan also attests to the other pull she was experiencing: that between her social conscience and her desire to serve her own needs, which would manifest itself again and again throughout her life. She could be blind to the most blatant of social realities despite her reforming tendencies. She had come of age during the white supremacy campaign and the social and legal codification of Jim Crow segregation that followed it. Nothing in her record suggests she was aware of the social construction of a one-party South that ripped the vote from black men's hands or the social and economic disempowerment of black men and women that occurred across the South.

Katharine was not alone in her blindness. For all of Normal's commitment to the common man and woman, race consciousness had been noticeably absent from its agenda. In a panorama for the state fair, Normal students from an eastern county created a tableau in which they dressed as black children and ate watermelons and did not give it a second thought.[149] In 1901, the students sarcastically referred to "The White Woman's Burden," a long skirt without pockets.[150] Sullins was even more removed from racial realities. Katharine received her education in the worst depths of North Carolina's white supremacy campaign, when Democrats used fears of miscegenation to undermine a Fusionist Party of Republican and Populist black and white voters and launched a horrific race riot in Wilmington to intimidate blacks, to secure political control and one-party domination. Katharine seems to have been oblivious to those realities, at a complete remove, isolated by her studies and her fellow students in a land of implicit white privilege. Although clever and smart, Katharine rarely used her education to challenge the presumptions of the southern cultural conservatism that surrounded her. As an adult, people marveled at her for being so thoroughly modern. She embraced the latest technologies, popular scientific knowledge, and progressive reforms with zeal. But she did so always within the larger framework of an inherent conservatism that rested on traditional social divisions across sex, race, and class.[151]

Katharine graduated from Sullins College in June 1902 and returned to her parents' home to teach china painting.[152] A pastel of a winter millpond landscape from this period, probably a lesson piece, suggests she understood basic composition and could create reasonable representational scenes. Its value lies in its poignant underscoring that Katharine could never have made a living as an artist in New York.[153] A natural leader with a forceful personality, Katharine had rejected the hard but important work of public school teaching to master the social conventions of the southern elite. She dreamed big about becoming an artist but then came to terms with her limitations, all by the age of twenty-one and with no serious suitors on the horizon.

Like other bright young women of her generation, Katharine stood on the brink of adulthood suspended between two vastly different cultural norms. On the one hand, she had inherited and even taken for granted the new attitudes, behaviors, and freedoms that an earlier generation of elite southern women, once bound to the gendered conventions of a slaveholding plantation world, had secured in the wake of the Civil War. On the other hand, new rules for white womanhood were still in the making. Normal taught Katharine how to make herself publicly useful as a smart woman in a changing world. Sullins taught her the social rules for private life among the southern elite. Both schools expected her to carry out conventional notions of white womanhood, including marriage. Hers was a world where white male authority still reigned supreme. Unmarried young white women, however, could use courtship to manipulate white male authority to their own advantage en route to marriage.

Although Katharine had admirers during her college years, they remain largely unidentified. One encounter during her Normal years, although not of an openly romantic kind, deserves relating, however. President McIver asked sixteen-year-old Katharine and her roommate, Emma Lewis Speight, to visit Katharine's cousin, R. J. Reynolds, during a school outing in Winston. While all the other young women rode their decorated bicycles in a parade honoring the Tobacco Fair, Katharine and Emma met with the famous tobacco magnate to request a donation for the new Students' Building. Speight recalled that R.J.R. "seemed quite impressed with his young cousin and sent the girls on their way with a box of candy apiece—plus the largest single check that was received for the new building." Their brief encounter, arranged by McIver, may very well have marked R.J.R.'s first meeting with his newly grown-up cousin. Not too long after that encounter, while wandering through Normal's Peabody Forest during a beautiful snow, Katharine confided to Emma, "When I marry, I shall go to Europe on my wedding trip. . . . And then I shall buy a great estate."[154] Had Katharine been thinking of her successful and distinguished cousin when she shared her romantic dreams?

Portrait of Katharine and R. J. Reynolds, 1914.
Courtesy of Reynolda House Museum of American Art. (frontispiece)

Hardin Reynolds, father of R. J. Reynolds. Courtesy of Reynolda House Museum of American Art.

Portrait of Nancy Jane Cox Reynolds, mother of R. J. Reynolds. Courtesy of Reynolda House Museum of American Art.

Zachary T. Smith and Mary Susan Smith, parents of Katharine Reynolds.
Courtesy of Reynolda House Museum of American Art.

R. J. Reynolds, 1872. Courtesy of Reynolda House Museum of American Art.

Mary Katharine Reynolds, ca. 1890. Courtesy of Reynolda House Museum of American Art.

R. J. Reynolds observing the arrival of the first airplane to Winston, ca. 1911. Courtesy of Reynolda House Museum of American Art.

Main Street looking south, Blue Ridge Hotel on the right, Mount Airy, early 1900s. Courtesy of the Photo Collection of the Mount Airy Museum of Regional History.

Downtown Winston, ca. 1900. Courtesy of Reynolda House Museum of American Art.

R. J. Reynolds, bottom row left, with his four brothers: eldest brother A.D. in the middle, Harbour on A.D.'s right, Will standing on the right, Walter standing on the left. Courtesy of Reynolda House Museum of American Art.

R. J. Reynolds with brothers Will and Walter in his office at R. J. Reynolds Tobacco Company. Courtesy of Reynolda House Museum of American Art.

Winston citizens with a Gatling gun; the Winston mayor borrowed Charlotte's Gatling gun during the 1895 race riot. Collection of the Wachovia Historical Society; photograph courtesy of Old Salem Museums and Gardens.

R. J. Reynolds, far right, standing outside the building of the Wachovia National Bank that served the R. J. Reynolds Tobacco Company, with James A. Gray (middle) and George Henry Brookes, probably in the early 1900s. Courtesy of the Forsyth County Public Library Photograph Collection.

New York City studio portrait of R. J. Reynolds, cigar in hand, ca. 1915. Courtesy of Reynolda House Museum of American Art.

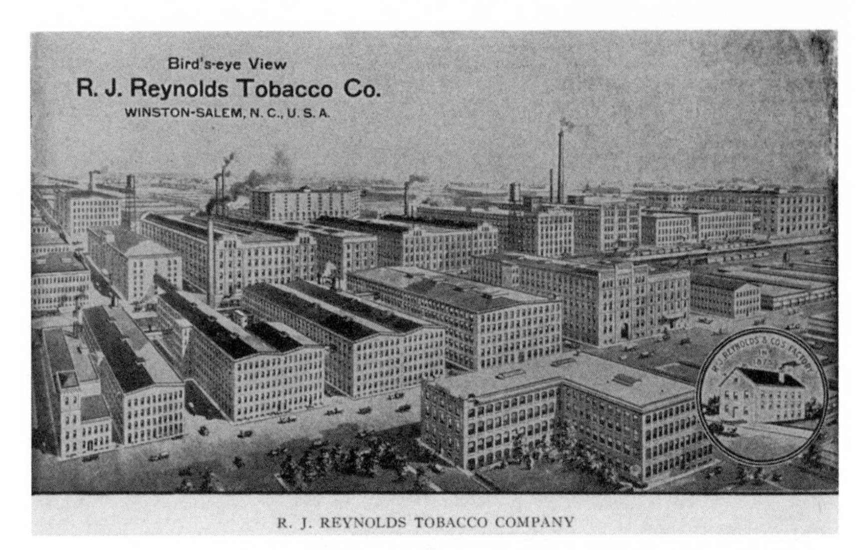

Bird's-eye view of R. J. Reynolds Tobacco Company. This is a composite view of the factories, 1918. Courtesy of Forsyth County Public Library Photograph Collection.

Aerial view of R. J. Reynolds factories and rail line. Collection of the Wachovia Historical Society; photograph courtesy of Old Salem Museums and Gardens.

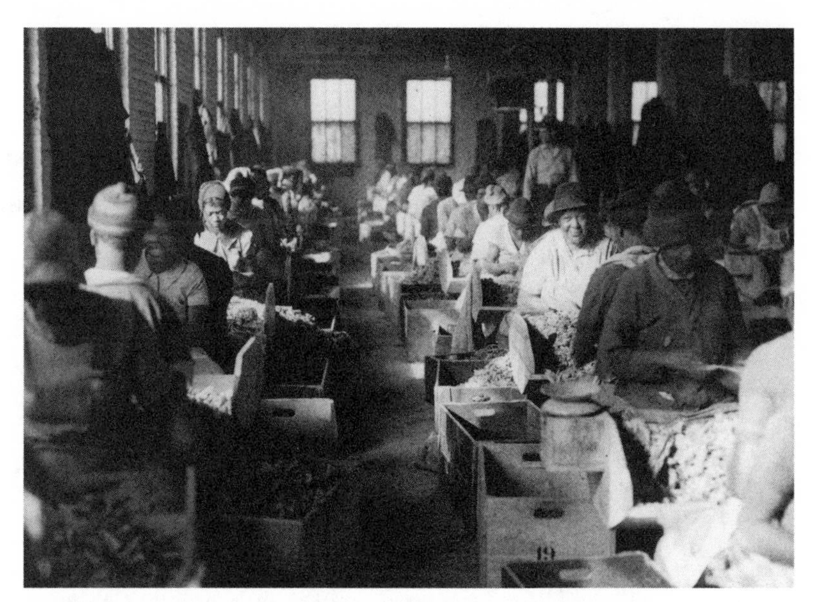

Tobacco stemming room, R. J. Reynolds Tobacco Company, 1938.
Courtesy of Forsyth County Public Library Photograph Collection.

Workers at wood box shop, R. J. Reynolds Company.
Courtesy of Forsyth County Public Library Photograph Collection.

EARLY BIRD
TOBACCO.

Tobacco sale in a Winston warehouse. Collection of the Wachovia Historical Society; photograph courtesy of Old Salem Museums and Gardens.

R. J. Reynolds Tobacco Company workers heading home. Collection of the Wachovia Historical Society; photograph courtesy of Old Salem Museums and Gardens.

Slater Hospital for Negroes, built in 1902 with matching funds from R. J. Reynolds. Courtesy of Forsyth County Public Library Photograph Collection.

African American World War I veterans parade in Winston-Salem. Collection of the Wachovia Historical Society; photograph courtesy of Old Salem Museums and Gardens.

Dr. Simon G. Atkins and Mrs. Oleona P. Atkins seated with the postgraduate department students in front of the Slater Industrial Academy and State Normal School. Courtesy of Winston-Salem State University Archives—R.G. 8.2, WSSU Photograph Collection—Graduate Department (1916).

The Reynolds home on West Fifth Street.
Courtesy of the Forsyth County Public Library Photograph Collection.

Katharine and R. J. Reynolds with their first child, Dick Jr., in Palm Beach, Florida.
Courtesy of Reynolda House Museum of American Art.

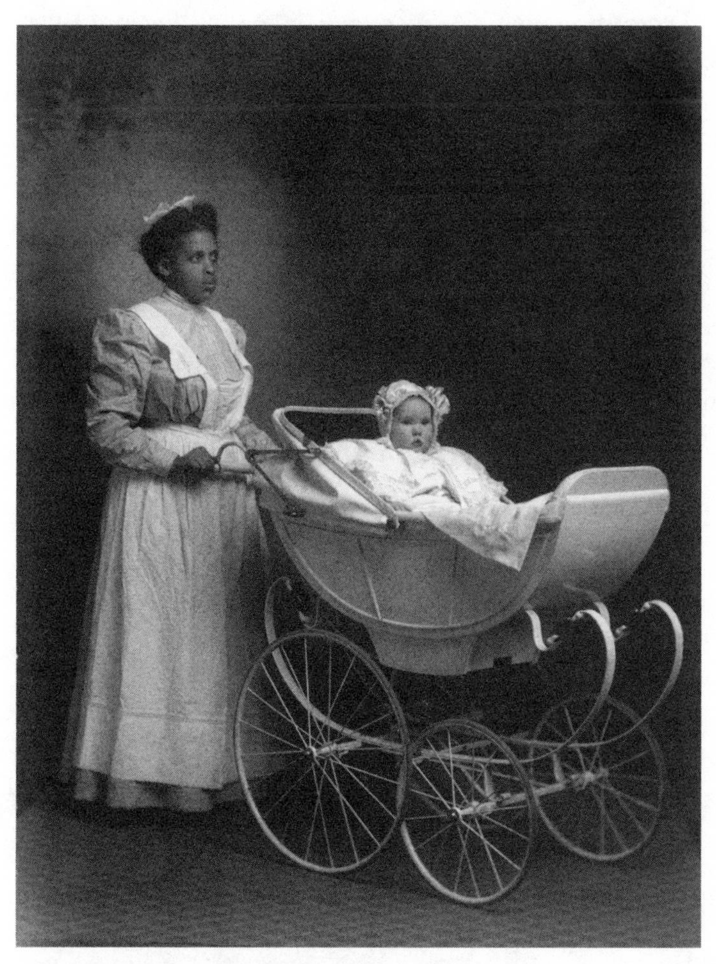

Nursemaid "Mammy Lula" with Mary Reynolds, 1908.
Courtesy of Reynolda House Museum of American Art.

R. J. Reynolds with children.
Courtesy of Reynolda House Museum of American Art.

R. J. Reynolds and family with chauffeur fording the Yadkin River.
Courtesy of Reynolda House Museum of American Art.

Katharine Reynolds with children.
Courtesy of Reynolda House Museum of American Art.

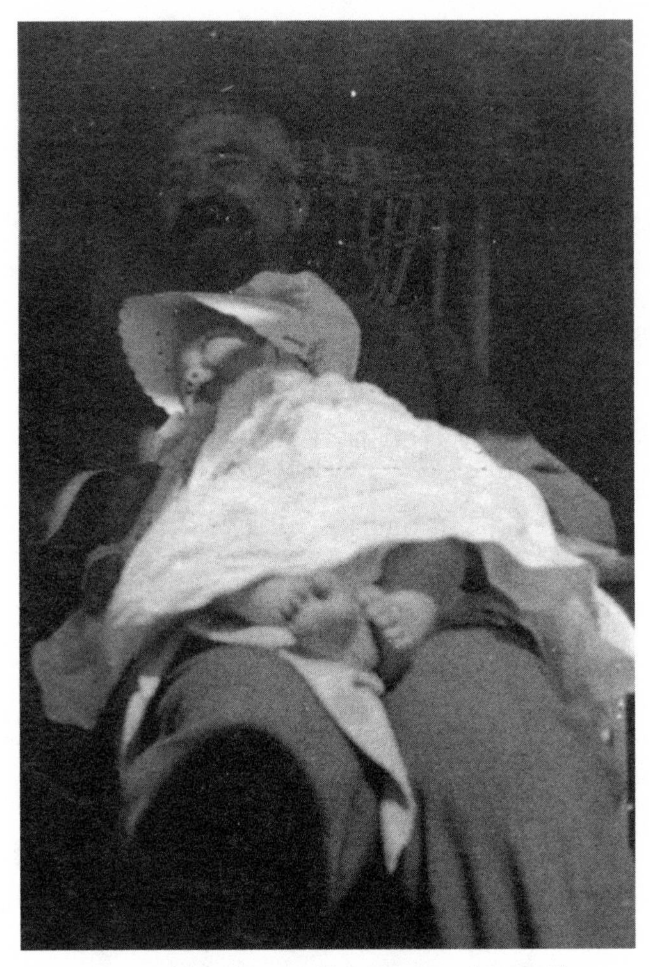

R. J. Reynolds with youngest child, Zachary Smith Reynolds, 1912.
Courtesy of Reynolda House Museum of American Art.

Family portrait, 1914. Courtesy of Reynolda House Museum of American Art.

Nursemaid Lizzie Thompson with the Reynolds children on the boardwalk at Atlantic City in a candid photo probably taken by Katharine Smith Reynolds, ca. 1913. Courtesy of Reynolda House Museum of American Art.

Henrietta Van Den Berg, the German-born, Johns Hopkins–trained nurse and governess to the Reynolds children and companion to Katharine Smith Reynolds. Courtesy of Reynolda House Museum of American Art.

Katharine Smith Reynolds used her own funds and secured convict labor and the aid of the Department of Transportation to hasten the paving of Reynolda Road alongside Reynolda Estate. Courtesy of Reynolda House Museum of American Art.

John and Marjorie Carter, the head butler and head cook at Reynolda House; the family called John Carter "the majordomo." Courtesy of Reynolda House Museum of American Art.

Lovie Eaton, the first teacher at the Five Row School for African American children on the Reynolda Estate. Courtesy of Reynolda House Museum of American Art.

Children in the Five Row School on the Reynolda Estate. Courtesy of Reynolda House Museum of American Art.

The Reynolda Estate, 1927, including bungalow home, Reynolda Farm and Village, and Lake Katharine. Aero Service Corp. of Philadelphia photograph, courtesy of Reynolda House Museum of American Art.

Contemporary photo of R. J. Reynolds's study in Reynolda House; note the ashtray in foreground and Katharine and R.J.R. portraits in background. Courtesy of Reynolda House Museum of American Art.

Contemporary photo of Katharine Reynolds's study, where she dictated letters to her secretary and kept her accounts. Courtesy of Reynolda House Museum of American Art.

Reynolda Presbyterian Church, at Katharine Reynolds's insistence, one of the first buildings erected on the Reynolda Estate. Courtesy of Reynolda House Museum of American Art.

The dairy on the Reynolda Farm sported some of the best-bred Jersey cows in the nation and state-of-the-art milking equipment kept sparkling clean to ensure hygienic dairy products. Courtesy of Reynolda House Museum of American Art.

The Young Women's Christian Association building on the corner of East First and South Church Street in Winston-Salem, 1918. Katharine Smith Reynolds was one of the founding members of the YWCA in 1908. Courtesy of Forsyth County Public Library Photograph Collection.

Katharine Smith Reynolds, family members, and officers of the North Carolina Federation of Women's Clubs in Katharine's beautifully decorated chauffeured car during the NCFWC annual convention meeting in Winston-Salem in 1912. Courtesy of Reynolda House Museum of American Art.

Portrait of Katharine Smith Reynolds, ca. 1920.
Courtesy of Reynolda House Museum of American Art.

J. Edward Johnston, Katharine's second husband, 1922. Courtesy of Reynolda House Museum of American Art.

Katharine Smith Reynolds, wedding portrait, 1921.
Courtesy of Reynolda House Museum of American Art.

J. Edward Johnston with J. Edward Johnston Jr., 1924.
Courtesy of Reynolda House Museum of American Art.

R. J. Reynolds High School and Auditorium, 1927; Katharine Smith Reynolds purchased the land, hired the architects to design the buildings, and funded the state-of-the-art auditorium. Courtesy of Forsyth County Public Library Photograph Collection.

3 Making Money

While Katharine was growing up in Mount Airy, going to school and dreaming about her future, R.J.R. was transforming Winston into an important southern industrial center. Boyish, clean-shaven, and thin as a rail when he first arrived, he grew more imposing with each passing year. He was maturing into a bear of man with a shaggy head of dark hair, a fulsome beard, and a portly belly. R.J.R. was part of a new generation of southern men with little interest in rededicating themselves to the past. Like dozens of other young men, he had been drawn to Winston for two key reasons: the presence of the North Western North Carolina railway branch, however modest, and the town's location as the buckle of the bright-leaf tobacco belt. Many years later, Virginians would compare Winston's growth with Danville's decline during this period, and they would add a third factor to Winston's appeal. Unlike Danville's boosters, who would not deign to advertise their community or their special soil or work at producing tobacco products that appealed to developing tastes, Winston's young industrialists were quite willing to be braggarts and innovators.[1]

By 1880, Winston had a boomtown quality. Sixteen tobacco factories and auction houses lined the streets, and four more were under construction. The population had increased tenfold over the last decade, numbering 5,706 inhabitants in Winston and Salem all told. About 40 percent were African Americans, many newly arrived, drawn to the seasonal wage work available to them in the multiplying tobacco factories.[2] Housing was in short supply, and new buildings were being thrown up in every direction to meet the growing need.[3] All this expansion depended on the national taste for bright leaf.[4]

By the mid-1800s, Europeans preferred milder-flavored leaf over the typical heavy, fire-cured U.S. tobacco of the era. Although farmers elsewhere in the United States had experimented with new methods to produce more leaf bearing this taste, it was the poor, siliceous soil of southern Virginia and Piedmont North Carolina that grew the best thin tobacco. In an ironic twist, the so-called Bright Belt, an especially impoverished region, sparked North Carolina's latest economic boom.[5] The state was benefiting from technological developments that accelerated mass production, better railroads to transport manufactured products to national markets, and greater risk taking among a second generation of tobacco manufacturers. The fact that cotton prices were declining in other southern states helped North Carolina's new national prominence too. The South's oldest crop, once the progenitor of the region's first rural elite in the colonial Chesapeake, was turning out a new class of wealthy men almost three hundred years later.[6]

R.J.R. understood that the emergence of the bright-leaf tobacco market signaled a major opportunity, and while he had benefited greatly from the knowledge and networks he had gained from his family in Virginia, his move to Winston allowed him to shape his own fortune at long last by putting himself at the heart of the action.[7] He brought with him a respectable amount of cash, about $7,500 (the equivalent of $136,000 today), with which to build his future empire. R.J.R.'s first company purchase in Winston was an unpretentious one, a one-hundred-foot lot on Depot Street, acquired from the Moravian Church for $388.50. The location put him close to the railway spur to Greensboro and its critical connections to the Richmond–Danville railway system.[8] He built a thirty-six-by-sixty-foot factory for $2,400, employed a dozen workers, and produced 150,000 pounds of plug that first year. He was so intent on saving money during this period that he slept in the factory.[9] Not only could he save the cost of paying for a room at a boardinghouse, he could keep a watchful eye out for fire, cured tobacco's biggest enemy. The R. G. Dun correspondents agreed that R.J.R. was making good progress, describing him in 1879 in the following glowing terms: "entirely responsible," "of good character and habits and stands high here, is doing a good business and making money."[10] Reynolds was tireless. Whenever his plant hit capacity, he expanded. "About every other year this factory was built on top, bottom and additions made to each end, until the business was increased to 1,000,000 pounds, having taken eighteen years to reach this volume," he later recounted about his first two decades as an industrialist.[11]

Initially R.J.R. employed a handful of men on a seasonal basis to make twist for wholesalers and affix other contractors' brands and tags to his product. Most of these employees were African American. In fact, black memory in Winston-Salem holds that R. J. Reynolds received so much help from African American residents during this early stage of his business that he expressed his indebtedness to those first wage workers for the remainder of his long career.[12] The fourth tobacco manufacturer to arrive in town, he managed to catch up with and then surpass the other three, Major Brown, the Bailey brothers, and the Hanes brothers (who would exchange tobacco for textiles in the early twentieth century and build a highly successful set of manufactories themselves). The *Winston Union Republican* and the *Winston Western Sentinel* touted Reynolds as the man to watch from the start, documenting for their curious readers each and every building addition and technological improvement he made. By 1881, R.J.R. had bought a twenty-five-horsepower steam engine. His investment in this technology immediately cemented his reputation as one of the city's "most industrious, go-ahead tobacconists," able to "manufacture an immense quality of weed" at considerable profit.[13] By 1883, he had become such an institution that the newspapers began to refer to him simply as R.J.R. He was smart enough to register those well-known initials for corporate use three years later.[14]

New South booster Henry Grady, the editor of the *Atlanta Constitution*, would have been proud of R.J.R.'s accomplishments. R.J.R. certainly practiced what Grady preached. Advocating industrialization as a panacea for the worn-down, war-torn region, along with thrift and hard labor, Grady had boasted in his famous 1886 speech before a room full of New England movers and shakers in Manhattan that southerners had "sown towns and cities in the place of theories. And put business above politics," asserting, "We have fallen in love with work." Dedicated to enterprise and unflagging in his work ethic, R.J.R. personified Henry Grady's New South man. Part of a larger movement that looked upon the old planter class and its slave labor and agricultural economy as a backward system, R.J.R. recognized that the diversification of agriculture, commerce, and industry built a healthier society, one able to incorporate blacks as well as whites. He wanted to be one of that core group of talented business leaders who orchestrated the creation of the New South. Grady's oration before the New England Club in New York City must have been one of R.J.R.'s primers: "The new South presents a perfect democracy, the oligarchs leading in the popular movement—a social system compact and closely knitted, less splendid on the surface, but stronger at the core—a hundred farms for every plantation, fifty homes for every palace—and a diversified industry that meets the complex need of this complex age."[15]

R.J.R. believed southerners could transform themselves into industrialists and businessmen, because he had done it himself with his own labor and ingenuity as his main resources. He was pleased by the spread of successful tobacco, textile, and furniture plants across the Atlantic South, the rise of new cities like Winston, and the new urban elite (including himself) that developed within these emerging metropolises. He knew firsthand what a city on the move looked like. The Fries Manufacturing and Power Company opened the Idol Hydro Station in Winston, the first hydroelectric dam in North Carolina, in 1890.[16] This construction allowed Winston to be the first town in the state to sport electric streetlights and one of the first in the country to operate electric streetcars.[17] In fact, Thomas Edison, an investor in the electric plant, attended the downtown celebrations that accompanied these exciting developments.[18] Winston had transformed itself into a prosperous place, with 225 mercantile establishments and 34 tobacco firms. The R. J. Reynolds Tobacco Company now employed five hundred hands in its brand-new six-story building; its facilities were considered the biggest and best in the state.[19] By 1896, the Winston population had grown to ten thousand people, and the number of tobacco factories had risen to 50.[20]

More than twenty years after his death, R.J.R.'s younger brother Will stated that R.J.R. was not a political man. R.J.R. believed that political activity was valuable only insomuch as it served "a high state of industrial and business acumen and the welfare of the citizens." He judged government on the basis of its helpfulness or hindrance to "the welfare of the citizens which in his thinking could be worked out soundly and permanently only through the establishment and maintenance in this country of fair conditions encouraging the development of the highest possible industrial and business activity."[21] Will got it wrong. R.J.R. was highly political in every sense of the word. He learned early in his career how to manipulate his business cohorts and the city council. He paid close attention to state and national politics, and he used his influence through his friendships and as an industry leader wherever he could.

Young R.J.R. had moved quickly to assert himself as a leader in this new class of urban power brokers. So successful were his efforts that his brother Harbour reported to family members back home in Patrick County that R.J.R. had become "the Virginia Carr in Winston."[22] R.J.R. was a master at making money through the impersonal workings of the market. He understood that investing his profits not only back into his own business but also into local stocks, real estate, transportation, and infrastructure enhanced his business and his political networking. He appeared frequently before the Board of Commissioners.[23] He sank money into local public-utility and transportation ventures. He had invested in the Winston Water Works by 1880 and took an active interest in the development of all local public works thereafter, actions that benefited his own ambitions while transforming Winston into an important industrial center. Following in his father's footsteps, he also bought land and properties left and right but went one step further by acting as a real-estate developer. He rented out the tenement houses he bought, acquired timberland, renovated commercial properties such as the downtown Merchant's Hotel, and owned nearly three dozen tracts of land around Winston before he turned forty.[24] He had holdings in the Piedmont Land and Manufacturing Company, the Winston Development Company, the North Winston Development Company, and the West End Development Company.[25]

Young R.J.R. displayed all the characteristics of the American entrepreneur. As committed as he was to developing the infrastructure of Winston, which ultimately served his own business interests even as it delighted most residents, he was also investing on a much larger scale. By the 1890s, R.J.R. owned property and stocks in multiple business pursuits, including the Damascus Enterprise Company, Conway Land Investment Company, Elkins Land Investment Company, Roanoke and Southern Railroad, Southern Chemical Company, and Orinco Company, and property investments in Gadsden, Alabama, as well as Martinsville and Bristol, Virginia.[26] He invested in textile mills around the South. By 1901, he was purchasing significant amounts of stock from national companies, including U.S. Steel, Southern Pacific Railroad, and Virginia-Carolina Chemical, the chemical fertilizer company.[27] Open to potential opportunities and willing to embrace change, he was aggressive in his business decisions and tenacious in the extreme.[28] Although he trusted his own judgment most, he understood the value of building stalwart social networks too. As the new man in town, he had joined one fraternal association and benevolent society after another.[29] These connections gave him access to valuable information about available properties, investment opportunities, and general knowledge about the other movers and shakers too.

Even as R.J.R. embraced business development and industrialization with a vengeance, his eyes wide open to financial opportunities that either served his tobacco manufactory or reduced risk by spreading his investments into other potentially lucrative avenues, he remained a grounded man, literally. Although he always lived in town, first in his company's loft, then in boardinghouses and hotels, and later in the family Victorian mansion built at the turn of the century to accommodate his brother Will, Will's new wife, Kate Bitting, and himself on Fifth Street, he also owned a farm he named Skyland in east Winston.[30] Here he relished cultivating crops and raising outstanding livestock. The tobacco industrialist was most at home in the countryside, despite his growing wealth and extensive national connections. R.J.R., one of the shrewdest and most farsighted of modern businessmen in the nation, remained a nineteenth-century man at heart, preferring his connectedness to the land and personal relationships over urban systems that his very embrace of industrial capitalism helped spawn in the New South.

R.J.R. also cultivated an interest in public office early in his career, although that career began and ended inauspiciously. Becoming involved in local politics was a shrewd decision on his part. As a city commissioner, he could shape votes on infrastructure and investment options that served his business interests well. In his first election in 1879, he lost the race for city commissioner. Undaunted, he ran again and won in 1884. He served on the fire and sanitary committees and was appointed supervisor of roads in 1886. His political career, however, was short-lived. In an ironic turn, R.J.R. and his fellow white Democrats lost to the Colored Men's ticket in 1890. His loss reflected two inextricable realities: demographic changes in the downtown ward as rural blacks flocked to the city for wage work, and the growing politicization of those same new workers.[31]

The Democratic Party had begun to dominate city politics by the 1870s and, with the exception of the 1890s, would do so until the end of the twentieth century. The hundreds of poor farmers and their families, white and black, who had left the fields to take new industrial jobs in Winston were so dependent on their wages that most felt pressured into supporting the dozen or so manufacturers, all Democrats, who had descended on Winston to make their living, much to their whiggish Moravian neighbors' dismay. The new industrialists, including R.J.R., were able to use their workers' votes to get themselves elected to city office almost immediately, and these same new men became full participants in party caucuses as well. Within a generation, however, these industrialists began relegating those roles to their relatives and junior associates and partners, puppeteering them from afar, as R.J.R. himself did following his 1890 loss. From the outset, this group of industrialists, who included the Hanes and the Moravian Fries families, publicly presented all government measures that aided their businesses as unselfish advancements in the city's progress and prosperity and embraced public roles as benevolent paternalists.[32] R.J.R. was no exception. In 1879, the year Winston was formally chartered, he was one among several tobacco manufacturers who petitioned the city for forty thousand dollars to construct two railroads departing from Winston, ostensibly to serve all residents, though he stood to be the biggest beneficiary by far.[33] R.J.R. advocated for strong transportation links for the rest of his life, as well as any and all other measures that assured strong business growth.

This coterie of industrialists did not advocate industrial development exclusively. They also promoted progressive initiatives that they thought served the larger population. Because they ran the local government and kept taxes low, public funds were limited. The paternalists used this situation to determine which public institutions they most wanted to support as private philanthropists and then sought matching funds from the larger population to complete these initiatives rather than raising taxes. This strategy put the cash-strapped black community at a special disadvantage.[34]

The improvement of educational opportunities for whites and blacks alike was one of the first initiatives they pressed for. By 1883, city leaders had secured enough votes for a public school system for the education of all classes and races, along with the taxes needed to support it. R.J.R. had worked hard for these changes. His name topped a list of thirty-nine petitioners calling for new property and poll taxes to establish graded schools presented to Mayor Albert Gorrell in 1878. Because Winston's leaders were willing to make this commitment, key North Carolina educators were subsequently drawn to the city. Calvin H. Wiley (1819–87), known as "the father of education" in North Carolina for his unflagging commitment to common schools and his appointment as the first state superintendent of common schools, even made Winston his home upon his retirement, such was his belief in its commitment to schooling. A youthful Charles D. McIver was equally impressed with Winston's promise. When the first graded school in Winston was erected, an impressive two-story structure, northern educators and philanthropists poured forth their praises. A. D. Mayo, the editor of the *New England Journal of Education*, commended the local industrialists for their commitment to education: "The new city of Winston, N.C., has done the most notable work among southern towns of its size in the establishment of a system of graded schools. . . . Only four months from its organization the West End Graded School, with all the disadvantages of the mixed population of a new manufacturing community, is a model and is thronged with visitors from all over the Southern country." Several city leaders, including banker James A. Gray and tobacco manufacturer W. A. Whitaker, not only supported the establishment of this system but subsequently took a firm hand in shaping the school curriculum, cementing widespread perception of paternalist intervention.[35]

Although the 1868 state constitution legislated free public schools for black as well as white children, limited progress was made on behalf of African Americans, even though they comprised 58 percent of the city's population by 1890. At first, support for black schools came almost exclusively from within the black community. Then northern Quakers financed salaries for two northern white women to teach in the black public schools, though their efforts were limited to primary and industrial education. In 1887, black leadership and northern philanthropic resources pressed for the establishment of the Depot Street Graded School for Negroes, a stone's throw from the tobacco factories. Winston superintendent Julius S. Tomlinson had actually traveled to the major cities of the Northeast seeking funds for this endeavor. Reynolds Tobacco Company workers' children subsequently flocked to the modest structure for their schooling, with reports of as many as 1,000 jammed into a small structure run by a principal and two teachers, while 533 students attended the white school.[36]

With the hiring of a gifted young black principal, Simon G. Atkins (1863–1934), to head the Depot School in 1890, R. J. Reynolds began to work publicly with African American city leaders, and especially Atkins, to improve black educational opportunities throughout Winston.[37] Educated at Livingstone College by talented black leaders, Atkins wrote opinion pieces on education for the *Star of Zion*, the AME Zion Church's weekly publication. He also worked with members of the North Carolina Teachers Association to persuade the state legislature to approve an institution of higher learning for African Americans. He shared this intention with Reynolds upon his arrival in Winston, citing Reconstruction amendments to the Constitution as argument for a black college equivalent to the recently approved North

Carolina Industrial and Mechanical College for whites. Reynolds committed five hundred dollars to Atkins's vision, and the black middle-class community secured another two thousand dollars, offering their own development property in Columbia Heights for the site, but the Greensboro black community outbid them with the promise of fourteen thousand dollars and eleven acres.[38] Undaunted, Atkins and his supporters opened their own academy anyway, with help from the northern-based John F. Slater Fund, established to uplift "the lately emancipated population of the southern states by conferring on them the blessings of an industrial education."[39] The duly named Slater Industrial Academy, inaugurated in 1892, marked the first black school of its kind in North Carolina dedicated to producing skilled craftsmen "to uplift the status of the ordinary colored laborer."[40]

Atkins was following in the steps of Booker T. Washington (1856–1915) and his Tuskegee Normal and Industrial Institute. Washington, born a slave, had come of age in Reconstruction (as had Atkins). After securing an education at the Hampton Normal and Agricultural Institute and studying at Wayland Seminary, Washington headed a newly established school for blacks at Tuskegee. Because Washington believed that the best path for most African Americans' success in the post-Reconstruction South lay in economic independence, he used his school to teach craft and industrial skills. Washington advocated that black institutions of higher learning dedicate themselves to training sharecroppers' children in these skills, cultivating thrift and enterprise in the process, while putting off the pursuit of civil rights and political power in exchange for wealth and security. His views, which he wielded to secure funding for Tuskegee and other black schools across the South, were warmly received by white industrialists, politicians, and philanthropists alike, turning Washington into a national spokesman on race. By 1900 critics like the black intellectual W. E. B. Du Bois decried Washington's outlook. His position, they argued, did nothing to stem the bloody tide of white supremacy that was institutionalizing racism across the South. Atkins himself was privately distraught by these developments too, and the failure of this black economic self-help movement to halt it, but publicly he continued to advocate this conservative vision of racial uplift, largely because it secured his Slater school considerable support, and especially from its best patron. R.J.R. Reynolds funded many black educational initiatives led by Atkins over the course of his lifetime. The two remained respectful of each other right up to Reynolds's death in 1918, despite the hardening of the color line and the institutionalization of Jim Crow segregation by the turn of the century.[41]

R.J.R.'s giving was decidedly local and piecemeal in contrast to the direction philanthropy had begun to take nationally. The number of millionaires in the United States ballooned from several hundred in the 1870s to over forty thousand by World War I. Many of these newly wealthy, like Mrs. Olivia Sage and John D. Rockefeller, delighted at the prospect of personally reshaping society with their new money. Their burgeoning interest in public welfare coincided with the rise of professional social-service agencies that sought to aid society with a more structured approach rather than the age-old tradition of charity. This marriage of philanthropists and social services exerted a powerful influence on social reform and public policy making by the turn of the century. That transition came more slowly to the South, instituted mostly by northern philanthropists, in the form of Rockefeller's eradication of the hookworm, Andrew Carnegie's public libraries, and widespread northern philanthropic interest in black higher education. Southern philanthropists were slower in the making and tended to pursue the advancement of higher education. James B. Duke donated funds for Trinity College in Durham, for example, while Coca-Cola magnate Asa Candler turned rural Oxford College into Emory University in Atlanta.[42]

R.J.R. did not provide endowment-making sums of money to colleges and universities. Instead, he gave small amounts to ameliorate need and strengthen the community around him in the nineteenth-century tradition of aid. His account books were full of examples of modest sums of money doled out to one social institution, reform association, or church after another, white and black, especially in Winston-Salem, but also across the bright-leaf tobacco belt. There was a method in his approach. As the largest employer in the area, R.J.R.'s funding of clubs, charities, orphanages, and churches brought greater social stability to his workforce and their families. It created more social bonds and allegiances. In particular, giving to social institutions in the black community helped discourage some black workers from heading north in search of better-paying jobs and less discrimination. R.J.R. did not rely on religious doctrine or church mandate to determine how to meet need; he was not even a member of a church until the last year of his life. Nor was he a visionary social reformer. His giving did not mark an effort to remake society. Instead, he wanted to improve the world around him to make it more stable in the wake of the urban and industrial transformations he had helped usher into the region. His company stood to gain by encouraging that stability. He built a reputation for himself as a generous paternalist as a side benefit.[43]

Although his strategy may not have been systematic enough to deserve the label "welfare capitalism," which came to characterize the new national pattern of corporate paternalism that emerged in the late nineteenth century and took root by the 1920s, his actions certainly suggest that he understood how industries could function as social institutions. By looking out for employee needs, he could avert labor unrest and discourage regulation at the same time. Over the course of his career, he continued directing his paternalistic benevolence at his employees' communities beyond the factory but eventually turned that benevolence inward too, providing on-site lunchrooms, water fountains, child care, sports teams, and women's clubs at his wife's encouragement.

R.J.R. personally benefited from directing so many of the changes that industrialization wrought on the Piedmont. The so-called entrepreneurial spirit that drove economic development so forcefully in this period and created so much individual gain at the expense of so many others drew its sustenance from the same culture that cultivated a belief in natural rights and democracy. R.J.R. supported black educational opportunity in Winston to serve his own ends rather than the simple pursuit of justice. But he believed that workers in America had more opportunities and better working conditions than their brethren in Europe despite the intransigent color line. "*Our* working people are better satisfied and much happier than the working Europeans," he observed. In R.J.R's mind Europe's violent workers' world was the fault of Europe's feudal past and its current rigid social hierarchy. America, by comparison, remained a society of Jeffersonian small producers. In the United States everyone had the opportunity to improve the quality of his or her life. Even in the economically strapped South, R.J.R. thought, new jobs in the cities brought poor whites and blacks alike higher standards of living and more access to a civil society characterized by the spread of schools, newspapers, clubs, and theaters.[44]

During Winston's earliest years, the black population had been relatively small. Rural whites had left their farms and villages to seek seasonal work in Winston in the tobacco and textile industries and in railroad construction, but the number of rural blacks seeking wage work quickly outpaced them. By 1880, the black population equaled the white population.

By 1890, it exceeded it by 10 percent. Black men, women, and children were arriving daily by the trainload in search of work while others walked all the way from Patrick and Henry Counties, and even Danville and Richmond, with hopes of finding work in Winston's tobacco factories.[45] R.J.R's own need for labor at his ever-expanding company had played a major role in driving this heavy migration. In the 1870s, he employed some 35 hands to produce about 150,000 pounds of plug between May and October.[46] By 1887, he was paying 300 hands to turn out as much as 750,000 pounds annually in his factory, which had quadrupled in size and now stood four stories tall.[47] But Reynolds was not the only tobacco industrialist dependent on black hands by a long shot. By 1890, the city employed 5,000 black tobacco workers, compared to some 750 workers, white and black, in the textile and wool factories, grist and sawmills, and ironworks of nearby Salem.[48]

The tobacco industry had always relied on black labor, first as slaves in home manufacturing enterprises like Hardin Reynolds's and in the late antebellum factories of Lynchburg and Danville, and then as free labor. Whites presumed black workers had a generational knowledge of tobacco work. They also embraced the illogical notion that black workers were better able to withstand its long hours, physically demanding expectations, and unsanitary conditions. These incorrect presumptions enabled whites to rationalize to themselves not only that blacks were fated to do what were clearly the least desirable jobs in the tobacco factories, but that they should be paid as little as possible for performing them.[49] There were benefits, however. Black farmworkers were fortunate if they earned $4.00 a month, but payouts for food and supplies gobbled that money up, rarely paid in cash anyway. A family working in a tobacco factory with a male breadwinner earning $1.25 a day, the wife 75 cents, and four children 50 cents each, all paid in cash, meant as much income in a single day in the city as a month of work in the countryside.[50] Years later, black educator Simon G. Atkins recalled that most black migrants came from places "where Negroes had little or no opportunity, and their object in coming to Winston-Salem was chiefly a bread and butter one."[51] The plentiful tobacco factories created a special culture. White visitors to the city gawked at "the ebon operatives" singing songs, their flying fingers matched to the beat, as they de-stemmed the tobacco leaves. The music was laden with meaning, whether offering critiques of their bosses or telling painful stories about their lives as unemployed hands. "Befo' I'd work fer Simkin, P.S. / I'd walk all night an' sleep all day; / Walk all night tu keep from sleepin', / An' sleep all day tu keep from eatin.'"[52]

Black labor and city politics have been inextricably linked at least since Reconstruction throughout the American South (if not before).[53] The origins of that complex relationship in Winston took shape in the crucible of late nineteenth-century industrialization. During the earliest years of tobacco manufacturing, seasonal labor was in great demand in this fledgling city. The workers, the majority of whom were African American, increasingly expressed disappointment at the low wages they received compared to white labor. In 1879, black tobacco rollers petitioned the tobacco manufacturers for living wages and recognition as citizens, believing justice economically and politically linked. But the number of people seeking work in the spring of 1880 so exceeded demand that the manufacturers ignored the rollers' demands. Although railroad construction jobs in the 1880s employed new numbers of unskilled laborers, the ever-increasing influx of rural black laborers seeking work in the city meant that manufacturers, including R.J.R., had no need to pay more competitive wages.[54] At the same time, R.J.R. and other city leaders took a paternalistic interest in the development of the black working class. As an elected member of the board of directors of the Twin-City Reform Club Room, R.J.R helped establish the Forsyth Five-Cent Savings Bank in 1888, borrowing the idea from similar efforts in New England to encourage black workers to save a portion of their wages.[55]

These industrialists must have prided themselves on their use of black labor, knowing the worker challenges the Dukes were facing in nearby Durham. Shortly after W. Duke, Sons and Company had installed their first Bonsack cigarette-making machine in their Durham plant, the 125 Polish and Russian Jewish workers whom the Dukes had hired from New York City threatened to destroy the new machinery, which they recognized rightly as their replacements. Fourteen of the émigrés then organized a local chapter of the Cigar Makers Progressive Union of America, the first of its kind in the Southeast, and in three months it counted over 70 of the 300 cigarette makers in Durham as members. At the national convention, the local chapter even went so far as to advocate "buying weapons and preparing for the coming revolution" in light of the Durham experience. James B. Duke eventually met with union officials protecting the Durham workers, but dissatisfaction with production quotas and wages, along with growing reliance on the Bonsack machine, persuaded the immigrant workers to return to New

York anyway, just as demand for cigarettes was growing. Appalled at their workers' escalating radicalism, the Dukes subsequently vowed to employ only "our own people" thereafter. By 1886, they wanted not only to replace but to enlarge their workforce and advertised for 500 white native workers.[56]

This series of events helped workers and employers alike in Winston understand that their manufactories were part of much larger economic and social worlds, and both groups hoped to leverage that reality to their advantage. African Americans sought to link their political identity with their working one. Although black men had secured the vote with the passage of the Fifteenth Amendment to the U.S. Constitution, ratified in 1870, black power did not begin its ascendancy in Winston until the election of the first black commissioner in 1881.[57] Then in 1886 the Knights of Labor, who were organizing new chapters across the country and in the new cities of North Carolina, organized both a white chapter and an African American chapter in Winston.[58] That year the Knights had held an annual national meeting in Richmond. When white hotels refused to house an interracial New York delegation, the group stayed in a black hotel. Grand Master Terence Powderly responded to this incident by asking Frances Ferrel, a black delegate, to introduce him at his opening speech. Powderly then warmly applauded the delegation for its insistence that color never divide its members. White newspaper editors in cities across North Carolina expressed their alarm at this story, all too aware that many of their urban working people had joined the Knights of Labor and needed to be disabused of this notion of social equality.[59] Yet in many quarters, well-to-do local whites informally sanctioned racial intermingling. Winston was no exception. The president of the local national bank, for instance, along with many other Winston and Salem elites, attended the wedding of an affluent black couple.[60]

Winston blacks were the main source of labor for the tobacco industry and the progenitors of a strong cultural community of their own making. Their fledgling political power, strengthened in part through their abortive Knights of Labor efforts, gained momentum in the years that followed. In 1889, Winston tobacco manufacturers followed the lead of Virginia manufacturers by reducing tobacco rollers' pay considerably. Local workers responded by organizing a strike in April, like their brethren at tobacco manufactories throughout the region. Crowds of African Americans gathered in Winston's downtown streets, while the strikers met at the Negro Knights of Labor Hall to debate their next steps. Meanwhile, the manufacturers had raised the pay for their prize hands (those who packed the tobacco) by twenty-five cents, convincing many of them to return to work. The rollers, who were losing as much as seventy-five cents for every hundred pounds they processed, held firm anyway. They launched a large public protest, marching through the streets behind a loud bass drummer and a fife player, "making the night hideous," according to white residents unnerved by the throngs of unhappy black residents. The manufacturers responded several days later by telling strikers that the wages paid to rollers in other North Carolina and Virginia towns were lower. Because Winston's wages, even the newly lowered ones, did prove better than elsewhere, the workers went back to work, and the strike ended.[61]

These battles for better wages had made their mark in an important political way, even if they did not change the wage structure. As in many other southern cities, Winston's African Americans by the 1890s had become well organized politically, better educated, and more willing to challenge white supremacy's demands than a generation earlier. The numbers of black businesses lining Winston's main streets and the number of black professionals, including teachers, lawyers, doctors, engineers, and ministers, had increased dramatically over the last two decades.[62] Black civic organizations now thrived, from fraternal organizations to bands to a fire-fighting company. Five black-built churches served the vibrant community.[63] Still, the community lacked a political voice, although African Americans now outnumbered whites. While the Republican Party sought black participation and allowed black men to run for office, the Democratic Party refused black participation but wanted black votes. But the Democratic Party was run by the industrialists, the very men who employed the majority of black workers. Although the Democratic Party had pledged to reduce black political power and black office holding across the state since winning election in 1876, urban black majorities in North Carolina, including Winston, actually increased the number of black officeholders over time.[64]

Leery of black political opportunity and responding to a new statewide election law, the Board of Commissioners redrew the three city wards. The new first and second wards contained almost all whites and together represented a third of the population. The third ward, in the factory and warehouse district, represented two-thirds of the town's population and was now disproportionately black. As a result of this gerrymandering, the white minority was represented by six elected commissioners, and the black majority by only three. In response, the black community organized a Colored Men's ticket in the 1890 municipal election in the third ward, as payback against the white-controlled first and second wards. This third-ward election swept out all three white incumbents, including R.J.R., although it left a majority-white council.[65]

Now the African American citizens could try to hold the industrialists accountable when it came to city policy making with their three black commissioners, but in all likelihood they would be outvoted by the six white commissioners. The emergence of a black political coalition on the heels of a public strike by black workers, even a failed one, signaled a sea change nonetheless. No longer were Winston African Americans content to limit themselves to wage work and relative isolation given the deprivation and dependence they had experienced as rural farm families and new urban workers. Southern cities by the end of the nineteenth century had produced a new world of horizontal race relations. Urban black men and women had more autonomy in cities, and more random and informal contact with whites in the factories, at the railway stations, on sidewalks and in restaurants, at theaters and in parks, in hotels and stores than ever before. But that freedom was increasingly contested by Winston whites.

The heavy patronage of the electric streetcars by the African American population led at least one editorialist to advocate adding a separate car for whites only. "On Sundays . . . the cars are literally crowded with the colored population, almost to the exclusion of the whites." [66] Thirty-one white women formed an association to establish a hospital and, although they claimed it would eventually serve all, immediately restricted it to whites.[67] Not only did the black community have to confront the institutionalization of white supremacy; so did R.J.R., along with the other Democratic industrialists, who were keenly aware of black political and economic demands for justice and the white intransigence that accompanied them.[68]

Local Democrats responded to African American demands for their political rights by openly disfranchising them. During the elections of 1892 and 1894, Democrats in Forsyth County used North Carolina election law to cut the number of black voters in half by denying blacks the right to register and challenging individual black voters on Election Day. The 1895 election to state office of the Fusionists—the Republicans and the Populists who had joined political forces to become a more powerful coalition—brought some measure of relief. The new North Carolina legislature voted to reduce the power of local registrars, allow colored ballots (to aid illiterate voters in distinguishing candidates), and guarantee representation by all parties at the polls.[69] But the local damage had been done. No powerful whites in Winston, including R.J.R., were willing to publicly defend equal rights for black citizens.

The public abrogation of those rights led to a formidable war between the races over the summer of 1895. When two policemen on the all-white force ordered a group of African Americans to disperse upon the arrest of a black man, nineteen-year-old Arthur Tuttle replied he would do so "when he got damn ready." A scuffle ensued in which Tuttle shot Officer Vickers with a gun passed to him by someone in the crowd. Tuttle, many people believed, had been especially resentful of police officers and the law that day, for he had just learned that an all-white jury had rendered another police officer "not guilty" in the recent death of his brother. Reaction to Tuttle's arrest splintered the city into factions. A plan for a lynching was rumored among whites, while a plan to free Tuttle from the local jail was spread by blacks.

Tuttle had expected whites to play by the rules. The all-white jury's sanction of his brother's murder by a member of the police department conveyed the utter absence of fair rules, and the police department's insistence on breaking up a black crowd during yet another arrest of a black man only enraged Tuttle all the more.[70] This was a society where white performances of civility toward blacks were few. White law enforcement ensured blacks few measures of postwar equality and especially not bodily protection from extralegal violence. In those last desperate years of the nineteenth century before whites once and for all abandoned the pretense of a biracial civil society and set up a regime of outright legal coercion instead, African Americans in Winston fought back out of desperation. When the fearful sheriff elected to send Tuttle to Greensboro to keep him safe, Winston blacks doubted his strategy would work. A reported two hundred African Americans "accompanied" Tuttle and the police on the train, while four hundred Greensboro blacks met the train at the station, bearing Winchesters and revolvers at the ready against would-be lynchers.[71]

Appalled at this huge racial rupture in spite of all his efforts to secure white support for racial uplift, Simon G. Atkins, the self-anointed peacemaker of the city, bemoaned all the "good feelings" between the races that black mob rule would undo. Atkins had just secured formal recognition from the state legislature for his rapidly expanding Slater Normal and

Industrial School as well as an annual budget of one thousand dollars.[72] Racial unrest of this magnitude in his own city denigrated this accomplishment. Still, while he swore blacks and whites were equal before the law, he also agreed that any man had the right to wield a weapon in self-defense if such rights were not respected.[73]

Fears for Tuttle's life were not diminished by Atkins's appeals, and Tuttle was moved to Mecklenburg County jail under armed guard. After the trial was set for August 12, he was moved back to town. Winston blacks raised five hundred dollars for his defense, and the city aldermen, in a highly unusual act that signaled their understanding of the larger repercussions of the trial, paid three white attorneys to defend him. On the evening of August 11, three hundred African Americans bearing weapons stood outside the jail prepared to fight off would-be lynchers. Though ordered to disperse, they did not, even when twenty police officers ringed them. Only when the sheriff ordered deputies and the Forsyth Riflemen to make arrests did the assembled blacks start firing. Forty-five African Americans were subsequently arrested by 4:00 a.m. Although injuries and deaths were reported on both sides, actual numbers were never made public. The sheriff subsequently ordered a Gatling gun, able to fire 1,700 shots per minute, sent up from Charlotte, while allegedly "thousands" of armed blacks collected outside the city. At the trial, the jury ruled Tuttle guilty, and the judge sentenced him to twenty-five years. The black community judged the sentence out of proportion when lesser sentences were consistently given to whites for similar crimes.[74]

The white community sought to downplay the whole series of events, denying that a "race war" as heralded in state newspapers had in fact occurred. "The affair is to be sincerely regretted. The colored people were foolhardy and hasty to act." In reality, argued the editors of the *Winston Union Republican,* "that mob of young negroes assembled on the streets near the jail" was "ignorant of the true situation of things." If the two hundred or three hundred present, who "thronged the streets in front, north and in the rear of the jail," had only returned to their homes as requested by the sheriff, peace would have been assured. Instead, although the leaders present agreed to disperse, when they did not do so in the time allotted and still were "all practically armed, and with their weapons in open display," the Forsyth Riflemen advanced. "The command was shoot to hit." Although three days later "the trouble" had been concluded, and the grand jury was certain "that the sheriff used no more force than necessary," the *Winston Union Republic* advised that the whole incident was "of such gravity . . . as to make the good men of both races and of all parties strive to prevent a reoccurrence in the future."[75]

In a society where white violence against blacks prevailed with so little governmental intervention, the willingness of the black community to defend Tuttle and the willingness of the white-majority city council to pay for a white defense team attest to the black community's power to force change.[76] But in the end, local black power did not prevail. The *Winston-Salem Journal*, founded in 1897, was proving a powerful organ for circulating Democratic Party ideas, especially white supremacy. Thus when the *Winston Union Republican* criticized a local resolution favoring white workers over black workers, the *Journal* fought back. "People will not invest in, or move into towns in danger of being dominated by negroes," wrote the editor, who then accused the *Union Republican* of championing "the negroes' cause" above that of white farmers and laborers.[77] Three days later, the editor concluded that only two parties existed in Winston, "the White man's party and the negro party, White Supremacy or negro rule. . . . Are you a White Man or a White Negro?"[78] On the eve of the election, employers spread word that workers who voted for Republicans would lose their jobs. White Democrats gathered by the hundreds at the polls to force potential black voters away and secured their victory.[79] Two weeks later even the *Winston Union Republican* had conceded to the Democrats. It carried a huge advertisement bearing the headline "White Men Wanted: To Come Live and Work in Winston-Salem." The ad stated, "We need them . . . to take the place of blacks in the mills and factories of Winston-Salem. In this, we have the backing of the best people of Winston-Salem."[80]

Compared to the politically driven racist vitriol in the local papers, Reynolds appears to have been moderate, largely because he said nothing in print on this issue. Whether Reynolds was one of the employers who threatened his workers with their jobs if they voted Republican, we do not know. Nor do we know if R.J.R. was one of the "best people" who approved the disfranchisement of black voters. It seems highly unlikely he had any interest in replacing his black workers with more white ones, however, from a cost-analysis perspective alone. Reynolds had worked hard to secure the support of the small black middle and elite classes starting to take hold in Winston, knowing that their leadership of the larger black community might influence some of his black workers. Although a lifelong Democrat, with the exception of the 1896 presidential election, when he voted for the businessman's friend, Republican William McKinley, he assiduously stayed out of the public eye during the "white men's party" politics that raged across the state and led to the brutal Wilmington race riot in 1898, the institution of one-party Democratic rule, the disfranchisement of African American men, and the racial segregation of public spaces, accommodations, and institutions that followed.[81]

Moreover, there can be no question that racist politics at the state level fueled Winston's ugly political scene. Democratic Party leaders had been working assiduously to regain political control after the Fusionists secured the house in 1894 and after Daniel Russell was elected the first Republican governor in 1896. Democratic Party champions had adopted a three-pronged approach to wrestle political power back from Governor Daniel Russell and the Fusionists. Their strategy turned on using their key leaders to the best of their abilities, some as writers, some as speakers, and others as "riders." Thus Democratic newspapermen like R.J.R.'s friend Josephus C. Daniels, editor of the *Raleigh News and Observer*, penned racist propaganda, while men like Furnifold Simmons (who had been elected to the U.S. House in 1896 and would be elected senator) and Charles Aycock (U.S. attorney for the Eastern District of North Carolina and future governor) delivered fiery addresses about black presumptions and improprieties that enraged white voters. Meanwhile, men calling themselves "Red Shirts" carried out intimidation tactics from horseback to terrorize blacks away from the polls and to force whites to vote for the Democrats. These architects of North Carolina's road to a segregation program used charges of black economic progress, interracial sexuality and miscegenation, and urban disorder to convince whites to "save" society from black encroachment by electing Democrats.[82]

The consequences of their successful campaigns were enormous. They removed African Americans from the election rolls based on literacy tests, adopted and enforced Jim Crow laws ensuring African Americans were second-class citizens, and controlled politics in North Carolina for some seventy-five years. No single event represented the intentions of the Democratic Party better than the horrific race riot in Wilmington on November 10, 1898. The impact of the Fusionist legislature had been especially apparent in the state's largest city, Wilmington, where middle-class whites and African Americans had cultivated a thriving economy and secured political office. Following the successful victory of the Democrats in Wilmington and across the state, a group of Wilmington whites drew up resolutions demanding that black newspaper editor Alex Manly—whose earlier editorial in the *Wilmington Record* challenging white notions about interracial relationships had touched off white indignation—leave the city and shut down his black newspaper. The group also called for the resignation of the mayor and the chief of police, all by the next day. The following morning as many as two thousand whites broke into the *Record*'s offices and burned down the building. Arguments and then escalating violence between whites and blacks quickly ensued, and several black men were wounded or shot dead, creating widespread terror and flight in the black community. The fallout from the Wilmington race riot, as African Americans left their property behind them and relocated in other states out of desperation, and the victory of the Democrats in subsequent state and local elections shelved the Republican Party in North Carolina for decades.

It is important to consider R.J.R.'s sustained public efforts to support black churches, benevolent organizations, and schools in light of one of the most repressive climates for African Americans in North Carolina history. Reynolds, a small boy during the last years of slavery, undoubtedly internalized the social mores of racial paternalism. Even more to the point, he had adapted them to a social and political world in rapid transition. He was no city-bred postwar pup inexperienced in the unspoken social understandings that had shaped racial and class hierarchies in the agricultural South for two centuries. Reynolds knew how to impose a benevolent kind of paternalism when it came to his employees, black and white, even in this new, wage-earning, urban setting.

While R.J.R. was comfortable exploiting black labor and finding it quite profitable, many white residents balked at the new society his business practices were creating. Like other new Piedmont towns, Winston had turned into a place where the new horizontal nature of social relations nurtured "the highest stage of white supremacy." This white racist reaction against black opportunity manifested itself in the severe escalation of white-on-black violence and was followed by the blanket imposition of political disfranchisement and racial segregation. This degree of virulent racism did not occur, by contrast, in the older cities and countryside, where the unwritten hierarchies were so rooted in place that everyone, regardless of his or her position on the social ladder, knew how to maneuver within them.

Winston differed little from the other New South cities of the day. Racism was rampant from the post–Civil War period onward. Perhaps more than many other men of his time and place, R.J.R. understood that his black workers, denied the rights and opportunities of white men regardless of their social station, were not simply the cheapest source of ample labor available to him at that time. They were quite capable of protesting their working conditions and demanding political redress. Therefore, it was in his best interests to see his workers in a more complex light, as breadwinners, savers, spenders, consumers, renters, and in some cases property holders, even civic participants if no longer legally recognized as citizens after 1899. His black workers not only reflected his enterprise but were producers of future workers at a time when blacks were beginning to leave the South in unprecedented numbers in response to the stealing of their rights, rampant racial violence, and limited opportunities.

R.J.R. worked at being a benefactor to the local black community, not necessarily because it was the ethical thing to do or because he felt some moral imperative to do so, but because the more money he put into black churches, schools, and orphanages, the more he was creating a desirable and more stable world for Winston blacks to make their homes in. The impact of his giving proved twofold. Building a strong black community helped him retain and recruit enough black labor (and black labor was always cheaper than white, even as wages increased) to meet the growing national and international demand for his tobacco products over the long haul. At the same time, the more established the black community, and therefore the more self-determining and the more self-policed, the less fearful the white middle class, which was beginning to move out of the downtown area into the suburbs in new numbers in response to a growing black urban presence that struck them as menacing at times. The downside of Reynolds's support was white resentment of black opportunity and social ascension, especially considering the concomitant rise of textile manufacturing with its reliance on cheap white rural labor. But the "successful" local imposition of Jim Crow segregation took care of that challenge, for it only strengthened the significance of R.J.R.'s public efforts. Black men were now demoted to noncitizens, denied the civil and political rights so recently secured them in the Constitution, even denied equal access to public spaces. Now whites regardless of class could see themselves as part of a homogenous white race of Americans all eagerly pursuing opportunity for themselves and their families.[83]

Meanwhile, the black community could remain in debt to R.J.R. for committing important resources that ensured more of their members a better standard of living, if no real rights. Even if R.J.R. did not take part publicly in the actual establishment of Jim Crow in Winston, though he probably did behind the scenes, he benefited decidedly from the ways the new, slimmed-down version of the Democratic Party brought the mercantile, government, planter, and industrial elites together to rule the city.[84]

Meanwhile, the nation had legalized racial division with its 1896 Supreme Court decision *Plessy v. Ferguson*, setting the precedent for the constitutional separation of facilities for blacks and whites as long as they were "equal," justifying not just separate railroad cars but separate facilities in all aspects of public life (restrooms, restaurants, theaters, and public schools). The outcome of this decision created a culture that made it even easier for southern state legislatures and local governments to impose their own forms of segregation. The imposition of segregation in Winston by 1900, as a social system and as an ideology, did not bring rampant change in and of itself. The economic development of Winston since the 1870s, fueled in large part but not exclusively by R. J. Reynolds Tobacco, had unleashed processes of change that could not be halted. But segregation did create a system of control that maintained white supremacy in a way that the old traditions of the countryside no longer could. R.J.R. did not need segregation to maintain white supremacy at his company. He used his own incentives of wage work and a paternalistic personalism to meet his needs. The problem that R.J.R. never really acknowledged was that most other whites lacked those tools of control. As the black population of the city increased by leaps and bounds, in large measure because of the growth of his firm, and as that black population grew in political strength too and gave its allegiance only to white employers to the exclusion of other whites, the latter felt increasingly threatened. This situation was replicated across the new towns of the Piedmont, the places most virulently racist and the most committed to segregation in the South.

R.J.R. hired mostly black workers because they were available and were looking for work, because black labor was standard in tobacco factories, because processing tobacco was considered nasty work that most whites did not want to do, because black labor was cheaper, and because he himself was long familiar with black labor in a factory setting. He employed men, women, and children alike. In 1880, fifty-five of his workers were men over fifteen, forty-five were women over fifteen, and ten were children fifteen and under.[85] If white labor had been cheaper and more readily available, he undoubtedly would have hired white labor. R.J.R. was a businessman first and foremost. "City and factory are essentially neutral institutions, which bend with the social and especially the political wind," historian John Cell has explained.[86] As long as Reynolds could secure the labor he needed to turn a profit, he was content. Ironically, it was his need for labor, coupled with black migration to the cities and black politicization, that generated white pushback in Winston and contributed to the local construction of Jim Crow. This racial segregation at the hands of a political elite of New South capitalists further divided the region into town and country. It also gave the elite unchecked dominance over not only African Americans but also poorer whites, many of whom had been stripped of their political rights along with blacks. These changes, all occurring between 1894 and 1904, hardened the South into a lean single party run by a handful of urban and rural elites from one county and city to the next.

R.J.R. was a moderate progressive or a moderate segregationist depending on one's outlook.[87] He shared the same racist culture with the extremists, benefited from it, and not only took the ideology of white supremacy for granted but gained economically from it. R.J.R. can be viewed as a moderate only if we accept that his social interactions with blacks and the ways he sought to improve the everyday lives of blacks and their long-term prospects can be viewed as a challenge to the New South's racist order. John Cell and other historians accuse the moderates of tacit collaboration with the extremist racists. Without the moderates, they argue, the extremists would have been marginalized by their own fanaticism. It is ironic that R.J.R.'s racial paternalism, rooted as it was in the rough plantation world of his southern Virginia youth, was perhaps less virulent than the rabid racism of his peers in Winston. Was it "a more flexible, a more intelligent racism," as John Cell has argued about moderates? To support that argument necessitates identifying the intentions behind R.J.R.'s actions. The tobacco magnate benefited from the respect many Winston African Americans bestowed on him as their caretaker and protector, but it was also the only way he had ever known to interact with African Americans. If he could have determined how even more rabid racism would have secured him more profit, he might very well have traveled down that road. His personal dealings with all people, white and black, rich and poor, male and female, regardless of their station in life, did reflect his interest in them and some measure of respect. His apparent decency in his interactions with all people, despite the profits he made from a segregated social system, made him appreciated for his benevolence, however self-serving, across social classes and even in the black community during the nadir of race relations.

Above all, Reynolds relied on his own independent assessment of the world around him. Other young North Carolinians of some education and wealth were establishing fraternal orders in an effort to direct post-Reconstruction ideology and politics across their state. They sought to influence "the moral and material advancement of North Carolina." The most influential of these new fraternal orders was the Watauga Club of Raleigh, which counted among its membership such notables as Walter Hines Page, Josephus Daniels, and Thomas Dixon Jr. But R.J.R. eschewed these groups, preferring to focus his energies on building his business and fostering a political economy that favored industrialization. Although he did not to any degree publicly advocate the value of industrial education, he put industrial education into action through his commitment to local schools, and not only for whites, the goal of political groups like the Wataugans, but for blacks as well.[88]

But by the 1890s, local and state political and social challenges paled next to the business realities that R.J.R. found himself facing. He had even considered retirement as his net profits moved closer and closer to one hundred thousand dollars as he turned forty. He had worked round the clock since arriving in Winston, throwing himself into growing his company at lightning speed, puppeteering one civic pursuit and regional development effort after another, and becoming a highly visible presence on the local social scene. His younger brother and right-hand man, Will Reynolds, had married Kate Bitting in 1899 and set up his own household.[89] R.J.R. and Will had been living in boarding hotels for years. Now R.J.R. was alone, renting a room in the Fountain Hotel on Main Street close to his company. Well into middle age, he had yet to marry and make a home himself. Although he seems to have taken stock of his personal situation in 1890 and considered slowing down or even selling out, in the end this man who lived on adrenalin-inducing risks did not retire. Instead, he rose to the waves of challenges the 1890s threw his way, including a national depression, the undercapitalization of his company, and Buck Duke's insatiable appetite for competing tobacco businesses.[90]

During the 1870s and 1880s, R.J.R. had built a thriving but relatively small regional tobacco manufactory. During this same period, James Buchanan (Buck) Duke, another enterprising son of a tobacco farmer turned manufacturer, transformed himself from head of a similarly small-time Durham tobacco factory into chief executive of a tobacco manufacturing trust that commanded more than 90 percent of the U.S. cigarette business.[91] R.J.R.'s success was certainly quite modest by comparison. Still, his company's physical size, number of employees, and output had grown at least sixfold between 1874 and 1890. Winston residents recognized that Reynolds had developed a strong regional market, selling more tobacco in Baltimore than any other two North Carolina firms combined. R.J.R. had begun advertising in print in 1892. Newspapers across the region soon bore catchy ads with phrases like "RJR tobacco has come to stay. Try it." His skillful integration of modern business practices coupled with his masterful manipulation of popular desire ensured his success.[92] He approved all the copy and all the graphic images for his ads from the beginning and would continue to do so over the next nearly three decades. His chewing brand names and the ads promoting them were always evocative, whether of place, taste, sensuality, or sentiment; Belle of North Carolina, Maid of Athens, Caromel, and Strawberry Twist were several of the earlier ones. The labels bore powerful imagery. Gold Cord Twist Tobacco showed a young man mounted on a fast horse gleefully outrunning a train. A Caromel label displayed a handsome mustachioed man in a straw hat rowing a boat and kissing a lovely young blond woman in a ruffled blue dress, while an equally attractive red-haired girl swirled her fingers through the lily-padded lake waiting her turn.[93]

By this time, youngest brother Walter as well as Will had joined the company at R.J.R's invitation. The three brothers pressed forward with the intention of making this company "the largest manufactory of flat goods in the world," signaling R.J.R.'s decision to stay in the game. R.J.R. filed articles of incorporation for R. J. Reynolds Tobacco Company on February 11, 1890, organizing the firm with $190,000 in capital stock, almost all of which was in his own name.[94] The legal act of incorporating ensured limited liability. Because R.J.R. owned the majority of the company and managed it too, he was in effect freeing himself up to take even bigger risks.[95] He had integrated new technologies, changed his relationship with growers, bought up or developed over six dozen of his own brands of chewing tobacco, and sold them through new wholesale outlets that reached well beyond North

Carolina. He had always lacked capital and had always secured it piecemeal, either from his family members or from his Baltimore tobacconist friends.[96]

Those months in Baltimore at business school had taught him more than accounting. R.J.R. had worked one-on-one with the big tobacco wholesalers there on behalf of his father's enterprise, and he had learned about the power of big banks in financing southern businesses. The tobacco business in particular necessitated heavy capitalization. Because processing tobacco was time consuming, requiring purchasing, transporting, storing, stemming, and remoisturizing, a great deal of money was needed up front, long before the manufactured product could be sold for profit. Neither his family members nor the local banks could finance his expanding ventures, but his Baltimore connections gave him access to capital that proved critical at this stage of his business and for the rest of his life.[97]

At this point in his career, R.J.R. personified the nineteenth-century definition of an entrepreneur. John Stuart Mill labeled entrepreneurs the fourth dynamic necessary for economic development, behind land, labor, and capital, because they marshaled resources and managed production in innovative ways. Noted economists have labeled such men as important forces of "creative destruction." By 1890, Reynolds remained the man to watch among some two dozen competitors in Winston. He was becoming increasingly influential in the regional economy as well. He evinced all the personality traits of risk-taking self-made men. Achievement-oriented, self-confident, and optimistic, he was independent, flexible, and comfortable with uncertainty. Those qualities, coupled with his extensive knowledge of the national tobacco business and its developing markets, had put him at the top of his game. But he wanted more.

Economic historian Alfred D. Chandler Jr. has linked the rise of big business in late nineteenth-century America with the accompanying emergence of a professional managerial class as a formidable development in modern capitalism. The R. J. Reynolds Tobacco Company had arrived at that watershed moment when R.J.R.'s leadership, long characterized by its nimbleness and creativity, was arguably less useful to the company's future than a strong management structure that sustained growth, trained and supervised staff members to take on critical roles in specialized sectors of the developing company, established a formal relationship with investors, and put together policies and procedures, ensuring long-term profitability. In fact, few entrepreneurs have had the personality traits and leadership characteristics needed to make this kind of transition, which is why so many entrepreneurs start successive new businesses, sell them off, and then start all over again. Entrepreneurs have always recognized business opportunities that others could not and have been willing to take risks to make them happen because they enjoy the challenge.

That R.J.R. hesitated on whether to stay at the helm of his company in 1890 indicates a great deal of self-knowledge as well as business acumen. In the end, though, he elected to soldier on, deciding to work even harder at being the country's top plug producer. He made the transition from entrepreneur to manager, but not without taking some serious knocks. During the next decade, he was thwarted by but did not succumb to the economic depressions of the 1890s. He struggled mightily with too little capital to support the growth he needed to be profitable. Forced to the mat by real financial pressures, even as he was building the largest, most modern plug-tobacco factory in the South, he then brokered a deal with James B. Duke and the American Tobacco Company that should have been his undoing. Instead, this relationship helped transform R.J.R. from brash entrepreneur into a superbly talented managerial leader who went on to build one of the top three tobacco companies in the country, but not until the government broke up American Tobacco in 1911.[98]

This path to R.J.R's great success was by no means an easy one. Entrepreneurs who manage to create large industrial firms all too frequently find themselves in a quandary, and R. J. Reynolds was no exception. Neither R.J.R. nor his brothers and his closest associates could manage the multiple and complex tasks of production, marketing, and distribution of plug tobacco on a national scale as their output grew in the 1890s. But because R.J.R. owned the vast majority of the company stock and therefore controlled the cash flow, and because he continued to look upon his business as his own personal empire, he did not feel compelled to adopt what Alfred Chandler Jr. has called "the systematic, impersonal techniques of modern top management" considered requisite for the emerging modern business enterprise.[99] Fellow North Carolina tobacco tycoon James Buchanan Duke offers a spectacular case in contrast. Duke could have followed R.J.R.'s path, resisting integration and the imposition of a management structure to maintain personal control at all costs.[100] Instead, following his successful gamble on the incorporation of the Bonsack cigarette-making machine into production in 1885, Duke moved quickly to set up selling and distribution offices in the biggest American commercial centers, explore entry into foreign markets, put together an extensive purchasing network, and build a new plant in New York City.

By 1890, Duke's was the largest cigarette firm in the country, but that did not stop him from orchestrating the collapse of his four biggest competitors into his own enterprise.[101] The American Tobacco Company that resulted, the largest tobacco business in the world, operating as a huge new integrated cigarette enterprise, was administered from New York City, where top management devised strategies for sustained profit and growth. Still Duke was not content and formed the Continental Tobacco Company in 1898, capitalized at $75 million, which gave him a platform from which to capture over 60 percent of the smoking- and chewing-tobacco business too.[102] A year later, the Continental and the American Tobacco Companies combined took in twenty-five independent manufacturers, increasing production by 100 million pounds in a single year.[103]

Duke managed his huge empire from 111 Fifth Avenue, where his talented management team integrated all facets of the merged firms and then centralized their actions. The R. J. Reynolds Tobacco Company marked one of the few exceptions to this full-scale integration. Plug depended on a special kind of leaf, which allowed R.J.R. to avoid Duke's big net for a number of years. But by 1899, even the R. J. Reynolds Tobacco Company had succumbed, albeit quietly, to Duke's insatiable hunger for tobacco ventures. Unlike most acquisitions, Duke did allow Reynolds Tobacco to maintain its own purchasing department independent of American Tobacco's mega-department, a significant act in and of itself.[104] Plenty of evidence also indicates that Duke respected R.J.R.'s command of his business and its market, and therefore he let him keep more control than the presidents of other firms he acquired. Duke had no experience with chewing tobacco, just smoking tobacco and cigarettes. This unique arrangement provided Reynolds with enough autonomy to experiment with smoking tobacco himself, despite Duke's strictures against Reynolds entering the smoking market. R.J.R. would actually press forward with marketing plans to launch his Prince Albert tobacco in 1908 while still under the trust.

R.J.R.'s independence while under the Duke monopoly was noteworthy. It ensured his company would be extremely successful by World War I. But it was Reynolds's maneuverings behind the scenes and his manipulation of the Duke acquisition story that deserve closer scrutiny. Although those who knew that R.J.R. had entered the trust assumed his company had been steamrolled under the Duke machine like all the other small tobacco businesses around them, this was not exactly the case. R.J.R. was not so much a victim of this monopoly building as a clever and ultimately successful gambler in its development.

R.J.R. had elected to expand his facilities in the early 1890s, making them the largest and most modern in North Carolina and increasing production by over 400 percent over the next decade.[105] Henry E. Harman's decision to move the *Southern Tobacco Journal* from Danville to Winston in 1891, wooed there by R.J.R. to underline the centrality of his company to the business, underscored the new impetus of the R. J. Reynolds Tobacco Company and indeed the whole town of Winston. A total of thirty-eight tobacco firms by 1896 meant that Winston had eclipsed all other North Carolina cities in tobacco production. But it was during this decade that R. J. Reynolds Tobacco Company rose to the head of the pack. R.J.R.'s bold ambitions were becoming legendary, as was his seeming commitment to the welfare of North Carolinians with their more modest hopes and dreams. This was no coincidence.

Reynolds, like dozens of other tobacco manufacturers, had been drawn to Winston because of its location in the bright-leaf tobacco belt. The first rail connection had been established in Winston just a year before R.J.R. relocated there, and indeed had persuaded him to do so. The Salem spur to Greensboro, linking the town to Danville and Richmond, served as the only rail connection for the twin cities for the next fifteen years, however, despite numerous efforts by city leaders, including R.J.R., to secure more lines.[106] Because this Salem line, not especially well organized or well run, had a monopoly in the region, it charged high rates despite poor service. Frustrated with these challenges and unable to secure a competing line, R.J.R. threatened to organize his own wagon drayage system for heavy freight, promising to make his rates so low he would put the spur line out of business. The railroad promptly lowered its charges, benefiting not just R.J.R. but many more-modest customers as well. When people asked R.J.R. if he really would have created a wagon business if the Richmond and Danville directors had refused to back down, he shot back a one word answer, "Sure."[107]

Not until 1889 did a Roanoke and Southern spur line finally tie Winston to critical markets in western Virginia.[108] Three years earlier, the Winston

Board of Trade, with R.J.R. at the helm, leaped at the opportunity to help finance a spur that would connect Winston, Martinsville, and Roanoke. The Virginia and North Carolina Construction Company, chartered by the Virginia legislature, bragged it had secured three hundred convicts and subscriptions totaling half a million dollars to get the project under way. R.J.R. himself, present in Danville for the announcement of the charter, traveled to Stokes County, north of Winston, where he urged residents to vote in favor of subscription at a public meeting. Described by those in attendance as "the most level headed man there," R.J.R. argued that northern capitalists had invested heavily in western railroads in the years after the Civil War, pulling thousands of people from the North and the South to the West in search of opportunity, and generating vast new wealth for these western people in the process. If northern capitalists continued to turn their attention southward as they were now doing at long last, the bonds voted by Sauratown residents would prove a propitious investment.[109]

When the last rail tie was laid in 1891, R.J.R. and dozens of other residents celebrated the fact that Winston and Salem were at long last connected "with the rest of the world." R.J.R. even bet that local real-estate values would be increased by a gargantuan 4 million dollars in less than ten years.[110] After the completion of the 122-mile extension from Roanoke to Winston, it was almost immediately taken over by the Norfolk and Western and then became the Southern Railway. But ownership of the line was less important than the new functionality it brought to Winston and Salem manufacturers, who could now ship east and west without relying on the Richmond and Danville system.[111]

R.J.R.'s conviction that railway service could make or break individual manufacturers and their towns led him to pitch a fight against a corporate behemoth in 1897. Although he lost the battle, his reputation as a man of the people received new confirmation. Financier J. P. Morgan, the organizing force behind numerous railroad empires across the United States, had acquired the greatly mismanaged and financially strapped Richmond and Danville, which was about to fold in the wake of the 1893 panic. He had invited the three principal stockholders, who had applied to Morgan's bank for help, to surrender their shares and give him control in 1892, but they had declined. The panic forced them to reconsider. Within a year, Morgan had organized the Southern Railway Company into a gigantic corporation serving the entire region, which prompted a political battle in the North

Carolina legislature. The Fusionist government fought unsuccessfully to repeal Democratic governor Elias Carr's ninety-nine-year lease of the state's railroad assets to the Southern Railway conglomerate. Over the next decade, the Southern Railway added new track and new railroads, made hefty improvements, and provided good service to shippers and passengers alike, a transformation described at the time as "one of the noteworthy achievements of American railroad history" and "a new era" for transportation in the South.[112] But in 1897, R.J.R., as frustrated with the railroads and as dead set against monopolies that did not serve his interests as any Populist, expected no such outcome.[113]

Reynolds publicly supported Governor Russell's efforts to repeal the ninety-nine-year lease. When the hearings were under way, he sent a telegram to legislators urging that the lease be annulled. R.J.R. then offered to lease the road himself, arguing that the price of the lease was much too low. Under the 1895 agreement, the state stood to gain $260,000 annually for the first six years and a meager $286,000 total for the remaining ninety-three. During this protracted fight in the legislature, *Raleigh News and Observer* editor Josephus Daniels was called to testify, and he sided with the repealers. Miffed at his opposition, the Southern Company withdrew Daniels's free train pass, a courtesy hitherto extended to all newsmen. When this news reached R.J.R., he promptly delivered a one-hundred-dollar check to Daniels, urging him to use it for his train travel and praising him for fighting "in the interest of the people of North Carolina for three generations to come." Daniels responded by putting a facsimile of the check on the front page of his newspaper and penning an editorial titled "Mr. Reynolds and His Kind Offer." In it he thanked R.J.R. for being a wealthy man who still stood with the people. That same day, Winston and Salem city leaders passed a resolution calling for the repeal too. When Daniels did not cash the check, R.J.R. purchased twenty copies of the *Observer* for all his friends to convey his support for the editor.[114]

R.J.R. and Daniels also joined forces to attack Buck Duke and American Tobacco. R.J.R. resented the monopoly's impact on his suppliers and customers. According to Daniels, R.J.R. provided financial support to enable Daniels's paper and the *Webster's Weekly* of Reidsville to fight the Tobacco Trust. Meanwhile, R.J.R. spoke directly to the farmers. Wrote Daniels, "He told the farmers what they might expect, and he saw himself what he might expect . . . if the trust carried out its plans." He noted, "[R.J.R.] was even more severe on Buck Duke than my newspaper and endeared himself to the farmers by his plain talk."[115] Tobacco farmers sang R.J.R.'s praises for years to come.[116]

The Daniels-R.J.R. alliance is a troubling one. The two remained friends for the duration of R.J.R.'s life. Daniels not only fought Buck Duke during this period. The staunch Democrat had also joined party leaders in their use of racism to dismantle the Fusionist Party of Republicans and Populists in the 1898 election. The battles waged by the *Raleigh News and Observer* and its allies against American Tobacco were occurring at the same time that Governor Daniel Russell (1897–1901), a Republican, had been elected by "fusion" with the Populists. Duke was a well-known Republican and thereby aligned with the political party of blacks and big business. The Democrats, eager to dislodge the Republican Party, resorted to championing the legalization of white supremacy to win white voters. Daniels himself, who used his paper not only to attack American Tobacco for hurting small farmers but to champion white supremacy, all in the interest of strengthening the Democratic Party, implied in his memoirs that his efforts were emboldened by R.J.R.'s public support. Daniels had attached himself to the Democratic Party's 1898 and 1900 campaigns to wrest power from the Fusionists and bring victory to the Democrats using white supremacist arguments. Although R.J.R. never publicly supported Daniels's racist propaganda, R.J.R. remained his lifetime friend and, as a staunch Democrat himself, publicly used his influence with North Carolina farmers to turn their backs on anything Republican.[117]

R.J.R. had fought against J. P. Morgan's railroad monopoly and against Buck Duke's trust. Although he lost both battles, he had gained the farmers' trust. He remained a New South booster. He believed local and state government needed to support entrepreneurship and infrastructure building, and that such acts would lift the boats of rich and poor alike. In many ways, despite his growing wealth, his widening influence, and his big ambitions, he still saw himself as a North Carolina everyman. He had reason to do so in one crucial respect by the 1890s. He had set out to grow his company into the biggest plug-tobacco manufactory in the state if not the country. But his inability to raise the amount of capital he needed, a challenge worsened by the panic of 1893, reminded him of what had been a perennial struggle throughout his business career, and remains so for most business owners. He had always been in debt to friends and family members, and he had always trusted he could secure more loans from them in times of need. He had learned to go to banks, but not always successfully. In fact, he had had to threaten the president of the local Wachovia National Bank that he would take his business to Danville to secure the additional credit he needed in the 1880s.[118] But the scale of his business aspirations had now changed, along with the scale of his credit needs too.

By 1889, R.J.R's competitors were thriving too. B. F. Hanes of Model Tobacco Works began erecting a new storeroom, and P. H. Hanes and Company began improvements as well, including a new brick warehouse and seven "mammoth" factories. The Whitaker, Wood, and Lucile tobacco companies followed suit. R.J.R., never one to be outdone, announced on March 19, 1891, that he had ordered one million bricks to begin building "THE tobacco factory of the South." He hired C. R. Makepeace and Company of Providence, Rhode Island, to design the plans for a six-story-high factory that could hold up to nine hundred workers with a brownstone front that could withstand fire, thereby cutting his insurance costs in half. Reputedly the most modern factory building in the state, it opened in the spring of 1892, replete with steam power, electricity, and a large Hahn clock. The equipment for each stage of tobacco production was assigned to a specific floor, and tunnels and tramways were built to move leaf, all in the name of convenience and efficiency.[119]

R.J.R. began creating a sales department and pursuing serious advertising at the same time, prompting business historian Nannie M. Tilley to label the year 1892 as pivotal in the transition of the company to a large-scale operation.[120] R.J.R. was not the first tobacco manufacturer to embrace modern business practices, including advertising, on a larger scale. Buck Duke had paved the way a decade earlier and was well known for his aggressive cigarette sales promotion. In short order, the whole tobacco industry would be famous for its unparalleled advertising outlays.[121] But R.J.R.'s commitment to moving his operation into the big leagues was a serious one, and he embraced this more vigorous management system with a vengeance. By 1896, the home office had issued multiple guidelines and policies, from when and how to use R.J.R. advertisements, to meeting daily and weekly expectations of mailed-in reports, and to paying as much attention to small retailers as big ones.[122] His investments in advertisements quickly paid off, prompting him to put warnings in trade journals against infringements on his trademark products.[123] He issued calendars, circulars, and signs and distributed samples by mail. He decorated railroad cars with the R. J. Reynolds Tobacco Company name and brands. He bought up billboard space.

No use of spectacle was too over the top. In Elkhorn, West Virginia, one salesman nailed an R.J.R. poster to the tree on which a man had been lynched recently. R. J. Reynolds Tobacco was the sole North Carolina exhibitor at the 1895 Atlanta Exposition, one of three tobacco exhibitors, and the only tobacco exhibitor from the South. R.J.R.'s company was commended for his "proper spirit of enterprise and progress" compared to his fellow tobacconists so noticeably absent. His exhibit, filled with a railcar's worth of Reynolds tobacco products, was complimented for its "tasteful arrangements" and use of the familiar R.J.R. trademark.[124]

R.J.R. incorporated technological improvements as well and was the first in the business to adopt the Adams machine, with its ability to weigh plug accurately. He had begun experimenting with smoking tobacco throughout the 1890s, and if he was not the first tobacco manufacturer to work with saccharine, he was the first to develop a new type of chewing tobacco with a new aging process for the leaf that depended on saccharine's chemical role in the process.[125] Reynolds worked hard to protect trade secrets, collaborating with chemist Emil A. De Schweinitz, who entrusted him with half the rights to his tobacco-preservation formula through the U.S. Patent Office in 1897.[126]

Unfortunately for Reynolds, the more tobacco he produced to meet the growing demand he was generating, the greater his company's debt. His expansion into so many new areas—facilities, sales and marketing, equipment, research and development—was a costly risk, even if increased demand signaled that his company was well on its way to establishing a national market. The growing debt was real, spiraling upward from $27,688 in 1890 to $101,276 in 1895 to $269,978 in 1898. Although R.J.R.'s spending made sense from a business perspective, when viewed in a larger light it seemed counterintuitive. A nationwide credit shortage had led to a U.S. depression in 1893. The financial crisis originated in Europe, where a bad economy had prompted many Britons to sell their American investments and redeem them in gold. This set of actions in turn depleted America's gold reserves, creating rampant fear in the United States. Many American businesses, banks, and railroads failed as a result, generating large-scale unemployment and protests. In the midst of this economic challenge, tobacco production dropped precipitously.[127] The panic proved a severe and protracted one for the tobacco industry in general, and most manufacturers, if they did not fail outright, adopted a survival strategy of dormancy, laying off employees and cutting operational and capital expenses sharply.[128] The depression, coupled with the competition they faced from Buck Duke's behemoth, meant that tobacco men everywhere—manufacturers and farmers alike—faced bleak prospects.[129]

In addition to these serious structural realities, R.J.R. suffered a surprise crisis in leadership. Following the state's incorporation of the company in 1891, Reynolds had inaugurated factory expansion in facilities and production so quickly that he had needed to rethink his management strategy. Until now, he had relied on two people besides himself to head up his leadership team: his brother Will, the vice president, who had joined the company full-time in 1884 to oversee leaf purchasing, and Henry Roan, secretary and treasurer, who had started his employ at R. J. Reynolds Tobacco as a part-time evening bookkeeper sometime before 1882.[130] These two men, plus R.J.R., represented the sum total of the company's officers and stockholders.[131] In 1892, the three officers added Thomas L. Farrow, a longtime manager who supervised the prizing department. Less than a year later and just before the full effects of the panic had been felt, both Farrow and Roan tendered their resignations, convinced that Reynolds was "a reckless plunger."[132] The curiously named Orthodox Creed Strictler, a traveling tobacco buyer for Reynolds, recalled that R.J.R. sought out his advice at this time. His assets, he told Strictler, amounted to only ten thousand dollars, but did not Strictler agree, R.J.R. argued aloud, that it was worth the gamble to sink it all into marketing? No wonder Farrow and Roan departed.[133]

R.J.R., always strategic and always hands on about all aspects of his business, was not daunted by the defection of these two officers with whom he had been so close. Reynolds quickly replaced Roan with his brother-in-law Robert Critz. R.J.R. then asked his youngest brother, Walter, to fill in for Farrow. Critz and Walter had spent the last three years operating a plug and twist factory in Bristol, Tennessee, where their oldest brother, A.D., had made his home and fortune, and where R.J.R.'s future wife would finish college.[134]

Meanwhile, R.J.R. had committed his company to fast-paced growth moored to little more than big dreams and ambitions despite limited capital and intense competition. Although two of the three men on whom he had most relied to support his ambitions had fled the company in protest of what they believed to be a series of rash financial acts, R.J.R.'s response was to circle the wagons and fill them with his kin. Not only were his new officers members of his family, but they had each been trained by his own father, a consummate risk taker and entrepreneur extraordinaire of the old school. The new leadership kept the company marching forward despite the panic and despite the deepening need for more capital.

During the North Carolina legislative session of 1899, a bill was introduced authorizing the Reynolds Tobacco Company to increase its capital stock. It was followed shortly thereafter by an announcement that the capital stock of the company had been increased dramatically, and that the incorporators were not only brothers R.J. and Will Reynolds, but James B. Duke and three other outside men as well. Reynolds Tobacco was now associated with Continental Tobacco. The news circulated quietly, and those in the know were astounded. They had watched dozens of tobacco companies fall under the scythe of American Tobacco. But R. J. Reynolds Tobacco had held strong. "Those who thought that Reynolds was more than a match for Duke," recalled newspaperman Josephus Daniels, were astonished by the switch. Daniels, now a longtime friend, told R.J.R. how disappointed he was by this news. He told R.J.R. he "had sold out" to the Tobacco Trust. Reynolds replied, "Don't you believe it. Sometimes you have to join hands with a fellow to keep him from ruining you and to get under hold yourself." R.J.R. had stood by as Duke bought out the Hanes and Blackwell tobacco companies and many others. "I don't intend to be swallowed," he told Daniels. "Buck Duke will find out he has met his equal, but I am fighting him now from the inside. You will never see the day when R.J.R. will eat out of Buck Duke's hands. If you will keep your eyes open, you will find that if any swallowing is done R.J.R. will do the swallowing. Buck tries to swallow me he will have the belly-ache the balance of his life."[135] In fact the pressure from the panic facilitated Duke's buyouts and ultimately benefited R.J.R. enormously. Smaller competitors were wiped out across the state, leaving Duke to dominate the industry in Durham, and Reynolds in Winston.[136]

Despite Reynolds's claims to the contrary to Daniels, there is every reason to believe that R.J.R. actively sought out Duke rather than let Duke steamroll him. Under the supervision of the Continental Tobacco Company, essentially a holding company for American Tobacco, R. J. Reynolds Tobacco secured enough capital to expand dramatically, acquiring smaller plug firms throughout North Carolina and Virginia, constructing a factory building that eclipsed its last one in size and function, to become the biggest plug-tobacco business in the country. But R.J.R. did not go to Duke until 1898, once the Continental Tobacco Company had been formed.

The American Tobacco Trust, Continental's predecessor, had garnered widespread public disapproval for its voracious business strategy. It had muscled smaller concerns to sell out to it, pressured wholesale tobacconists to do business with it, and coerced farmers into selling it their leaf at bargain-basement prices.[137] Duke and his financiers, aware of their bad reputation, created a new trust with Continental and took a different tack. It did not buy companies outright as American had done but purchased majority shares instead, making these firms Continental subsidiaries. This strategy irked fewer people and cost less too. By letting the local company retain its name and officers, as well as its local reputation, it ensured a strong customer base and decent profits.[138] The R. J. Reynolds Tobacco Company joined Continental as a subsidiary, so to all appearances it retained its public autonomy, and indeed some North Carolinians never knew that Buck Duke sat on the Reynolds board beginning in 1899. In fact, at R.J.R.'s death, nineteen years later, the only newspaper to document his association with James B. Duke was the *Wall Street Journal*.[139]

Duke himself testified during the antitrust hearings a decade after the acquisition that Reynolds had come to him seeking the relationship, which was not surprising given the debt Reynolds was carrying.[140] Duke told him he would take two-thirds of the company at a price Reynolds named, provided that Reynolds stay and run it, for Duke's people had no expertise in plug manufacture. Duke testified:

> Mr. R. J. Reynolds is a very able tobacco merchant. After the Continental Tobacco Company was formed he came up with the idea of selling his business to them. I personally told Reynolds the [company] had no organization to manufacture, or knew how to manufacture his style of goods and that I would not favor buying it unless he should stay and run it, and that I did not think he was the kind of a man to run a business that he had no interest in—a rich man. I told him we would take two thirds of it at the price he named because I thought it was a good investment and manufactured an entirely different class of goods from what the Continental Tobacco Company manufactured. They are sold in the Southern States and I did not consider they were in competition with the Continental Tobacco Company's plug because it is in a different class of goods.[141]

Reynolds agreed to these terms but kept the deal dead quiet, even when an agent from Continental admitted to curious residents that he was in Winston to acquire local factories for his firm.[142]

The R. J. Reynolds Tobacco Company formally joined Continental on April 4, 1899, opening up a new chapter not just in R.J.R.'s business but in his life. His company was now a national one, reorganized in New Jersey and responsible to Duke and his men at 111 Fifth Avenue. But Duke was true to his word; he made R.J.R. president, himself vice president, and quickly removed his original appointees on the company board so that R.J.R. could reappoint his old leadership team, his family members. Duke bumped up their modest annual salaries in the process. R.J.R., who had never earned more than $2,500 a year, now received the princely sum of $10,000.[143] Meanwhile, R.J.R. wasted no time. Upon his return from New York, he determined he would increase production from 10 to 15 million pounds and construct a mammoth new building replete with state-of-the-art automatic machinery and swanky offices.[144]

As Duke and Reynolds built manufactories meant to capture ever-greater shares of the national and international market, their success brought greater prosperity and significant economic development at the local and state levels, from waterworks and utilities to schools and colleges to banks and insurance companies. The companies spawned subsidiary industries like paper and box companies and encouraged artisanal enterprises like wagon works and machineries. Those new economies of scale that afflicted so many tobacco entrepreneurs made quite an impact. Many of them were forced to turn to textiles instead. They imported borrowed methods, capital, and skill sets from the long-established industry giants in the Northeast, on one hand, ensuring broader local development than tobacco could generate by 1899 and, on the other, indebting them to outside creditors.[145]

R.J.R. had worked like a dynamo from the moment he had arrived in Winston through American Tobacco's acquisition of his company in 1899. In fact, the rise of his company offered a valuable lesson in microcosm about moneymaking in the American capitalist system of the late nineteenth century.[146] Entrepreneurial by nature, R.J.R. had learned how to buy, produce, and market a local agricultural crop into a desirable consumer good with relatively unskilled and certainly undervalued local black labor, increasing scales of efficiency all along the way and taking advantage of rapidly developing financial and legal resources to do so. By the 1890s, not only had he incorporated his company and secured more loans, but he was also squeezing his competitors out of business. Duke, who had moved to incorporate new technologies more quickly than Reynolds and who had a bolder vision for national markets, had beaten him at this game, ultimately driving him into a Duke subsidiary.[147] But that does not diminish all that R.J.R. had accomplished over those twenty-five years. As one admirer astutely observed, R.J.R. had "the power, seemingly, to make capital out of what to a weaker man would be misfortune, and herein lies the thing that distinguishes him from, and gives him an advantage over, other men."[148]

R.J.R. was the consummate entrepreneur. Historian Joyce Appleby writes about such men in U.S. history: "Retrospectively, the lives of successful entrepreneurs appear boringly similar. . . . As boys they excel at whatever jobs they take at fourteen or fifteen, thrive as precocious self-improvers, display a determination to set up their own businesses, persevere assiduously to some level of prosperity, attract the attention of sponsors, and then launch themselves into new industries, all along divining the direction of economic growth."[149] Entrepreneurs like R.J.R. thrive on uncertainty and are willing to take risks because of the thrill they get pursuing new opportunities. Their discipline and energy are contagious, affecting everyone they work with. Men like R.J.R. pursue little beyond their business interests and do not relish spending their wealth, whether at leisure activities or in conspicuous consumption. They prefer instead to use their gains to seek out even newer challenges.[150] Self-confident in the face of shifting circumstances, they are imaginative in their commitment to discovering a better or less expensive product that satisfies a unique need. Entrepreneurs typically have a very difficult time, however, turning their innovative ideas, piloted on a small scale, over to a much larger enterprise, where management structures, comprised of policies and procedures, must necessarily take precedence over the personalism of the smaller effort, where the entrepreneur has a strong hand in every single aspect of the business.

R.J.R. was a classic entrepreneur. Those very distinctions in personality assured him multiple achievements by the time he had turned fifty. His financial coups and public actions as a businessman, a politician, and a city booster were well documented in local and state newspapers. But his private life in those years has almost vanished from the historical record and public memory. There is a notable absence of his personal correspondence in the Reynolds Family Papers, and the few stories still circulating about R.J.R.

during his lengthy bachelor years rarely hold up to documentation. The man who does emerge in this period is enigmatic and even contradictory.[151]

Physically, he had retained his imposing presence. He had also cultivated a piercing gaze over the years. Despite cutting such an impressive figure, he still managed to make all kinds of people feel comfortable around him. Indeed, he always seemed to have time for everyone, a skill honed as a backwoods salesman when he talked to rural men and women from all walks of life. His office waiting room filled daily with folks from company and town eager to discuss work challenges and employment opportunities, to secure his financial support for benevolence and church work, and to seek out his advice on politics and the economy.

R.J.R. was so likable, remarked a friend, because he was as "unaffected as a boy [and] hospitable as a king."[152] Through the last few decades, he had been something of a man-about-town when he wasn't working round the clock, and he did make time to attend the key social events of the day. The dark-haired bachelor was groomsman at innumerable weddings and escorted the best daughters of the city down the aisle. But there was another side to Reynolds that is important to document too. An undated photo, probably from the late 1890s, shows him sitting on some outdoor steps surrounded by well-dressed men and women at Roaring Gap, a North Carolina mountain resort founded and patronized by wealthy Winstonians. R.J.R., though not the sole object of the photographer's lens, stands out, perhaps because he looks off into the distance. Even more telling, his companions have left a space all around him. However likable most people found him to be, he always cultivated a strong sense of his separateness.[153]

It is hard to pinpoint the origins of this separateness. R.J.R. was one of the wealthiest men in town, a real power broker as he moved into middle age late in the nineteenth century. But he was also an unchurched southside Virginian who stood out in comparison to the long-settled pious Moravians across town. He was unpretentious, choosing to reside in unassuming hotels known more for their hearty meals than their luxurious accommodations.[154] A local editor noted, "Reynolds was a unique character—apparently didn't care much as to what other men thought of him; never courted the lime-light; always was honest and always paid attention to business."[155] The shrewd entrepreneur paid minimal attention to his dress and was known to hold his clothes together with a safety pin rather than replace a lost button.[156] Sympathetic observers could chalk this up to the absence of a wife.

Critics pointed to his rural roots. True enough, R.J.R. seemed a country man at heart, however much he finagled the establishment of a national company and a New South city.[157] He loved hunting in his limited spare time. Reynolds paid property taxes on farmers' lands throughout the Piedmont to secure hunting rights and was never happier than when he was chasing down squirrels, quail, turkey, possum, and deer. He consistently bred the best hunting dogs around.[158] Although a cartoon in the local paper poked fun at "The City Boy in the Country," dressed in plaid suit, spats, and deerstalker cap with cocked gun in hand, unable to make heads or tails of his quarry, R.J.R. was the opposite, always the country boy in the city.[159]

An avid lover of horseflesh, he relished driving a fleet team of handsome trotters across town. At tracks where his mares raced—rumored to be the fastest horses in the South—he was famous for letting out "the Patrick whoop on some good track, [so that] it would make you think that a full grown Texas tornado had broke out in your immediate vicinity."[160] In one of his few acts of extravagance, he built an expensive octagonal brick stable on his factory lot to stable seven horses, with a nonfreezing hydrant and a patented automatic feeder, all of which cost far more than most people's homes. Similarly, locals were astounded that R.J.R. paid a horse trainer forty dollars a month to maintain his string of twenty-two racehorses.[161] Reynolds's purchase of the splendid stallion Matador, known throughout the Southeast for his speed and gaits, provided yet another testament to his adoration of fine horses and his willingness to indulge himself in his passion for them.[162] His well-known penchant for fast horses was not without its share of humbling moments, however. One day he left his favorite trotting mare hitched outside Dr. Shaffner's gin. When she spooked, broke free, and fled home, mangling the vehicle behind her, the man known for never slowing to a walk had to follow on foot. The event brought local residents much amusement. It was not often that folks witnessed R. J. Reynolds left behind in the dust.[163]

In an editorial that seemed only half in jest, the *Winston Union Republican* pointed out that R.J.R. spent so much time and money on his horses that he would make an ideal husband: "A man who would go to such an amount of expense and trouble for his four-footed pets, in our opinion would make an estimable liege lord to some fair maiden. Although she is yet to be found, we bespeak for her a lavish disposal of means and affections, which by the way, are very essential necessities to domestic welfare and happiness."[164] But

R.J.R. did not seem particularly concerned about finding a bride, even when he turned fifty with the arrival of the new century.

For most of his adult life, and certainly while a bachelor, R.J.R. paid little heed to those conservative southern evangelicals and Victorian naysayers who warned against the illicit temptations of gambling, drink, loose women, and tobacco.[165] R.J.R. was rumored to partake of them all. He indulged in his own plug, preferring Brown's Mule over all other brands and switching to more socially acceptable cigars only late in his life.[166] He always tried to sit in close proximity to a cuspidor, for as one employee recalled, "Mr. R. J. was never without a chew of tobacco in his mouth."[167] He enjoyed his single state and assumed the role of showman on occasion. "The biggest blood in Winston," as his brother called him, attended a Mother Goose dance dressed as one of Old King Cole's fiddlers three, and on Saint Patrick's Day he paraded with other revelers through the streets with enough pints under his belt to give his cheeks a ruddy glow.[168]

R. J. Reynolds embraced life. He purportedly named several of his brands after his favorite girlfriends (including Bessie, Lula, Lottie, and Annie).[169] Over a hundred years later, local stories continue to circulate about his dalliances as a single man. Winston's white and black communities recount several oral traditions about R.J.R.'s sexual relationships with black women in particular, although the same stories are often attributed to his younger brother Will too.[170] Dr. John Howard Monroe, the son of the dairyman who once worked at the Reynolda Estate, did recall that "Mr. Reynolds was said to have had some 'outside children.'" But his elaboration of that particular story seems too farcical, too crafted to make a point about rich blood and social class to be true. "One [of R.J.R.'s alleged black 'outside children'] gave him a little bull that was cross-eyed and had a crooked horn . . . the ugliest animal he'd ever seen. . . . Someone turned that bull loose and messed up all the pure blood that he had imported from Kentucky. . . . Someone had ruined the finest herd in the whole southeast."[171]

Only one illegitimate child can be documented, and he was white. Indeed, R.J.R. acknowledged within his own family the existence of this son, John Neal, whom he supported emotionally and financially for much of his life. Family lore holds that while hunting on a Mooresville farmer's land with Major Huske, R.J.R. seduced the farmer's daughter. When he discovered she was pregnant, he sent her to Stokes County to have the child. Born in 1887, John Neal grew up in an orphanage in Oxford, North Carolina. But there is anecdotal evidence that he later spent considerable time with R.J.R. and with Will and Kate Reynolds too. On one such occasion, R.J.R. and Will took young John on a hunting excursion. Left behind to play near a train track, whether with a servant or alone is unclear, the child was pinned by a sliding set of cars. The accident severed his leg, which he subsequently lost.

The historical record is limited when it comes to John's childhood. Account books show that by the time the boy was in his teens, R.J.R. was buying John's clothing and financing his education. R.J.R. had him collect local rents and paid him a percentage of the take, giving him some hands-on business training. R.J.R.'s commitment to John's welfare was commensurate with, and in some cases exceeded, his generous and long-standing commitment to his nieces and nephews, for whom he also paid their tuitions and expenses and gave out generous cash gifts at Christmas.

One farm employee remembered about R.J.R.'s relationship with Neal that "Mr. R.J. was particularly fond of him, and he was a very friendly fellow." In 1900, Will Reynolds was listed as his guardian. At that time, John had left the orphanage and was living with Will and Kate. Later, John was hired by the Reynolds Tobacco Company. He received one-thousand-dollar gifts of stock from his father and uncle, as well as twenty-five thousand dollars from his father's estate. His name, birthday, and death date are listed in the R. J. Reynolds family Bible.[172]

Biographers presume that knowing the private life of a person explains his public accomplishments. We tend to believe that the private person is the real one, while the public person is an elaborate act.[173] R.J.R. presented himself as an all-American success story southern style. His performance depended on his dual identity as a country boy from the Old South and a New South entrepreneur. That performance was wearing thin as he neared the half-century mark, if not to his audience, at least to himself. His marriage, at the age of fifty-four, to his cousin Katharine Smith revitalized him. In the wake of his winter wedding in 1905, R.J.R. the all-American icon faded a bit from the public eye and was replaced in some critical respects by his alter ego, his new wife, Katharine Smith Reynolds.

4 Dearest of All

R. J. Reynolds had never been a romantic. He preferred shrewd deals and hard living to sentimentalism. But his love for his first cousin once removed, Kate Smith, his "dearest of all," proved deep and abiding.[1] Her decision to marry him brought the fifty-four-year-old industrialist great joy. He believed it was "gods blessing" that he had waited so late in life to marry so that Kate, thirty years his junior, could be his bride. He delighted in imagining their future together at a time when most men had begun to dwell on their mortality. As much as he loved Katharine, and he did so with the abandon of a far younger man with many fewer responsibilities, he also judged her carefully. Because she was such a "good" young woman, well suited to be his partner, he believed there could be no "sweeter or better wife" in the world. Her strength of character made him appreciate what an extraordinary helpmate she would be. He was grateful to her for accepting his hand. In return he promised her a future filled with his love, his respect, and the very best of all things.[2]

A "great individualist" according to her college roommate, Katharine as a young woman was generous, spirited, and opinionated, striking rather than beautiful, with black hair and sparkling eyes.[3] R.J.R. may have been deeply smitten, but he was nobody's fool. He had long skirted matrimony, and marrying anyone at all was a daunting undertaking given his many years of independence. His commitment to expanding his business through good times and bad had discouraged him from settling down. He had not considered the farmer's daughter who bore him a son suitable to be his wife, though he had eventually accepted responsibility for the child. In typical Victorian fashion, his role as favorite son and bachelor caretaker for his extended family had postponed his decision to have a family of his own.[4]

Around 1900, R.J.R., Will, and Will's wife, Kate, had moved into their enormous new Victorian home, with its multiple porches, turrets, and dormers, on Fifth Street. His sister Lucy and brother-in-law Robert Critz lived a block away. His mother, Nancy Susan Reynolds, lived with her daughter and son-in-law nearby. Widowed in 1882, she had moved to Winston in the early 1890s, vowing never to return to Patrick County. R.J.R. was deeply attached to her. When she died in 1903 at the age of seventy-seven after a long illness, he was heartbroken, he explained in a letter to his cousin Kate. He reported, "[She] called me to her and said that she loved me so much she hated to part with me, that I had done everything that could be done for her, and that I had been such a good son to her. . . . Her loving words of appreciation more than compensate for what I have done for all others, or my hope to do during my entire life." He added a self-recrimination: "I have been so much absorbed in business that I feel much grieved from the fact of my . . . [not] spending more of my time with my dear beloved mother."[5]

R.J.R. buried his mother per her wishes—"wherever [R.J.R.] expected to go"—in the Salem Cemetery.[6] Her death, given R.J.R.'s expressions of sentiment to his cousin as well as his subsequent actions, must have opened his eyes to the passing of time and emotionally freed him to consider marriage. He immediately began pursuing Katharine, who did not mind his attentions in the least. She had spent the last two years since graduating from Sullins living at home in Mount Airy. She wrote R.J.R. quickly after learning his sad news. "Dear cousin, I was so sorry to hear of aunt nancy's death. I knew she was very sick, nevertheless her death was quite a shock to me." Apologizing for her absence at the funeral, she explained she had received the message too late to catch the train.[7] His hasty reply filled with his mournful thoughts was followed by another letter ten days later inviting his "Dear Cousin Kate" to join his niece, Nannie Critz, and himself on a trip to New York. "It will give me great pleasure to have you with us," he wrote.[8] The three of them, joined by Kate's friend Nancy O'Hanlon, subsequently traveled up the coast by train, staying at R.J.R.'s favorite hotels, the Belvedere in Baltimore, the Traymore in Atlantic City, and the Plaza in New York.[9] R.J.R. had taken all his nieces and nephews to Atlantic City for a few weeks each summer in previous years. He had taken John Neal, his illegitimate son, to Atlantic City too.[10] But this trip with Kate seemed less a gift of a vacation from an avuncular cousin than an exciting, though chaperoned, adventure for a twenty-two-old woman with a handsome, wealthy, older man.[11] Ten years later, Kate referred to this trip as the beginning of their courtship, a time when Baltimore became to her "all wonder and beauty."[12]

Why was R.J.R. so drawn to Kate? The most reductionist of interpretations would focus on their kinship. Marrying Kate Smith, the eldest daughter of his first cousin, meant he could keep his great wealth in the family, an age-old strategy for protecting fortunes. But if this had been his only criterion for choosing a bride, other cousins would have filled the bill much earlier in his life. Kate Smith was more than kin. She was an exceptional young woman. R.J.R. respected her force of personality and ultimately loved her for it. If Reynolds epitomized Henry Grady's New South man, his wife-to-be embodied the next generation's New South woman. Intelligent and determined, emboldened by familial affluence and the benefits of higher education, she used this set of attributes to secure considerable autonomy for herself, albeit through conventional means—first as an elite, single white woman in the early twentieth-century South, then as an elite married white woman.

Although R.J.R. had lived for several years in the big Victorian on Fifth Street, he had spent the three preceding decades in boardinghouses and hotels. He had not been part of an established household run by a woman for the majority of his life. As he contemplated marriage, he may have recalled the example of his oldest sister, Mary. She had died prematurely in 1888, and her husband, Judge Lybrook, with whom R.J.R. had always been close, had mourned her passing by extolling her considerable domestic virtues. "Her home was a model of order, neatness and refinement and content. As a wife her patient devotion had no limit. As a mother her daily sacrifices for twenty years for her children bears testament to her great solicitude for their welfare and honor."[13] If R.J.R. expected Katharine to create such a haven in a heartless world, he would be mistaken. She proved far more inclined to pursue domesticity in a businesslike way, following the lead of R.J.R.'s sister-in-law Kate, who ran such a tight ship that she charged her brother-in-law and his horses for board. While Katharine understood expectations for married women of her social class in the South and delivered them in full, she did so in her own inimitable style, pursuing many other interests that stretched well beyond southern women's traditional housekeeping role.

Although family lore holds that R.J.R. and Kate had known each other since her childhood, and that he had given her a bracelet when she was ten, their first documented meeting occurred in 1899 when President McIver sent her to R.J.R.'s office to request a donation for Normal Institute.[14] There is no evidence that the two exchanged letters or spent time together before R.J.R.'s grief-filled note to Katharine about his mother's death. Following their trip to Baltimore, Atlantic City, and New York in the spring of 1903, R.J.R. invited Katharine to work for him as one of his personal secretaries. Her willingness to take this position hints at her commitment to a more complex self-determination. Winston was a big city compared to Mount Airy. But it was also a world in which young women of her race and class had been newly confined to narrowed feminine roles to justify the exclusion of black men from the body politic. On the national scene, women were just beginning to enter the professions, including teaching and nursing, but also as department store clerks and business secretaries. Though these new opportunities were increasingly available in the urbanizing South, they were not necessarily socially sanctioned ones for respectable young ladies. The prevailing racist ideology justified its public vilification of black men and the removal of their civil rights as the best strategy for protecting vulnerable white womanhood. Young white women's presence as paid workers in public places complicated that argument.

As R.J.R.'s secretary, Katharine could experience the new freedoms that came with employment while under the protection of the most important man in Winston. She discovered a youthful city in the throes of rapid demographic and economic growth, much of it due to the impact of the R. J. Reynolds Tobacco Company. Over seventeen thousand residents called the twin towns of Winston and Salem home by 1900. Nearly a third were employed in the tobacco factories nine months out of the year. The city embraced the ambition generated by the industry. In one week alone, the local papers bragged, the city shipped out 800,000 pounds of plug tobacco on twenty-nine railcars, breaking all world records.[15]

Katharine also found a cultural milieu in Winston that Mount Airy lacked. Salem Female Academy and College had long upheld the importance of education, and women's education at that. Plays, concerts, operas and operettas, musical comedies, vaudeville, and minstrel shows were commonplace in the downtown. Silent motion pictures were shown at Nissen Park on summer evenings.[16] Booker T. Washington gave a public speech raising money for the R. J. Reynolds Slater Hospital, with orchestra seats reserved for whites and the balcony for African Americans.[17] Katharine found herself in a vibrant new community, full of innovation and contradiction. She rode the segregated streetcar to the management office, shopped in the new downtown department stores, and worked with three male secretaries on the Reynolds accounts.

Despite the novelty inherent in Katharine's new home, with the thrill of modern capitalism at full tilt and plentiful arts to entertain her, she still had to think about her reputation and her social circles. Protecting her reputation as a single working girl living away from her immediate family mattered. As another educated young woman who also worked in a local Winston business politely noted about this period, "It was not so generally accepted then as it is now for a girl to go into an office."[18] Although she had stayed with her Reynolds cousins on earlier visits to town and was close to Kate Bitting, Katharine lived in the home of D. Rich and his wife on 657 West Fifth Street rather than at her cousins' house.[19] Her temporary residence was just down the road from the Reynolds home on the lovely tree-lined street known as "Millionaire's Row."[20]

Katharine's stay with Mr. and Mrs. Rich not only ensured that she was carefully chaperoned but gave her considerable insight into her cousin's tobacco company. D. Rich had worked as a tobacco hand in a Mocksville factory before coming to work at Reynolds Tobacco at the age of twenty-two. He had learned the bookkeeping system by day and worked in the factory by night, eventually becoming head bookkeeper, employment manager, and treasurer. R.J.R. respected Rich's work ethic, his mastery of the company's finances, and his ambition. Living with the Riches helped Katharine grasp R.J.R.'s predilections all the more.

During her time in the office, she also got to know George C. Coan, treasurer of the Reynolds Tobacco Company, extremely well. He had brought considerable expertise to the Reynolds table as a former banker, tobacco manufacturer, and highly trained bookkeeper and had become R.J.R.'s trusted advisor. Her very proximity to these key company leaders and to R.J.R. meant that she was exposed to all aspects of company decision making, including the reorganization of management, the expansion of the sales and advertising departments, and the institution of a formal filing system. R.J.R.'s nephew, Richard S. Reynolds, was receiving much the same education at the same time as Katharine. It proved so valuable that he was able to launch his own successful aluminum company with it in due time. In contrast, Katharine would use her business education to become her husband's most trusted advisor.[21]

Intelligent, meticulous, and hard-working, Katharine started her wage-earning career on April 16, 1903, and quickly distinguished herself.[22] The twenty-two-year-old kept the books on significant accounts, including R.J.R.'s holdings of hundreds of thousands of dollars in his own and those of other national companies, and kept records of his much smaller stock purchases, usually ranging between one thousand and thirty thousand dollars. She made only one error in her nearly two years of keeping the books, posting R.J.R.'s farm account twice.[23] In 1904, R.J.R. awarded Katharine a cash prize in a competition for the best letter promoting R. J. Reynolds Tobacco Company's products. Local lore holds that this award signaled R.J.R.'s romantic interest in her. The gift account entry in his day journal reads simply: "To Katharine Smith. Gave to Katharine Smith $100.00 which I offered as a prize for a satisfactory letter to jobber's salesmen." Katharine probably had produced the best letter and was already conveying her strong aptitude for this business, but R.J.R. did propose to her shortly after the contest. Incidentally, Katharine's youngest daughter reported years later that Katharine thought the proposal late in coming.[24]

R.J.R. and Katharine had signaled their romantic interest in each other long before this prize competition.[25] Kate began keeping R.J.R.'s ledger books on May 1, 1903.[26] She received a salary of thirty-five dollars per week through early September, when it was increased by ten dollars a week. R.J.R. paid his nephew, Richard S. Reynolds, future CEO of Reynolds Aluminum, fifty dollars a week during the same period, and he was a year younger than Kate.[27] She knew all the salaries because she kept the books, so it is perhaps not surprising that by February 1904, her salary was raised to fifty dollars and increased four months later to sixty-five dollars, now higher than R.J.R.'s favorite nephew.[28] Unlike the other assistants and secretaries in the office, she and Richard were paid out of R.J.R.'s private account, indicating his personal relationship with them.[29]

R.J.R.'s romantic interest in Katharine notwithstanding, he clearly respected her aptitude for numbers and tutored her closely in the world of investments. On March 1, 1904, he sold Katharine 100 shares of Greene Copper Stock at $10 a share. Less than a month later, at R.J.R.'s request, his commission house, W. M. Patterson and Company in New York, "sold for [his] account for Katharine Smith" those shares, making Katharine $225.[30] She subsequently purchased more stocks with R.J.R.'s help, or as he stated in his books, "[I allowed her] the buying of 200 shares Colonial Fuel and

Iron (CFI) bought for herself with 200 shares which I bought for myself. This reduces the cost of her stock by $387.50 and raises mine by the same amount."[31] By that fall, R.J.R. had helped her purchase $10,000 worth of CFI shares.[32] She sold 100 shares of CFI a month later and pocketed an impressive $4,500 profit.[33] She also sought expert help from others on her own, consulting with Francis H. Pattisant at W. M. Patterson on Wall Street's method for calculating interest. "Once known," Mr. Pattisant assured her, "you will find it easier than the way taught in schools."[34]

A quick study, she had parlayed her initial thirty-five-dollars-a-month salary into well over ten thousand dollars' worth of stocks in less than eighteen months.[35] Less than 5 percent of Americans owned stock at this time; the majority of those who did were exceptionally wealthy, given the high margins and brokers' fees of this era. Katharine's willingness to invest in the nation's financial markets under R.J.R.'s tutelage long prefigured the huge increase in people of more modest means who would begin investing during and after World War I.[36]

R.J.R.'s encouragement was not aimed at Katharine alone. He long had made a habit of encouraging family, friends, and employees to purchase Reynolds stock. But although he bought shares for John Neal and persuaded managers to purchase theirs, his account books do not show consistent support, including use of his own commission houses and his own knowledge to gain entry into this new world of investing, to any single individual except Katharine. R.J.R. delighted in Katharine's avid interest in the stock market and her aptitude. Katharine must have delighted in this new challenge and the guidance and financial backing she received from R.J.R. Moneymaking can be an aphrodisiac. It could easily have peppered their growing affection and respect for each other. Both R.J.R. and Katharine entered into their relationship as employer-employee with ulterior motives. Like a growing number of other women of her age and era, she could experience wage work in a fast-paced, formerly male-only business environment. She could live relatively independently in a busy city. But she could also pursue romance, for her first cousin once removed was a handsome, vital man despite his age and certainly the wealthiest, most prominent bachelor in all of North Carolina. That Katharine was intentionally exploring the possibility of romance with R.J.R. seems just as likely as R.J.R.'s intentionally bringing her to Winston to work for him so he could assess her as a prospective wife.

Marriage to R.J.R. enabled Katharine, in the end, to craft a marital ideal that patched pieces of the ideal Victorian lady to the whole cloth of the New Woman. She secured a companionate marriage despite a thirty-year age difference because her husband truly loved her and respected her aptitude for business and numbers. He also must have recognized how much he benefited from her social knowledge and her cultural sensibilities. Katharine studied current fads and fashions and all the other predilections of the new world of conspicuous consumption. That knowledge was invaluable to R.J.R., a man whose biggest successes turned on his ability to understand the power of marketing and the fickleness of taste.

While Katharine was receiving a lightning-fast education in accounting, investments, and the tobacco business, she and R.J.R. were falling in love. R.J.R. admitted that he stopped by the Rich home whenever he passed in hopes of seeing her.[37] A family story reveals Katharine's strong sense of self-worth at this stage of her life. On the day she took her first streetcar ride in Winston, the conductor came up to her and said, "Fare, lady." Katharine smiled but ignored him. Although he repeated the request several times, she lowered her head and looked out the window. Finally, a male passenger paid her way, and suddenly Katharine blushed with shame. She thought the conductor had been calling her a "fair lady."[38]

Katharine had a number of beaux besides R.J.R. during her two years as a single working girl. She received many courtship tokens during this period, including boxes of candy and bouquets, but the identities of these young men remain unknown, as does the extent of Katharine's interest in them. R.J.R. stood out from these others. He chose a different strategy for expressing his intentions by sending her fresh milk to demonstrate his commitment to her good health. His unconventional but caring gesture distinguished him immediately from her more conventional admirers.[39] Meanwhile, Katharine traveled within the extended Reynolds family circle. She joined the First Presbyterian Church, where R.J.R.'s sister-in-law Kate B. Reynolds worshipped. Many top Reynolds Tobacco Company managers were listed among the First Presbyterian congregation as well, although R.J.R. was not one of them.[40] Katharine also took on a more personal role in R.J.R.'s life. The daybook that Katharine kept for her future husband uncharacteristically began listing expenses for such domesticating items as towels, curtains, and rugs once she was in his employ.[41] New entries also appeared for expenses related to the pressing and cleaning of R.J.R.'s clothes by downtown companies. Over and over again, these accounts convey a growing intimacy between the two. R.J.R. provided Katharine with one hundred dollars' worth of credit marked "gift account."[42] Katharine wrote President McIver requesting confidential information about Normal's former gardener when R.J.R. expressed interest in employing him.[43]

In the spring of 1904, R.J.R. bought outright the home he had been sharing with his brother Will and Will's wife, suggesting his confidence that Katharine would consent to marriage.[44] That summer he began listing her name "on account" for frequent purchases and cash allotments. In December 1904, Katharine must have requested a reassessment of her time worked and wages paid, because a new entry states she was being "credited back for lost time" for four weeks' worth of wages across four different months totaling $72.49.[45] Her last entry in this journal, just weeks before her marriage, listed receipt of $4,040.73 from her cousin Richard S. Reynolds, to be deposited in the Wachovia National Bank in her name.[46] The future aluminum czar was repaying her with interest for a loan she had made him. On the eve of her wedding, Katharine had won the heart of one of the most successful men in the state, learned the basics of the tobacco business, and grasped how to make money in the modern world. Her two-year apprenticeship to one of the largest tobacco manufacturers in the country had not been in vain.

Although only a handful of love letters from R.J.R. to Katharine have survived, they are remarkable in their sweetness and sincerity and show a different man than the affable but powerful figure the public recognized. After Katharine wrote him that she would be his wife and proposed a wedding date, he immediately replied by the next post:

> My Dearest of All, I frankly set my perusle [*sic*] of your most highly appreciated letter of the 6th inst naming the 28th day of March as the day you will be my wife, giv[ing] me the greatest undescribable pleasure & the very highest appreciation of the confidence you have placed in me. I feel that no one on earth . . . is blessed with a more noble earnest sincere lovely & sweeter or better wife than I will have in you. I love and respect you so much more than I ever did any one else, that I realy feel that I never before knew what real true love was, & it must be gods [*sic*] blessing in having me to wait for you & receive more happiness than earlier marriage would have given me.[47]

R. J. Reynolds, who rarely wrote anything down, trusted Katharine so implicitly he poured out his heart with no concern for his lapses in grammar and spelling.

The wedding was held at 8:00 a.m. on a Monday in late February 1905 (earlier than originally planned) in Katharine's parents' home in Mount Airy. R.J.R. had filled the Smith house with expensive fresh flowers and plants: palms, ferns, American Beauty roses, and pink and white carnations.[48] The bride wore a "beautiful and becoming tailor-made" suit of navy-blue wool trimmed with navy-blue chiffon, white silk, and lace.[49] The bride and groom entered the parlor to the piano strains of Mendelsohn's "Wedding March," and the Reverend D. Clay Lilly, minister of the First Presbyterian Church in Winston-Salem, presided over their exchange of vows.[50] The two received "a number of beautiful and costly gifts." R.J.R. gave Katharine a watch and pin set with rubies and a necklace with rubies and diamonds.

The wedding had been held in relative secret. Three days after the event, the *Mount Airy News* reported that one of its favorite daughters had been married off to a familiar tobacco scion. The article described him as "probably the most wealthy man in North Carolina," noting, "He is supposed to be worth 3 million dollars. . . . No man is more highly esteemed in all this section." With particular pride, the paper boasted, "Miss Smith is one of the state's brightest daughters." Even Katharine's willingness to work was deemed honorable. "She was reared in a home of plenty and there is no reason why she should aspire to work for wages. . . . The R. J. Reynolds Tobacco Co. employed her as a stenographer and she saved her money and judiciously invested it until she was worth several thousand dollars in her own right at the time she was married." Katharine's investment talents, if underreported, were now public knowledge. Despite her Sullins years, she was no typical southern belle but a rather extraordinary young woman in the eyes of her hometown.[51]

Almost immediately after their early-morning wedding, the newlyweds caught the next train to Greensboro and then made their connection to New York. Ever practical, Katharine remained clad in her navy wedding suit, set off with a smart-looking beaver hat, to stay warm and disguise the grime of train travel. They departed the next day aboard an ocean liner bound for Liverpool to begin their "grand tour."[52] Taking Katharine to Europe to see the great cities, enjoy the best restaurants, attend the theater and opera, and stroll through famous gardens and down legendary boulevards broadened not only Katharine's horizons but R.J.R.'s too. It also signaled their arrival as Americans of considerable economic standing.

It had been Katharine's dream to take a European honeymoon. R.J.R., however, had expressed little interest in cultivating the cultural traits and consumer habits that distinguished the American elite in the late nineteenth and early twentieth centuries. The long-standing bachelor not only had devoted most of his energy to growing his chewing-tobacco company but had worked hard to appeal to a broad swath of customers disinclined to value displays of elitism on his part. His marriage to Katharine changed his outlook significantly. No longer was he content just to invest in his racehorses, the only real expressions of his wealth before his cousin Kate moved to town. Following their marriage, the man who had lived in boardinghouses throughout his adulthood, had bought the mammoth Fifth Street home from his brother and sister-in-law for twenty thousand dollars.[53] Now with a new wife of his own, whom he adored and to whom he had promised the best of all things, he was intent on providing her with the accoutrements of the high life in his pursuit of her gratification.

It is a revealing personality trait that Katharine, having saved about ten thousand dollars from her working-girl salary and her subsequent stock market investments, prepared for this voyage by sewing her own honeymoon negligee.[54] This European tour marked an enormous transition. Putting their frugal tendencies aside, both R.J.R. and Katharine embraced an outrageously extravagant culture new to both of them. Their fourteen weeks in Europe began with their transatlantic voyage aboard the *Baltic*, a twenty-four-ton, 725-feet-long, twin-screw steamer, owned by the White Star Line, the same company that later commissioned the *Titanic*.[55] In their first-class berths, with stewards catering to their every whim, even the drawing of their baths, the newlyweds built their intimacy amid a lifestyle as remote from their daily responsibilities as it was lavish.[56] After landing in Liverpool, the two traveled to London and began building their cultural knowledge of Europe city by city: London, Paris, Marseille, Cannes, Nice, Genoa, Pisa, Rome, Naples, Florence, Venice, Milan, Como, Lugano, Lucerne, Zurich, Munich, Salzburg, Cologne, Brussels, and back to Paris and London.[57]

In this small world of Americans abroad, captured so aptly in the literature of Henry James and Edith Wharton, R.J.R. and Katharine Reynolds did not go unnoticed. The Paris edition of the *New York Herald* documented their arrival, including their stay at the Carlton Hotel in London. They were observed attending a variety show at the Alhambra Theatre in London's Leicester Square that included a ballet divertissement titled "My Lady Nicotine." The segment showcased a Virginia tobacco plantation; dancing American, Turkish, and European cigarettes; and a "smoker's waltz."[58] That their homegrown Piedmont product could have such enormous cultural reach across the Atlantic and in one of the most sophisticated cities in the Western world must have been an especially compelling discovery for them both, massaging their growing sense of their own self-importance.

The honeymooners not only took in shows and reviews but purchased paintings and furniture.[59] In Paris, Katharine bought two custom-made belle epoque gowns at the House of the Compagnie Lyonnaise. The height of early twentieth-century Paris spring fashion, the dresses were practical as well as beautiful, suitable for numerous occasions, from afternoon visiting, receptions, and dinner to the evening theater. R.J.R. hired famous studio portraitist C. Pietzner, official photographer of Emperor Franz Joseph and the Austrian imperial court, to capture Katharine in her pink taffeta gown, long white kid gloves, and matching hat trimmed in roses and plumy ostrich feathers. The lovely young woman dressed in all her new finery looked straight into the camera lens. She strikes the viewer as young and unsure of herself, not quite ready to take on the mantle of one of the newest members of the southern elite.[60]

Yet her subsequent actions belied the tentativeness in the photograph. R.J.R. arranged to ship their many purchases home, writing D. Rich that he must receive these goods, inspect them, and "please observe on each paper the notes made by Katharine." She was already taking charge.[61] R.J.R. was not surprised. He joked early in their marriage that he had married Katharine to secure her excellent advice and fine suggestions for free. He also observed that "she was going to break him," invoking Katharine as horse trainer and he himself as a wild mount.[62]

There was some truth in those statements. Insistent that he present himself appropriately to the world, she made sure he dressed well, "like a dandy," recalled a former servant.[63] Relatives and employees alike recalled that Katharine loved to run things. "Katharine wanted to plan everyone's lives. She got upset if she was not listened to."[64] She also retained her desire to obtain her own financial independence. She traded just as many stocks after her wedding as before, her name now listed in the entries as Mrs. Katharine Smith Reynolds.[65]

In a strikingly parallel universe, Buck Duke too was marrying late in life, at age forty-eight, and also honeymooning in Europe. Unfortunately for Duke, he quickly initiated divorce proceedings. Katharine and R. J. Reynolds's early marital years were decidedly storybook by comparison. The smart young wife and the wily tobacco industrialist were clearly in love and building a new kind of marriage based on mutual respect and complementary talents. Katharine Reynolds represented a new generation of southern white women with a whole array of new choices about their future.[66] Her parents had left plantation farming behind at the end of the Civil War, drawn to life in town and the opportunities they could create for themselves and their children there. They were able to provide all their offspring with good educations and nice things thanks to the living they made from their multiple ventures with people from all walks of life, from the mountain folks who sold them their tobacco to the wealthy resort-goers from the mid-Atlantic. Katharine received an incomparable education from this early exposure to moneymaking and social relationships. It left her with a dual outlook about her identity. Although she relished wealth, she retained some empathy for those without it.

In this time and place, marriage provided the only route for Katharine to realize her ambitions. The right marriage offered her the surest path to security and prosperity, even power and control. Katharine had never seriously considered pursuing adult life as a single woman. She was too pragmatic and too driven, only briefly entertaining her single flight of fancy—moving to New York to paint—before setting her sights instead on marriage like virtually all young elite white women of her generation. But she had much higher expectations than most about what she wanted out of marriage. Katharine was a decided catch in the southern Piedmont world she inhabited, and she knew it. Pretty, educated, and ambitious, she would have made an ideal wife for a smart young manager or entrepreneur, offering sound advice on business negotiations and able to perform as a charming hostess to boot. Such a marriage would have been severely constricting for Katharine, however, who wanted more than anything to put her ideas and beliefs into action in the world around her. Marriage to R.J.R. created myriad opportunities for Katharine to be in charge. As the wife of one of the wealthiest men in North Carolina, Katharine gained the money, authority, and perhaps most importantly the social sanction to influence many people's lives, shape multiple institutions, and even determine the form and function of the physical landscape around her.

R.J.R., the desirable tobacco titan of Winston-Salem, had sidestepped marriage for many years and so entered the venerable institution in 1905 with eyes wide open. To this vigorous man with such strong appetites for work and play, the union of man and woman as husband and wife sanctioned by God and the law had one formal purpose above all else: the assurance of legitimate heirs. At fifty-four, the time had come for R. J. Reynolds to have bona fide descendants. But R.J.R. understood that exchanging his relative freedoms as a bachelor for a vivacious young wife whom he truly loved had other benefits too; it brought him a clever and thoughtful companion at a time when his business was experiencing significant change, a companion who could also care for him as he inevitably grew old.

Katharine understood all these expectations, and she handled them with aplomb throughout their marriage. She loved R.J.R., but she had not entered into this marriage blindly either. She understood that as R.J.R.'s wife she had significant work to perform. It was her obligation to meet those gendered responsibilities typically relegated to middle-class and elite American wives by the turn of the century, and then some. These critical duties turned on subordinating herself to her husband's needs; making him happy; being his confidante; managing his private life; organizing their large, complex household; handling myriad social expectations; and most importantly, bearing and raising their children. The scale of Katharine's responsibilities as R.J.R.'s wife far exceeded the domestic duties typically outlined in the Victorian primers on household management that she read so devotedly. This was acceptable to Katharine, however, who always relished bigger challenges and quickly came to define her "wifely" duties as more encompassing, taking on more and more control of the world around her in the process.

Katharine's domestic duties began with the Reynoldses' Fifth Street house, a "very handsome Victorian" well designed for entertaining. A spacious hall welcomed guests, opening to a parlor on one side and a family sitting room on the other. These front rooms were set apart from the hall by sliding doors that could be pulled back to make one contiguous space for parties. Behind these rooms lay the dining room, the kitchen, and the conservatory. The master bedroom had walls covered in a sumptuous pastel-blue silk with its furniture painted blue to match. The upstairs, where the children and the nurse and governess slept, was devoted solely to bedrooms.[67] The house was a showplace.[68] "Oh, it was plush, beautiful, and you'd see things there you wouldn't see anywhere else," recalled house servant Elizabeth Wade. It even had one of the first refrigerators in the region at a time when everyone else relied on iceboxes.[69]

Katharine relished entertaining. Putting parties together gave her an opportunity to pamper her guests, warmly welcoming them into her home and creating a memorable occasion, one that also underscored her originality and fine taste. She was always on the lookout for special party favors, house gifts, and bridge prizes, purchasing them by mail order from Baltimore and New York.[70] She kept her home filled with flowers appropriate to the seasons and holidays—freesias, cyclamens, roses, poinsettias, holly, narcissus, hair ferns, carnations, Easter lilies, asparagus fern, lilacs, tulips, daisies, daffodils, sweet peas, jonquils, hydrangeas—purchased from local florist Annie Grogan and cut from her own extensive gardens.[71] Katharine and R.J.R. held a Halloween party every year at the Fifth Street house for all the Winston socialites, who showed up in outrageous costumes. One year, a banker dressed as Robinson Crusoe, shirtless, in buckskin breeches to everyone's surprise. He won the prize for best costume.[72] Nothing slowed Katharine and R.J.R. down, including the enactment of a state prohibition law by their good friend Governor Robert Broadnax Glenn that preceded national prohibition by a decade. To ensure he had a well-stocked liquor cabinet for entertaining, R.J.R. adopted a twofold strategy. Under North Carolina law, families were allowed a bottle of liquor a week. R.J.R. bought all his nondrinking friends' requisite weekly bottles. He also kept a wine cellar in Baltimore and transported "a bottle in every suitcase" back to Winston to get around the law.[73] No wonder that the Reynoldses' parties were always hits. "I know how full your hands must be," wrote good friend Mary Daniels after another wonderful party. "How in the world did you ever gain sufficient courage to give a 'breakfast party'—know it was a grand success, for you are the one person who knows no such word as failure."[74] Myra Ludlow observed of Katharine, "You have the art of making people happy and it is a blessed gift."[75]

Katharine enjoyed attending social events as much as giving them and worked hard to make time for all the invitations she received.[76] They were plentiful, ranging from local events to the Corps of Cadets dances at Virginia Military Academy to the twenty-fifth wedding anniversary of Mr. and Mrs. Joe Mitchell Chapple in Boston.[77] Although not an inveterate gossip, she did spread the word on occasion. When she learned "one of the Langhorne beauties" was expected to visit Mrs. Noell for several days, she shared the news with her best friends.[78]

Meanwhile, during the first few years of her marriage, Katharine had begun to formulate a plan for a working farm. She eventually created an entire model estate with the help of architect Charles Barton Keen and landscape architect Thomas Sears. What made this effort distinctly her own was its undergirding in her reform ambitions. This estate, which came to encompass more than one thousand acres including an expansive "bungalow" home, with mammoth flower and vegetable gardens, a greenhouse, a farm, a church, and schools, allowed her to realize many of her boldest dreams. This commitment to the estate meant that her "domestic work" increasingly extended well beyond her family and the usual social obligations, giving her a slew of new roles, including that of reformer, Democrat, and patriot. All the while, her husband's visibility as a leading North Carolina businessman and her growing visibility as his wife and as a business and community leader in her own right drew new public attention. Katharine's decision making as manager of their home had considerable impact on her family, her friends, Winston-Salem, and beyond. It secured her far more influence than virtually any other southern wife commanded during this era.

Toward the end of his life and some seventy years after his mother's death, Katharine's youngest child noted without a trace of irony that his mother "was a businesswoman at heart."[79] Marriage to R.J.R. had given Katharine the opportunity to run a world ostensibly centered on her special responsibilities as his wife. She used her unique role as head of the Reynolds household to widen her sphere of influence, beginning with her own home, which she ran like a well-oiled machine, but stretching well beyond its borders. She employed excellent management skills, imposed a solid organizational structure on all her efforts, clearly designated work duties and expectations for all her employees, integrated the latest technologies to maximize efficiencies and create desirable living conditions, and instituted hard-edged accountability for her employees balanced with generous bonuses for top performers.

This business of domesticity marked a new kind of role for southern married women. It was a far cry from the plantation mistress of the nineteenth century, who worked hard but had limited rights and limited control over the plantation, even over her household—restrictions that left her at best mediating relationships between the master and their slaves, and with no public identity whatsoever. It bore little relationship to middle-class American women's role as the moral caretaker of home and society in the late nineteenth century. In a few instances, educated married women without children could embrace companionate marriages as did Madeline McDowell Breckinridge of Lexington, Kentucky, but such examples were relatively rare.[80] Nor did it have any correlation with the domestic worlds of the new American elite. The marriage of James B. Duke offers a case in point. Duke's marriage nine months after R.J.R.'s to Mrs. Lillian McCready, a forty-year-old widow and socialite, ended in divorce in less than a year. Rumors abounded that Mrs. Duke not only despised her new husband's 2,500-acre estate in Somerville, New Jersey, but preferred the glamorous social world of Manhattan, where she had allegedly carried on an extramarital affair in her own tony residence on Sixty-Eighth Street.[81]

Katharine eschewed all these models. She had no interest in being a latter-day plantation mistress, a reforming mother, or a socialite testing convention's boundaries. She understood that she would be called to play those parts at various moments in her married life, but her energy and ambition lay elsewhere. Instead, she established her own model of domesticity, one that had a larger purpose than simply ensuring efficient home organization, even on the grand scale her estate eventually commanded. Katharine used her consummate management skills for a specific purpose, to further the interests of the R. J. Reynolds Tobacco Company, thereby helping her husband ensure its continued growth and success. In taking on this role, she was in essence operating a new branch of the company. R.J.R. had learned to encourage and then rely on specialization in critical sectors of his corporation—buying, marketing, research, and so on. Katharine's leadership on the home front and its extended reach into more-public realms through her social engagement with her husband's managers and business colleagues was in some respects just as essential to the company's achievements as the more conventional departments.

The world that Katharine built stood in sharp contrast to that of her husband's enterprise. In his grimy factories, black and white workers and their barefooted children performed repetitive and often dangerous tasks at their noisy machines. At risk for tuberculosis in the damp, germ-ridden air, they produced coffee-colored tobacco products that were sold across the country and ultimately smoked down or spat out at the end of their material lives. In all her pursuits, Katharine sought beauty and a simple elegance, manifest first in the redesign of the Fifth Street house interior and its gardens and then in her one-thousand-acre estate on the outskirts of town. She reified good health and cleanliness, as well as pastoral landscapes and the virtues of village living. By the end of her life, Katharine had constructed a quasi-utopic world. Though built with tobacco gains, it could be read as an implicit critique of the tobacco city her husband's ambitions had wrought.

When R.J.R. married Katharine in 1905, he was the richest man in Winston and one of the richest in North Carolina, but his several million dollars' worth of wealth paled next to Buck Duke's, which was rapidly approaching the billion-dollar mark. Although the future of R.J.R's company was tied to Duke's apron strings at this stage, his private life was decidedly not. Duke's decision to put his company's headquarters in New York and his country estate in New Jersey ensured that he was at the center of the nation's industrial and financial action and in the middle of a fast-paced social milieu as well. Although R.J.R. had incorporated his company in New Jersey to accommodate the Duke buyout, actual tobacco production as well as his own office and home remained in Winston.

While the national press delighted in documenting all aspects of Duke's private and professional life, vilifying him for crushing the little man and envying him for his huge financial success, R.J.R. lived much more quietly at the edge of Duke's long shadow. While news of Buck Duke's pending divorce made him more human and therefore more interesting to the public, R.J.R. calmly juggled his business and relished the new joys of being a married man. Compared to Duke, R.J.R. was just one among many relatively successful businessmen in the new business climate who attracted limited interest from the trade journals, a few mentions by the national press, and occasional references in the state papers. Not until he launched Prince Albert Smoking Tobacco and broke free from Duke's Tobacco Trust did R.J.R. receive substantial media attention, most of it generated within his own industry. This meant that R.J.R.'s family life, for the most part, was largely insulated from the national eye, if not the local one, and he preferred it this way. R.J.R. had always made some time for social pursuits but had never let them dominate him. Even when Prince Albert and the Camel cigarette made R. J. Reynolds a household name, he did not seek national celebrity. Instead, he and Katharine continued to work hard to control the public image of the R. J. Reynolds Tobacco Company, traveling in smaller social circles with people whom they trusted.

Although Katharine and R.J.R. developed a powerful partnership based on their mutual dedication to their tobacco company, their strong appeal to each other lay at the core of their relationship. In marrying Katharine, R.J.R. had secured an attractive young lover. She was pregnant at least five times over thirteen years and bore four children in six years. In marrying R.J.R., Katharine had secured a devoted lover, an affectionate father for her children, and ample financial security. Despite the difference in their ages and despite the decidedly different attributes and experiences each brought to the marriage, the two shared many qualities. Both believed in hard work and an active life of purpose. Both were meticulous in all their pursuits and happiest when planning, organizing, and executing ideas. They loved the challenge of leveraging their resources and making money. They were down-to-earth and practical to a fault. Although their wealth depended on modern industrial production, each derived great pleasure from the land, as farmers and cultivators, as livestock breeders and horse people. Finally, both were deeply committed to their family and kin.

Over the course of their marriage, the two worked together to put the tobacco company in the best light, Katharine adding important new dimensions by virtue of her more youthful and feminine attentiveness to developments in consumer culture and social reform. Over time, that very attentiveness, combined with the widening political and business circles in which they circulated, pushed R.J.R. and Katharine closer toward greater interaction with national figures, from wealthy socialites to politicians. But early in their marriage, the two acted out public roles mostly at the local level. Because Katharine was well attuned to these social expectations and had received superb training in that role from her mother, from her exposure to the social world of the Blue Ridge Hotel, and especially from her year at Sullins, she began pursuing an exacting domesticity and a demanding social schedule almost from the start of her marriage.

Katharine and R.J.R. returned from their several-month honeymoon in Europe early in the summer of 1905, and by late June Katharine was pregnant with their first child. The two began their new life together at 666 Fifth Street, in R.J.R.'s grand Victorian. Theirs was a well-to-do uptown neighborhood about six blocks west of R.J.R.'s factories. They were surrounded by the leading business families in the city, including other Reynolds relatives as well as R.J.R.'s closest advisors and officers.[82] Brother Will and his wife, Kate, lived next door, and Bowman Gray, a Reynolds manager, and his wife, Nathalie, just beyond them. Close by on Spring Street lived R.J.R.'s sister, Lucy Critz. Some years later, Katharine's sister Maxie married and moved across the street.[83]

Although Katharine had kept a low profile over those first summer months of her marriage, probably suffering from morning sickness, she emerged a highly visible participant in the life of the social elite of Winston by early autumn. The wives of company officers, including D. Rich's wife and William Lippfert's wife, were quick to invite her to their homes.[84] Katharine in her turn rapidly assumed the role of gracious hostess. Despite her advancing pregnancy and relative inexperience, she staged dinners and parties, her lifelong penchant for drama and spectacle much in evidence. During her sister Maxie's visit, Katharine arranged for six wagons to take a merry party of friends and family to Nissen Park for a sumptuous dinner under beautiful trees twinkling with a thousand brilliant lights, an event the likes of which most Winstonians had never before imagined.[85]

Katharine gave birth to her first child, Richard Joshua Reynolds Jr., on April 6, 1906. R.J.R. was delighted. He had always valued family highly, caring for his mother, brothers, sisters, cousins, nieces, and nephews for years. He now threw all that attention upon this child and the three that followed almost like clockwork between 1906 and 1911. He spent the remainder of his years balancing his rich new family life with the biggest business challenges of his entire career. The flood of telegrams that followed R.J.R. Junior's arrival conveys just how interwoven Katharine's and R.J.R.'s public and private lives had become. By 1906, everyone understood that R.J.R. was the one and only head of the company, for younger brother Will was too casual and brother Walter too timid to ever take the reins. Such was Will's affability and appeal that all the children in the neighborhood called him Uncle. Though he was adept at purchasing the highest quality tobacco and had a good head for business, Will lacked R.J.R.'s drive. He was personable and charming, ultimately preferring to spend his time with women and horses. Walter lacked not only R.J.R.'s ambition but also the family penchant for risk taking. Careful to a fault, even after the incredible successes of the Reynolds Tobacco Company with Prince Albert and the Camel cigarette, he owned fewer than five hundred shares of Reynolds stock after decades in the company's inner circle, whereas Will owned nearly five times and R.J.R.

thirty times that number.[86] The three brothers got along well despite their differences. Tobacco broker E. J. Brown recalled "the beautiful devotion that existed between the brothers and [their] congeniality and concerted action in business [together]." That mutual respect contributed to the company's long-running success and also meant that each brother understood his own strengths and weaknesses.[87] Still, there was no clear successor to R.J.R.

Thus, the birth of R.J.R. Jr. was a significant occasion for the Reynolds family and the R. J. Reynolds Tobacco Company, for the town, and for the tobacco business and subsidiaries as a whole. Although R.J.R. surrounded himself with intelligent, talented, hardworking business associates, he was old-fashioned enough to believe that family meant everything, especially when it came to company leadership. The birth of his son resolved any doubt concerning the future of R. J. Reynolds Tobacco. "Here is to the future president of R. J. Reynolds Tobacco Company," crowed one telegram cabled from across the country after another.[88] W. E. Brock, president of Trigg Candy Company Manufacturers in Chattanooga, captured in his cable what everyone was thinking: "Junior may be admitted to firm immediately it will add fifty percent increase on our stock."[89]

Little Dick's arrival symbolized continuity and stability for the R. J. Reynolds Tobacco Company. No wonder then that the company engaged in a well-orchestrated effort to communicate the good news across the industry. Telegrams announcing the birth of the new crown prince of plug went out to all the buying and selling branches, the jobbers and middlemen, the vendors and wholesalers, and even company competitors. The births of the three children that followed were similarly announced. Mary Katharine Reynolds, named for her mother, arrived August 8, 1908. Nancy Susan Reynolds, given the name of her paternal grandmother, was born on February 5, 1910, and Zachary Smith Reynolds, named for his maternal grandfather, arrived on November 5, 1911.[90]

Katharine gave birth to four children in five and a half years. She had experienced heart trouble during these pregnancies, probably because she had suffered from rheumatic fever during her childhood. Bearing children put extra strain on her heart, a condition not diagnosed until her second or third pregnancy. By her third pregnancy, she had experienced enough health challenges that the family hired a highly recommended young nurse from Johns Hopkins University to care for her: Henrietta Van Den Berg, who had emigrated from Germany with her family in 1879 and had graduated from Hopkins in 1899. Although she had been reluctant to leave Baltimore to nurse "an invalid mother," Miss Van Den Berg became an ideal nurse, counselor, and home manager for the Reynolds family over the next eleven years. Only a few years older than Katharine, she evolved into her ersatz mother and confidante over the course of their close relationship. The children adored Miss Van Den Berg, whom they nicknamed "Bum," and remained intimate with her long after they had grown up. Van Den Berg offered each of the children abundant love, comfort, and stability.[91]

Katharine, supported by R.J.R., sought to protect her family at all costs. Even before bringing Van Den Berg to Winston, she had arranged for a top pediatrician and a top surgeon to practice in a town that until then had only general practitioners. Based on strong recommendations from Johns Hopkins Hospital, she invited Dr. Wingate Johnson, a pediatrician, and Dr. Arthur Valk, a surgeon, to build practices in Winston, guaranteeing them their living expenses for the first two years to get them started.[92] Ironically, both Katharine and R.J.R. agreed that smoking cigarettes was an unhealthy practice. Katharine never smoked, even when increasing numbers of well-off women considered it fashionable by the early 1920s. R.J.R., although he chewed tobacco and smoked cigars, forbade his children from smoking and always warned them against it. Like many grown children, the four offspring ignored their parents' advice in adulthood.[93]

Katharine's commitment to health consciousness extended to diet as well. Both R.J.R. and Katharine insisted on growing their own fruits and vegetables. They ordered fruits they could not grow themselves or could not buy locally in sufficient quantity, including exotics like guava and kumquats, but also bananas, cantaloupes, pears, apricots, cherries, lemons, oranges, and grapefruit.[94] The couple had good reason to be wary about disease in this time and place. Airborne illnesses were so ubiquitous that doctors advised parents to restrict their children's attendance at parties, dancing schools, and even kindergartens to avoid contamination.[95]

Katharine, who had received fresh milk from R.J.R. during their courtship as a sign of his commitment to her, worried incessantly about providing their children with safe, healthful milk. This concern may explain why she nursed all her children much longer than most mothers. Her daughter remembered that Katharine was embarrassed when she realized that she had breast-fed her children much longer than "modern" recommendations and more like "country people," who nursed until their children were "real big."[96] Katharine refused to take the children when they were small to see their grandparents because Walter Gordon Laboratory Milk, the only milk she would let her children drink because it was sanitized, was only available in Washington, D.C., and Baltimore, and not in Mount Airy.[97]

Despite all her best efforts, Dick Jr. during his first year of school at Salem Academy had come down with measles, diphtheria, and whooping cough.[98] Katharine and the other children caught the measles too. Domestic matters ground to a halt in the weeks following Christmas. Unfortunately Katharine did not rebound as quickly as her children. Plagued by colds and tonsillitis, she finally traveled to Baltimore for a tonsillectomy in May. Illness, often serious, threatened the family constantly.[99]

In the spring of 1914, when Katharine was pregnant a fifth time, her health problems proved troubling enough that she was admitted to Johns Hopkins Hospital. Here she had a series of heart attacks. On the fourth day, the doctors aborted a male fetus. In a letter conveying Katharine's ordeal to Miss Van Den Berg, who was in Winston caring for the children, Katharine's nurse described her patient as "the most brave and wonderful little woman I have ever known." Katharine had begged the doctors to let her remain pregnant, "but after the heart attack she was perfectly resigned and realized it was the only thing to do."[100] It was at this point in Katharine's life that her doctors advised her to have no more children, a directive she later ignored.

Katharine's growing frailty throughout these years made Miss Van Den Berg's role an especially important one. Van Den Berg became much more than an exceptional nurse to the Reynolds family. In short order, Katharine gave her nurse the authority to discipline the children as she saw fit. Van Den Berg also came to fill the place of the children's often-absent mother and to be a confidante for Katharine too.[101] Van Den Berg even ran the household and gave the staff orders in Katharine's absence.[102] The letters exchanged between the accomplished nurse and the mistress of the house are illuminating. They also convey the scale of work performed on a daily basis. After Katharine had been absent for many weeks caring for her hospitalized husband in the last year of his life, Van Den Berg finally reported to her with relief, "Things are beginning to run much more smoothly."[103] She meant that Christmas preparations—securing gifts for friends, employees and family; decorating the house; managing the cleaning, the silver, and the linens; purchasing and preparing six dozen young chickens, turkeys, and hogs, grapefruit, oranges, dried fruit, sugar, and all the other necessary ingredients to create sumptuous holiday feasts—had been taken care of. Van Den Berg was even handling the finishing touches for a holiday move into Katharine's planned bungalow—without Katharine there. The accomplished nurse had her hands full managing a daunting set of tasks in her employer's absence, ensuring that the workmen on the estate completed their assignments, that the glitches in the bungalow's new heating and electrical systems were fixed, that R.J.R.'s room was outfitted with comforts to ease his invalid status, and so on.[104]

Miss Van Den Berg could handle these challenges. She tended to boss everyone around, including Katharine. In fact, she may have been the only person able to do so. Katharine and R.J.R.'s youngest daughter, Nancy, recalled that Katharine could sometimes be jealous of Miss Van Den Berg in her role as de facto mother. It was Van Den Berg, for example, who explained menstruation to Nancy, after the young girl thought she had unknowingly injured herself.[105] "Mother had so much to do that she couldn't have done it [alone], it was really too much for her," Nancy explained. Katharine and Van Den Berg remained close despite these tensions. "Mother liked her very much," Nancy concluded.[106] Van Den Berg looked after Katharine and found her a heart specialist in Baltimore in 1917 when R.J.R. was too ill himself to care for his wife.[107] Van Den Berg was not as close to R.J.R. as she was to Katharine and the children, perhaps because Van Den Berg and R.J.R. competed in the role of Katharine's confidante, or perhaps because R.J.R. was less than pleased that Van Den Berg played so large a role in his children's upbringing. When R.J.R. fell seriously ill, Van Den Berg assiduously avoided nursing him, despite Katharine's entreaties. Though she could surmount her "personal indisposition" if necessary, Miss Van Den Berg felt it would be in R.J.R.'s best interests to be nursed by a stranger.[108]

Her refusal to nurse R.J.R. notwithstanding, Van Den Berg's otherwise invaluable support meant that Katharine did not let child rearing or her health problems slow her down. Katharine also supported Van Den Berg in her special role as governess-nurse by hiring a nursemaid, Scottish émigré Lizzie Thompson. "She was kind of jolly, and not as well educated," daughter Nancy recalled. "But she'd do whatever Van Den Berg told her to do."[109] The demands on Katharine's life were extensive, from running the household to managing the construction of the Reynolda Estate she was building in the suburbs to advising R.J.R. about the company to organizing her siblings' and parents' lives to meeting the social demands of entertaining (and being entertained) to engaging in numerous reform projects, clubs, and societies. Katharine loved her children dearly and was alert to their needs, but her ability to focus on them to the exclusion of her other perceived responsibilities was limited. Thus, when Miss Van Den Berg returned to Baltimore for a protracted stay for gallbladder surgery and recovery, Katharine was not pleased. "I was not only quite distressed about her [Henrietta], but quite distressed that she was obliged to leave the baby right in the beginning of the summer, when he is teething," she wrote Senah Critz. Instead of hiring someone to replace Van Den Berg, which Katharine realized was impossible, she elected to care for Smith herself. "I suppose that I am very much spoiled, but it does seem very hard to find someone who begins to take Miss Van Den Berg's place."[110]

With her children so well cared for, Katharine could pursue her estate building, reform work, and social activities in full force, slowing down only when her own illnesses temporarily felled her. On the whole, her youthful energy and willingness to engage in so many social activities brought an added measure of glamour and importance to a town that derived much of its livelihood from an industry long considered dirty and mean. While she spent the lion's share of her time caring for family and planning her model farm, she hosted innumerable breakfasts, lunches, dinners, and parties for R.J.R.'s management and sales teams, visiting dignitaries like Virginia governor William Hodges Mann and his wife, Etta, leading her social and reform clubs, and catching up with her friends. Katharine consistently threw the most desirable parties in the entire Piedmont.[111]

Katharine and Henrietta Van Den Berg were the principal caregivers for their children, but R.J.R. was a doting father, and his children worshipped him. When they were little, the children woke up one night to a raging downpour that scared them badly. "So we all jumped into Daddy's bed," youngest daughter Nancy recalled. "And then he told us some wonderful tales and we completely forgot about the thunderstorm."[112] They never forgot the comfort and love he gave them. One summer Katharine took baby Mary and toddler Dick Jr. to the Inn at Roaring Gap in the North Carolina mountains to escape the heat. R.J.R. wrote her frequently, eagerly asking about baby Mary's health. He told Katharine, "[I] could not go to sleep under one hour after laying down without thinking about how my sweet Dick and Mary is and the loansome [*sic*] home without all. I do not know the words to tell you how much I miss & love you and the children."[113] He delighted in the time he did get to spend with his offspring. While Katharine was out of town, leaving him home with Mary, he wrote her almost gleefully about his little daughter: "She loves me much better now than she does when you are here or seems to be much gladder to see me. She can walk without any assistance."[114] Photographs of the family always depict an affectionate, graying father with a wide smile stooping to pick up one of his brood to toss high in the air or kneeling down on the ground to play alongside them. Daughter Nancy said about her father, "I was only eight when he died, but my feeling and recollection of him is the pleasure he got out of having children. In some of the pictures you see that, grinning from ear to ear when he picks us up, laughing when we pull his hair. So I have a warm feeling when I think about him; I feel a little more distance from my mother."[115]

Perhaps because R.J.R. felt he could fully father these four children, in a way he could not with his nephews, nieces, and illegitimate son, he was never the disciplinarian in the family.[116] Instead, that role largely fell to Katharine or to Miss Van Den Berg in her absence. Daughter Nancy Reynolds stated emphatically that "her mother was the boss of the house—she handled the discipline." In contrast, she explained, the children were R.J.R.s "entertainment." It was her mother, Nancy pointed out, who "would take the whip to Dick and Smith" making her "cringe."[117] Katharine ran a tight ship. Not only did she have high expectations about her children's behavior, but she dictated their activities too.[118]

Both R.J.R. and Katharine insisted that their children develop a strong work ethic and appreciate the value of money. Their father put them to work. He brought home pipe tobacco, small bags, and pieces of cord, and the children strung the tops of the little bags of pipe tobacco with the cord. They were paid by the piece, for extra money, and understood that black families earned extra cash working from home in the same way.[119] Although the children remembered going to their father's office several times, they never actually went to the factories. It is interesting that R.J.R. himself maintained this dividing line that kept even his own family away from the behind-the-scenes, gritty world of the workers and his machinery.[120]

The children, although privileged, did not expect extravagance. They considered oranges in their stockings a great Christmas treat.[121] Although the Reynolds offspring would engage in lives of excess as young adults after their parents' deaths, all four siblings genuinely strove to please them as children, especially during R.J.R.'s lifetime. Dick was attentive to his parents and respectful of the values they preached, including self-sufficiency, salesmanship, and citizenship. At age eleven, he proudly wrote his parents that he had sold all his Liberty Bonds during World War I and would be receiving a medal for his accomplishment. Meanwhile, he was happy to note that the chickens he was raising were thriving.[122] Nancy, a Girl Guide, once went with her troop to Raleigh for a convention, during which she and the other troop members stayed in the homes of private families. Nancy's hostesses were seamstresses, who kept feeling the material in her dresses and asking her if she were one of the "tobacco Reynoldses." She denied any connection. Nancy simply wanted to fit in, to not be "conspicuous."[123]

The children led an ideal life in many respects, especially while both parents were alive and in good health. Like all children they delighted in special occasions and spectacle. Katharine made sure they had a flashy, smart-stepping pony they could drive around town.[124] The whole family loved the children's involvement in pageants and shows at school and church.[125]

The development of the Reynolda Estate provided the children with their own personal playground long before they actually moved there. One summer the whole family even camped out by the Reynolda spring while the bungalow was being built. The children could all ride. The girls ventured out on their ponies for hours at a time, making a huge circuit beyond the estate on dirt roads and stopping at a little store for an Orange Crush before heading back.[126] Katharine sometimes joined them on her beloved white mare, Kentucky Belle. Smith reported to his parents during one of their absences that he anticipated swimming in the lake as soon as the water warmed up a bit. He was thrilled that the workmen had just built a sliding board into the water and that he had camped in the woods with older brother Dick and his friend Bosley, setting rabbit traps and catching possums. The boys had cooked out over a fire, making splendid meals of bacon, eggs, and cocoa. Since it was almost summer time, Smith wrote for permission to go barefoot or at least to forgo socks, since they made him look like a "sissy."[127]

Katharine and her family embraced a developing national commitment to active participation in sports and recreation, part of the new suburban lifestyle. She turned up her nose at more urban, working-class pastimes. She never attended the movies, even when D. W. Griffith's *Birth of a Nation* opened in Winston to much hoopla in 1916, and did not allow her children to attend. Nor did she ever go to ball games.[128] She did enjoy hunting. She and R.J.R. even chaperoned a "possum hunt" near the Yadkin River comprised of some of the wealthiest young people in the city. Katharine's embrace of more elite leisure pursuits included golf, in which she was quite competitive, even writing her instructor to inquire whether she or R.J.R was the better player. Her coach replied tactfully that both were talented, and he hoped both were keeping up their game.[129]

Katharine and her family also relished travel in their automobiles. Most local trips took them to Mount Airy to see Katharine's grandparents once the children were old enough to travel and the roads improved.[130] But they took other treks too. A garage owner in Statesville recalled repairing one of the finest automobiles he had ever seen for a handsome family—a pair of well-dressed parents with four well-behaved children all decked out in goggles, linen dusters, and caps. The driver and head of the brood, a large, striking man with an abundant beard, turned out to be none other than R. J. Reynolds himself.[131]

Vacations factored heavily into the Reynoldses' lifestyle. R.J.R. had long traveled by railroad from Winston to Greensboro to Baltimore to Philadelphia to New York, and back again, a route he knew well by the time of the dissolution of the Tobacco Trust. Katharine soon learned the choreography of this familiar journey too. They preferred the Plaza Hotel in Manhattan and often stayed at The Stafford in Baltimore. As much as Katharine enjoyed the opportunity to shop in these cities or take a train from Philadelphia to Atlantic City for a breather, business was usually at the core of these treks. The family also pursued more relaxing holidays away from business, often taking advantage of the healthy air in the North Carolina mountains. At Roaring Gap, the resort community frequented by wealthy Winstonites, they took rooms in the Greystone Inn.[132] Because the Reynoldses enjoyed their creature comforts, they were the first on the mountain to have plumbing installed in their suite of hotel rooms, much to the amazement of the local folks, who came in droves to see their first bathtub.[133]

R.J.R. bought a 2,500-acre hunting preserve in Alabama perhaps in the hopes of pursuing more rustic adventures, but that proved a rarity given his demands.[134] Instead the family made an extended trip to New Orleans for Mardi Gras and then on to Texas and Hot Springs, Arkansas, in 1907. Several months later, they toured New England by chauffeured automobile, stopping in North Hampton, Massachusetts, and Bretton Woods, Mount Washington, and White Mountain, New Hampshire, then on to Portland, Maine, where they stayed at one lovely resort after the other, replete with liveried

African American servants, before heading back to Atlantic City for a short stay.[135] That same year, R.J.R. applied for passports for his family members and the family nurse to travel to China and Japan, where the company was developing business connections, but the trip was later canceled. They did travel to Nassau in the Bahamas, where they stayed at the Colonial Hotel. The following year they vacationed in Palm Beach, Florida, after stopping in Jacksonville, at the encouragement of Ethel Reynolds, their niece from Bristol, Tennessee.[136] In 1910, the family now included infant Nancy, as well as the toddlers Dick and Mary, but that did not stop Katharine and R.J.R. from taking all of them on a long chauffeured car trip to Thousand Islands, in Canada, with Miss Van Den Berg.[137] In 1913, the family debated going to California, or at the very least to Tampa or Augusta, but did not manage any of the trips, probably because of Katharine's poor health and the need to supervise the building of the estate as closely as possible, while planning the advertising launch for the Camel cigarette the following year.[138]

In fact, the family stayed close to home for the next several years, with the exception of trips up the Atlantic coast to Baltimore, Philadelphia, and New York. In 1917, the family traveled to Belleair, near Tampa, and to Jacksonville and Palm Beach as well, staying the whole winter in Florida, the first real vacation outside visits to Atlantic City in a long while.[139] It was Atlantic City, however, that claimed the Reynoldses most frequently. R.J.R. had taken his nephews and nieces to Atlantic City for years; he and Katharine did the same with their children. Both considered Atlantic City a place to regain their health, as did many other North Carolinians. Katharine told her friend Mollie Bernard that she was planning to go to Atlantic City for two weeks "for a little strengthening up."[140] Nathalie Gray invited Katharine to join her soon in Atlantic City "to enjoy doing the Boardwalk" and gain a pound or so a day as she had since her arrival.[141]

The notion of Atlantic City as a healthy escape had originated in the post–Civil War era when mostly Philadelphians made day trips to the ocean to avail themselves of the benefits of salt water. The train ride took two and a half hours each way and was almost as much a part of the adventure as stepping waist deep into the waters in full-length bathing clothes to be gently lifted by the swells for bodily restoration. As word spread, and growing numbers of wealthy New Yorkers and Washingtonians flocked to Atlantic City to take the cure too, entrepreneurs built family resorts to meet their needs, throwing up French-inspired Second Empire–style wooden hotels. By the late nineteenth century, Atlantic City promised its guests—increasingly a middle- and working-class clientele, and not just an elite one—a whole host of amusements and pleasures, from elegant hotel dining to performances by escape artist Harry Houdini, from fishing expeditions to bizarre exhibits of "the incubator babies."[142]

By the early twentieth century, the Garden Pier section of the boardwalk with its beautifully landscaped gardens offered upscale visitors a calming stroll. B. F. Keith's theater provided one of the finest venues for moviegoers in the country (and it was no small irony that *Tobacco Road* premiered here years later, in 1941). Although the boardwalk was central to shaping this unique landscape, the dozens of hotels flung up against it contributed mightily to this sense of marvel too. The Reynoldses stayed only at the "best" hotels centrally located on the boardwalk. The Traymore, with its long-standing reputation for serving the well to do, was the largest hotel in the city at fourteen stories with six hundred guest rooms. The Marlborough-Blenheim, the other hotel the Reynoldses engaged, was even more visually amazing by virtue of its massive Moorish-style dome and turrets.

By the 1900s, the chamber of commerce began promoting the city as "the" locale for convening fraternal societies, political parties, labor groups, and professional organizations. By the second decade of the twentieth century, Atlantic City was drawing an estimated ten million people annually and had turned into a convention destination.[143] The value of using Atlantic City to generate team spirit and hawk products was not lost on industry leaders. Pierre du Pont held his general sales convention meeting of the Du Pont Company in Atlantic City in 1918 and at the same time made sure that Du Pont products were exhibited in stores and shops up and down the boardwalk.[144] R. J. Reynolds's own sales force had worn Prince Albert swimsuits on the beach to bring new attention to their product several years earlier. Katharine herself understood the novelty of the place and its potential for promoting products. In 1913, she wrote R.J.R. that she was disappointed to find that no shops displayed Prince Albert in their windows.[145]

Throughout their busy lives, Katharine and R.J.R. retained their love and affection for each other. "My Dear sweet wife," R.J.R. began a letter written on company stationery during his family's travels up the East Coast, "I arrived here [in Winston] safely," adding, "I hope you will write me at once and let me know about the health of your sweet self and our lovely children."[146] In their tenth year of marriage, Katharine gave R.J.R. a beautiful pair of sapphire cuff links for Christmas, stating, "I only wish I could give you something that would give you even a small part of the pleasure that your gifts always give me, but the little that I can give is with a heart overflowing with love."[147] They disliked being apart. R.J.R. wrote his new wife from the Madison Hotel in New York in 1905, "Leaving under the voice 'Miss Katharine is crying' certainly was the most painful task I ever performed and I feared crying myself if [I] saw you shed tears."[148] Two years later, he wrote from New York, "I would have much grieved over parting with you and Dick looking so mad at me, if I had not looked on the bright side as I always try to do. . . . I will assure you nothing could give me greater pleasure than to always have both of you with me. I will never go without you unless I am compell[ed] to do so."[149] In still another letter, he lamented leaving her in tears yet again in Winston: "I regret that I had to come to NY without my dearest of all. . . . [It] certainly was the most painful task I ever performed."[150] Throughout their marriage, R.J.R.'s letters conveyed how desperately he missed Katharine and the children when they were separated, and Katharine, who despised their leave-takings, expressed the same sentiments.[151]

Katharine worried about the toll that running the business took on her husband, while R.J.R. assured her things were under control. "You must not think I am worried when I look serious as I always look serious when I have a difficult business problem to work out," he told her. "I will always be happy so long as I receive some love and good treatment as heretofore from you the one I love & respect more than I do all others. You have made me happy & I will certainly do all in my power for your happiness also for the good of our children."[152] Meanwhile, he wanted to ensure that she lived in high style and completely made over the Fifth Street house at her direction in 1910. "I think you will be delighted with your house[.] [T]hey are doing high class work[.] [T]he changes you ordered made will add largely to the comfort of the house & I am delighted over your plans. When completed I will feel you have the most delightful home in NC & all of us will be proud of our home with a hart full of love from your husband for you and our children also highest regard to Miss Van Den Berg Your devoted husband RJ Reynolds," he wrote his wife.[153]

In fact, R.J.R. humbled himself before his vivacious young wife over and over again.

> You have been such a sweet lovely wife to me & [it] gives me greater & more pleasures during our four years than I have ever received from every body during my entire life. When ever you see I have made a mistake you know how to correct me in such a sweet lovely way that I always appreciate what you say & words will not tell how I am grieved over my utter failure to do likewise or as good for you. . . . I want you to tell me when you think I have made a mistake [my] prair [*sic*] will be in asking the lord to teach me how to express myself to please instead of displeasing you.[154]

In each letter expressing his affections, he also shared with her news about business meetings, expectations, and sales.[155]

Within this special marriage, Katharine secured considerable autonomy. R.J.R. adored her and wanted to fulfill her hopes and expectations. His wealth meant she had the financial wherewithal to dream big and the domestic support that freed her to pursue her dreams. Because he was a workaholic, and because his business was growing exponentially during their marriage, she could choose to involve herself in his work as much or as little as she liked. Early in their marriage, the two appeared to be working together to urbanize downtown Winston. In early 1909, R.J.R. was contracting with the Fogle Brothers to build a handsome, twenty-thousand-dollar department store on Liberty Street to be occupied by a leading merchant, while Katharine was purchasing property at the western edge of the city where she planned to build a nine-thousand-dollar apartment building, replete with "every convenience, including janitor service and heat."[156] Because R.J.R. was a self-confident man, he had no need to place limitations of any kind on Katharine, and in fact he encouraged her ambitions and explorations.

Her freedom was perhaps most obviously demonstrated in her mobility—literally. Leaving Winston for the day or for weeks on end allowed her to escape some or all of her many familial responsibilities and public duties, renew her sense of independence, and gain new experiences and insights. She probably was the first woman in the North Carolina Piedmont to own a car, a Cadillac "Thirty" Roadster that cost $1,870 in 1909. Although she was always chauffeured, an important nod to her social status, she used her vehicle for duty and for fun—to visit her family in Mount Airy, to take the children during the hot and sickly late summer months to Roaring Gap, to catch the northbound train in Greensboro, or to head south to the new golf resort at Pinehurst.[157] Her automobile gave her a kind of freedom few southern women would secure for themselves for at least several more decades.[158]

Katharine relished travel. She journeyed frequently and often far from her home.[159] She was as likely to travel alone, especially once she could entrust the children to her highly capable nurse, as with her family.[160] In an undated letter to R.J.R., Katharine even implored, "Don't let [the children] forget me."[161] By the time she was in her thirties, she knew the "best" spots up and down the Atlantic coast, spending significant amounts of time in New York and Atlantic City especially, but also in Miami, Baltimore, Washington, D.C., and Philadelphia, and at resorts in Roaring Gap, Asheville, and Pinehurst, North Carolina, in the mountains of upstate New York and New Hampshire, and along the coast of South Carolina.[162]

Although Katharine savored the opportunity to travel and the freedoms it gave her, she remained committed to her domestic responsibilities and took pride in her mastery of her demanding household duties. She raised her daughters to embrace the so-called habits of the southern hearth. Some were decidedly gendered, including the virtues of devotion and self-sacrifice and the aesthetics of taste and beauty. Others were not, though they had a decidedly southern orientation: the civility of good manners, graciousness, and poise. Katharine internalized all these habits with aplomb in the course of her lifetime as head of the Reynolds household. Her Achilles heel lay in her penchant for organization and detail, leading her to run her home and her life like a business. Only occasionally would she relax enough to enjoy that sense of irony and play that comes with a good mind and a fine sense of humor.[163]

Seriousness of purpose was evident in Katharine's reading practices and her library. R.J.R. read every newspaper he could get his hands on, from the local and state papers to the *Wall Street Journal* and the *New York Times*, but Katharine was an inveterate reader in her own right, especially of popular magazines and advice literature. Her literary interests were catholic, and like R.J.R. she embraced a decidedly national outlook. Her tastes, more than her husband's, ran toward deciphering trends in popular culture and conspicuous consumption. She subscribed to the leading political and cultural journals of the day: *Harper's Magazine*, *Theatre Magazine*, *Current Literature*, *Century Magazine*, and the *Christian Observer*. Katharine and R.J.R. also read *Motor Age* and *Motor* religiously. She devoured *Vogue* and *Dress*. She studied gendered domesticity with subscriptions to magazines like *Woman's Home Companion* and *Boston Cooking School.* She gave her children *St. Nicholas* and *Little Folks,* covertly training them in mass culture. She also read journals about gardens, farming, and suburbia, including *Country Life in America, Suburban Life,* the *Garden Magazine,* and the *Progressive Farmer.* The materials she perused were jumbled together across categorical and ideological divides. Consistency in outlook was less important to her than the didactic information she collected and applied to her world.[164]

Like her taste in popular literature, her taste in books was eclectic. In one year alone, she purchased over two thousand dollars' worth of books: biographies, histories, literature, and reference works, including Russell's biography of Gladstone, the *Lover's Yearbook of Poetry* in two volumes, Coxe's *House of Austria,* Clodd's *Childhood of the World,* Greeley's *American Conflict,* Eves's *West Indies,* Adams's *History of Japan,* and McClintock and Strong's twelve-volume *Biblical and Theological Cyclopedia.*[165] She filled her library shelves with beautifully bound classics, including a multivolume set of Lacroix covered in green Moroccan leather, and even owned Mark Twain's collected works.[166]

Those selections stood juxtaposed against another genre Katharine consumed almost obsessively, one that could be called "the scientific business of domesticity." These purchases included *The Library of Work and Play* put out by the Country Life Press.[167] Other titles examined domestic science, home economics, and home nursing, such as Lucy Maynard Salmon's *Domestic Service* (1911), a series of bulletins from the Housekeeping Experiment Station in Stamford, Connecticut, on topics like "Housekeeping Efficiency," and *The Chemistry of Cooking and Cleaning* (1912).[168] This category included Katharine's penchant for books on gardening, landscaping, architecture, and interior design, and here she selected the standard texts: Charles Edward Hooper's *Country House* (1909), E. T. Cook's *Gardening for Beginners* (1907), Andrew Jackson Downing's *Landscape Gardening* (10th ed., 1912), Peter Henderson's *Handbook of Plants and General Housekeeping* (1904), Gertrude Jekyll's *Color Schemes for Flower Gardens* (1914), and Alice Lonsberry's *Southern Wild Flowers and Trees* (1901). She consulted all these works in her development of the Reynolda Estate, and the landscaping and design of her estate reflect the advice she garnered from them.[169]

Katharine adapted into her household organization many contemporary ideas from her voracious reading of this popular literature. She believed in efficient operations based on "scientific principles." Because protecting her family's health was a top priority, cleanliness and nutritious cooking mattered deeply to her. At the same time, she valued beauty in all its forms. She prided herself on creating a home away from the grime of the working-class tobacco world she knew all too well, one that let her family thrive and that warmly welcomed her many guests and visitors.[170] She served hearty foods such as pickled carrots, apple butter, salmon croquettes, Brunswick stew, creamed sweetbreads and chicken livers, and delicious treats like sweet potato pudding and butterscotch pie that put her company at ease and sated their appetites.[171] Monogrammed linens, bedding, and china reminded guests of her taste and wealth.[172]

Katharine was never completely selfless in her commitment to this idealized standard of living. Not only did she sometimes escape her duties with extensive travel, but she also had a penchant for drama and could be imperious. She insisted on breakfast in bed each morning, her tray piled high with fashion magazines, before she arose to greet the new day.[173] Dressed in her peignoir, she lay surrounded by "gorgeous sketches from the fashion designers in New York, the most famous ones. And the most beautiful," daughter Nancy recalled.[174] Katharine insisted on receiving kisses from each of the children first thing in the morning while she was still in bed and scolded Nancy many times for forgetting. "But a couple of times I'd go and she'd still be asleep, so that was always my alibi."[175]

Managing this household was no easy task, nor was it one Katharine could pull off alone. She needed far more support than Miss Van Den Berg or Lizzie Thompson, the children's caretakers, could provide. The Reynoldses maintained a retinue of servants, one that grew over time. Katharine's household staff, first at Fifth Street and then at the Reynolda Estate, proved instrumental in the smooth functioning of the Reynolds home. The staff members were divided by occupation and race. The children's nurse and the nanny were white, a practice long adopted by many elite families in the South.[176] Katharine's personal secretary, who opened her mail, typed all her correspondence, paid her bills, kept her books, and organized her calendar, was white too.[177] But the rest of the staff—the cook, the butler (whom the family called the majordomo), the maids, the laundress, the telephone operator—was African American. Katharine dressed her servants in uniforms appropriate to their particular form of service and purchased from New York houses. Charles, the chauffeur, wore a regulation full suit, dress shirt, and collar from the Rogers-Pete Company. The butler wore a coat and apron from O'Neill's. For young telephone operator Savannah Webster, Katharine and Miss Van Den Berg sought out staff member Pluma Walker's advice, not quite sure of the cap and apron appropriate for this new position.[178]

Appearances were critical to Katharine. Her servants represented her own values to the world; therefore her staff's presentation mattered. Their clothing needed to represent their respective occupations but also, and more importantly, their seriousness of purpose and professionalism. In a disease-laden society, they also needed to be spotlessly clean, signaling Katharine's commitment to sustaining good health. Such dedication to sanitation was part and parcel of the Progressive Era, a characteristic concern of women of her class and time. So critical was hygiene to Katharine that she built her own laundry at her estate, much to the chagrin of local laundries eager for her patronage.[179] The proprietor of Zinzendorf Laundry even sent Katharine a handwritten letter observing that although he knew she had her own private laundry, he thought he might persuade her to rely on his company instead. He promised her that he was familiar with "the labor troubles which usually attach to Laundry work, wash women and wash men" and could alleviate them for her, while ensuring that his laundry's "perfectly sanitary methods . . . at the forefront of any city" would protect the good health of the Reynolds family.[180] But Katharine preferred managing her own staff and her own laundry for the bulk of her needs. In a big bare-bones building in the village on her estate, her servants washed the linens, including the bedsheets, in huge washing machines virtually every day. Enormous mangles that took up half the space, dangerous because of their heft, rolled the linens smooth. Almost nothing was sent to the commercial cleaners, despite their entreaties, except Katharine's own clothing, which she shipped as far away as Baltimore to secure the best services.[181]

Katharine's embrace of domestic management was a major undertaking given the number of people and responsibilities it entailed under the aegis of her estate. But she spread her duties even further by including her extended family under her definition of household too. She offered her home to a favorite niece for her wedding and sponsored a distant cousin whose career path had taken him from missionary work to law school and most recently to enrollment at Union Theological Seminary.[182] This generosity was characteristic of all her relationships with her relatives, but she heaped her greatest commitments on her sisters. She bought them clothes, paid their medical bills, and held soirees for them.[183] She financed their educations.[184] Katharine kept abreast of her brothers and parents as well. Her letters are filled with concern over her mother's health and her hopes that her mother will be well enough to join them at Reynolda for a visit.[185] She bought clothes not only for her sisters, but for her mother, father, and brothers.[186] Katharine did press her family members on occasion to mend their ways, especially where money matters were concerned. Although she gave generously to her sisters, because she understood that their "success" in life depended mostly on the circles they traveled in and the likelihood of their marrying well, she was tougher on her brothers. Although she bought them the occasional suit and sent them cigarettes and candy during their basic World War I training, she was a stickler on money issues.[187] In one instance, she loaned her brother Matt one hundred dollars, which he repaid with interest. He borrowed another one hundred dollars from her six months later and paid her three dollars interest the following month, a steep rate from a family member to whom one hundred dollars meant so little. Matt even felt compelled to assure his older sister that he would not "overcrop" himself that year, limiting cultivation to only twenty-five acres and doing most of the work himself, to make sure he could pay her back.[188] Katharine's interest in the financial well-being of her Smith family members was so strong that she even managed a number of their accounts at the Wachovia National Bank.[189]

Katharine's keen commitment to purposefulness was reflected not only in her family relations but even in her attitudes toward entertaining. Although she enjoyed it, it was almost always in the interest of bettering something—usually her husband's business relationships or her progressive reform efforts. Whereas her childless sister-in-law, Kate Bitting Reynolds, and other women of Katharine's social class spent their spare time pursuing club activities and pastimes that brought them considerable personal pleasure or status, from competing in horse shows to participating in the local chapter of the United Daughters of the Confederacy, Katharine directed her energies toward others' happiness and amusement rather than her own and usually for a larger purpose.[190]

Katharine was purposeful about cultivating her friendships too, and these women were always important to her. She wrote letters to her friends with surprising frequency given her hectic schedule, thanking them for the gifts they had sent and their kind cards filled with their news, while updating them about her own family and especially their health.[191] Katharine had considerable influence on the women around her. The amount of independence she wielded in her marriage, including her access to significant amounts of money, astounded most of her friends. Nor was she afraid to challenge male authority. Her old friend and chaperone D. Rich, now the R. J. Reynolds Tobacco Company treasurer, refused to give his second wife and Katharine's good friend cash of her own. Nor did he let her have a bank account. Katharine was appalled, telling him that he needed to give his wife money to use as she liked. Rich refused, but he did let his wife put purchases on credit for the first time. Not to be outdone, Katharine persuaded her friend to go to the store, buy a hat, but have the store charge her for two hats and give her the difference in cash. The clever strategy worked. Mr. Rich was never the wiser.[192]

Katharine was a wheeler-dealer. She knew what she wanted, and she figured out how to get it. She handled all the business accounts associated with her family and mastered all the details. She had no compunctions about negotiating prices, finding the best deals and holding professionals, suppliers, and contractors accountable. In 1912, she hired L. L. Miller of Somerville, New Jersey, landscaper for the Duke estate, to design her city lot on the Fifth Street property. Their subsequent letter exchanges show she was attentive to the smallest details, and in one instance, calculated her local gardener's error in laying out hedges, its ramifications for Miller's plans, and her own proposal for a middle-ground solution. She assessed the grading angles, reminded the landscape architect that her husband's stable needed to be much larger than originally outlined, and agreed a "dear little fountain" called "Music of the Waters" would be a lovely addition. Still, she demanded to know the actual price before committing to buy the fountain, despite Miller's vague promise that "it [was] not very costly." Katharine relished beauty, but she wanted projects completed in a timely way, and she was economical. She had already balked at a bid she considered too high for a pergola Miller had proposed, despite his advice to accept it. He thought the bid low given that the suppliers were "the most reliable and most experienced builders of pergolas in the trade." Katharine had none of it, telling Miller in a subsequent letter that Mr. Reynolds had found local craftsmen willing to build the same pergola for $119 less.[193]

Katharine was strong, even tough. No wonder then that R.J.R. rarely took the lead on domestic projects of any sort, leaving the negotiations to her.

He also rarely offered advice, although in 1910 he did suggest she consider buying leather-covered chairs for his smoking room rather than the cloth ones she liked, as he had once accidentally set his chair on fire at the Plaza Hotel with his cigar.[194]

Katharine's penchants could often seem to be at war with one another. Like her husband, she could be down-to-earth and practical, committed to economizing and making do. But she also had a fondness for self-indulgence. This divergence in values manifested itself in her relationship to clothes and fashion. Katharine was raised a thrifty daughter of an increasingly well-off merchant family. Growing up, she usually sewed her own clothes, including her midnight-blue wedding suit. Once married, she continued sewing whenever she could, but she also employed local seamstresses to make her undergarments and tailor her outfits. She hired Miss Annie Jean Gash, expert in domestic science, to come to her house to teach her, along with her circle of friends and family, dressmaking skills and domestic skills in general.[195]

Katharine loved clothes and had used fashion to signal her status and sophistication at least since college. As a married woman, she developed a keen enthusiasm for shopping in Baltimore at the best dressmaking establishments and, after 1910, shopped almost exclusively in New York City. The local newspaper described the first lady of Winston's attire whenever possible. Katharine's fashion choices helped feed its local readers' desire for glimpses of wealth and exoticism. In the end, Katharine learned to balance her love of fashion with her frugal origins. She adored clothes and wanted the latest styles.[196] She relied on a phalanx of seamstresses, dressmakers, and boutiques from near and far for her wardrobe and was never above some sewing herself. She wrote her Baltimore dressmaker, Miss A. M. Hall, about scheduling a date to travel up the coast and view "the Spring Models" in time to have her selections ready by Easter.[197] She kept local women busy too. One spring, Mrs. Farrar sewed a total of ninety-four hours for Katharine over a sixteen-day period in Winston.[198] Mrs. T. W. Hancock, owner of a downtown millinery, sold Katharine ribbon, cloth, ready-made clothes, and hats.[199] Unlike most women of her class, Katharine was not above buying some of her undergarments ready-to-wear.[200] She asked a local seamstress to duplicate a princess shirt she had purchased in New York some years earlier.[201]

Penny-wise or not, Katharine enjoyed fashion. She understood its multiple meanings and functions, as a way of displaying status and wealth, of expressing beauty and taste, and of generating sensuality. She owned a nearly transparent dress trimmed in monkey fur. She wore big hats adorned with long beautiful feathers, knowing, as did all women of the period, that when she walked, the movement of the feathers could be arousing. Once the Audubon Society convinced well-dressed American women that their penchant for wide-brimmed chapeaux covered with feathers had endangered too many species, Katharine changed her ways, but she did not forgo the sexual elements. While she adopted more conservative hats, she had them trimmed with rich, alluring adornments like ermine. She followed national fashion trends and their relationship to politics closely. Her hats became smaller and smaller, and her haircuts and hemlines shorter and shorter over the course of World War I and into the early 1920s, even as she was growing older.[202]

Katharine was not a classically beautiful woman, but she had a strong penchant for beauty, and she understood that attention to her body and how she presented herself could make her more beautiful. Like many women of her class and time, she worried about her weight. In 1912, at age thirty-two, with four pregnancies behind her, she told Miss Van Den Berg that she weighed 161 pounds and promptly sought help from the experts. Chicagoan Susanna Cocroft, originator of the Physical Culture Extension Society, promised Katharine she could help her regain her figure and restore her to splendid health without the use of drugs "and thus be of greater use to those whose love and respect she would command."[203] But Katharine never expressed concern that R.J.R.'s love for her would be diminished by her appearance. It was her own sense of self that directed her down the women's self-improvement road.[204] Because she enjoyed her body and her femininity, she was not opposed to indulging in high fashion and expensive beauty treatments.[205]

Not surprisingly then, for someone who believed clothing shaped inward and outward perceptions and gendered ones too, Katharine had some expectations for her husband's attire. She had begun dressing R.J.R. while she was still single, pressing him to purchase eighteen shirts, collars, and handkerchiefs; three pairs of suspenders and gloves; and three hats six weeks before their wedding and honeymoon.[206] She continued purchasing his clothes once they were married, increasingly choosing tailors in Baltimore and New York City over local ones.[207] One Reynolda staff member recalled of R.J.R., "He was dressed like a dandy whenever his wife was taking him out somewhere."[208] But his displays of sartorial splendor were modest by Katharine's standards. While she owned enough furs to keep a chest of them in storage, R.J.R. had one greatcoat, a full-length wool topcoat lined with mink. It was a practical choice. The mink lining kept him warm, and though the coat was fashionable, it was not a flagrant display of wealth.[209]

Katharine's command of her world and the people in it came at least in part from her belief in the power of her self-presentation. Longtime African American household staff member Elizabeth Wade captured Katharine best in this regard when she stated, "She was so beautiful, and wore such beautiful clothes, and so intelligent—she was the last word, that's all I've got to say about her, she really was. And she was a lady, every inch of her, she really was."[210] Katharine could act as if she were born to the manor. "I mean you would just think she was born in a gold pit, the way she deported herself," added Wade. "You never saw Miss Katharine when she wasn't dressed to kill. As my grandmother said, she had quality."[211]

She bought beautiful things for herself, for her family, for her friends and employees, for her home, and for her estate. In essence, consciously or not, she used her numerous and conspicuous displays of "good" taste to justify her privilege and superiority. The wealthy have always used their "tastes" to help substantiate the "rightfulness" of their social power and authority. As Pierre Bourdieu has argued so convincingly, expressions of taste, supposedly uniquely personal to the individual expressing them, in fact have long defined social class. Taste, always dynamic, competitive, and strategic, encourages disdain and one-upmanship. Expressions of taste become a means to social dominance. Katharine could transcend her social status as a tobacco merchant's daughter and a tobacco-factory owner's wife in the North Carolina Piedmont through her expressions of taste—whether through the clothes she wore and her hair styles, all from Fifth Avenue; the parties she held; the architecture, interior decoration, and landscaping of her homes; or the creation and aesthetics of her largely self-sufficient estate.[212] All these acts, however different in scale and scope, when threaded together manifested her social importance, which was especially important to her as a woman denied the kind of access to the newest forms of power and privilege that most white men considered their birthright. Katharine cemented her self-importance and elite social position in other ways too, including commissioning photographers and artists to take formal portraits of herself and her family members.[213]

Katharine's "tastes" were unique in the Piedmont but not always the most cutting edge in the most socially elite circles. She relied on Edward Belmont of the John Wannamaker Department Store in Philadelphia to help her furnish her bungalow, writing him for his recommendations, including the right Victrola for a cabinet, noting that she had purchased "the best Victrola on the market in New York City several years ago for $500." For all her desire to have the top of the line, Katharine remained an inveterate comparison shopper and expected the people she employed to respect this trait.[214] Her correspondence with her Bristol niece, Ethel, must have been irksome. Ethel persisted in telling Katharine which resorts she should visit, whose homes were the most beautiful, the best musicians and orchestras to seek out, and the latest purchases by various elite social sets. She wrote Katharine from Miami stating, "I want you to have your tennis court fixed as large as Mrs. James. Her place is Paradise. Grounds immaculate. House Japanese. With many pillars, covered walks . . . just everything that taste, genius and money can do, her grass like a velvet carpet under your feet."[215] Katharine was not persuaded. She had her limits.

Chock full of contradictory preferences and identities, Katharine was a devoted but independent wife, a loving but often absent mother. She enjoyed entertaining and giving parties but relished quiet time to read and indulge. She adored her extended family but strove to shape them around her own values and expectations. She could be economical but loved beauty and opulence. She drove hard bargains but delighted in spectacle and sensuality. While R.J.R. was breaking free of Buck Duke's Tobacco Trust and relying on Katharine's good ideas about marketing to launch Prince Albert tobacco and Camel cigarettes, Katharine was creating Reynolda Estate, the one place where she could put all her paradoxical sensibilities and predilections into practice.

5 Brains and Backbone

R.J.R.'s business thrived during the period in which he had entered into marriage and fatherhood. Thirty years earlier, he had built a barn-red tobacco warehouse in Winston. He had spent the last three decades transforming his tobacco business into one of the leading economic engines in the South. All the while, he had been cultivating external displays of character that ensured him public respect and admiration. It would be easy to argue that R.J.R. was a smart nineteenth-century man who had used his inherent self-discipline to best advantage in a late-blooming regional economy. But R.J.R. represented more than a reductionist all-American, rags-to-riches cultural ideal. He also represented the archetypal southern good ol' boy, a bushy-bearded, womanizing, tobacco-spitting, liquor-loving, possum-hunting, horse-racing charmer who read the weather signs to know when to sow his seeds and harvest his crops for bumper yields. Both depictions, whether as Benjamin Franklin throwback or bastion of southern masculinity, relegated R.J.R. to a bygone era. By the turn of the century, they made him a man of the past, one who had made good in a particular time and place when economic opportunities had been omnipresent, and one who looked backward more than ahead.

Meanwhile, a modernizing America was in the works. The Gilded Age with its crises of character and faith, its social Darwinian blessings on corruption and greed, and its tortured birthing of the management model and the corporation, had choked to death most nineteenth-century entrepreneurial men's ambitions. But R.J.R., though married at long last and settling down, wanted to face the future. The political and racial challenges that he confronted on his home turf, as well as the national business contests he encountered in the larger American economy, left him unfazed. He was prepared to reinvent himself and his business at least one more time, and his late-in-life marriage to Katharine Smith both underscored that fact and aided him.

By 1900, R.J.R. understood, having watched Buck Duke's acquisition of dozens upon dozens of small tobacco manufactories, that the American social system had become far more closed than Horatio Alger's beloved stories suggested. The popular dime novels where poor boys always made good had an important but often unspoken subtext—the weighty role of the older male benefactor of some means. R.J.R. understood that in this new day and age rich men were not only the fictional but the real catalysts behind individual opportunity making, and he fully embraced that notion, mentoring smart, capable boys and men with real commitment. He benefited from this role personally, for he molded the best of these young people into his own talent pool of salesmen, marketing men, and managers. At the same time, while he appreciated the skills and abilities that individual men could bring to the table, R.J.R. also understood that the timing of larger economic forces like the panic of 1893 and the advent of such technological innovations as the Bonsack cigarette machine had shaped human destinies far more than personal ambition and moral character. No wonder that he eschewed the cosmology of American Protestantism, wherein a good God promised a good life as reward for moral and material self-discipline. To R.J.R., late nineteenth-century arguments for positivism made substantially more sense. Success in the world of tobacco trusts and corporations rested increasingly on a competitive ethos of positioning that was dependent on salesmanship, self-confidence, and dynamism. Industry and frugality, totemic in the nineteenth-century entrepreneurial world, were overrated in this emergent twentieth-century culture. It was the hard-nosed art of skillfully, even "scientifically," manipulating others—customers, shareholders, workers—along with adaptability to change that ensured sustained business success in this new environment.[1]

R. J. Reynolds's brilliance lay in his ability to straddle two fundamentally different worlds, one on the wane and the other in the throes of creation. He made a considerable financial success of it, while appeasing the great majority of people who preferred the old to the new. R.J.R. had been the quintessential nineteenth-century entrepreneur, able to turn a small piece of money into a profitable business through hard work, frugality, and ambition. By reaping the fruits of his own labor, Reynolds had made good in a society steeped in the virtues of a republican political economy. A nation of small producers had inexorably given way to big business. Between 1880 and 1920, the corporation had rooted itself in the American economy and played havoc with the American psyche in the process. R.J.R. understood that monumental shift taking place and decided to engage in it himself, while managing to convince most naysayers that he remained on their side.

As consolidation swept the country in the railroad, banking, oil, and even tobacco industries, producing unprecedented wealth in the hands of a very few—the Vanderbilts, J. P. Morgan, Andrew Carnegie, John D. Rockefeller, James B. Duke—the rest of the nation looked on with apprehension. The independent producers with their manifold small shops found themselves replaced by huge companies that dwarfed the economy and the government alike. In case after case, hundreds of employees and hundreds of shareholders rolled under the control of one small group of men intent on squelching labor unrest, raising product prices, and eliminating competition through monopolies.

Suddenly all the benefits of a republican political economy of small producers, not the least of which had been the encouragements of social and political equality, paled next to the enormous wealth that these large enterprises secured for the nation. Meanwhile, social and political costs be damned. Men like Carnegie explained that they distributed their riches as they thought best based on their unique vantage point in society and the special knowledge it gave them. American fears of monopolies and the men who puppeteered them were only further exacerbated by the news that the frontier was dead, as historian Frederick Jackson Turner had pronounced in 1893. The absence of new land with new resources on which to build an independent life through hard work and imagination regardless of one's social origins struck a heavy psychological blow at a time when monopolies and trusts were sweeping up smaller concerns left and right, wiping out small businessmen, and smashing workers' wages.

R.J.R. realized that he could stand to gain from this transformation if he could grow his business big enough. Ever the pragmatist, he was more concerned about his own opportunities than the greater good of the American population. Nor did he feel compelled to uphold American Revolutionary principles of democratic republicanism. Yet he countered his shrewd economic maneuverings, many of which he sought to hide from the public, with public support for the antimonopolist position. He had decried J. P. Morgan's monopolizing interest in Southern Railroad as well as James B.

Duke's craving for small tobacco firms. He had painted himself as an unfortunate victim of the American Tobacco Company (ATC) once news of the acquisition of Reynolds Tobacco got out, although Duke's buyouts had eliminated all his competitors and ultimately secured him enormous benefits. Still, R.J.R. continued his disavowals of Duke and monopolists in general right through the Supreme Court decision to bust the American Tobacco Company Trust, when he emerged in the eyes of the public as the victorious underdog. So great was his identification with the common man that he stood at his door in his nightshirt to tell reporters that he believed the newly instituted U.S. income tax was a just piece of legislation. Because he had the money, he told the reporters eager to record his first reaction, he had an obligation to pay. Those who didn't have the money didn't need to, he added, a position in sharp contrast to most wealthy men. He concluded, "It's a good tax," and then closed the door and went back to bed.[2]

R.J.R., the master of consumer sensibilities when it came to nicotine, was also the master of public predilections. He understood that so powerful, frightening, and impersonal were the forces of corporatism that many Americans decried them. Their entry into the Populist Party and its local variants in record numbers had made this point a half generation earlier. These same citizens were now reexamining their relationship with their one-time nemesis, the American government, and demanding intervention in this laissez-faire economy where the mighty few trounced on the vulnerable many with impunity.

The politicians responded to the people's fears, rolling out Progressive proposal after proposal to regulate the market and even nationalize it. Their work resulted in a new system of governmental bureaucratization that monitored food and drugs, busted trusts, established a federal income tax, and assured fair trade. Because the public now viewed capitalism conducted by large-scale corporations as bad, R.J.R. increasingly bent over backward to diminish the perception of the R. J. Reynolds Tobacco Company as a corporation. He did so through the force of his own personalism and his many paternalist actions on behalf of the greater public good. Despite his remarkable ability to construct a modern business structure out of one of the oldest and most stagnant of business models in U.S. industry—Reynolds Tobacco was replete with extensive hierarchical structures for buying, producing, marketing, and selling plug tobacco, pipe tobacco, and cigarettes by the

1900s—R.J.R. generally earned respect and admiration locally, across the state of North Carolina, and from the nation as a whole.[3]

What Reynolds grasped with exceptional acuity was not only the importance of the corporation as a means of ensuring huge efficiencies to generate great profits but its ability to satisfy consumer desires. This new understanding had just begun to creep into the twentieth-century American mind-set of wealth creation. It spelled the death knell for a labor theory of value that presumed the biggest profits came from the hardest workers, and replaced it with a marginal utility theory declaring that those most able to meet consumer preferences secured the greatest rewards. Corporations, having eschewed an open, competitive market and instead opting for trusts and monopolies, raced to meet those tastes. They relied on hierarchical organizational structures in which older values of character, thrift, and labor meant little, and social networks, family connections, verbal abilities, accounting knowledge, and relational skills meant advancement. In this new world, the few at the top ordered the lives of the others down the entire chain of command. Leadership favored idea people over skilled hands, talent in mathematics and science over moral commitment, machinery and technology over job creation.

The rise of management with its specialized tasks and opportunities for individual advancement generated by this corporatism produced a new white-collar class that reveled in the idea of a national corporate economy.[4] Working as a salesman in corporations like DuPont and International Harvester with their extensive sales structures meant lucrative paychecks and opportunities for professional growth. Complex hierarchies spawned sales managers, district managers, assistant managers, accountants, technicians, clerks, secretaries, advertisers, sales agents, and actual salesmen.[5] These same corporations worked exceedingly hard to ensure that their sales forces, now spread out across the country and in some cases even across the globe, extolled the same message about their products. All learned a "science of service." This training was designed to ensure all employees understood that their company's product met an integral societal need and that their dedicated, honest, energetic salesmanship was the best route to building a strong consumer base. The R. J. Reynolds Tobacco Company copied these new structures and new mind-sets from industry giants with lucrative results.[6]

Although R.J.R. remodeled his company into a corporation serving a national market, he refused to change his locale, which meant Winston and the Reynolds Tobacco Company became increasingly inextricable in the early twentieth century. As R.J.R. ramped up production to meet a wide-open market, outsiders reported that the city around the factories buzzed with commotion and disorder. Still, a closer look from the vantage of a downtown street corner revealed a far more regulated society where race largely determined social place. At noon and 6:00 p.m., the streets surrounding the factories filled with voices as African American tobacco workers headed home for dinner and supper. The air was always pungent, from the sickly sweet smell of tobacco, especially in the fall, but also from the overpowering spell of human waste that black drivers transported out of the city on two-wheeled carts. Chained convicts, almost all black, repaired the streets and constructed new ones under the watchful eye of an armed guard.

Industry and commerce thrived in this racially ordered world. Horses snorted and neighed almost round the clock on city streets, their iron shoes striking sparks on the cobblestone as they worked through the night and into the morning. Wagon after wagon loaded with boxes of tobacco, cotton, vegetables, ice, and furniture thumped back and forth between the depot and the growing numbers of factories, stores, and homes mushrooming out from the town center. On special occasions, the whole city came together across race and class, when the circus and Wild West shows came to town and for band concerts on the courthouse lawn.[7]

Winston's reputation was improving with its growth, even if racial segregation remained entrenched. One booster after another bragged that "the people of Winston-Salem ha[d] not only kept pace with progress but abreast of it." The *Winston-Salem Journal* asserted, "They have done well. . . . The people of Winston-Salem are a working people. All of them work. . . . This applies to the negroes as well as to the whites, and as a result of honest industry, the people are happy and contented."[8] Winston and Salem's population combined, only 4,194 in 1880, had more than tripled to 13,650 by 1900.[9] Whites now made up the majority; blacks constituted a third of the population. The mean age of city dwellers was twenty-five, and nearly two-thirds were single. Women slightly outnumbered men. Nearly nine out of ten residents had been born in North Carolina and the rest in nearby Virginia. Among the black population, about one in five had come from Virginia, as rural migrants seeking wage work in the tobacco factories.

A generation earlier, thousands of African Americans across the South had fled the stark racism of the region to head to the West in search of freedom and opportunity. The vast majority of southerners, white and black, however, remained in the countryside. They had not even ventured to southern cities, as opportunities remained limited in the post–Civil War urban South. The proportion of the South's manufacturing establishments compared to those of the nation as a whole and the value of their output had changed little between 1860 and 1900. Moreover, moving long distances was expensive, and few families had the resources to do so. Moving also broke families apart at a time when families represented one of the few wellsprings of comfort and hope for poor whites and blacks in such a strained world. Industry jobs, because they paid poorly, drew limited numbers of migrants from the southern countryside or elsewhere for that matter. Whether in lumber and mining in the Appalachians, textiles across the southern Piedmont, or tobacco in Virginia and North Carolina, industry leaders believed their jobs needed little education and few skills, justifying low wages, especially compared to those paid in many industries outside the region.

Thus, Winston's fast-paced manufacturing growth in the early twentieth century and the accompanying rise in the number of jobs and in wages signaled an important shift in economic development. Before 1900, Winston had taken shape organically, growing by leaps and bounds without a master design, but always in response to economic demands. Makeshift structures had been thrown up for stores, residences, churches, and warehouses, and when they proved too small, they were torn down and replaced with larger edifices. As opportunities for work increased, thousands of black and white men, women, and children trekked to the city. Moravian leaders in nearby Salem watched in amazement, no longer able to control the pace or culture of the community around them. Careful builders of their own planned church community, they found themselves making uneasy deals with the new industrialists on the scene, who increasingly took over the reins of decision making. The inappropriately nicknamed "twin cities" of Winston and Salem forged their first formal alliance with the establishment of a shared chamber of commerce in the 1880s.[10] The consolidation of the post offices in 1899 signaled the next big step toward merging the congregation town and the rowdy county seat.[11] The local governments finally united in 1913. Salem's leading industrialists had come to recognize that they had too much in common with Winston's industrialists, bankers, and lawyers to fight consolidation, though the middling class of Salem professionals, tradesmen, farmers, and storekeepers believed otherwise.

R. J. Reynolds, a master at pulling strings behind the scenes, had helped engineer this realignment. In a rare interview, he explained that consolidation would benefit both communities by drawing new businessmen with money to their shared community. A pair of towns united by nothing but a single road, he contended, is not attractive to the shrewd investor who wants to feel confident about sinking his capital into a place full of promise. Consolidation would not only draw new moneyed men, but it would be much more efficient to run a single government and a single set of town services, reducing costs. Finally, property values would rise in both places, he predicted, because more people would see Winston-Salem as an up-and-coming community with a growing population. He promised taxes would not increase, and he added he was the biggest taxpayer anyway and swore that any potential tax profits from consolidation would be earmarked for the education of Salem children. He concluded his interview by conveying his deep respect for "the German race that built Salem."[12]

This industrializing set of cities was racially segmented by work and neighborhood. Salem boasted the Arista Mills, owned by the Moravian Fries family, where white rural workers, mostly women and children, produced fifteen thousand yards of cloth a day.[13] Brothers Pleasant Henderson Hanes and John Wesley Hanes had been successful plug-tobacco manufacturers in Winston for twenty-five years, only to be bought out like so many other local manufacturers by R.J.R. under the guise of the Continental Tobacco Company.[14] The Hanes brothers subsequently turned to textiles.[15] John Wesley Hanes built Shamrock Hosiery Mills, a sock manufactory, while P. H. Hanes founded P. H. Hanes Knitting Company, which made underwear. Both companies employed white workers almost exclusively. As P. H. Hanes himself observed, "No Negroes save janitors are employed in Hanes Cotton Mills." He brought his employees under his wing by establishing Hanestown, a mill village that replicated the paternalistic system first made manifest in the United States in early nineteenth-century New England. Hanestown offered its 180 white employees houses for rent, access to a full-time nurse, community vegetable gardens, sports teams, its own police force and churches, and a company store.[16]

While Winston and Salem combined, and race segmentation increasingly characterized the towns' workforces, R.J.R. continued to manipulate local government and business alike. But he put the bulk of his energy in the first years of the twentieth century into consolidating his holdings, merging some and acquiring others. Not all of his actions proved as surreptitious as he might have liked, and not all of his buyouts turned out as well as the Hanes one. The editor of the *Winston-Salem Journal*, almost always R.J.R.'s public booster, noted the numbers of local businessmen leaving the tobacco business and tried to put these changes in a good light. While "there are plenty of [tobacco men switching to other industries] we should think it quite in the city's interest that we should have diversified industries instead of the specialty as in former years when Winston was principally a tobacco manufacturing town."[17] In contrast, the Statesville paper bemoaned the acquisitions. "This is bad news to the tobacco men of North Carolina, both growers and manufacturers. . . . It looks like the plug industry of the state will be absorbed by one company [R. J. Reynolds]; as has the cigarette company. The smaller factories will be forced to sell or go out of business. When this is accomplished the tobacco farmers will be forced to sell all their tobacco to one concern. . . . The future of tobacco in North Carolina is gloomy indeed."[18]

The Statesville editor was merely repeating what tobacco farmers had been claiming for some time. On January 17, 1900, representatives from twenty-six North Carolina counties and several Virginia counties declared themselves the "North Carolina Tobacco Growers' Association" and named their objective "to increase the price of leaf tobacco by legitimate competition in trade." In a rousing speech, J. F. Jordan of Guilford County condemned the Tobacco Trust and James B. Duke, but not R.J.R. "You must either give your tobacco away to the American Tobacco Company or else quit raising tobacco," he told his fellow aggrieved farmers.[19]

Despite these buyouts, orchestrated as much or more by the local leaders of the Reynolds Tobacco Company rather than the directors of the trust, R.J.R. seemed to retain most of his populist following. But the escalating succession of buyouts stunned the Piedmont nonetheless. In late November 1900, the local papers learned that the Brown Brothers Company, including its tobacco, brands, machinery, buildings, and stock, was to be sold to the R. J. Reynolds Tobacco Company, although R.J.R. himself stated he knew nothing about it.[20] In early December, the newspapers announced that the Reynolds Company had just bought both Hanes factories in one of the largest tobacco deals in the history of the city. R.J.R. also purchased T. L. Vaughan and Company at this time. These purchases essentially doubled the output capability of the Reynolds Tobacco Company.[21]

Less than three years later, Reynolds secretly secured enough stocks to control the Winston-Salem firm of Liipfert, Scales and Company and build a new company out of it. Then in 1905, the Rucker and Witten Tobacco Company of Martinsville, Virginia, which had been buying up smaller operations in Mount Airy and Richmond, sold its entire operation to Reynolds Tobacco.[22] The Reynolds Tobacco Company could afford all these purchases through a combination of stock issues, earnings, and the borrowing of substantial amounts of money totaling almost $10 million between 1902 and 1905.[23] By the time it began producing the Camel cigarette, the company boasted dozens of plants across Virginia, North Carolina, and Kentucky in addition to its mammoth hive of factories and warehouses in Winston-Salem.[24]

The 1909 *Report of the Commissioner of Corporations on the Tobacco Industry* only corroborated what critics had been observing for years. The creation of Duke's tobacco monopoly had as its principal objective establishing "a dominant place in the tobacco business of the United States, with the result that it ha[d] a nearly complete control of it. . . . Many weaker concerns ha[d] been virtually driven out of business or forced to sell out to the Combination."[25] The combination's purchase of the R. J. Reynolds Tobacco Company in 1899 gave the trust absolute control of eastern "plug" manufacture.[26]

Farmers everywhere felt vindicated by the report's corroboration of the debilitating effects of the monopoly, but the editor of the *Winston-Salem Journal*, increasingly a mouthpiece for the Reynolds Tobacco Company, countered in the ATC's defense. The demand for leaf at the Reynolds's factories was so enormous, he argued, that a fair price was assured. Reynolds would never drive prices so low that it would force tobacco farmers to stop growing the crop and shut the factories down. Nor would Reynolds ever consent to pay the huge freight costs to ship tobacco from elsewhere and thereby undercut the North Carolina farmer. "This would be sheer idiocy. . . . The tobacco industry in Winston is in its permanency. No short sighted suicidal policy will be adopted by those in control. . . . The farmer and the manufacturer are mutually dependent upon each other. Neither can stand alone," he reassured his audience.[27]

Reynolds justified his buyouts in terms of the unique challenges he faced as a plug manufacturer, challenges that smoking tobacco and cigarette companies did not encounter. His product was a long-standing one, with many more competitors, and had to be sold at a considerably lower average price, he reasoned. His rates of return were always lower than those of Duke's own tobacco company by comparison.[28] The only way for Reynolds to break out of this cycle was to eliminate as much competition as possible and use scales of efficiency along with heightened demand to make more money. His explanation, like his actions, did not generate widespread support. Some critics began to accuse him—and not Duke—of selfishly swallowing up other manufacturing concerns whole.[29]

R.J.R. was in a tough spot. He needed to keep one eye on the federal watchdogs that had begun circling the tobacco trust like buzzards and the other on North Carolina tobacco farmers. The latter had been none too pleased with the buyouts and failures of so many manufactories over the past decade. Nor was it clear how long Duke would be willing to be the scapegoat or how long the public would continue to trust Reynolds. In 1908, the industry journal *Tobacco* reported that three thousand North Carolina growers had vowed to fight the Tobacco Trust at their annual convention in Winston-Salem, right on R.J.R.'s home turf. They also intended to employ agents in every tobacco-growing county in North Carolina to boost membership and political influence. R.J.R. countered by claiming himself Duke's victim too. Once again, he promised farmers that their best interests were aligned with his interests and against those of their shared enemy, James B. Duke.[30]

City boosters showed little sympathy for the tobacco farmers. Well aware of the growth of the R. J. Reynolds Tobacco Company and its centrality to the functioning of the city economy, they unleashed counterarguments of their own that celebrated and encouraged industrial diversification. The twin cities had been taking off financially at least since the 1890s, they pointed out. Industrialist Francis Fries had helped launch the profitable Wachovia Loan and Trust Company, and both the Nissen and the Spach Wagon Works thrived from the runaway tobacco trade, their wares no longer bearing pioneers and their dreams but farmers' golden leaves.[31]

In 1902, J. K. Norfleet, president of the chamber of commerce, bragged that Winston had received the highest possible rating from the Dun reports. Their once-sleepy community now boasted "more opportunities than ever before or than any neighboring city," all thanks to the thriving tobacco industry. Wages paid by these mushrooming manufactories, Norfleet observed, were instrumental in the spreading of that prosperity across the South.

However rosy the boosters considered their town's future, laborers in the tobacco factories often believed otherwise. They were as skeptical of corporate tobacco's promise as the farmers. Even R.J.R., for all his charm and hands-on attention, could not diffuse labor challenges. In 1900, forty black machine boys went on strike at his company, leaving two hundred more men and boys, white and black, who worked as wrappers, stemmers, weigh boys, and cappers, each assigned to a machine, unable to do their jobs. The machine boys wanted five cents more a day for their work. R. J. Reynolds balked, telling reporters that the boys had been inexperienced when first hired. They had since received a raise and would receive another when they became more proficient. "At the same time they give us lots of trouble and seem to think they should receive as high wages as the experienced man at our old factory," Reynolds stated; therefore "we will employ men in their places."[32]

The striking boys had been influenced by the recent organization of the Alamance factory workers under the National Union of Textile Workers two counties away. When the Alamance owners demanded that their employees rescind their membership, the employees declined, prompting the owners to let them go. The mills not only closed, but hundreds of men, women, and children lost their homes as well as their employment. At first, Winstonians expressed sympathy for the Alamance workers as well as the Reynolds machine boys.[33] On January 10, 1902, the local papers announced, "There is a strong possibility that every branch of labor will be systematically organized in Winston Salem before many months." Other cities, including Raleigh, Charlotte, Wilmington, and Asheville, had met with considerable success when labor representatives had come south to organize their workers, and the editor expected likewise. The anticipated results would include better wages, better hours, better citizens, more housing, and more spending. Citizens should be encouraged to help the working classes by supporting this cause, the editor concluded.[34]

Ever mindful of R.J.R.'s omnipresence, the editor carefully argued that organized labor could be valuable to employers too.[35] In subsequent issues, the paper extolled the virtues of trade unions, carried a letter from Samuel Gompers on the principles of the American Federation of Labor (AFL), and quoted Robert E. Ely, secretary of the League for Political Education, on the near impossibility of working people supporting their families on the average U.S. wage.[36] The *Journal* even inaugurated a regular column titled

"Union Labor" that supported the AFL, the dignity of the working man, and the power of unions to generate arbitration. Two local railroad employees, the paper announced, had been so moved by this national climate that they had demanded pay for working overtime, and when they had not received it, they quit. The paper was decidedly sympathetic to them.

Reynolds Tobacco was also fighting growing public disapproval of child labor.[37] The company not only hired children, its safety record on behalf of minors was less than stellar, and its skirting of the 1903 North Carolina child-labor law well publicized. R. J. Reynolds had employed children almost from his company's inception. At least 10 of his 110 employees in 1880 had been children. Despite a weak statute passed by the state legislature in 1903 discouraging employment of children under twelve, their presence continued in factories throughout Winston-Salem and the state. Former employees from the second decade of the twentieth century recall that children who worked at Reynolds Tobacco usually had mothers and fathers working there too. In fact, their fathers typically collected their wages on Saturdays. Despite the obvious presence of their parents on the factory floor, the foremen disciplined the children, often with whippings.

In 1903, Willie Thrift died after a beating from his "factory boss." Although the case went to trial, the superintendent who delivered the corporal punishment was exonerated. That same year, a Reynolds Tobacco minor sued Reynolds Tobacco after losing his hand in a factory accident. The defendant won his case in the Forsyth County Superior Court two years later, making this the first such case heard at the level of the state supreme court since the adoption of the child-labor law. Less than three months later, Dempsie Archie, an African American boy, had three fingers crushed in a machine at Reynolds Tobacco. Because of a new company policy adopted in the wake of the *Rolin v. R. J. Reynolds* suit, Archie received free medical care from Slater Hospital. Reynolds Tobacco had elected to set a new standard for industrial responsibility given the increasing social scrutiny.[38]

In some respects then, R.J.R. found himself confronting an increasingly labor-friendly climate. He also had to realize that his workers had come to grasp their connectedness to a wider world and could envision themselves as part of a larger labor movement. Although he fought unionization to the end of his days, he began incorporating more and more incentives to support his wage laborers, from incentive raises to lunchrooms to nurseries to affordable housing to loans for stock from this period forward, in an effort to avoid lawsuits, organizers, and strikes. He also funded sports teams, like the Prince Albert Pond Giants baseball team first organized in 1914.[39] In these actions, he was mirroring a widely used strategy adopted by industrial capitalists across the country. This welfare capitalism—the paternalistic efforts of employers to provide social-welfare benefits to ensure worker loyalty—discouraged worker unionization and the imposition of state regulation too. The wily paternalist of the Old South had reinvented himself as the welfare capitalist of modern America.[40]

The divide between capitalist and laborer was complicated by race in this period. Winston's black population, most of whom were employed in the tobacco business, lived and died in the shadow of their workplace from one generation to the next. In 1900, 80 percent of black and mulatto laborers lived in tenements and boardinghouses in a twenty-one square block encircling the tobacco district in downtown Winston.[41] A thriving black commercial community had taken shape between Liberty and Depot (later Patterson) Streets, a stone's throw from the tobacco district. Black-owned drugstores, theaters, cafés, funeral homes, churches, along with doctors' and lawyers' offices, birthed what local residents called "a black mecca."[42] By 1920, a vibrant middle class had taken hold here as well and had even begun to build new neighborhoods beyond the factory district. Still, almost two-thirds of the city's twenty thousand African Americans remained employed in the tobacco industry.[43]

The rise of this black professional class notwithstanding, white Winston harbored a disparaging attitude toward black Winston. Local newspapers consistently fanned white fears of black violence and incipient urban danger. Typical was the article on a "Colored Tough" named Murcur Dobney, a recently arrived factory worker wanted for gambling, fighting, and other misdemeanors.[44] "Murder in Salem," screamed another set of headlines when a white man was allegedly shot and killed "by an unknown negro."[45] Coverage of the hanging of an accused black murderer in Roanoke covered the entire front page, replete with photos of the doomed man.[46] Even the mundane drew editorialists' attention, including columns pointing out the number of black families in court over "family rows."[47] Debauched black men were selling enough cocaine "to run twenty-five negroes crazy." Judges were slapping black men and women, one right after the other, into jail and on to the road crew for months at a time for vagrancy.[48] Prostitution was a growing problem and not just in the black section of town. City officials had been increasingly forced to acknowledge that not only did a sizable sex trade exist in which black and white women provided favors, but one in which "young white boys [were] openly invited to get into hacks . . . and [were] taken to dives where immorality [ran] riot and where whiskey flow[ed]."[49]

At the core of this mounting immorality lay the presumption that racially inferior African Americans were to blame. The most prominent racist themes that white editors harped upon were black obstruction of white justice and the violent nature of black life. A "desperate negro" bit off an officer's finger after a police confrontation, read one report.[50] Historian Clement Eaton, the mayor's son, accompanied his father to the city courtroom as a young boy where a "high yellow" woman, accused of murdering her boyfriend with a razor, ran down the center aisle and leaped from an open window to her death on the street below. Eaton also remembered his family servant Neelie taking him to the jail to see her lover.[51] These stories suggest not so much the predominance of black-on-white violence and justification for white fears and the enforcement of Jim Crow as the hardships of black life, the escalation of white police brutality and black desperation to escape it, and the construction of racist narratives to justify white-supremacist attitudes. When one reads between the lines, the despair of the black community bleeds through, as in one incident in which a black Winston-Salem man accused of stealing a bicycle was confronted by two police officers with weapons drawn. The alleged bike thief shot himself out of the situation and took flight, rather than face the armed police.[52]

The continued growth of the black population in response to the expansion of the tobacco industry meant that black neighborhoods had begun to spread beyond the tobacco district. Some developed in east Winston, including the black suburban neighborhoods of Richmond and Baltimore. A poor tenant community known as "The Pond" developed to the northeast.[53] Housing was proving problematic across the city, in white and black neighborhoods alike, given the city's expansion. "1000 Houses Needed," shouted a typical newspaper headline. "Among the laboring classes there are three or four families to a house, while many other families who desire to come to the city can find no place to live."[54] This dearth of housing meant significant movement back and forth across unofficial racial lines in many new neighborhoods. While subtle at first, the change in formerly white neighborhoods generated white public pushback. In one notable instance, whites burned down a house at the corner of Eighth and Woodland after a black woman moved in.[55]

In 1913, a tobacco worker named William Darnell, while attempting to build a house on a corner lot at Eleventh Street and Highland Avenue, was arrested because he was black and all the other residents on the street were white. The legal case that ensued, *State v. Darnell*, resulted in a surprise victory for Darnell and an unexpected defeat for Jim Crow segregation. The defeat also speaks to the behind-the-scenes power of R.J.R. and his company to override Jim Crow when it served the company's own interests. Two years after Baltimore had adopted the nation's first residential segregation ordinance, Winston-Salem had adopted one too. The pace of population growth and the incessant demand for housing had fueled a boom real-estate market in the tobacco city. Some white residents had drawn up restrictive covenants as early as 1890 to prevent buyers from selling or renting to African Americans. The real-estate explosion prompted some whites to demand stronger prohibitions against racially mixed neighborhoods by the 1900s.

In 1911, whites living in the East Fourth Street neighborhood petitioned the board of aldermen for a residential segregation law because they felt increasingly divided from the white neighborhood on the western end of Fourth Street (Millionaire's Row, where the Reynoldses and most other industrialists lived). The burgeoning numbers of African American tobacco workers who lived in the low-lying part of Fourth Street near the railroad lines separating the two white neighborhoods alarmed them. So did white neighbors who ignored restrictive covenants and sold East Fourth Street homes to blacks. The aldermen concurred with the petition makers and made it illegal for any white person to occupy a residence on a majority-black block and vice versa, to the tune of a fifty-dollar fine and thirty days in jail for each day of offense. The passage of this local residential segregation law indicated that neither R.J.R. nor his company completely controlled the city commission *just yet*.

The aldermen may have been the de jure leadership of the city, but as Clement Eaton stated in his childhood recollection, R.J.R. and the management at Reynolds Tobacco were the de facto authorities.[56] What is clear from the events that unfolded in the wake of William Darnell's arrest is that certain prominent men in the legal system understood the larger economic ramifications of this local law and sought to put an end to it. In the wake of Darnell's arrest in 1913, the well-known law firm of Watson, Buxton, and Watson defended his case. Renowned Democrats with strong political resumes, connections to R.J.R., and outstanding records as attorneys, Cyrus B.

Watson and John C. Buxton were old-school paternalists, and Buxton, a huge man with a big mustache, had frequently provided legal services for African Americans facing criminal charges. When the jury returned a verdict of guilty in the 1914 superior court retrial of the Darnell case, Watson and Buxton immediately appealed the decision to the state supreme court. Although the law was clearly on the side of the prosecution, Supreme Court Chief Justice Walter Clark overruled the decision, citing an unorthodox states' rights argument that thwarted a black exodus when late nineteenth-century labor agents attempted to lure North Carolina blacks to the North.

Judge Clark had good reason to make this comparison. The Democratic legislature had repealed or amended 33 sections of the North Carolina legal code and passed more than 150 laws between 1895 and 1898. It had instituted the state's first Jim Crow law segregating streetcars and gerrymandered Winston-Salem wards into predominantly white ones. Many disheartened African Americans had left North Carolina, heading to other states to work on the railroads, in the mines, or wherever else they could secure manual labor under less punitive white supremacy laws. Black leaders like Simon G. Atkins pleaded with blacks across the state not to flee, but it was hard to make the case to stay. The rest of the nation recognized that Jim Crow was generating a mobile labor pool. Agents from as far away as Peru, Indiana, arrived in Winston to recruit dozens of black workers at a time.

Winston businessmen worried, local newspapers played up the disadvantages of living and working in the North, and an ordinance was passed requiring all labor agents to obtain a five-hundred-dollar license.[57] Political violations against blacks had prompted the exodus, and the legal denial of the vote to black men exacerbated the out-migration. By election time in November 1902, only twenty-eight black men were registered out of a population of over five thousand. Whites had responded with enthusiasm to these developments, at least at first. White workers even demanded that R. J. Reynolds establish a stemming plant operated only by white men and women. But then white wives began to complain about the overwhelming number of domestic duties thrust upon them without black women domestics, and businessmen mourned inadequate numbers of black wage workers.[58]

As black leaders like Simon Atkins encouraged African Americans to stay in North Carolina, and as demand for laborers in the tobacco factories increased, the exodus slowed, and the black population eventually rebounded and grew. But the city had been scarred by this experience. African Americans had lost the little faith they had in white leaders along with their political rights. Whites, ignoring the implications of denying black men their citizenship, recognized only that the black working population could vote with their feet. When labor agents showed up in Winston once again in 1912, they were promptly jailed and fined and left town immediately upon their release.[59] Two years later, Judge Clark overruled the residential segregation law in an effort to encourage African Americans to stay in Winston. Citing the Irish exodus from Great Britain and Jewish emigration from Russia, Clark declared that Winston's residential segregation law was "contrary to the legislature's will," and he overturned Darnell's conviction.[60]

Meanwhile, forced to contend with the realities of black migration north in the wake of the Jim Crow laws, the Reynolds Tobacco Company had begun heavily recruiting potential workers in rural South Carolina.[61] The editor of the *Winston-Salem Journal* even reported that while South Carolina was importing white labor for its textile mills, it was exporting "unskilled negro labor for more simple employment elsewhere." The *Columbia State* observed, "The exchange is entirely satisfactory."[62] Loaded up in railroad cars and transported to Winston, unskilled black South Carolinians, many of them farmhands and failed tenant farmers, were lined up on Fifth Street and examined like slaves in an auction house. Once hired, they were often assigned the most boring and dangerous jobs at the factories. Although they welcomed their five-dollars-a-week wages, their treatment by established workers left something to be desired. Old hands looked askance at the rural émigrés, surprised by their accent and their insistence on calling the factories "mills." As Slater Institute founder Simon Atkins observed, the newest black workers came from rural conditions "where Negroes had little or no opportunity, and their object in coming to Winston-Salem was chiefly a bread and butter one."[63] R. J. Reynolds was clearly taking advantage of rural poverty to build a massive workforce. As a result, the number of African Americans in Winston nearly doubled between 1890 and 1910, from 4,868 to 7,828.[64]

The manufacturing process that new workers encountered differed little over the years despite the introduction of machine improvements. Tobacco needed inspection and grading before it went to the casing room, where men in bare feet stomped on the leaves to mix in flavorings like sugar, saccharin, and licorice. Stemmers then ripped the leaf from the stem.[65] Although characterized as unskilled labor, stemming demanded considerable talents and took three to four weeks to learn. The best stemmers had learned the skill as children. One manager bragged that his black workforce had "all been brought up in stemmeries and [knew] how to handle tobacco."[66] Rollers took the stripped leaves, cut them to form a plug, and wrapped them up. These plugs were dried in large boxes for half a day or more. Then boys with nimble fingers attached a metal brand tag to each one. The compression of the plug with a steam hydraulic press marked the next-to-last stage in the process. The plug was then boxed, and a revenue stamp, images, and brands sealed onto the box, which weighed between ten and sixty pounds.[67]

While new generations of rural African Americans transitioned to urban wage workers, earning enough income to change the trajectory of their lives, established generations of black elite and middle-class residents despaired. Educated blacks, stripped of their political rights and denied equal access to public transportation, education, and social spaces, found little solace in the thriving tobacco economy. Nationally known educator Simon G. Atkins mourned privately in his correspondence what he dared not say in public: "I sometimes hardly know with whom to be most disgusted—the white people who seek to destroy us, or the Negroes who are willing to accept this destruction."[68] Atkins realized that the white-supremacy campaign had unleashed a mind-set that pressed beyond the spirit of separate but equal as mandated in the 1896 Supreme Court decision. "The Jim Crow car is bad enough, but it is not the Jim Crow car that troubles me, it is the spirit of public sentiment which demands the Jim Crow car. . . . The fact that the word 'Jim Crow' itself is paired in connection with the [railroad] cars shows that it is not separation that is desired and demanded, but humiliation."[69]

What frustrated Atkins and black men and women like him most were the white public outcries—against black men in general, against cohabitation between the races, and against miscegenation. What hypocrisy, these black leaders argued, especially when it was white men who sexually exploited black women. Black men were actually in favor of miscegenation laws to protect black women and the black race. "The better thinking colored men in my State . . . have been making an effort not only to educate the race, to lift it up, to improve it, Christianize it," observed Atkins. "But so far from seeking anything like social equality, we have been seeking to restore and maintain the identity of the race. We have been making progress in that direction, for the race has been gaining its original color."[70] Atkins, like so many prominent black leaders of the era, including Ida B. Wells, was acutely aware of southern black men's vulnerability to horrific white violence in response to alleged white male fears of black men's sexual relationships with white women.[71]

Atkins attempted to use his Slater School to help frame white racist assumptions about the black community. In 1909, Slater commencement exercises opened with a sermon by Rev. J. D. Chavis on the importance of "True Womanhood and Manhood" as the touchstone for "good heart, pure Mind, the Godly soul." The address that followed was given by Rev. Neal L. Anderson of the First Presbyterian Church (where Katharine and Kate Bitting Reynolds worshipped).[72] Atkins's approach to fostering better race relations helps explain R.J.R.'s perspective on the politics of race. Some scholars have labeled Atkins a black conservative for his willingness to accept Jim Crow humiliations publicly and for building an industrial institute rather than a bona fide academy. There is some truth to that critique.

Atkins believed that while the black community hungered "for true manhood, sterling integrity and good citizenship," these attributes and rights were impossible to achieve as long as whites permitted the extralegal lynching of black men, denied blacks trial by jury, and refused black men the vote.[73] His insistence on inculcating black working people's embrace of nineteenth-century republican values, while reassuring to white advocates of black acquiescence to white authority, represented an increasingly anachronistic ideology. Like Booker T. Washington, Atkins wanted his school to imbue young African American men and women with the dignity of labor by providing them with dual academic and manual-labor educations to elevate their minds and their opportunities. But in point of fact, skilled wage work as an entrée into the proprietorship of small workshops and businesses was passé in a modernizing world where corporate property holding and labor relations had begun to predominate even in the American South.[74]

Intent on securing enough financing for Slater Academy to construct new buildings, build more programs, and enroll more students, Atkins sought help from R. J. Reynolds. The tobacco king committed a five-thousand-dollar pledge to Atkins, with the stipulation that the black educator raise another five thousand dollars. By the autumn of 1899, Atkins was hunting for contributions across the South to match R.J.R.'s pledge. His pitch differed little from community to community. "I think that you will agree with us that the proposal of our wealthy townsman, Mr. Reynolds, to give Five

Thousand dollars . . . is remarkable; Mr. Reynolds, being a southern white man and a Democrat."[75] He wrote Professor P. P. Claxton, editor of the *North Carolina Journal of Education*:

> Mr. Reynolds is not a man who desires publicity given to his contributions to charity, but this proposal of his is, in my mind, so unique that the public should know about it. . . . This is the largest amount, so far as I know, that has been tendered by a southern white man for the benefit and training of colored youths. This proposal of Mr. Reynolds distinguishes him as the representative of that large class of southern white men who believe in helping humanity and who have a friendly and generous feeling toward the colored people of the South. . . . This offer signifies that the best white people of the State believe in giving the negro this preparation and not only that, but also that they believe in the education of the negro as an integral part of citizenship, and it is an important factor in bringing to the State and to the South prosperity which it is so thoroughly capable of. This . . . in a community where the relation between the races is cordial and where . . . the continued sympathy and aid of its leading white citizens . . . [means] good citizenship . . . for our manhood and womanhood.[76]

While the Democratic Party, led by political men with whom Reynolds allied himself, was putting the last nail in the Fusionist coffin and finishing touches on their own white-supremacist ideology, and while Atkins was despairing of blacks' future in North Carolina, Reynolds was throwing African Americans a lifeline. He was quite publicly supporting a school for young black men and women. Not only did Atkins use R.J.R.'s name liberally among southern black and white friends, colleagues, and other possible benefactors, but he employed him in his letters to northern philanthropists as well. In a letter to Rev. B. J. Burrell in New York City, he stated, "I think this proposal of Mr. Reynolds' marks a new era in the history of our school; that a southern white man right here in the community where the institution is best known should make such a proposal." Sadly, Atkins suggested it was white men's responsibility as citizens to provide black men and women educational opportunities even as they denied black men citizenship.[77]

Atkins enclosed a printed slip with R.J.R.'s offer in each of these request letters, noting that the money would be used to create a nurse training academy and possibly a hospital (there was no hospital for blacks in Winston-Salem), and he added that this generous gift marked "only the beginning of Mr. Reynolds's interest."[78] Atkins even wrote a friend close to President Roosevelt, urging him to tell the nation's leader about Reynolds's gift and invite him to come to Winston. "No place would offer the President a more interesting view of southern conditions." He then proceeded to describe R.J.R. as "a white man of this community, to the manor born, who himself formerly held slaves" as testament to the power of white men to revise their thinking on race and support education for African Americans.[79]

In November 1900, Atkins announced that he was close to matching R. J. Reynolds's five-thousand-dollar gift and had instituted a board of managers for a hospital he would build upon completion of the fund-raising campaign. Five out of the six newly appointed members were prominent local white men, and three of them were Reynolds kin: brothers Will and Walter Reynolds and their nephew J. A. Lybrook. Atkins was the only African American member. The board acknowledged the deep need for the black community to have access to a hospital and a nurse training school. The local paper declared the Slater School and the R. J. Reynolds Hospital Fund "the most pronounced evidence of good feeling between the races to be found anywhere in the South."[80] Yet despite the successful campaign for the black training hospital and R. J. Reynolds's important role in making it happen, the imposition of Jim Crow laws remained devastating to black men and women in Winston and across North Carolina.

Atkins appealed to African Americans "to be hopeful and not to contemplate leaving the State."[81] He even supported gubernatorial candidate Charles Aycock as the lesser of two evils once Aycock pledged to provide public education for all the people of the state.[82] Despite his public position, Atkins continued to privately despair about blacks' future in North Carolina. "The election is in progress today, and it looks as if after this the only civil status the Negro will have in the state will be in what the Democratic Party sees fit to give," Atkins bemoaned. "We are in the midst of an awful condition of affairs, and I sometimes indulge in the vain inquiry whether God is dead. Some of us who have been conservative and hopeful are almost ready to throw up the sponge."[83]

Over the summer of 1900, the white Democrats in Winston began holding well-attended meetings of as many as five hundred men. They elected officers, adopted the same constitution and bylaws as the state's White Supremacy Club, and called themselves "The White Man's Club."[84] When three city registrars were arrested for refusing to register "unqualified negroes," the new club found its purpose. The arrests had been initiated by Republican congressional candidate E. Spencer Blackburn, and the warrant sworn by the post office's black janitor, Turper Peddiford. The White Man's Club planned a torchlight procession to which all white men were invited, with special provision for white "ladies" to observe from the porch of Salem Academy. This march was planned for the evening after the arrests. At a rally later that day, an angry speech by one of the arrested registrars fanned the flames. "It makes my blood boil when a man shall for the sake of office hurl indignities in the face of his own race," stated someone in the crowd. Congressional candidate Blackburn "should hang his head in shame and go off and live with the negroes," exclaimed another. Registrar J. T. Thompson told the assembled throng that 6,700 unqualified black votes had been cast in recent elections. "It seems that any man who will be honest with himself will come out and take up the white man's cause," he observed.[85]

The court case that ensued received plentiful local coverage. Multiple witnesses, all black, were called to testify against two of the accused registrars. Each black man gave a statement indicating that he had not been allowed to register because he had not brought someone to vouchsafe for his age. Richard Reynolds, an employee of the Reynolds Tobacco Company and perhaps a descendent of a Reynolds homestead slave, testified that he had not been able to get the four white people best able to identify him at the designated time and place for registration. Those four people—Phil Lybrook, Walter Reynolds, Richard Lybrook, and Will Reynolds—were key leaders in the R. J. Reynolds Tobacco Company. Richard Reynolds must have presumed that being able to cite four of the leading citizens of Winston before the polling officer and on the courtroom stand was powerful evidence.[86] By July 13, 1900, the editor of the *Winston-Salem Journal* was begging the White Men's Club to practice more patience and good sense. The white men's "red flag of riot," the editor insisted, pressed a white-supremacist viewpoint but needed to be replaced by "the white ermine of rights and justice."[87]

Within weeks, the Democrats swept the state, with a majority of more than fifty thousand votes, making Charles Aycock the gubernatorial candidate. Democrats won Forsyth County by five hundred votes.[88] The *Journal*'s editor subsequently lambasted the alleged "reign" of the Populists and the Fusionists in the Old North State over the past six years. He crowed that the final symbolic blow to white Democrats had come when "a white face, black hearted Legislature" had adjourned in honor of Frederick Douglass's passing, but not for Lee's.[89] The turnabout Democratic victory meant that any expression of biracial equality was contentious. Racist hyperbole abounded. A Forsyth County grand jury was forced to investigate a claim that black and white convicts slept in the same bunk in convict work camps outside the city. The rumor proved false. "If it were true [it] would be a disgrace to the county," worried the *Journal*'s editor.[90] No black public activity went unnoticed despite the formal codification of racial hierarchy with Jim Crow laws. When Winston's African American population celebrated Emancipation Day, the event incurred critical white commentary. Not only did whites believe that all black progress since slavery was the result of the new commercial and industrial opportunities that white leaders had generated, not black self-help; whites also wanted to shape the tenor of the celebration itself. "We trust that they will conduct themselves in such a manner today as to make their white neighbors respect their motives and rejoice with them that they are no longer slaves."[91]

In the end, for all their political posturing, most whites did not just support the denial of black men's political rights. They also ignored the harsh realities of black life in Winston. As the numbers of tobacco workers increased, overcrowding and unsanitary conditions multiplied, especially in the tenements around the tobacco factories near Chestnut, Sixth, and Depot Streets. Unsanitary wells, a breeding ground for typhus, were commonplace in this part of town, an area most white residents now called "the Negro slums."[92]

R.J.R. understood white hypocrisy better than most given his proximity to black working-class experience. Although he made multiple efforts to improve the living standards of the black community, he refused to challenge white supremacy with the exception of his behind-the-scenes tinkering with the residential segregation law in the Darnell case. Reynolds depended on racial inequality to keep his workforce low waged. He also had to pacify local working-class whites with deep-seated fears about their own limited economic opportunity. Those fears were undoubtedly tangled with psychological fixations about black mobility, miscegenation, and social chaos, as they were throughout the early twentieth-century South. R.J.R. grasped these fears better than most white leaders. His was a specific rationale for lying to reporters that "he had risen from an ordinary hireling to president of the R. J. Reynolds Tobacco Company." His story underscored the point that he had served as a laborer himself before becoming the boss.[93]

He understood that his most important constituency may not have been his majority-black workers but white working-class men and women. They had long constituted the majority of his customers, and it was to them as much or more than any single cohort that he owed his considerable success. He had learned long ago how to market to their emotional needs and appeal to their tastes. He was in their debt in many respects. After all, plug tobacco was by no means a necessity; it was a luxury, albeit a small one, for most poor white families across several generations after the Civil War. While black families purchased plug tobacco too, the long and short of it was that rural white working people were R.J.R.'s core customers.

Poor whites were the bulk of his suppliers too. He sent his tobacco buyers all across the state and indeed the region in search of the best tobacco they could find. Although the price of that tobacco could fluctuate wildly with supply and demand, it was in the company's best interests to pay the least it could get away with. The tobacco consolidation of the 1890s meant less competition for the leaf and lower prices for the farmers. Individually these farmers could do little to alter the prices, but they could work together collectively through the formation of cooperatives and at the ballot box to generate resistance. It was in R.J.R.'s decided best interests not to rile the farmers, and he worked hard to keep himself in their good graces. He had gone out of his way to distinguish himself from Buck Duke and his tobacco-monopoly henchmen, despite his actual indebtedness to the ATC. He had tried to "protect" the farmers from J. P. Morgan and his Southern Railroad empire, although his company would have actually benefited as much or more from thwarting Morgan than the farmers themselves.

R.J.R. also realized that an implicit cultural understanding beyond these economic realities bound him to rural whites. In North Carolina, where poor whites had long been the majority, their needs and desires came first in the political economy. The white common folk ruled in a state that had spawned not one but two U.S. presidents, Andrew Jackson and Andrew Johnson, both from common-folk families themselves. North Carolina men had fought and died in disproportionate numbers in the Civil War. The centrality of North Carolina's common whites to the state's self-conception, even if more myth than actual political practice, was national knowledge. In 1901, John Gilmer Speed argued in *Harper's Weekly* that the Emancipation Proclamation had freed not only the slaves but the South's poor whites as well, for the latter had been denied access to opportunity for generations. The exception to this rule, Speed pointed out, was North Carolina, where "the poor white ha[d] always been in a more congenial environment than elsewhere in the South." According to Speed, "He does not feel lonesome there, he has never known that he was despised. There, poverty and illiteracy are and have been the rule."[94] R.J.R. had no intention of despising his suppliers, his customers, or the majority of his state's voters. These very same voters had once cast their lot with the Populists and the Republicans "turned" Fusionists, entered into biracial alliances, shown their abhorrence of their political abuse, and ignored racial divisions long enough to wrest local and state political control from a moneyed elite. The Democratic Party elite, his friends and acquaintances, had responded by using white fears about black sexuality and miscegenation as well as black political domination to fell the Fusionists with racist rhetoric. The sad result was a Democratic Party impervious to challenge. Its imposition of black disfranchisement and white supremacy laws assuaged fearful whites that they now had greater access to opportunities than blacks.

Ever the pragmatist R.J.R. rode right along in the roiling wake of the Democrats. In fact, white supremacy served his business interests well. It meant he could continue to pay his majority-black workers substandard wages compared to whites, and no one could or even would be able to successfully challenge him. Most whites believed blacks were getting what they deserved, a lower wage that reflected their inherent racial inferiority. Most blacks believed they had little recourse in the wake of the violence launched their way and the political rights torn from them, although that sensibility would change by World War I. In the end, black workers could either accept low wages paid in cash on a regular basis and the relative opportunities that came with city living alongside the always-present reminders of their base apolitical status, or they could leave Winston and head north.

These realities forced Reynolds to balance white and black interests carefully. He had to make factory work and urban life acceptable enough for his black employees to keep them in Winston, but he could not give them too much without making whites suspicious—many of whom worked in the local textile factories for low wages too. His strategy was ultimately a simple one, placating everyone, whites and blacks, as equitably as possible within a Jim Crow world while serving his own needs.

That Winston-Salem is a product of R. J. Reynolds's paternalism should be no surprise. All quarters of the community concur that Reynolds's commitment to a benevolent paternalism shaped the twentieth-century history of the city in critical ways, and especially its rise and fall as an economic powerhouse for businesses and wealth generation. This paternalism extended to all of R.J.R.'s workers—white and black, male and female—and it took multiple forms. First, R.J.R. made a commitment to live and work in the town that his tobacco business had built. He kept his factories in Winston, even when Duke forced him to organize his corporation in New Jersey. He kept his home in Winston too, even when his business interests compelled him to frequent Baltimore, Philadelphia, and New York, and his wealth could have secured him a fine estate outside any one of these cities. Indeed, Buck Duke had paved the southern industrialists' way north with his beautiful country home in Somerville, New Jersey, and many successful southern businessmen had followed suit.[95]

Second, R.J.R. was interested in providing opportunities for working people to improve their positions. He was particularly sympathetic to hard-working, ambitious young white men starting on the bottom rungs of the employment ladder. He singled them out and mentored them, often well into their adulthood. His treasurer, D. Rich, born in nearby Mocksville, is a prime example. Rich had learned tobacco manufacturing as a boy and had come to Winston in search of work; he was employed in the Reynolds factory by night and learned accounting by day before advancing into the management ranks and ultimately into senior leadership. R.J.R. also sought long-term security for his employees. In a society where few middle-class let alone working-class people had access to the stock market, R.J.R. purchased Reynolds stocks on loan for his management team and eventually provided all his employees with opportunities for profit sharing and Reynolds stock purchases on loan.[96]

Third, although R.J.R. accepted the rules of Jim Crow and tacitly agreed with the white-supremacist belief in the social separation of the races, he also was committed to black uplift within the system and used his money to fund black schools, orphanages, and churches. As scholar Guion Griffis Johnson argued more than fifty years ago, southern whites had adapted the racial paternalism of slavery after emancipation with ease. Yet that paternalism could take multiple shapes by the early twentieth century, from the rabid racism of South Carolina politician Ben Tillman and Georgia congressman Tom Watson, which turned on presumptions of perpetual racial inferiority, to a "modified egalitarianism" whereby white paternalists argued that blacks needed only education and white support to come closer to whites' capabilities in certain arenas. R.J.R.'s thinking, while still avowedly white supremacist, followed these latter lines.[97]

Although R.J.R. did not encourage the social mingling of the races outside his workplace and maintained race divisions in certain occupations and in the company lunchrooms, he acted on the belief that it was his duty as a prominent businessman and citizen to support the economic and social development of black families in Winston. He had learned from childhood that African American men could be as capable and talented as white men. As a planter's son, he was comfortable working with black men, women, and children, and his postwar experiences had not changed his attitude. In fact, he may even have harbored some respect for black political and civil rights aspirations in the wake of his favorite brother-in-law's fight against the Patrick County court for denying two young black men their right to a trial by a jury of their peers. Regardless of his attitudes, however, white southern paternalism in any form was increasingly untenable after 1914. Once black men began to exchange the rural South for the urban one, and then the South for the North—change that World War I precipitated—their families followed them, and the black exodus northward accelerated over time. Other African Americans stayed in the South and used labor organizing to build larger struggles for black opportunity and political rights. No amount of white paternalism could halt this transformation.[98]

Many white paternalists in the early twentieth century began to argue that the newest generation of African Americans lacked the work ethic and the willingness to commit to new educational opportunities that an older generation had once embraced. Meanwhile, critics like Thomas Nelson Page condemned many blacks for their failure to use new opportunities like industrial education to advance themselves.[99] R.J.R. supported industrial education through his contributions to Slater Academy, but he did not offer any public opinion on black work habits, or on white work habits for that matter. He was all too aware that the majority of white people wanted black men to know their places as manual laborers at the bottom of the social rung, reinforcing antebellum presumptions of racial inferiority and continued justification for black subjugation. No wonder Booker T. Washington's insistence on industrial education was highly palatable to so many whites. Reynolds seems to have understood that the most threatening sector of society in the early twentieth century was not black people but white working men unable to remake themselves in the midst of so much change. Blacks had to be cast as society's subordinates in order to bring artificial uplift to that large class of demoralized whites.

R.J.R.'s tacit approval of white supremacy alongside his moderate racial paternalism was reflected in his politics. His support of North Carolina governor Robert Broadnax Glenn (1854–1920), a fellow Winstonian, offers a case in point. Glenn attributed his personal and political success to R.J.R. "Mr. Reynolds gave a poor struggling young man his start in life and help[ed] make him what he is. . . . Until I was elected Governor I was his attorney and know what his life meant to Winston-Salem and his state. . . . Generous in his dealings with his fellow man. Honest and straightforward in all his business operations."[100]

Glenn served as Democratic governor of North Carolina from 1905 to 1909, after defeating his Republican opponent by a wide margin. Winston-Salem claimed him as its own, declaring him a brilliant jurist, distinguished orator, and faithful friend who embraced "the sturdy manliness" of North Carolina's good citizens.[101] The editor of the *Winston-Salem Journal* intoned, "The history of R. B. Glenn from 1876 to the present time shows unremitting toil to lift the people from the terrible conditions brought about by reconstruction, carpetbagism, and negroism, and his heroic efforts throughout the length and breadth of the state, have made his name familiar in every home."[102] A supporter of white supremacy ("Bob Glenn took upon his shoulders the fight of the people for good government, for sane government, and above all, for white supremacy"), he was a strong advocate for public education and poured new funds into public health.[103] He argued that a state's progress must be measured in the quality of its schools. He also believed that black schools had to be strengthened and that supporting them only with taxes secured from African Americans was unjust. "Taxes should be divided in a manner which is equitable and just," he stated at his inaugural address.[104]

Glenn, like R.J.R., supported white supremacy but sought some measure of uplift for blacks within that racist system. He had been the only governor from any southern state to visit the African American hall at the Jamestown exhibition in 1907 and actually addressed the black audience about the Old North State exhibit he viewed the next day. When a Salisbury mob tore from prison five black men who had been accused of murdering a local family and then brutally mutilated and lynched them, Governor Glenn traveled to the town to restore order and punish the ringleaders. One white perpetrator was even convicted and sentenced to jail for fifteen years at hard labor in the state penitentiary. White public outcry against the governor's actions was vociferous, especially after he issued an executive order that all county sheriffs and state militia shoot to kill if any white mob threatened violence against prisoners anywhere in the state. The *New York Times* predicted correctly that Governor Glenn would not be reelected as a result of his actions, though his prohibition legislation contributed to his defeat as well.[105]

At the same time that R.J.R. was juggling state and local politics to support his interests, he was strategizing about how best to deal with Buck Duke and the American Tobacco Trust. Although Duke and R.J.R. had worked out the future of the R. J. Reynolds Tobacco Company cordially, privately R.J.R. was not satisfied. He had told his friend Josephus Daniels that he would never let Buck Duke get the better of him, and he did not.[106] At the same time, his close study of Duke and his mighty corporation benefited his own company greatly. Duke had been quick to adopt cigarettes as his tobacco product of choice in the late nineteenth century and had embraced the latest labor-saving technology in the form of the Bonsack machine to mass produce them. This innovation considerably reduced his need to rely on human labor, a boon to Duke, who resented labor costs and labor politics. This technological breakthrough, with its fantastic economies of scale and rapid production rates, necessitated rethinking the traditional structure of tobacco manufacturing, from the organization of the factory floor to retail sales and marketing.[107]

Duke solved his new problem of overcapacity by developing a larger market. He used the latest marketing and promotional techniques to do so. Tobacco manufacturers had long relied on billboards, discounts, coupons, premiums, and collectible cards covered in memorable images promising consumers action, adventure, exoticism, and sex. In fact, tobacco's marketing strategies had contributed significantly to the rise of the modern advertising industry. R.J.R. had always been keen on the use of such imagery to market his products and had proved particularly talented at identifying the images that would best compel people to buy them. As head of one of the first multinational corporations, Duke transferred that approach from the smaller, more localized chewing- and smoking-tobacco firms like R.J.R.'s to his cigarettes and quickly developed a national sales force, with salaried executives coordinating departments and salesmen, to get his smokes to market. Duke's reorganization not only solved the problem of overcapacity but also created a new model for business management that helped launch a new middle-class culture on the cusp of the twentieth century.[108]

Thus Duke was inspiration and goad to R.J.R. as much as boss and competitor. The two were respectful rivals, learning from each other over the course of their careers. After all, the R. J. Reynolds Tobacco Company was the most important American Tobacco subsidiary producing plug tobacco, an accomplishment achieved through the consolidation and acquisition of eleven different manufacturing businesses.[109] Even after the ATC trust had been broken up, Duke continued to appreciate Reynolds's capabilities and personally held 4,350 shares of R. J. Reynolds Tobacco Company stock.[110] Much to R.J.R.'s chagrin, Duke not only held a substantive amount of company stock but the American Tobacco Company itself controlled almost two-thirds of the Reynolds Tobacco Company common stocks after the trust breakup. Duke had great faith in the continued profitability of R.J.R.'s company.[111]

By 1906, the R. J. Reynolds Tobacco Company operated two plants in Winston, with an average of 2,863 employees combined, and a smaller plant in Richmond. Including Liipfert-Scales production, in which Reynolds had controlling interest, Reynolds produced nearly 25 million pounds of plug tobacco that year and just under a million pounds of smoking tobacco.[112] Reynolds's leading brands included Brown's Mule, Schnapps, Suncured, Early Bird, Red Apple, Hanes Natural Leaf, R.J.R., Apple Jack, and Hill Billy. The Richmond plant's best brands were Humbug, Maritania, Rustic, and Apple, while Liipfert-Scales's major brands were Red Meat, Black Mammy, and Wild Duck. All told, the R. J. Reynolds price list sported fifty-seven different brands.[113] The R. J. Reynolds Tobacco Company enjoyed considerable independence compared to other subsidiaries under the combination because it was the dominant manufacturer of plug tobacco in the United States and had command of that market. This expertise convinced Duke to let Reynolds market his own goods directly and to buy his own leaf. To support its leaf purchasing, Reynolds Tobacco maintained rehandling and storage plants in Martinsville, Danville, and Richmond as well as Winston, along with receiving stations throughout Virginia and North Carolina. The company also operated a huge stemming plant in Winston.[114]

By 1906, thanks to Duke's machinations and R.J.R.'s growth, the number of plug- and twist-tobacco manufactories in the United States had been cut more than half from a high of 393 independent factories in 1897. About 50 of those factories had been acquired by the combination. The remaining 150 had been squeezed out of business.[115] Meanwhile, R.J.R. and his company had prospered. He was one of the top fifty-two stockholders in American Tobacco, with one thousand shares to his name.[116] Confident in his company's future, he had even upped his own annual salary to twenty thousand dollars.[117]

R.J.R. had good reason to be self-assured. He was about to introduce a new formula for a smoking tobacco made of Kentucky burley. He had named his new product himself, calling it Prince Albert after the popular Prince of Wales turned British monarch, Edward VII. He had sent his marketing team a photograph he had ripped out of a newspaper—R. J. Reynolds was an avid newspaper reader—that showed Mark Twain attending a royal tea and King Edward turned out in a frock coat.[118] R.J.R.'s company had been working on a recipe for a desirable smoking tobacco for almost two decades. Its work resulted in a patented formula comprised of different grades and ages of burley leaf, as well as secret flavorings.

Despite the threat of a lawsuit by the trust, R.J.R. was not tentative about introducing his new product in 1907. He launched an out-and-out hard-hitting marketing campaign with the help of N. W. Ayer and Son, who helped him make Prince Albert the first national tobacco brand. Ubiquitous ads promised readers they could buy "the national joy smoke" everywhere—Saint Paul, New York, Tampa, Winnipeg, Seattle, Five Corners, Kankakee. They assured customers that their new favorite tobacco was "sold *universally* throughout America, even in the littlest store fartherest back in the wilds."[119]

R.J.R. relied on talented artists as well as clever slogans to promote Prince Albert. Gorgeous images laden with emotional appeals had served his plug well over the decades, not only in print ads but on posters, billboards, bonuses, coupons, and prizes. To sell his latest product, Prince Albert's avuncular face beamed out from mass-market magazines everywhere, including the *Saturday Evening Post* and *Collier's Weekly*. The full-page ads showed a happy gent in suspenders smoking merrily away on his pipe, "the national joy smoke" slogan to one side of him and a can of the tobacco on the other. R.J.R. had put his many years of marketing know-how into his newest product, and it showed. With Katharine advising him at his side, R.J.R. had approved all the design and copy himself.[120] His wife had been as invested as R.J.R. in Prince Albert's success and reported to her husband when tobacco stores were not displaying Prince Albert in their windows.[121] She had nothing to fear. Prince Albert's sales brought the company its four years of fastest growth in what had been a steady upward climb for the past twenty-five years.[122]

R.J.R.'s ingenuity kept that latest growth curve steep. Originally selling Prince Albert in five-cent red bags and ten-cent red tins, Reynolds Tobacco had been the first company to sell smoking tobacco in half-pound and full-pound allotments in specially designed humidors.[123] By 1914, ads promoted a pound of Prince Albert in one of R.J.R.'s "handsome glass humidors" as an ideal Christmas gift. The favorable public reception was enormous. *Tobacco* reported, "Sales the past few weeks have broken all previous records."[124] Meanwhile, R.J.R. even sanctioned putting Prince Albert's jolly visage on a huge billboard above New York City's Union Square in flashing lights. It bore the words "Prince Albert—The Nation's Joy Smoke, R. J. Reynolds Tobacco Company, Winston-Salem, N.C." Duke's men were none too happy as they watched the Prince Albert phenomenon from their Fifth Avenue perches.[125] In fact, the American Tobacco Company tried to block the brand, threatening a suit if R.J.R. did not turn Prince Albert over to the ATC.[126]

But the Tobacco Trust was about to confront much bigger concerns. It had not been the only major industrial merger in the late nineteenth century. Oil, copper, lumber, and railroads had all been consolidated too and had made men like Rockefeller and Vanderbilt mega-rich. The majority of Americans were increasingly resentful of the unalloyed power of these monopolies and of the men who ran them seemingly at the public's expense, for these trusts manipulated the free market and generated high prices. Meanwhile, the public's mounting dissension was attracting political interest. Government officials did not like the fact that monopolies enabled corporations to control the markets even through downturns in the economy. This set of realities prompted Congress and the courts to step in, albeit slowly and carefully. The courts, while they were loath to run the corporations, were generally friendly toward competition. Although Congress had passed the Sherman Anti-Trust Act in 1890 with the express purpose of limiting corporations, it did not invoke the act with any success until President Teddy Roosevelt rolled out his "trust-busting" campaigns in 1904. That year, the Supreme Court upheld the government suit against the Northern

Securities Company. Standard Oil and the American Tobacco Company were next in line.

By 1907, the year R.J.R. launched Prince Albert, Duke's monopoly controlled 80 percent of the tobacco business and was the third-largest corporation in America, behind U.S. Steel and Standard Oil. No wonder that under Roosevelt's watch the Justice Department quickly slapped American Tobacco with a violation of the Sherman Act. When the federal court found American Tobacco guilty in 1908 and banned the trust from interstate trade, it appealed to the Supreme Court. But so did the prosecution as the legal decision had exempted United Cigar Stores, Imperial, and British Tobacco. Three years later, in May 1911, the Supreme Court ruled the American Tobacco Company in violation and ordered the trust dissolved on the same day it broke up Standard Oil.[127]

R.J.R. had always cooperated with the ATC, though he did so somewhat dismissively, referring to new policies handed down to him as the latest "song and dance."[128] He continued to do so during the hearings. Although both Duke's and R.J.R.'s top management testified that R.J.R. visited New York City five or six times a year, they added that R.J.R. did not meet with Duke to confer on business. They were stretching the truth. Duke and R.J.R. had met, and R.J.R. met with Duke's top leaders as well. R.J.R. and Katharine had socialized on occasion with Duke, visiting his farm in Somerville, New Jersey, and were so intimate that they secured advice and plants from Duke's head gardener. Still, R.J.R. was correct when he claimed that the management of his company was for all intents and purposes independent of the combination. Duke himself testified during the hearings that R. J. Reynolds "directed the affairs of the R. J. Reynolds Tobacco Company, and not any one in the American Tobacco Company, and no one but R. J. Reynolds had ever done so, and that R. J. Reynolds owned his own leaf company and sold his own goods, both 'independent and on his own account,' and had his offices in Winston-Salem where the selling was done."[129]

Throughout the hearings, R.J.R. worried unceasingly about the impact of the case on company stock. He visited Wall Street frequently to hear financiers' opinions.[130] Fairly typical was the letter he wrote Katharine from the Plaza Hotel on August 11, 1909, about his upcoming meeting with Caleb Conely Dula (1864–1930), a director of the American Tobacco and Continental Tobacco Companies who supervised Reynolds Tobacco. "I spent part of the day on Wall Street and every body I saw are bulls on stock. I delivered the bonds and will [join] Mr. Dula and his wife out of city on a pleasure trip."[131] Between the hearings and the launching of Prince Albert, R.J.R. had entered a particularly demanding phase of his career. With long lines of men waiting to meet with him in his office, he was often too busy to write Katharine when she was out of town.[132] "I have had so much important business before me that I was forced to look after, that I have not written you as often as I desired to write."[133] Katharine was concerned for his welfare and urged him to cut back on his commitments. He tried to reassure her. "You must not think I am worried when I look serious as I always look serious when I have a difficult business problem to work out."[134]

The suit resulted in the dissolution of the American Tobacco Company and its separation from the R. J. Reynolds Tobacco Company.[135] Louis Brandeis, who followed the case very closely, was unimpressed by the outcome, arguing that it essentially "legalized" the trust by dividing the monopoly into the same parts to be delivered into the same hands that had put the trust together in the first place. He was correct. R. J. Reynolds received his company back, as did the heads of Liggett and Meyers, P. Lorillard, and American Tobacco. Only one new company would emerge into the ranks of big-time tobacco after the dissolution: Phillip Morris.[136]

When local reporters rushed to his office to ask R.J.R. how the Supreme Court decision would affect the nation, he stated nonchalantly, "Oh, the country will run along all right." Feigning ignorance, he added that he had not yet fully studied the situation and therefore had to defer a full interview for the time being. Still, he assured his eager audience that he suspected the American Tobacco Company would be reorganized and tobacco manufacturers would go on about their business, with minimal impact on the tobacco market.[137]

R.J.R. lost no time pushing his company into its next phase of development. Under the combination, he had beefed up all his offices, especially sales and marketing, and added new ones for research, legal, and payroll. By the summer of 1911, he had erected a new office building and purchased real furniture to replace the licorice boxes the managers and accountants had used for chairs and filing cabinets. "We are now placing beautiful mahogany furniture in our office," R.J.R. wrote Katharine. "We have such nice comfortable offices I now invite you to come to us often also getting our factories so clean that I can now invite you to go over the factory when you return."[138] Throughout this period, in the wake of the Supreme Court decision and before the formal dissolution process of the trust was announced, R.J.R. worked unceasingly. He returned to his home only to eat and sleep.[139]

On August 12, 1911, R.J.R. explained to Katharine, "I will have to go to New York the last of this month. . . . Attorney General has agreed on the general plan of complying with the terms of the court and will sell the stock of my company. Let me know how many shares you will buy and the limit price you will pay per share."[140] Although the dissolution did not become formal until November, R.J.R. was eager to get his company's shares in the hands of North Carolinians and thereby reduce the power of "the New York crowd" who owned two-thirds of it as holders of American Tobacco common stock.[141] Meanwhile, he remained personal friends with Duke, who sent R.J.R. and Katharine a congratulatory note upon the birth of their fourth child, Zachary Smith, the same month the dissolution was finalized.[142]

None of the four ATC corporations—R. J. Reynolds Tobacco, Liggett and Meyers, P. Lorillard, or American Tobacco—knew which brands would ultimately rule the market in the coming years, but each knew capturing that market was key. Each emerged from the trust ready to fight over market share; they pumped huge amounts of money into cigarette advertising and adopted publicity techniques we have come to identify as quintessential to modern promotion. The emerging cigarette industry would continue to bank on traditional approaches for decades thereafter—pursuing mass markets, marketing to youths, and capitalizing on tobacco's addictive qualities. The new cigarette industry cultivated whole new markets, ultimately integrating cigarettes into the very makeup of twentieth-century American identity despite strong political and cultural opposition.[143] R.J.R. understood well the power of compelling publicity linked with tobacco cravings. He cautioned his own children never to light a cigarette, let alone smoke one.[144]

Independent at long last, R.J.R. watched his company's stock like a hawk. As profits began to rebound in the months after the ATC dissolution, R.J.R. was pleased that his stock prices began to climb as well, signaling renewed confidence in his company. In late June 1912, he wrote Katharine announcing his safe arrival in New York City, wishing that she and the children were with him to enjoy the glorious weather and reporting good news. He then gloated, "A big advance today of forty five dollars per share in the selling price of our stock, now two hundred and eight five dollars per share, bid."[145] Still, although R.J.R. appreciated the price surge, he wanted most of all to increase the amount of locally owned stock to offset the controlling influence of the New York crowd.

R. J. Reynolds had resented the combination's controlling interest in Reynolds Tobacco stocks from the beginning. Even he found it difficult to buy Reynolds stock in the early twentieth century, since 75 percent of the company had been secured by Duke and his trust in 1899. R.J.R. also resented having to talk large "Yankee" brokerage houses and big individual stockholders into selling him their Reynolds Tobacco shares. He brokered virtually all his purchases in two respected New York investment houses; Lazarus Hallgarten, a native of Hesse, Germany, had founded Hallgarten and Company in 1850, while Dominick and Dominick had opened in 1870, one of the earliest firms on the New York Stock Exchange.[146] It was at this point that R.J.R. came up with a unique plan shared by no other tobacco company at the time. He purchased 2,800 shares of Reynolds stock for $287,000 in 1902. He kept 2,265 shares for himself and bought another 535 shares for fifteen of his top managers, who repaid him between $1,500 and $5,000 depending on their subscription.[147]

A decade later, R.J.R. broadened his strategy of keeping Reynolds Tobacco stock close to home. He created an incentive plan for all his employees that allowed him to take advantage of the bonanza in Reynolds stock after the breakup of the trust.[148] Undaunted by the fact that Buck Duke and his Wall Street buddies owned the biggest block of stock right after the trust bust, R.J.R. pressed the board to increase the number of shares by 25 percent. The shareholders voted in favor, and the Wall Street crowd finally lost its limited influence. At that point, he created the lucrative profit-sharing plan for his senior officers and followed it up with a plan open to all his employees, an idea advocated in theory by U.S. progressives as early as the 1880s.[149]

Former R.J.R. employee Orthodox Creed Strictler had purchased tobacco for the company for many years. After his retirement, he had kept an autographed photo of R.J.R. on his mantle. While he amassed a considerable fortune working for the tobacco magnate, he had always refused to purchase stock, calling himself a conscientious objector. To his chagrin, however, he watched all the men around him grow enormously wealthy from the company shares they had purchased at Reynolds's suggestion.[150] The wife of a factory hand recalled that while her husband worked in the factory from 7:00 a.m. to 6:00 p.m. weekdays and until noon on Saturdays, without any breaks, the trade-off for his demanding work schedule was his succumbing to the company pressure to purchase stocks. Those stocks brought significant wealth to the couple later in life. "All those young men who would work for Mr. R. J., they would make them put aside so much every week and buy stock. . . . Well, they encouraged them to, they didn't force them to."[151]

Shortly after R.J.R. began his program, forty-eight officers and employees owned Reynolds Tobacco stock.[152] Those numbers grew quickly over time. R.J.R.'s daughter Nancy recalled that her father loaned money routinely to friends as well to get them to invest in Reynolds stock: "He wanted to be sure his friends also got on the bandwagon and didn't lose money. He would loan money to come invest in his company, and that's why there are so many millionaires in Winston. Even if you had nothing to do with the company, if you wanted to buy Reynolds stock he would loan you the money to do it."[153] Sometime after 1910, R.J.R. invited his old friend, the famous *Raleigh News and Observer* editor Josephus Daniels, to come to Winston-Salem and work for his company. "I'll make you rich," he told Daniels. The editor demurred but affirmed that R.J.R. had made many North Carolina men rich over the course of his own long career by pressing his stocks upon them.[154] Reynolds was certain that this "participation stock" would thwart speculation while inducing loyalty and commitment from all his employees, from top managers to unskilled wage workers, black and white.[155] In 1918, the company introduced category "B" common stock. Its appeal was solely in its robust dividends, for it carried no voting rights. Investors devoured it, even trading out their regular common stocks for the new "B" ones and thereby transitioning over even greater control of the company to Reynolds and his officers.[156]

Ironically, the *Tobacco Leaf* journal claimed that R.J.R. "was one of the few men of great wealth who absolutely ignored the stock market, and it [was] said of him he rarely ever glanced at the Market Exchange. He knew what his company could do and what his stock was worth, and except as it was an accurate reflection of his company's achievements, he did not care what price it was quoted at."[157] But this was simply not the case. R. J. Reynolds paid close attention to his stock's prices, just as he worked assiduously to build up his own Reynolds Tobacco shares and those of his family, friends, and employees in order to gain more control.[158] Ever the careful investor, he continued to diversify his assets by speculating on a number of profit-making concerns beyond his company. These included mining land in Ashe County, multiple cotton mills, American Sugar, Amalgamated Copper, American Cotton Oil, Seaboard Airline, Southern Railway, Seaboard Air, Tennessee Coal and Iron, U.S. Steel, Virginia Carolina Chemical, and Virginia Southwestern Railroads.[159]

Meanwhile, Reynolds remained supremely successful at cultivating personal relationships with his men. Throughout his career, he persuaded his employees that looking out for his company's best interests meant looking out for their best interests. He welcomed all his employees to visit him in his office and frequently wrote Katharine that long lines stood in his anteroom waiting to speak with him.[160] At his death, the *Raleigh News and Observer* noted, "He was most democratic in his bearing, and ever ready and willing to listen patiently to a constructive suggestion from any of his subordinates. He believed firmly in 'giving the young men a life,' and never failed to encourage them whenever the opportunity offered."[161] R.J.R. mentored many of his salesmen and managers personally. They consistently remarked on "the force of his personality" and his helpful career and business advice.[162] He practiced, according to worker R. E. Horn, "perfect fairness in all of his business dealings with men of all classes and his impartial interest in all in his employ." Horn added, "He was my best friend." Employee W. M. Armistead stated that R.J.R. not only was his best friend but had filled the enormous hole that his father's early death had left in his life.[163]

R.J.R. carefully cultivated those relationships and the loyalty they secured him. He invited his salesmen to his own home for dinners and socializing, often asking Katharine to take on the burden of planning these important large-scale events, but not always. One summer, while she was at Roaring Gap Resort with the children, R.J.R. explained that he had invited "the boss men [from the factory] . . . to take dinner with [him] Sunday" and was delayed in joining her.[164] On another occasion, R.J.R. wrote his wife that he had entertained the company salesmen while she was in Bristol. He thanked her for training the servants so well, for the evening had been a great success.[165] He held one of his most memorable company events in 1916. R.J.R. invited all his salesmen east of the Mississippi to the Reynolda Estate, where he held a huge barbecue, butchering his own hogs, for some five hundred people alongside Lake Katharine.[166] Whether entertaining a single guest or hundreds, R.J.R.'s hospitality was legendary.[167]

R.J.R.'s warm embrace of his white-collar employees, and especially his salesmen, did not prevent him from incorporating the latest strategies for even greater sales successes. Despite the growing web of salesmen he had spun out across the country, he was insistent that his managers always knew their salesmen's whereabouts, their sales numbers, and their customers. His years under the ATC had taught him the value of weekly updates, quarterly reporting, and careful financial analysis. He also insisted they respect the letter of the law—within reason. All Florida salesmen, for example, were notified by letter that the distribution of cigarette papers in any form to a minor was illegal. "Therefore, in distributing samples of Refined you should be very careful not to give some to boys under 21 years of age."[168] But Reynolds's marketers did not want to lose out on the youth market completely. In September 1915, division managers were instructed to tell their salesmen to stock up on their supplies and "meet the demand of the students." Framed by the language of the chase, salesmen were encouraged to "leave nothing undone to place [the company's] goods with all dealers patronized by students." They were instructed to hunt down bookstores, campus shops, and especially the fraternities because they had "stands at their houses for smoking tobacco and cigarettes, and . . . should be encouraged to purchase Reynolds brands."[169]

Perhaps Reynolds's greatest strength lay in surrounding himself with top officers who complemented his abilities. Because he built relationships that lasted lifetimes, management's loyalty to R.J.R. and to his company helped ensure its long-term success. Bowman Gray (1874–1935) was a critical member of R.J.R.'s inner circle. The son of a merchant, Gray exchanged his secure position as a teller at Wachovia National Bank in 1895 for the unstable one of Reynolds Tobacco salesman. For his first two years, Gray was assigned to Georgia, where he proved a standout. R.J.R. was so impressed with his selling prowess that he made him eastern sales representative and stationed him in Baltimore, where he married Nathalie Fontaine Lyons of Asheville. The couple returned to Winston in 1912 so that Gray could manage the sales department. R.J.R. then made him a vice president.[170] Gray had a good memory for faces, a charming personality, and consummate persuasive skills. He was also a workaholic, approaching shop owners while on vacation with his family in an effort to convince them to carry Reynolds brands. Although Gray's foreign language skills were negligible, Reynolds sent him to Europe, where he managed to build good relationships with business partners nonetheless.[171] Gray and Reynolds became confidants, and their wives dear friends. R.J.R. frequented the Gray house on Sunday afternoons to discuss business, with brother Will Reynolds sometimes accompanying him.[172]

The Reynolds Tobacco Company had its share of challenges even after the trust breakup. Labor problems arose after 1910, while World War I created significant supply and price problems, but some of the most worrisome concerns turned on the quality of Reynolds tobacco products.[173] The process of making plug tobacco was not especially hygienic. Nor did it meet the highest quality-control assurances. Letters abound from private individuals and lawyers seeking redress for physical problems that customers suffered upon biting into chewing tobacco laden with "surprises." Occasionally a metal tag, whole or in pieces, found its way into a shipment. One man alleged he had found a fingernail in his chaw, another small bone fragments. One customer experienced sharp burning pains after biting into a plug of Apple Tobacco and suffered weeks of abscesses and eventually significant tooth loss. W. M. Miller, a Hattiesburg, Mississippi, man, sued the tobacco company for gross negligence in 1914. He testified in circuit court that after buying a plug of Brown's Mule, he had "taken a chew and was made deathly sick, and at the same time his teeth came in contact with a hard substance, which on being examined was found to be the end of a human finger." R.J.R.'s legal department worked behind the scenes to resolve these cases, keeping them as far from the public as possible.[174]

R.J.R. believed deeply in the powers of advertising to shape consumer opinion and invested accordingly. In a 1915 interview, he told reporters that his company spent a minimum of 3 percent of its earnings on advertising each year. Newspaper ads were critical to his company's success: "In establishing brands, we cover the country section by section. . . . When you consider the number of newspapers that go daily into the home and how dependent we all are on them for the world's news, it would be hard to depreciate their value as an advertising medium." So valued were newspapers to their marketing efforts that the company actually spent more, not less, on ads when war broke out in Europe. "As a result," Reynolds observed with pleasure, "we are doing the largest business in our history."[175]

Tobacco had been an American staple crop since the seventeenth century. It played an essential role in the development of the American economy and the maturation of slavery as a labor system. It had shaped the social behavior of the many Americans who smoked and chewed tobacco. But the rise of the cigarette in the twentieth century greatly expanded the market for tobacco consumption and inextricably linked cigarettes with the emergence of modern America's economy and culture.[176]

By 1900, the weakened economy of the 1890s had adversely affected the tobacco industry. Rates of consumption had slowed precipitously over the previous decade, and a new market for tobacco products was swinging away from plug tobacco and toward cigars. Sales for cigarettes had leveled out. Taken as a whole, there was good reason to hedge one's bets by selling not just one but two or three of these products. Not surprisingly, R.J.R. was developing a cigarette of his own (in addition to developing a smoking tobacco) despite his agreement not to compete with American Tobacco. As usual, his read on the developing market was dead on. Over the next decade, the biggest growth in consumption occurred in cigarettes, so the timing of R.J.R.'s introduction of the Camel cigarette several years after introducing Prince Albert could not have been better.

Although Americans had considered European cigarette smoking effeminate—"a miserable apology for a manly pleasure," noted one pundit—they had taken up the new tobacco pastime with a vengeance by 1880. At that time, cigarette sales jumped from 42 million to 500 million in a mere five years mainly because of advertising. Innovative packaging provided room for promotion and emboldened manufacturers with their efficient technologies to pursue national marketing for the first time.[177]

Advertising, with its images of cheesecake girls and its cheap giveaways, secured some new consumers, but so did the ease with which cigarettes could now be purchased and smoked, especially when compared to the inconvenience of pipe tobacco. Meanwhile, tuberculosis outbreaks led to growing public protests against spitting chewing tobacco in a number of major cities. Newspaper after newspaper, including those in Winston-Salem, carried advertisements for sanitariums where the ubiquitous disease could be treated.[178] Cigarettes were not only more suitable for urban living;

Table 1. Increase in tobacco consumption, 1870–1920

	U.S. population	Tobacco	Cigars	Cigarettes
1870–1880	30%	48%	107%	2,844%
1880–1890	25%	73%	72%	446%
1890–1900	20%	21%	30%	18%
1900–1910	21%	56%	32%	198%
1910–1920	14%	(–5%)	26%	546%

Source: adapted from Werner, *Tobaccoland*, 137.

they were also more social. They begged to be shared, and elegant people loved to smoke them over coffee or drinks.[179]

It was in this changing climate that R.J.R. introduced his Camel cigarette in 1913, one of four new brands he was test-marketing at a time when cigarette smokers were still few and far between. By late 1912, R.J.R. was buying cigarette machines. By early 1913, he told the Winston Board of Trade that he would be producing cigarettes. Eager to capture a national market, just as he had with Prince Albert, he played with the same blends that had made "the national joy smoke" so popular—plentiful burley, a generous smattering of bright leaf, and 10 percent Turkish. The formula took the bite out of straight Turkish blends but retained enough exoticism to capture people's taste buds and imaginations. Turkish cigarettes were virtually unknown in the United States before the appearance of the Camel. In contrast, the La Ferme factory in Saint Petersburg had manufactured Turkish cigarettes since the 1850s and was selling them in Dresden by the 1880s. That same decade, Turkish cigarettes could be found in Constantinople soon after the Ottoman government monopolized the tobacco trade. Although they had become commonplace in Europe, Turkish blends were only beginning to penetrate a small segment of the American market, principally among "the more cultured smokers" willing to pay higher prices. R.J.R. had found a way to make the exoticism and desirable taste of the Turkish blend affordable to the masses.[180]

But he had hedged his bets, developing three other brands at the same time: the classic Virginia tobacco named Reyno, ten to a box for a nickel; another Turkish blend called Osman; and a Turkish straight with a cork tip called Red Kamel, a brand name bought from a New York firm that sold ten to a pack for ten cents. Camel, with its touch of Turkish leaf and plenty of sweetener, was a bargain at ten cents for a pack of twenty.[181]

Although the marketing department tossed around multiple names for their new cigarette, including Kaiser Wilhelm, in the end they settled on Camel. What made the Camel cigarette so appealing was its promise of an exotic and pleasing Turkish blend of tobacco at an affordable price. How better to convey that exoticism than by invoking the tobacco's origins, in a land profoundly different from the bright-leaf and burley-leaf worlds of the American South. So Reynolds adorned his packages with symbols that Anglo-Americans associated with the Middle East—a minaret, mosques, an oasis, two pyramids, three palm trees, and a one-humped camel in the foreground set against a golden desert. This packaging was decidedly distinctive, a far cry from the Victorian imagery with its nostalgic Americana sentimentalism that the tobacco industry had relied on over the previous fifty years. It was also strikingly different from the winking countenance of the mild-mannered Prince Albert caricature marketed only five years earlier.

The camel image itself was central to the packaging. It gave the brand an easily distinguishable image among illiterate consumers, a trick that plug manufacturers had used for decades. There is some debate about why the company settled on the Camel name. Camels had long been associated with the Ottoman Empire. In fact, camel drivers had long forced their pack animals to inhale tobacco smoke to keep them moving day and night without rest on extensive treks.[182] The story that the company tells about the origins of the iconic Camel image is prosaic by comparison. In 1912, the Barnum and Bailey Circus arrived in Winston while the marketing department was debating what kind of camel image should sell the product. R.J.R.'s secretary raced to the big top with a photographer to capture a dromedary named Old Joe on film. When the handler slapped the animal to get its attention, the camera man captured the image recognized the world over even today—a one-humped "camel" with tail and head raised, ears flat against its head, and eyes tightly shut.[183]

The relationship between the Barnum and Bailey Circus and the resultant Old Joe image deserves a bit more scrutiny, because it reveals a basic truth about R. J. Reynolds's marketing genius. R.J.R. had an inherent grasp of what people enjoyed regardless of their birth, education, status, or income. Like all leading businessmen of this period, he wanted to move away from selling numerous brands aimed at local markets to selling more universally desired ones. Efficiencies of scale ensured cost savings, while strong transportation guaranteed market reach. But all the benefits of developing national markets were fruitless without widespread yearning for the product. R.J.R. was singularly attuned to grasping those needs. He was an observer of human behavior. He knew that when Ringling Brothers, Barnum and Bailey, or any circus came to town and foreign animals paraded through the streets alongside cavorting clowns and calliope music, rich people and poor, black and white, stopped in their tracks and made a beeline for the nearest curb. The camel, a popular circus animal, appealed to mass audiences, for all its strangeness: its peculiar physical shape and way of moving and its evocation of desert people and their culture.

Once again employing top advertising firm N. W. Ayer, Reynolds drew up one of the most novel and ultimately most successful national advertising campaigns of all time. Once R.J.R. had settled on Camel as the brand to promote, he allegedly spent $1.5 million in advertising that first year.[184] The October 13, 1913, release of the Camel brand had been preceded by a set of teaser ads. The first pictured Old Joe, the camel, and merely stated the word "Camels." The second ad announced: "The Camels Are Coming." The third and final ad guaranteed, "Tomorrow there'll be more Camels in this town than in all Asia and Africa combined." Competitors thought the whole campaign was a joke, but Camels immediately swept past older brands as the new cigarette of choice. Reynolds Tobacco Company sold a million Camel cigarettes in its first year, leaping to 6.5 billion in 1916, and then a whopping 14 billion, earning $10.3 million in profits two years later.[185] By 1918, Camels alone had captured 40 percent of the market.[186] By 1921, one-half the cigarettes smoked in America were Camels.[187]

Family members hold that Katharine was responsible for the wording on the Camel cigarette package. It is also reported that she consulted with R.J.R. and the Ayer firm each step of the way. In fact, Katharine and Mr. Ayer became good friends.[188] Regardless of who contributed the most to the campaign's development, "The Camels Are Coming" teaser heralded not only a new cigarette but also an extremely effective and well-planned rollout of a new product.[189] The trade journal *Tobacco Leaf* was so impressed with Camel sales that it praised the R. J. Reynolds Tobacco Company for its confidence in America and its people. Reynolds showed not just "implicit faith in the future prosperity of the country but in the present and existing buying power of the American people." The editors lauded Reynolds Tobacco, "one of the oldest and most reliable manufacturing concerns in the tobacco line," for "having the brains and backbone to plan and get into operation a business venture on such a magnificent scale." It predicted that the whole Camel enterprise would mark "a distinctive achievement in tobacco history."[190]

The promoters relied heavily on mass-market popular literature, changing images and the text for Camel ads on a monthly basis to draw renewed attention.[191] The company placed ads in a variety of print media, from popular magazines like *Town and Country*, *Life*, and *Puck* to such trade journals as *Smoke*, *Tobacco Leaf*, *Tobacco*, and the *U.S. Tobacco Journal*, and even the *Army and Navy Journal* and the *Army and Navy Register*.[192]

Reynolds told his jobbers that they would benefit from committing to the

Camel too. "We feel about this cigarette game just as we felt about Prince Albert," Reynolds promised them. Camel emerged as their new best seller, and Reynolds's commitment to Camel and his belief in its marketability were evident in the advertising campaign, "as broad and convincing as that which ha[d] won fame for Prince Albert." He declared to the jobbers and merchandisers, "We are prepared to spend thousands to quickly put Camels into the mouths of smokers, because we believe they will be preferred to any other cigarette." Reynolds appealed to the jobbers' savoir faire. "You didn't cut your eye teeth last week; you have lived long enough to know something about cigarette selling methods." In a vernacular tone, Reynolds added, "Well, get this. . . . Camels will be sold to you . . . with all the cards on the table—a fair, living business profit for both of us." Go ahead and bet on Camels, Reynolds suggested, and trust in the company that had "smashed wide open the door to better things in the trade," and planned "to keep on smashing while the smashing [was] good."[193] R.J.R. was meticulous about all aspects of the marketing campaign. Shop owners who sold Camels received detailed instructions on installing a Camel Cigarette window display, including eight critical steps, specifications, and a correct example. The company warned storekeepers, "Every display will be personally checked by a Camel salesman and all the displays not according to specifications will be rejected."[194]

Competition between tobacco companies was fierce, and Reynolds was not above the fray. In 1915, the R. J. Reynolds Tobacco Company publicly accused Liggett and Meyers of designating their new Smokarol brand as smoking tobacco, not a cigarette, to save money on federal taxes.[195] Meanwhile, R.J.R. believed that one of his competitors had struck a particularly low blow when rumors spread slandering his ultra-successful Camel cigarette. Although the exact source of the defamation is not known, gossip circulated that saltpeter was being added to Camels to give them their distinctive flavor, and also that workers in the Reynolds plant had been stricken with terrible communicable diseases like syphilis or leprosy. The company fought back by offering five-hundred-dollar rewards to the first twenty people who revealed the origin of these false reports. The instigators were never identified, but ironically enough the reward ads generated renewed interest in the Camel cigarette.[196]

Despite wartime challenges, the company prospered. It built a new five-story factory in 1916 to eliminate the night shift and, a year later, a new plant in Maysville, Kentucky. The company released a statement that it was "undeterred by the war and increasing its plants on an enormous scale," and it had several other manufacturing plants under construction.[197] Meanwhile, *Tobacco* reported that the number of Camels "consumed" in 1915 could stretch from the earth to the moon, and forty thousand miles beyond. The number of Camels produced during the same period could circle the globe about eleven times.[198] Thanks to Reynolds, North Carolina now manufactured more chewing tobacco and smoking tobacco than any other state and was second only to Virginia in cigarette production. That same year, Winston-Salem replaced Saint Louis as the top tobacco-manufacturing city in the world.[199]

The R. J. Reynolds Tobacco Company now employed ten thousand people, with all but a few hundred connected with the Winston plant. It operated four manufacturing plants and forty-seven storage facilities and owned a total of 121 buildings. Its bold foray into national advertising with Prince Albert had secured it much fame and even bigger sales. That success was repeated and augmented with the novel campaign for Camel cigarettes so that literally billions of the smokes were now being manufactured in Winston-Salem. With the decision to eliminate coupons, the company inaugurated another big switch from the tobacco industry's past. "Don't look for premiums or coupons, as the cost of the tobaccos blended in Camel Cigarettes prohibits the use of them," read the inscription on the package.[200] Demand continued to skyrocket despite the absence of these enticements, necessitating more expansion plans notwithstanding World War I shortages. The company purchased an enormous timber tract in Washington County, North Carolina, in 1917, for example, with the intention of clearing 2,500 acres immediately to make tobacco cases and boxes rather than rely on suppliers compromised by wartime demand.[201]

The tobacco industry as a whole realized that soldiers' addiction to cigarettes gave Reynolds a huge bonanza. One trade journal observed that it was easier for soldiers to go without food, clothing, and shoes than without tobacco and noted that tobacco had been a form of exchange between soldiers and across enemy lines in every war America had ever fought. In fact, American soldiers in France actually demanded more Camels than the War Department had provided them, a request delivered to the Reynolds Tobacco Company by General Pershing himself.[202]

Wartime exigencies challenged the company on several fronts, despite the high sales figures. Roy Haberkorn, frustrated by his inability to find foil for wrapping, experimented religiously with alternatives. He interrupted R. J. Reynolds during his convalescence in Atlantic City to let him know that he had located "a paper that [was] absolutely impervious to moisture" and identified a dozen or so paper mills that could supply it.[203] In March 1917, the company directors voted to increase preferred stock from $2.5 million to $5 million to raise capital.[204] In May 1917, Reynolds raised wages by 10 percent across the manufacturing departments, announcing, "This will apply to every man, woman and child." This marked the third wage increase since the start of World War I. The bonus system remained in place even with the increases. Operatives judged "loyal and attentive to their duties" received a 4 percent bonus each December.[205] R.J.R. needed to hold on to his experienced labor as best he could even if it meant providing escalating incentives.

Winston-Salem demographics had changed dramatically over the first two decades of the twentieth century. The black population had increased greatly. In 1900, blacks had made up just over a third of the population. But the enormous growth in Prince Albert tobacco and Camel cigarette production and the concomitant need for more tobacco workers turned African Americans into the majority population by 1920. The makeup of the city was changing in other critical ways too. In 1900, 87 percent of residents had been born in North Carolina. That percentage had dropped slightly to 85 percent by 1910, but plummeted to 68 percent in 1920. Rural African Americans recruited from South Carolina now made up 13 percent of out-of-state migrants. Over half the population was male, youthful (the mean age was twenty-four in 1920), unmarried, and black. Although the divorce rate remained low (less than 1 percent), the number of divorces increased fivefold between 1900 and 1920. A full third of the population worked in the tobacco industry in 1910; nearly two-thirds of these workers were African American. No other occupation came close to rivaling the tobacco trade's central role in the local economy. Although Winston-Salem had changed dramatically by the late nineteenth century as a result of tobacco's predominance, the city became a bona fide urban center only in the second decade of the twentieth century, in the wake of the R. J. Reynolds Tobacco Company's blockbuster successes with Prince Albert and Camel.

The trade journal *Tobacco* captured R.J.R.'s professional accomplishments over these first two decades of the twentieth century:

> In knowledge, judgment and achievement, R. J. Reynolds may well be regarded as one of the greatest men in the tobacco business. But he is the first to admit that in his mighty undertakings he has been ably aided. As president of the company, he has as co-workers men who most thoroughly understand every detail of the tobacco industry. This is the day of efficiency and specialization. The demand is for men who understand a particular line, men knowing thoroughly every detail of each duty they have to perform, men of broad ability and deep insight, men who develop rapidly, yet who endure the strain of responsibility, the strain of hard work. Of the official family of R. J. Reynolds Tobacco Co., each member is a man of proven worth. Their intelligent planning, their arduous labors help to account for the unusual success the R. J. Reynolds Company has achieved.[206]

R.J.R. had made outstanding decisions. He had been supported by a cadre of ambitious, talented men whom he himself had mentored. *Tobacco* failed to mention the role that his wife, Katharine, played as R.J.R.'s biggest supporter, confidante, and advisor, however.

The R. J. Reynolds Tobacco Company, for all intents and purposes, was a man's world. Its products were perceived as masculine; cigarette smoking had yet to be feminized. Its working environment was masculine. Lower-class women were barely visible in the most unskilled of positions at the lowest wages, and only half a dozen women provided secretarial and clerical support in the offices. Katharine Reynolds was the sole woman able to exert influence on the company. She knew its details as intimately as any of R.J.R.'s best men, but she nonetheless had no formal role to play alongside them. Katharine's part in making the R. J. Reynolds Tobacco Company such a success deserves attribution. Documenting her presence in the actual decision making of this critical era in the company's history is difficult. While public memory and family recollection hold that she was instrumental in shaping the Camel campaign, for example, no written record confirms this. Nonetheless, R.J.R.'s actions took on a new boldness, and his ambitions reached new heights once Katharine entered his life. Indeed, recent studies by economists in fact confirm that marriage alone enhances the productivity and success of men, although researchers cannot pinpoint the causal explanation for their findings.[207]

R.J.R. and Katharine Reynolds complemented each other's strengths and weaknesses. Katharine did not limit her pursuits to the R. J. Reynolds

Tobacco Company, despite her interest in the business and her role as R.J.R.'s confidante. She was deeply invested in a series of social reforms at the same time that her husband and his tobacco products were becoming household names. She also put tremendous time and energy into building the Reynolda Estate, and subsequently created an empire of her own.

6 A Thousand Cattle on a Hill

Even as a young woman, Katharine had dreamed big. She once told her State Normal and Industrial School roommate Emma Speight, "When I marry . . . I shall buy a great estate . . . and I shall have a thousand cattle on a hill . . . and flowers all around."[1] Katharine's ambition to be mistress of a grand property was not an original one. Nor did it challenge the social or political status quo in any fundamental way. But she did put herself in charge of making her dream come true. She told Emma that it would be she herself, not her husband, who would buy an estate one day. She was intent on being the master of her own world, regardless of the more subordinate roles society expected her to play as a wife and mother. In a culture where women's aspirations and authority remained constricted, even for wealthy women, Katharine had fixed upon a pursuit that suited her imagination, predilections, and talents. Although it took her twelve years, and she never amassed a full one thousand head of cattle, she built a one-thousand-acre estate, complete with a superbly designed landscape of forests, pastures, gardens, a pool, and a man-made lake, all sculpted out of the thinnest of soils and worn-out gullies. Despite the family's long history with tobacco, not a scrap of it was cultivated here. Fruit trees, flowers, and vegetables abounded instead. The completed estate included a spacious colonial revival residence, a greenhouse, a working farm, a golf course, and tennis courts. It had a working village of quaint English-style residences for employees, a blacksmith shop, a dairy, stables, a mule barn, a henhouse, a cattle barn, a smokehouse, a corn shed, a garage, a heating plant, a laundry, schools, and a post office. Formal gardens incorporated southeastern native plants with Japanese architectural elements and classical European designs. An ivy-covered timber-framed Presbyterian church presided over the village community. The completed estate was a marvel—one of the showcase properties of the Southeast featured in *House Beautiful*. "Your home and surroundings," wrote Katharine's friend Ella McGee Geer, "are a perfect dream of loveliness.[2]" By 1918, the year R.J.R. died, Katharine had succeeded in making her own world, and she had managed the creation of this whole enterprise largely by herself.

Katharine had captured the imagination of the wider community around her in the act of building Reynolda, beginning in 1912. Just as R.J.R. was heralded for bringing modern industrialization to Winston-Salem, Katharine was celebrated for bringing modern scientific management to rural agriculture. "Reynolda is destined to become one of the great factors in the development of rural life," crowed the *Winston-Salem Journal*.[3] Miss Bell Lee, a visitor to the city, left convinced that the commercial future of the South was bright indeed if a tobacco metropolis could bring such fecundity to the land and prosperity to the people, based on her tour of Reynolda. "No more magnificent home in a more beautiful location is to be found in the South and surely there is not another in the whole world that is more suggestive of freedom and joy," she wrote. Lee was astounded by the beauty and order of the place, and its attendant "air of independence" secured through its apparent self-sufficiency. Gardens produced "tender young plants" that were turned into delicious, wholesome dinners. The dairy produced the richest and most healthful milk and cream in the state as well as pound after pound of "the purest butter." Scientific management and expertise were in abundance, from the mechanics who maintained the cars to the blacksmiths who repaired farm implements and shod the giant Percheron workhorses to the poultry man whose immaculate yard was filled with the best breeds in the land. Set against this exceptional management and efficiency was the arresting sight of "dozens of modern little white bungalows with climbing roses and stately hollyhocks cluster[ed] around the Presbyterian Church where Mrs. Reynolds worship[ped]."[4] Katharine's estate took aesthetic orderings of the landscape from the past, along with their attendant hierarchical social relationships, and bridged them with the future by incorporating the latest advances in agriculture and technology.

The beauty and efficiency of her accomplishment astounded the larger Piedmont community and filled local citizens with pride. Her estate seemed to suggest new possibilities for the future welfare of the region. If Katharine could create her own version of a modern garden of Eden shaped out of ruined southern soil, the region could still be a land of plenty for all, she seemed to be suggesting through her spectacular example. Her vision for Reynolda reflected reform ideas already widely in circulation. This country-life movement, although it never captured the attention of the nation as a whole or of the majority of rural dwellers, aimed to transition farmers into landed businessmen so that they could keep step with the new national economy. The problem with this movement was that it served only those farmers with business proclivities to begin with, and especially those who owned their own land and had access to capital and credit. Tenant farmers and sharecroppers stood to gain nothing from it.

Country-life reformers had strong national advocates with ties to Katharine's world. North Carolinian Walter Hines Page had been a contributor to the president's report of the Country Life Commission released in 1909. The Department of Church and Country Life of the Presbyterian Board of Home Missions, organized in 1909, proved to be one of the most effective of the many country-life initiatives in its commitment to country church improvement. Led by Warren H. Wilson, a minister trained in sociology, the department pursued sociological surveys, printed informational brochures, held country conferences, and prepared ministers for service in rural churches.[5] Katharine's commitment to establishing her own country church, Reynolda Presbyterian, dedicated in 1915, was simultaneously taking root at this time.[6] Country-life reformers eventually claimed some large-scale successes, including the creation of the Farm Bureau Federation. Other new national legislation reflected some of their concerns as well. The Smith-Lever Act of 1914 brought about the consolidation of schools, as well as extension teaching, while the Smith-Hughes Act of 1917 ensured the teaching of agriculture and home economics in the school curriculum. These reforms benefited some rural Americans, but they failed to address the deeper structural realities of property holding.[7]

Country-life reformers wanted to slow urbanization and discourage rural migration to the cities. They made no real inroads on this front, however. In fact, their insistence on turning farmers into businessmen expedited the latter. The reformers did nothing to alter the prevalence of tenant farming. Though they did help make rural churches more responsive to community needs, the introduction of the automobile, the telephone, and better roads helped rural people far more. Their advocacy of rural free delivery, while generating better communication networks for rural people, helped kill community spirit. Folks no longer needed to go to the nearest village or crossroad to get the mail and catch up on "the news." Though rural schools incorporated more nature-study courses and scientific agriculture at the insistence of the reformers, these classes did not nurture enough love for the country to stop young people from leaving for the city and seeking out what seemed to be better opportunities there.

The reform movement worked at cross-purposes, juxtaposing the business and technological virtues of agricultural reform against the social aspects of rural life, including the values and traditions that made agricultural living a particularly worthy pursuit to preserve. The movement was never radical enough to make significant change. Although it acknowledged the great handicaps that the nationalizing economy created for farmers, especially monopolies and tight credit, it generated studies to assess them rather than putting pressure on key leaders to pursue new legislation. The movement also relied too much on education as a change agent. Finally, it did not confront "the Negro Problem" in the South, as W. E. B. Du Bois explained in 1908 to L. H. Bailey, a member of the Commission on Country Life. It would be too easy, Du Bois warned, to put the future of the movement in the hands of the very same large landholders who perpetuated racial inequality in the countryside.[8] In the end, the country-life effort was overshadowed by the Progressives, whose spectacular exposés of government corruption and business monopolies dwarfed country-life work and reform.[9]

Katharine drew inspiration from this movement, however, because it married the two great ideological contradictions in her life. She wanted to preserve traditional agrarian values and the character traits she associated with them—independence, self-sufficiency, and hard work as the antidote to the growing evils of city life—but at the same time she recognized that the fruits of industrialization not only ensured her own creature comforts but also raised the standard of living for many Americans, including the working class. The country-life movement offered a solution to this dilemma. It argued that adapting agriculture to the modern age through scientific knowledge preserved the best agrarian values while bringing the economic benefits of capitalist competition to the countryside.

The country-life movement was never well organized. It comprised a broad constituency of land-grant-college educators, state and federal agricultural bureaus, rural school and rural church reformers, and those with economic or social-gospel interests in rural reform. Katharine's world overlapped with all these constituencies in a variety of informal ways.[10] Her world also overlapped with that of urban reformers and women's club work. Like her husband she was generous with her money and her time and often donated to worthy causes. Her largesse included new seating for a small church, a banquet for workers at the hospital on Thanksgiving Day, and Christmas dinner for the needy at the county home.[11] She was an active member of several state and local women's organizations committed to maternal benevolence and progressive reform. The city of Winston-Salem had been slow to make the transition from aid to reform that other cities were making by the turn of the century. The local Associated Charities run by the wives and daughters of the leading citizens of the city preferred hands-on volunteerism, with its case-by-case approach to helping "the deserving poor."[12] As a young mother, Katharine lacked the time and energy to join the older matrons on the Associated Charities board who attended to the needy. She may also have been critical of their approach. Her earlier education at Normal, with its more modern commitment to women's reform work rather than traditional charity, had suggested a more systemic approach to ameliorating poverty.

Though Katharine had received her degree from Sullins, Normal and its progressive values also remained important to her throughout her life.[13] When Normal president Charles McIver died suddenly in 1906, she led the effort to establish a monument in his honor, holding fund-raising meetings and making the first formal donation.[14] She stayed in touch with her former teachers and schoolmates and served on the school's board of directors as the representative from the Alumnae and Former Students' Association.[15] Her sustained Normal connections kept her in the swirl of social reforms and organizations that the school embraced, as did her growing status as the wife of R. J. Reynolds. The local Business Women's Association invited Katharine to become a member, stating, "We recognize you as the state's leading business woman."[16]

Like many progressive women of her place and time, she supported the North Carolina Federation of Women's Clubs (NCFWC).[17] This increasingly powerful network of early twentieth-century women helped North Carolina earn its reputation as the most progressive state in the South. They secured considerable political strength from their public work in large measure because they agreed with men about what society needed and did not challenge a political system that denied African American men their political rights. Meanwhile, African American women nurtured relationships with these white clubwomen in an effort to meet the most basic needs of their own black communities.[18] White clubwomen in North Carolina proved especially successful at creating a strong public role for themselves, and Katharine quickly tapped into their efforts. Because they presumed early on that electoral politics was white male territory, they delved into politics only when it most affected the female terrain of caretaking and social well-being. Their success lay in redefining civic obligation as women's work, thereby giving them an important back door into the public domain. They used that back door to support the incorporation of social services into the state system. Katharine benefited personally and politically from this work during her long-time association.[19]

The first Women's Club chapter in North Carolina was organized in Winston under the leadership of Katharine's friend Lucy Patterson (1865–1942), wife of Winston-Salem attorney Lindsay Patterson (1858–1922), who was best known for securing the acquittal of two Republican North Carolina Supreme Court justices against trumped up impeachment charges brought by the Democratic General Assembly in 1901. Lucy, who became a popular writer and served on the Republican National Committee, befriended Katharine soon after her arrival in Winston and probably introduced her to this local branch of the NCFWC.[20]

As was true for so many other members whose husbands, fathers, and sons were leading industrialists and businessmen, Katharine's earliest years in the NCFWC proved problematic.[21] The NCFWC tackled leading social issues of the day, and one of the biggest was child labor. Although textile-factory owners drew the bulk of national attention and white middle-class ire for hiring white children, tobacco factories did not escape their share of blame for their hiring of black youths. Katharine must have found herself torn between her commitment to the family business and the NCFWC's critique.

She could not have been the only NCFWC member caught between her social ideals and her family's business pragmatics. Despite serious efforts to generate child-labor legislation beginning in 1898, the NCFWC had ultimately backed off the issue by 1912, switching its energies to reforming "delinquent" children instead. The NCFWC, following in the footsteps of the General Federation of Women's Clubs (GFWC), which had unanimously passed a resolution against child labor in 1898, picked up the child-labor issue with the intention of putting more teeth into the mild legislation already passed. By 1905, the NCFWC had invited Dr. A. J. McKelway to give a keynote address on child labor at the annual convention in Goldsboro. That same year, the organization formed a Child Study Committee. In 1910, the committee was renamed Industrial and Child Labor but then lost its steam. Rather than either tackle the enforcement of the weak 1903 law or campaign for a stronger one, the NCFWC decided to charge itself with supporting a state institution for juvenile delinquents. A year later, the committee backpedaled even further, renaming itself the Constructive Philanthropy Committee. It subsequently gave one thousand dollars in support of the Stonewall Jackson Training School for delinquent boys, admittedly the first of its kind in the state, and a significant accomplishment, but considerably far afield from the political hot potato of child labor. While Julia Lathrop led the GFWC in pressing for juvenile-court law before being appointed to head the Children's Bureau at President Taft's request in 1912, the NCFWC was quietly tabling its pursuit of child-labor issues. Many of its members were the wives and daughters of the very industrialists who insisted on the practice of cheap child labor in their factories after all. Katharine was not the only NCFWC member who would have experienced these divided loyalties.[22]

Although these clubwomen publicly claimed their mission was to "uplift" the working classes, their efforts on working people's behalf tended to be moderate ones: beautification projects in the mill villages; educational programs for the working poor; the formation of mother's clubs and civic organizations; and the establishment of kindergartens and day-care facilities. They increasingly steered clear of pursuing structural changes like child-labor and minimum-wage laws to avoid tackling head-on the men who owned and ran the factories, in part due to their personal connections with them, and in part due to the political strength these men wielded.

Although organized women throughout North Carolina worried about the welfare of working women and children, "the commercial spirit deter[red] them," as NCFWC leader Sallie Southall Cotten volunteered. The active industrial lobby deterred them as well. North Carolina women made limited headway on child-labor legislation compared to clubwomen in other states. Moreover, they elected to press only for regulation rather than an outright ban. When Congress considered a child-labor bill in 1915–16, North Carolina manufacturers staunchly opposed it for multiple reasons, telling legislators that their own employees were against it and blaming northern textile competitors. They also opposed it because the movement was led by women and in an ancillary development began fighting woman suffrage for fear women would use the ballot against them. As a result, the North Carolina General Assembly would fail to mandate an eight-hour workday for children under sixteen until 1927.[23]

Meanwhile, at the Tenth Annual NCFWC Convention in 1912, held once again in Winston-Salem, the delegates spent considerable time discussing a report on the legal status of women in North Carolina. The NCFWC had recently requested permission for women to run for office in the school board election but had been told by the state attorney general, T. W. Bickett, that doing so would be unconstitutional.[24] In the midst of this important discussion, Katharine chaired the local hospitality committee for this convention. Aware that crafting image was an important part of power making, especially for women, she provided the NCFWC president with "a beautiful automobile with its attentive chauffeur dedicated solely" for her use during the gathering. Decorated with sprigs of pine tied with blue and white ribbon and labeled "The President's Car," it stood ready at the president's command, underscoring her importance and the Reynolds family's tacit support.[25] Katharine herself was photographed in the elaborately festooned vehicle next to her chauffeur and her younger sister Ruth on the front seat; the NCFWC officers, wearing serious faces and striking hats, sat behind them.[26]

The growing authority of the NCFWC was becoming obvious, a fact not lost on the male power brokers in the state. Manufacturers gave the group receptions in their honor, and politicians were always hospitable. Governor W. W. Kitchin welcomed a delegation to his mansion at one annual meeting. The NCFWC delegation held its business meetings in the hall of the House of Representatives at another. Seated in the chairs of the male-only legislators of their state and speaking from their lectern, the delegates were surely aware of the irony of their exclusion from the political process.

Although Katharine was committed to the NCFWC, she was not one of its visible leaders. This can be explained by at least three reasons. First, some of the issues that the clubwomen pursued early on (particularly child-labor laws) put her in a compromising position as the wife of one of the most prominent industrialists in the state. Second, the NCFWC was slow to embrace rural services and reform, Katharine's real passion.[27] Third, Katharine's social position was a particularly vaunted one, her time limited and her responsibilities many. The fact that one of the wealthiest women in the state publicly supported the NCFWC, whether or not she was an elected officer, underscored the importance of white women's commitment to incorporating social reforms into the body politic before supportive and hostile audiences alike.

Katharine adopted a much more hands-on approach with the Young Women's Christian Association (YWCA) by comparison. By the early twentieth century, the YWCA was providing education, leadership training, and services for women in city after city across the country. By 1920, it was the third-largest women's organization in the United States and the only one committed to bringing white and black women together under the umbrella of Christian sisterhood. Although YWCA clubs in southern states lagged behind clubs elsewhere in the United States when it came to grappling with the race problem, they were ahead of most other southern social-reform institutions, secular or religious, in encouraging interracial cooperation.[28]

White women in Winston began fund-raising to start a local YWCA branch in 1906, the same year the national YWCA was formed. R.J.R., at Katharine's encouragement, made a matching pledge of five thousand dollars to make the Winston club happen.[29] Two years later, Katharine was elected first vice president and founding board member of the new chapter. She played as active a leadership role as her complicated life allowed in the organization for the remainder of her life, far more than she ever had in the NCFWC.[30]

The degree to which her interest in the organization was mutually interdependent with her commitment to R. J. Reynolds Tobacco Company and its employees was already evident by 1912. The annual YWCA report that year noted that 750 white women and girls were employed at Reynolds, one-quarter of whom were boarders and therefore likely recruits for the local YWCA.[31]

Katharine focused her attention on the local chapter despite repeated requests to assume broader regional and national roles in the organization.[32] Elected president in 1916, she told the audience at the annual banquet that she considered this role "the most exalted and responsible position [she had] ever held," noting, "While I realize my own unfitness and inability to serve . . . I feel the keenest pleasure in an attempt to guide it through the coming year." She was convinced that the YWCA encouraged in young women a much broader social and intellectual outlook through its Christian mission and manifold educational opportunities.[33]

The Winston YWCA was especially concerned with the welfare of young, single white women arriving in the city by the dozens in search of wage work. Chapter leaders feared that the modern city lifestyle of single young women, who sported their own income and lived independently in boardinghouses, was a recipe for their moral ruin. In the absence of familial and community support, these girls would undoubtedly attend movie theaters and dance halls, leading to the moral degradation of one young woman after another. In this, the Winston chapter differed little from other local YWCA's across the country, whose goals were to find suitable housing for these female urban migrants and provide them with wholesome activities and useful education during their leisure hours. Although the local YWCA did help thousands of young women, the act of creating a support system for them also invested not only national but even local YWCA women leaders with political authority. This power was especially important in the South, where the actions of the YWCA leadership, like that of the NCFWC leadership, implicitly challenged the long-held political hegemony of southern white men. The carving out of whole new public spaces for women marked the most obvious manifestation of this development. In Winston, this meant a YWCA building for education, training, and sports. Meanwhile, black women created their own chapter in the city, with help from the white YWCA leadership, and established public spaces for themselves as well, an even bigger challenge given the realities of Jim Crow.

Although little in the public or private record documents Katharine's position on interracial reform, her lifelong involvement in the biracial YWCA suggests that she entertained a more moderate outlook than some of her peers. Moreover, when black educator Simon G. Atkins welcomed famous African American leaders like Booker T. Washington and Anna Julia Cooper to the community, everyone knew Katharine loaned her china to Mrs. Atkins to help her entertain them. Washington himself had remarked on this "interesting incident," as he called it. "In one case, in Winston-Salem," he singled out in a letter to Walter Hines Page, "the richest white lady in the city loaned her dishes and table ware to the colored family where our party was entertained." This act of intimacy was an important symbol of connection between an elite white woman and an elite black woman and their respective communities in the segregated South. As other historians have convincingly argued, Washington's desire to aid his own people increasingly led him toward speaking on behalf of whites with power, rather than on behalf of so many African Americans without it.[34]

Katharine was conversant in and led other social reforms as well. She was a member of the local Civic Improvement League and took a formative role in framing its constitution.[35] The goals of the group centered on "making Winston cleaner, more sanitary and more beautiful" by putting pressure on the local alderman to enforce city ordinances already in place and by improving school grounds and buildings.[36] Though she had declined an invitation to be a member of the South Atlantic Field League of the Civic Improvement League, the local league had formed "a colored committee" and sponsored an auxiliary organization for the city's black women by 1913 under her leadership.[37]

In 1912, Virginia governor Thomas Staples Martin (1847–1919) was well enough aware of Katharine's social interests to personally invite her to meet with the governors he had gathered from across the South to discuss pressing social reforms.[38] She also joined the North Carolina Conference for Social Service. This organization had recently been founded by a group of state leaders including Clarence Poe, editor of the *Progressive Farmer*. A noted southern Progressive, Poe had launched a plan to impose residential apartheid in the rural South in the early decades of the twentieth century.[39] He advocated outlawing black ownership of property in any rural or suburban neighborhoods where whites predominated.[40] It is not clear where Katharine stood on this issue, only that she had demonstrated a public commitment to support traditional black leadership that sought to aid black working families but did not challenge racial segregation. Regardless, it was the North Carolina Conference for Social Service, perhaps more than any other organization to which she belonged, that enabled her to tie together her interests in rural reform and social progress.[41]

Katharine's connectedness to these broader social currents gave her strength of purpose in her creation of Reynolda. Daughter Nancy recalled, "My mother was the one that really built Reynolda. I don't think my father had much to do with it. This was what she loved doing, and this was something that pleased her, and so he said go ahead, Katharine, you do what you want."[42] R.J.R. faithfully reported farm developments to Katharine whenever she was traveling, but the estate ultimately embodied her vision, and in the end she ran it.[43] Building Reynolda allowed Katharine to make her dream a reality, but more importantly, it let her act out all her ideas about an ideal social world, appropriating country-life ideals, progressive reform impulses, and historical tropes and blending them into her own version of "the good life."

Katharine borrowed heavily from multiple pasts as well as reform traditions. Not coincidentally, the estate co-opted some aspects of the plantation. Katharine and her husband built a big house to live in as the heads of the estate and constructed living quarters for African American agricultural workers at some remove. But she borrowed heavily from the English village ideal too. Her estate included a small community whose architecture, purpose, and physical layout resembled an English country hamlet. This village housed services that supported the estate (a blacksmith shop, a heating plant, a laundry, etc.) and the skilled white families and household servants she employed. She borrowed from the country-house movement, whereby wealthy new industrialists built working farms and estate houses on spacious land outside East Coast cities. Katharine also appropriated landscape traditions from around the world. Her aesthetically pleasing grounds were groomed to evoke Mediterranean vistas, New England lake scenes, the rolling English countryside flecked with Shropshire sheep, Italianate garden strolls, and Japanese tea gardens.

Into this romantic vision, she injected state-of-the-art technology. These amendments ensured that the estate operated as an efficient, healthful, hygienic, and physically comfortable family home as well as workplace and reform grounds. She consistently consulted agricultural experts in state universities and the federal government.[44] Viewed in this light, Katharine made Reynolda into an inherently conservative social commentary, one that stood in stark contrast to the factory world and its surrounds in a city created largely by her husband's ambition over the last four decades. In the factories that shook with mechanized noise and dripped the mess of tobacco production, the newest technologies stood side by side with poor people working long hours at monotonous, often dangerous jobs. Radiating out from the factories were the boardinghouses, flophouses, storefronts, churches, and dives that supported the private lives of formerly rural people, mostly African American, who had been flocking to the factories for wage work since the late nineteenth century. To elite white eyes like Katharine's, this was an unfit world for human habitation, a place that Katharine and R.J.R. never let their children visit.

Katharine's Reynolda Estate marked her attempt at a model corrective. Here the miracles of industry and science only enhanced the lives and work of the people who made this aesthetically pleasing place their home, full of soothing pastoral scenes that brought out the best of human character. Reynolda was a tightly bound community of carefully ordered people who knew their responsibilities and performed them in exchange for good wages, creature comforts, and homage from their boss. In this world, everyone knew his or her literal and figurative place, everyone knew the expected social and racial etiquette, and everyone tacitly agreed to act it out. From Katharine's vantage point, Reynolda was an apolitical world. Yet the irony of the origins of this world she had made could not have been lost on her. Reynolda could never have existed without great wealth. R.J.R. had secured that wealth by harnessing tobacco's production and mastering mass marketing. In the end, he bankrolled Katharine's utopian dream with his dirty profits. In just six months alone, he wrote her a check for twenty thousand dollars, followed by another one for one hundred thousand at Christmas, to support her beloved estate.[45]

As Katharine's college conversation with college roommate Emma Speight made clear, she had already made up her mind to build an estate years before her marriage to R.J.R. After their wedding, she prioritized its building over the next thirteen years of their marriage, despite health challenges, five pregnancies, young children underfoot, the growing demands of the tobacco business, her increasing social obligations, her civic leadership, and at the end, R.J.R.'s prolonged illness and death. She purchased her first piece of rural property within her first year of marriage and here established her own farm north of town called Maplewood, despite the fact that R.J.R. already had his own farm east of Winston, Skyland. In fact, husband and wife would maintain a friendly competition, each claiming his or her own crop the best.[46] Correspondence in 1908 indicated something grander was in the works: a "country mansion."[47] Always a supportive partner, R.J.R. not only supplied the substantial funds necessary for realizing Katharine's vision but stayed up late at night to pour over plats and architectural plans with her over the next few years.[48] Katharine eventually cobbled together twenty-seven land purchases to form a contiguous property. Most often she bought property in her own name, but sometimes in R.J.R.'s name, and in a few cases, she had her father in Mount Airy make the purchases, in the hope that the locals would not connect them and jack up the prices. In most cases, the land was registered in her own name alone, a rare legal act for married women in this period.[49] She directed a retinue of experts from around the country as well as hundreds of workers in its design and construction. Located only three miles from downtown, the very naming of the property—Reynolda, a feminized version of the Reynolds family name—publicly carried Katharine's imprimatur. R.J.R. himself consistently referred to Reynolda as Katharine's farm.[50]

There may have been some fits and starts to Katharine's dream. As late as 1908, R.J.R. and Katharine had not determined that they would settle permanently in Winston, despite family conversations about a future mansion. That spring, R.J.R. had toured the countryside outside Baltimore with the president of Merchants National Bank to view "all the beautiful farms for sale." R.J.R. promised Katharine he would not buy one without her approval.[51] A year later, the two remained frustrated with local Winston farmers unwilling to sell the properties the couple sought. "Land owners are much excited now over the growth of this city & wont price their land," R.J.R wrote Katharine, knowing his own company's success had helped generate the boom.[52] But several days later, he wrote her that they would be able to purchase the Grays' 90-acre farm at one hundred dollars an acre, the adjoining George Hodge's 74-acre farm at fifty-four dollars an acre, and Nandings' "old Grise [*sic*] mill pound tract about 125 acres." They even hired Mr. Dunn from the Augusta Golf Course to look at the land; he declared it ideal for a course.[53]

Although R.J.R. bailed Katharine out when her funds grew low, she remained responsible for the finances of the estate and kept her own accounts. The property taxes were assessed to her, for example, and she paid them herself.[54] While running her household and building the Reynolda Estate, Katharine continued investing in the stock market; receiving dividends regularly; consulting with Dominick and Dominick, her brokerage firm; and growing her shares in Reynolds Tobacco, although she held many stocks in a number of other concerns too, including cotton mills. She constantly worked her numbers, covering her checkbook margins with fine-penned calculations on investment returns, interest, and dividends. Although she did not always balance her books precisely and willingly went into debt, she was keenly aware of how much things cost and juggled her funds accordingly. There can be no question that the costs of Reynolda kept her constantly preoccupied. It was fortunate that building Reynolda coincided with some very good years for the tobacco company.[55]

By 1908, the R. J. Reynolds Tobacco Company was in the act of freeing itself from Duke control and beginning to make significant profits. That Katharine and R.J.R. elected to make their permanent home and build a country estate in Winston-Salem was a significant choice. They could have afforded to live in established communities outside the older and bigger cities to the North. Their decision to remain in Winston was not lost on its citizenry, who believed it affirmed R.J.R.'s commitment to their welfare. "He lived his life here with his fellow townsmen," the city remembered some years later. "He made his nest with his own people."[56]

Heavily farmed for decades, Katharine's new land, like so much of the rural Piedmont, was comprised of thin pines and sorry soil. It suffered from overgrazing, overcultivating, underfertilizing, and antiquated farming methods. But no problem was too big for Katharine, whose imagination and pocketbook were both capacious. To remedy this situation, she hired the New York firm of H. H. Buckenham and L. Miller in 1910. Englishman Horatio Buckenham had already developed quite a name for himself by creating "a veritable fairyland" on James B. Duke's two-thousand-acre estate on the Raritan River in Somerville, New Jersey.[57] That Katharine employed Duke's own landscape firm is not surprising. Katharine and R.J.R. had visited Duke's estate on several occasions. They had toured many other country estates as well, from the extraordinary Biltmore Estate in nearby Asheville to the beautiful suburban properties that ringed New York, Philadelphia, and Baltimore.[58] At Reynolda, Buckenham and Miller's first charge in transforming the property into an attractive working farm was to restore the soil. They began their work by planting peas and, rather than harvesting them at season's end, plowed them back into the soil. Because the nodules within the legume roots generate nitrogen, the plowed-under plants' decomposition cycled the essential chemicals ammonium and nitrate back into the earth.[59]

The landscape architects also laid out the sites for a future residence, a formal garden, a golf course, a man-made lake, a church, and a working village. Frustrated with the slow transformation of her land, Katharine eventually replaced Miller, who had separated from Buckenham, with Thomas Sears, a talented, Harvard-educated landscape architect.[60] Although Buckenham and Miller's work was masterful, it would be Sears who would tease out the beauty of the landscape with his artist's imagination. He encouraged Katharine, for instance, to naturalize around her lake by planting sixty thousand daffodil bulbs. The results left visitors waxing poetic.[61]

Katharine hired Philadelphia architect Charles Barton Keen (1868–1931), well known for his attractive country estates on the Mainline and across the Delaware Valley, to plan and execute the grand design for the Reynolda buildings in 1912. Keen and Sears had collaborated on a number of estates in Philadelphia before coming to Winston. Their successful partnership at Reynolda led to the spread of commissioned Keen homes and Sears gardens in new suburban enclaves across the North Carolina Piedmont. Thanks to their success at Reynolda, the two would secure a whole coterie of newly wealthy southern clients who would keep them busy for the remainder of their careers.[62] Their introduction of national architectural and gardening movements to the region connected these newly affluent southerners to the wider country-house movement and a broader world of wealth and prestige. In fact, one of Katharine's village houses was showcased in an essay on the American country house in the *Architectural Record* in 1918 because of its exemplary representative architecture.[63]

Winston-Salem's wealthiest families followed Katharine's lead with a vengeance over the next twenty years. In 1921, brother-in-law Will and his wife, Kate Bitting Reynolds, bought a big piece of land west of town along the Yadkin River and built a sprawling but plain main house along with a working farm, including extensive horse facilities to accommodate their passion for racing. They called their new estate Tanglewood. Robert Lasater, a Reynolds relative and an R. J. Reynolds Tobacco Company executive, built Forest Hills Farm, designed by Keen, west of the city too and not far from Tanglewood. Constructed in 1928, the two-story, hipped-roofed, stone Georgian revival totaled some twelve thousand square feet and offered sweeping views down to the Yadkin River.[64] Nathalie Gray, wife of Bowman Gray Jr., began constructing their Norman revival home in 1928 just across the street from Reynolda on land the Reynoldses had sold them. During the depths of the Depression, her interior designers plucked European treasures like Louis XIV paneling from the Hotel d'Estrades in Paris and glass chandeliers from Venice to create an opulence hitherto unknown in this tobacco town.[65]

The first of its kind in Winston and its surrounds, Katharine's ambitious estate-building project provided a wonderful opportunity for Keen and Sears to showcase their talents and establish their local reputation. They were fortunate in that Katharine's commitment to Reynolda knew few bounds. Achieving the two-and-a-half-acre, man-made lake that the Buckenham and Miller plan called for necessitated excavation work by dozens of men and mules over many months, as did the engineering of a massive concrete-core earthen dam. The completed lake and dam became one of the aesthetic hallmarks of the estate. Framed by native stone with a double waterfall cascading down native rocks, the dam was spectacular despite the challenging and costly construction. While Buckenham and Miller designed the expansive landscape and established all the building sites, it was Sears who brought exceptional beauty to their master plan. He preserved existing trees wherever possible, introduced great numbers as well as great varieties of others, including many native species, and with a painter's eye used all these plantings to frame wonderful views and vistas across the estate.[66]

In the course of rebuilding the soil and implementing their designs, the landscapers made a surprising discovery. Katharine's property had at least one ample resource after all, and it was a critical one—pure artesian well water. Well builders discovered a set of springs and, upon digging in the vicinity, tapped a deep aquifer that produced forty thousand gallons of running water a day. In a society where pure water was a rarity, and tainted water the source of many horrific diseases—Katharine needed no reminding of this after the typhoid deaths at Normal—the artesian well ensured not only a plentiful water supply but an exceptionally healthful one. The subsequent installation of water service to the buildings throughout the estate as well as to the man-made water features, and even the placement of fire hydrants to prevent a disaster, marked an impressive technological bridge between nature's bounty and human need. Katharine, as usual, was deeply knowledgeable about the design of the system and worked closely with the contractors on the technical challenges they faced in executing it.[67]

Katharine's passion for developing this landscape knew few limits. She scoured her library—replete with time-honored gardening and landscape books like Gertrude Jekyll's *Color Schemes for the Garden*, A. J. Downing's *Landscape Gardening*, and Alice Lonsberry's *Southern Wild Flowers and Trees*—for inspiration. She was drawn to a wide array of aesthetic influences, appropriating classic styles from many periods and cultures and blending them into her landscape. Although her formal gardens were structured in a classical revival or Italianate style, plantings and fixtures within them showed a decidedly Asian influence and included long avenues of Japanese cherry trees and cryptomeria, along with five Japanese-style teahouses with black wooden tables. Her correspondence with her landscape architects conveys her involvement in the garden-making process as well as her ultimate decision making. The results were spectacular. Her palm house, with its flanking wings on either side of the palm room, built by Lord and Burnham Company of Philadelphia for $16,600 in 1913, evoked national botanical houses like Kew in London.[68] Beyond the formal gardens with their Italianate and Asian influences stretched the more functional cut-flower, vegetable, and fruit gardens, as well as a rose garden with some three hundred varieties.[69] Framed by thick white-columned pergolas, the garden was designed to echo the look of the residence at the crest of the hill.

This beautiful setting with its bollard lights and dramatic spaces evolved into a public area. The children at Katharine's Reynolda School staged plays and operettas here. Local organizations like the YWCA and the Red Cross held chrysanthemum benefit shows at the Palm House.[70] Strategically located alongside Bethania Road, the garden was designed to be accessible to visitors, albeit only white ones, without disturbing the work of the farm or the privacy of the family. Because the garden was intended to highlight blooming annuals and perennials throughout the warm-weather seasons, delighted guests found all manner of colorful blossoms, including asters, larkspurs, phlox, veronica, calendulas, anthus, and daylilies galore no matter what the date.

At the edge of the garden was a playhouse for Katharine and R.J.R.'s daughters. The interior contained scaled-down appointments and furnishings suitable for a real house, including a working fireplace, twin beds, even a dining room. Made to look like an English cottage, with overflowing window boxes and a rustic shake roof, the playhouse was a space where the girls could act out domesticity yet was so lovely and so removed from our notion of playhouses today that long-term guests in later generations often resided there.[71]

Although the landscape and gardens were critical to Katharine's vision for her estate, her church was especially important to her. Traditionally, village churches have always been the center of village life, the place where the entire community comes together across their differences to celebrate life and death and find solace in their earthly existence. Katharine saw her church as a place where local farm families could secure spiritual succor and religious education. She and several of her friends from the First Presbyterian Church had begun holding mission Sunday school services at the Wachovia Arbor School House just north of town and about a mile south of the estate with First Presbyterian pastor Neal Anderson's blessing in 1912.[72] Katharine intended to build a large enough congregation to create a membership for the church she was building on her own property. She visited the construction site frequently and often found herself negotiating between

Keen and Anderson on the form and function of the interior worship spaces. For Katharine, religion was about doing good works. She was no doctrinal Presbyterian. Her faith turned on gratitude to God as expressed through the love and care of others. The presence of this two-story chapel, with its transatlantic Arts and Crafts features fused with some traditional pre-Reformation English elements, along with its critical placement across the street but facing the farm village, visibly underscored Katharine's belief in the importance of fellowship and community.[73]

Katharine used her commitment to the Presbyterian Church to pursue social benevolence and moral improvement over intellectual engagement. Although her denominational identity was important to her, her spirituality took a distant backseat to her religious reform work. She was especially interested in using religion to cultivate moral values that could improve social relationships in the larger world. She was interested in both the home missionary movement and foreign missionary efforts. She kept in close touch with Junia Graves, who supervised missionaries in the nearby mountains of North Carolina and Virginia sent to convert the poor whites of Fancy Gap, Mack's Mountain, Pilot View, and Deep Water to the Presbyterian faith. Graves's letters were filled with descriptions of the "dangers" in these places, populated with moonshiners and "rough mountain people" who "cut" and "shot," but even more worrisome to her were the "hard-shell" Baptists.[74] Katharine also supported Presbyterian missionaries in Africa, like Robert R. King, who pursued evangelical work in the Congo.[75] Katharine's Presbyterianism allowed her an important outlet for doing good work as an elite southern woman that was socially sanctioned.

When Reynolda Presbyterian opened in 1914, it counted thirty-two members drawn from the vicinity, many of whom Katharine had tracked down herself, going door to door, farm to farm, to invite them to join. Katharine taught classes in the Sunday school, giving gold stars to children who memorized the catechism. Shortly after the building was completed, the congregation asked Katharine to build an outdoor auditorium, and she put Thomas Sears on the task. He created a sunken garden set against the west facade of the church with its stained-glass windows and gabled wings; it proved a perfect staging area for outdoor services and weddings.[76] The church itself, with its stuccoed walls and half timbers, was charming. Already well known for his country estates in the Philadelphia area, where he used designs that combined the English Arts and Crafts movement, the

French Beaux-Arts, and the architecture of colonial Pennsylvania farmhouses, Keen brought that same look to Reynolda and especially to Katharine's church, which stood facing Reynolda Village like a moral beacon.[77]

The village across from the church took some time to build because it incorporated a working farm as well as staff residences, offices, and services supporting critical functions for the main house. The village was comprised of several dozen structures, and the choice of building materials, mostly wood frame versus stucco with stone foundations, and the placement of the buildings—the barns were put on elevated sitings—signaled Katharine's priorities. The cottages for the various farm managers were made of stucco and much larger than those for the stenographer and the chauffeur.

All the residences (gardener's cottage, horticulturalist's cottage, farmhouse, dairyman's cottage, servants' cottage, chauffeur's cottage, superintendent's cottage, electrician's cottage) were equipped with electricity, indoor plumbing, hot and cold running water, steam heat, and telephone. The cattle and dairy barns, made of stucco and stone, dominated the entire village landscape.[78] The post office, flanked by the gardener's two-story house on one side and the Palm House on the other, stood directly across from Reynolda Presbyterian and operated as the village center. It had a common reading room with a fireplace "for the men of the Village."[79]

This warren of buildings was designed for function. Barn entrances opened to pens. Back walls acted as fences. Each building had a relationship to the structures around it. The buildings repeated the use of river stone in their foundations, the Arts and Crafts white stucco on their walls, and the signature green tile roofs of the chapel and surrounding homes. Keen duplicated this look in the family home, making his structures seem almost natural to this Piedmont landscape. Thus Keen's style ensured not only that the village appeared as a unified whole, a working community characterized by equanimity, but that the family bungalow fit the pastoral picture as well. His decision to use white stucco and green roof tile on the family residence as well as many of the village buildings tied the sprawling estate together. It made the property sparkle in its newness even as its architecture evoked older traditions. The gardens, village, and church, situated next to the busy Bethania Road, embodied the public face of Reynolda, while the family's bungalow embodied the private one.

To reach the family residence, one had to pass through an entrance framed by natural stone walls and an iron gate. Visitors followed a winding half-mile road that curved in and out of open woods and the rolling hills of the nine-hole golf course before forking. One path led to the bungalow entrance, the other to the two-and-a-half-mile drive around the lake.[80] The long, inviting bungalow made of reinforced concrete and rebar and covered with white stucco and green roof tile sported a low, colonnaded porch that blended the residence into the natural landscape of azaleas, dogwoods, cedars, and pines that flanked the wings and driveway. The upper level had shutters and awnings to keep out the sun but invite the ventilation of fresh air. In springtime the home and its surrounds dazzled with one set of blooms after another, daffodils, then dogwoods and azaleas, flowering laurels, and finally magnolias. Inviting porches, multiple entrances, Italianate cedars, terraces, lily pools, fountains, and lighted paths encouraged romantic strolls at all hours of the day and night and blended indoors and outdoors. When the main residence was finished, a fait accompli that earned headline status on the front page of the *Winston-Salem Journal* alongside "Russians Cut Off from Railway Communications," Katharine's friend nicknamed it "The Palace Bungalow."[81] Stretched out long and low on a hilltop above the man-made lake, the home struck upper-crust visitors as both modern and modest.

Katharine's decision to borrow the landscape and architecture of the English village was a potent one. The English village remains fixed in the Anglo-American imagination as a good place with good people where nothing ever changes. It is a refuge and a dream where a church and cottages stand clustered together, with the manor house set on a pastoral landscape not too far distant. This picturesque scene strikes the viewer as time honored and natural, belying the strong human hand shaping it. Yet almost all English villages have been the creation of a landlord of some sort, one who could choose to bestow benevolence or act out of greed, but regardless created relationships of dependency among the villagers, despite the powerful imagery of self-sufficiency that the village exudes.[82]

Katharine balanced this potent imagery with exacting attention to functional details. Throughout the estate-building process, she communicated religiously in person and in letters with Miller, Keen, and Sears, conveying her intimate familiarity with each and every project under way at Reynolda, from determining the best source of stone for the barn foundations to requesting a "toilet room" for the children to getting her brother-in-law's advice on the size of horse stalls. She also made sure that design efficiencies were consistently incorporated. "The coal certainly should be chuted from wagon into coal vault. The ice should be moved directly on platform in front of [the] refrigerator," she wrote Charles Barton Keen.[83] Her involvement in the construction of Reynolda meant that she often acted like a general contractor. She had commenced the building phase of her estate fairly quickly, hiring local architect Willard C. Northrup to erect the first cottages in her English-style country village even before asking Keen to take on the bigger projects: church, bungalow, main village buildings, and barns. She hired Wiley and Wilson, consulting engineers from Lynchburg, to install certain engineering features on the estate including the refrigeration systems, demanding that Keen and Wiley and Wilson cooperate fully with each other under her guidance.[84]

Katharine was meticulous about all the details associated with her estate, and she was demanding. She articulated her expectations, gave deadlines, and wanted them honored. She was so intent on ensuring her golf tees met *American Golfer* standards that she walked the property herself to check. She instructed her golf-course designer not to have "a single weed standing on the entire course by springtime."[85] Golf was a surprisingly integral part of the Reynoldses' lives. R.J.R. taught his son Dick to play on the nine-hole course long before the family actually lived on the estate. Katharine played on a ladies' team of four.[86]

Katharine employed contractors by the dozen, bringing them from Lynchburg, Philadelphia, New York, and Boston. The contractors in turn hired hundreds of local workers. She charged the contractors with ensuring that all the mechanical and artisanal work be superb. An architect's assistant recalled that the quality of the work performed by these men was quite high as a result. "Everything was done 100% correctly by good mechanics. There wasn't a poor mechanic on the job."[87] Many of these hired workers not only learned to read blueprints for the first time but subsequently used their experience at Reynolda to go into business as tradesmen for themselves.[88] The work they performed was not easy and was often dangerous. Mechanic William B. Fulcher suffered a terrible injury from a steam-powered rock crusher. Katharine took responsibility for him after the fact and gave him a permanent job as a night watchman.[89]

Although she tried to be fair, Katharine was not only a vigilant boss but also a tough customer. Her letters to the companies and stores that provided her goods and services suggest her tendency toward imperiousness. She excoriated Philadelphia interior designer L. D. Wilkinson for laundering her curtains at an inflated rate and hemming them without being asked. "I cannot but believe a mistake has been made," she concluded. To Messrs. P. D. Schmidt and Company of Baltimore, she penned, "I write to let you know that I would not care for the wicker Governor's Cart, having found a new one cheaper than the one you offer me."[90] She even attacked the Southern Bell Telephone and Telegraph Company for failing to provide first-class telephone service to Reynolda, reminding the company that a contract with her promised "as large a revenue as many of the big business houses, and considerably larger than any other private house in this community." Katharine advised, "From my standpoint it looks like very poor business on the part of the Southern Bell Telephone Co. not to complete this job at once, and be drawing the money on work in which they already have considerable funds tied up."[91]

Katharine incorporated the management of the estate construction into her everyday life. She knew the details of each building inside and out, including all the materials, their quantities, and costs. The whole family picnicked on the grounds frequently so that Katharine could monitor what was being accomplished. Her excitement about building the estate was manifested by her willingness to hike out to the property with her "walking club" friends at 10:00 a.m. each day. At the farm, the young women played like children, wading in the stream, climbing trees, competing at mumble peg, and lounging about in the grass until, as Katharine wrote a friend, "the automobile comes out and brings us back."[92] Photographs of Katharine alone or in groups show her standing in front of buildings under construction and frolicking on the half-finished landscapes. Reynolda was Katharine's enterprise through and through. She went to great lengths to manage its construction and ensure it lived up to her imaginings.

Katharine had an ability to make things happen thanks to her energy and drive backed up by her husband's name and fortune. Buckboard wagons pulled by mule teams and Conestogas pulled by oxen and horses rumbled up and down Bethania Road, making huge dust clouds during dry spells and bottomless mud holes in the wet season. Visiting the estate by car was difficult, and the prospect of asking guests to endure these challenges, let alone the family handling them on a daily basis, demanded action as far as Katharine was concerned. Deciding it was high time that the road to the country estate of one of the leading southern industrialists was paved, she cut a deal with the North Carolina State Highway Department in 1916. She would pay the state ten thousand dollars and supply the paving materials. In return, the state would supply the convict labor and the supervision to construct a hard-surface road from Summit Street to Silas Creek, just beyond the entrance to her new home, village, and church. Katharine's commandeering of the state's resources and the private use of convict labor were nothing new in southern society. It does speak, however, not only to Katharine's problem-solving skills but also to her implicit comfort with the political maneuverings of this time and place, regardless of her gender.[93]

Elizabeth Wade, one of Katharine's domestic servants, described Katharine's tenacity on the paving matter in a different way: "Miss Katharine—she kept crying and begging, and she got it [paved]."[94] This interpretation suggests it was easy even for people who knew Katharine well to reduce her to a spoiled rich girl rather than a clever woman with enough resources to solve major challenges. This offhand comment may also underscore why Katharine worked so hard at controlling her world and mastering all its details. She resented assumptions that she resorted to southern-belle manipulations to get her way. Few women had access to the kind of power—let alone exercised it—that Katharine wielded with aplomb on any given day. She wanted to be respected for her abilities, not caricatured.

Reynolda was a place of pleasure and spectacle. The building of the bungalow had been slowed by World War I, when labor and materials were scarce, but the family finally moved in over the winter of 1917–18. Even before this date, though, the family had made the estate its own, camping out near the springs, boating and fishing on the lake, and playing golf. In 1916, R.J.R. held a Fourth of July celebration at Lake Katharine for all his salesmen and their wives from as far west as the Mississippi River. His guests dined on Reynolda garden produce and barbecued Reynolda hogs. The children camped out near the springs even before the bungalow was complete, all dressed up in Indian headdresses.[95] Katharine staged *Hiawatha*, the Indian passion play based on Henry Wadsworth Longfellow's poem, as a pageant on the bank of the lake, complete with teepees and dozens of children dressed as Indians, framed by Reynolda electrician Robert Gibson's theatrical lighting. Daughter Mary played Minnehaha while Bowman Gray Jr. played Hiawatha, allegedly to a local audience of five thousand. Acts were separated by dance intermissions in which pretty little girls danced as graceful wind phantoms, while less comely ones clad in burlap flicked their flashlights off and on from behind the shrubs.[96]

Reynolda also functioned as a model working farm. Katharine blended the traditional functions of the estate as a wealthy family residence with new ideas about progressive farming in a region of the South undergoing rapid industrialization.[97] She understood that most farmers in Forsyth County and its surrounds in the early twentieth century farmed tobacco on every square inch of their land. This overreliance on a cash crop meant that the county produced only a quarter of the food it consumed. The poorest families survived on little more than cornmeal, molasses, and pork. Observed one rural economist: "While your city flourishes, your farm regions languish."[98] Winston-Salem's success as a rising industrial city seemed to come at the cost of the county's welfare.

Katharine understood the challenges poor country people faced and especially those of rural women, for she received numerous heart-wrenching requests for help from them. "My husband has been in bad health for two years . . . so not able to help much," wrote Mrs. Richard Anderson.[99] Mrs. Mary B. Harrell from Ararat, Virginia, began her letter to Katharine, "Dear and Honered Lady," before describing her terrible straits: her home and all her property burned up in a recent fire, "a sickly husband," six children too young to work, and total incapacitation after the sudden death of their only horse:

> God knows how we will live but I don't know I am left pore [*sic*] without any dollar knowing that you are a very kind lady and very welthy [*sic*] I most humbly pray that you will help me some so I can buy some sort of cheap horse so I can have something to work to keep our little children from suffering winter is at hand and clothes to buy for eight in family no money nothing to hall [*sic*] logs to build some sort of house to keep my children from freezing . . . in hope the good People will help me some so with hard work I can care for my poor misfortunate family.[100]

Mrs. Lola James of Farmington appealed to Katharine: "Although a stranger to you I have heard many times what a good Lady you are to the poor. . . . I am writing to ask if you can help me and my children some." Mrs. James had eight children, seven living with her, and a sickly husband. Her oldest son had dropped out of school to cut wood with his father to support the family. "It is an awful thing to beg, and my people would be horrified," she added, requesting the dignity of anonymity.[101] Mrs. Willie Sugg of Goldsboro told Katharine that she had three young children and had been widowed for twelve long years; her husband had died of typhoid. She explained that if Katharine did not help her, she had no recourse but to put the children in an orphanage to ensure they received an education and grew up good Christians.[102] Lula Boyette of Warsaw penciled Katharine a note asking for work and clothes. "I am all most necked for under clothes & top ones too & I could work in your husband's tobacco factory making bags for smoking tobacco, or any think that would give my little boy and myself a few clothes, enough to keep from bein[g] hungry."[103] There is no record of how Katharine responded to these requests.

Given these appeals, it is no wonder that Katharine molded Reynolda Estate into a kind of progressive response to the human costs of rural poverty. Creating a "modern estate" that incorporated scientific farming and the latest technologies meant Reynolda could be a model for working farm families. Yet she never explored how to translate the shining example of her own working farm, with its educated management and wage-earning workers, into a model that poor farmers with no education and no resources could emulate.

This problem notwithstanding, as early as 1912 Katharine began seeking the expertise of state and federal government agencies for this purpose. She read the *Progressive Farmer* religiously. She tutored herself in the latest trade literature by subscribing to magazines like the *Breeder's Gazette*, *Horticulture*, *Fruit Grower*, *Country Gentlemen*, and *Country Life in America*.[104] Katharine's reform vision included making Reynolda Farm profitable; therefore, she marketed her crops and livestock. In 1911, she was selling her wheat for ninety-five cents a bushel. She cultivated orchards and vineyards in addition to grains.[105] Her lake was well stocked with little-mouth black bass.[106] Katharine had even consulted with the Bureau of Fisheries at the Department of Commerce on how to use aquatic vegetation to propagate spawning grounds for her fish and breeding grounds for their fry, as well as how to reduce mosquito infestation.[107] Her livestock program represented an important component of her farm practice too. By 1917, Katharine counted 11 horses and 1 colt, 60 head of cattle, 52 hogs, 121 sheep, and 95 lambs in her barns and pastures.[108]

Katharine frequently rode around the farm on horseback with Clint Wharton, the farm manager, to keep abreast of the crops and livestock. She was a talented equestrian, and her white horse, Kentucky Belle, was the most spirited in the barn.[109] In addition to the family's riding horses, she also kept five teams of Percherons—"huge big-hipped things"—considered by some to be the finest draft horses in the South. These animals worked their hearts out, plowing fields and hauling grains, hay, and rocks.[110] Both Katharine and R.J.R. were committed to building one of the best dairy herds in the region as well. Katharine had always been concerned about providing her family with the purest possible milk. R.J.R., who had met candy industrialist Milton Hershey in 1911, told Katharine "how clean and pure [Hershey's] candy was." He attributed this quality to Hershey's use of his own carefully bred cows.[111] By 1916, the Reynoldses had settled upon Jerseys as their breed of choice; they researched bloodlines and purchased the best exemplars of the breed.[112]

They were clearly influenced by their friend F. W. Ayer too, the self-made millionaire advertiser whose famous company R. J. Reynolds Company had hired to develop the enormously successful Prince Albert and Camel campaigns. A genius at advertising, Ayer indulged his true passion in his Meridale Farms Dairy. Enamored with the pastoral beauty of Delaware County, New York, Ayer had purchased farmland in 1888 and in short order turned his hobby into a million-dollar business, producing award-winning Jersey cattle and large quantities of outstanding butter and milk. Correspondence between Katharine and F. W. indicates that he provided them with top Meridale Jerseys, including a "herd leader." Ayer observed of Katharine's commitment, "You must be building a very fine herd." And indeed, Katharine and R.J.R. were, intentionally introducing the best pedigreed Jersey bulls in the region in response to appeals from agricultural associations to upgrade livestock in the South. The couple secured top stock not only from Meridale but also from a famous dispersal sale at Elmendorf in Lexington, Kentucky, to round out their herd.[113]

The Reynoldses also bred and raised hogs. In 1916, R.J.R. wistfully remarked to his farm manager that he would love to breed hogs "with meat as sweet as that of the long-nosed 'piney woods rooters.'" D. J. Lybrook did his homework and introduced to Reynolda a breed of hog known as the Tamworth, descended from Irish rooters, and known for their lean meat, thriftiness, large litters, and robust health. R.J.R. subsequently drilled friends and visitors to the estate on the merits of Tamworths. Gabriella Hart Dula, wife of Duke executive R. B. Dula, confided to Katharine in a letter after experiencing one of R.J.R.'s tutorials firsthand, "I was able to write most astutely to Mr. R. B. Dula about them [Tamworths], who I am sure was greatly impressed with my knowledge of this 'streak of lean and streak of fat' variety."[114] The Reynolds children recalled only the fun of the annual fall slaughter because they were given the hog bladders to blow up like balloons.[115]

Katharine had introduced sheep on her farm early on, and by 1916 her flock of purebred Shropshires numbered more than two hundred. Not only did they provide lambs and wool, but their year-round grazing kept the golf course greens closely cropped.[116] Katharine never realized her ambitions on the poultry front. She had intended on selling guinea hens to hotels in what would have been one of the biggest poultry-raising businesses attempted in the region. But World War I foiled her efforts. She was left raising white Leghorns to lay and Plymouth Rocks to broil instead. An admiring lawyer interested in establishing a much more modest chicken yard sought her advice, stating, "I know that you have gone into the matter with that thoroughness that characterizes all that you do or undertake." She explained her failed project and advised him to take up Leghorns and Plymouth Rocks as a more practical direction too.[117]

Besides her commitment to researching the best breeds and breeding the best animals, Katharine was also committed to practicing the highest methods of sanitation and hygiene known to the farm business. Ensuring the good health of her family remained a serious obligation for Katharine throughout her life. She had cared for her ill parents throughout her college years, and she and her children suffered multiple illnesses themselves. She had watched her mother grow thin and frail with tuberculosis, a disease that plagued the early twentieth-century South, attacked all classes, and ran rampant in the factories downtown, leading to the city's construction of a "pest house" for impoverished victims of the awful disease. Katharine understood that clean streets, clean air, clean water, and timely waste removal provided a powerful arsenal against infectious germs, but these weapons against disease were difficult to ensure in urban environments. National experts and their popular literature increasingly argued that suburbia offered the safest of all havens from disease.

Katharine made Reynolda a haven from contamination and disease as a result. Her incorporation of state-of-the-art technology and exemplary hygiene in her cow barn and milk room offer a case in point. Dairymen wore uniforms and had wiping cloths, both laundered daily in the laundry intentionally situated next door to the milk-processing barn. The cows were tested for tuberculosis twice a year, and Katharine's cow barn was one of the first to install experimental automatic milking machines. She even added an electric refrigerator plant to keep the milk cooled at a consistently safe temperature. Her commitment to hygiene knew few bounds. She kept the silo at Reynolda filled to the brim with corn stalks, legumes, and molasses, ensuring the absence of air circulation and heat to prevent bacteria and produce desirable moist silage at the bottom. She provided a public fountain at the Reynolda Village entrance to Bethania Road where passersby could refresh themselves and water their animals with pure water from her artesian well without fear of contagion. Together with open spaces to walk and ride and sleeping porches in her bungalow to secure fresh air, Katharine incorporated all the modern practices she could think of to keep everyone around her healthy and well.[118]

Katharine's commitment to science was not limited to hygiene. The son of Reynolda dairyman T. G. Monroe remembered that his father relished working for the Reynoldses because he could always persuade them to provide the most up-to-date resources for his charges. Monroe would call his former teachers from North Carolina State University, who then traveled to Reynolda to give him advice. Their recommendation that the barn be constructed to incorporate stanchions, a brand-new practice in the region, to assist in the efficient milking of the cows was adopted, making the Reynolda cow barn one of the first in the state to do so.[119] "The farm is flourishing now. I am acting Superintendent, and good management is beginning to tell," Katharine told a friend on November 10, 1912, following the dismissal of former manager R. E. Snowden, who could not keep his books accurately enough to please Katharine.[120] She replaced him with Clint Wharton and charged him with introducing the new agricultural methods of crop rotation and soil analysis to the estate as well as to the surrounding farmers. It was her desire to engage more "educated farmers" to cultivate the property.[121] Mary Martha Lybrook, Katharine's niece, marveled at her aunt's aptitude for this work. Katharine could sit down with farm superintendent Clint Wharton and talk about sheep husbandry or any other agriculture topic he broached. She felt Katharine "really had her finger on the running of the farm."[122] Katharine was committed to providing the best, and she expected the best in return.

Katharine probably first learned about progressive farming from Lucy Bramlette Patterson, the first president of the NCFWC. Patterson began writing articles for the *Progressive Farmer* a year later in 1904. It was undoubtedly Lucy who introduced Katharine and R.J.R. to Clarence Poe (1881–1964), the editor of the *Progressive Farmer*. Katharine became an inveterate subscriber to the *Progressive Farmer* thereafter.[123] Through her commitments to model farm practices, Katharine had introduced a progressive model of "land use" management to the surrounding Piedmont.[124] In the course of building Reynolda, she came to recognize the impact her application of scientific agriculture on the land could make on the larger community. By 1917, she believed that her estate was "becoming the experiment station to which students of agriculture, domestic science, dairying, livestock raising, etc. look[ed] for reliable and authentic information on farm problems." The public agreed, "Reynolda is destined to become one of the great factors in the development of rural life . . . [in] the entire Piedmont section of North Carolina. It is already the model of progressive farmers and their families throughout this section of the state, and many have made the trip from distant states for the sole purpose of looking over the splendid development and to study its methods."[125]

Katharine relied on expert help from government agencies, agricultural departments at colleges and universities, and nationally respected professionals, not to help her lead a local movement in radical agricultural reform, but to build a magnificent estate and a state-of-the-art farming business. But because she believed in the cult of the expert, because she wanted and could afford the best, and because she respected scientific methods as a college-educated woman, she discovered in the act of creating Reynolda that her estate could have a larger purpose too.

The nationwide mobilization of support for World War I was the real catalyst that moved Katharine to broadcast her Reynolda enterprise as an exemplar of progressive farming. Because she had embraced modern science at every turn to improve the fertility of her soil, grow her own fruits and vegetables, provide the purest dairy products possible for her family, and raise the best sheep, poultry, hogs, and cattle in the region, she had begun to grasp that her endeavor might have an even broader reach with a deeper meaning than the market. It was at this point that she "consented that a series of demonstrations [should] be conducted on her estate" for farmers and their wives. These 1917 demonstrations included how to use modern dairy equipment, and especially the steam sterilizing machine, to assist in canning. In the midst of the current food emergency, Katharine believed it was imperative to "be engaged in food production and food conservation." She intended Reynolda to put up thousands of cans of fruits and vegetables from the estate, and to do the same for families on adjoining farms. She was to be assisted in this endeavor by Ida Long, one of the directors of the canning clubs in the county department of farm demonstration, who would be assisted in turn by Lizzie Roddick, Forsyth County director of economics and domestic science. Katharine expected they would produce five thousand one-gallon cans of soup stock, six thousand cans of vegetables, and one thousand bottles of grape juice. The canning was to have been done according to government regulations, and the government was to have right of first refusal in case the foodstuffs were needed for army supplies. "If the government does not require any of it," Katharine added, "it will be disposed of to local industrial lunch rooms, hotels, or cafes. . . . There will be a large market for home-canned goods here this winter, and there is no danger of 'flooding the market.'"[126] Unfortunately, just as harvest season hit, R.J.R. became deathly ill, and the grand experiment was halted as Katharine relocated to Baltimore to be near her husband for his protracted stay in the Johns Hopkins Hospital.

Katharine's development of Reynolda, including its evolution into a model farm, mirrored almost to a fault the philosophy of the Woman's National Farm and Garden Association. Its membership was comprised of three categories of women: amateur gardeners and farmers; professional and commercial gardeners and farmers; and "altruistic and sociological" gardeners and farmers. Just as the Woman's National Farm and Garden Association increasingly linked itself to the patriotic cause, as exemplified by the statement, "Today our work in orchard, farm and garden is a vital necessity and now more than ever to win the war we must work and give," so too did Katharine. "We are helping women find a new vocation," proclaimed the association. Katharine was one of those women the association helped.[127] Throughout the war era, national publications urged women to recognize their responsibility as patriotic citizens by pursuing agricultural work. They pointed to the sterling example of women in Europe filling in for the male agricultural workers who had left for war. The presidents of the Garden Club urged club leaders across the country to work with the Boy Scouts and the Girl Scouts to train them in garden work. They urged women to secure help from the farm bureaus and state employment bureaus, state colleges of agriculture, women's colleges and alumnae associations, the Woman's National Farm and Garden Association, the YWCA, Women's Clubs, the National Women's Farm Laborers Association, and many other agencies. Katharine was familiar with the local branches of virtually all these organizations. Farming as war work gave her a new net in which to collect her disparate identities as club woman, reformer, farmer, and industrialist's wife together.[128]

In July 1918, the chairman of the national membership committee of the Woman's National Farm and Garden Association invited Katharine to act as subchairman of the membership committee for North Carolina.[129] That same month, the president of the association, Louisa G. Davis of Ambler, Pennsylvania, announced at the annual meeting that membership had tripled in the last year in response to the war effort. "We gave our best energies for our Allies and our country then. No group of women in the country showed a larger, more devoted patriotism than our membership." Canning food, helping their communities, and working on behalf of the Land Army of America all fostered a dramatic increase in the number of women seeking an education in agriculture and horticulture. The association believed this gave its members a special mission to pursue "with all earnestness and speed."[130] The association was committed not only to building its membership but to "creat[ing] a body of public opinion in regard to the unity of interest between the city and the country." Anticipating renewed national interest in agriculture, the association believed itself well poised to have "a valuable part to play in the reconstruction work."[131] The association continued to seek Katharine's leadership, even asking her to represent it at the Southern Congress for a League of Nations in Atlanta, February 25–March 3, 1919.[132] Seven regional congresses had been planned across the United States over the winter of 1919 to "stimulate and consolidate American public opinion behind the League of Nations project now taking shape in Paris," as an article in the journal *Outlook* explained.[133] This invitation from the association spoke to the national respect Katharine had earned for her exemplary work as a woman agricultural reformer.

Katharine's many ambitions could never have been realized without abundant help. She employed dozens of people to aid her in running all aspects of her estate, including farmhands, artisans, mechanics, farm managers, and household servants. It was a community, according to retired employee Harvey Miller, where "everyone knew everyone."[134] Farm workers gathered at the horses' watering trough on weekday mornings to receive their orders for the day and on Saturdays to collect their pay.[135] Word spread quickly that good wages could be had here, drawing rural wage laborers and tenant farmers from miles around, many of whom were African American. Ellis Pledger willingly walked twenty miles round-trip each day for nine dollars a week, three times his normal rate, to work at Reynolda. Eventually Ellis gave up the lengthy foot commute and moved with his wife, Flora, to the estate.

By 1915, Katharine was setting aside a special community for her black farmhands. Called Five Row, it was "the best place," declared Flora Pledger, that she had ever seen.[136] Five Row stood at the far end of the estate and a quarter-mile walk from the village. Black farm workers left their jobs at the end of the day and headed northwest, not past the greenhouse and gardens or down the driveway of the bungalow to get to Bethania Road and on to town by jitney, the way most workers left Reynolda, but past the heating plant and its companion piles of coal at the edge of the village, hidden from the bungalow's view, and down a dirt road past the quarry, a yawning pit with jagged stone walls. Right before hands lit explosives to crack open the granite, a piercing whistle warned people to run inside to escape flying rock debris.

In short, Five Row was situated in the least attractive quarter of the estate, but Katharine worked assiduously to improve it. The black community encompassed two lines of a dozen or so modest cabins and a tiny church near Silas Creek.[137] Five Row houses had front porches and privet hedges. Katharine held contests for the prettiest flower gardens and provided plants and flowers to help residents beautify their yards and houses. Inhabitants had artesian well water piped into a single community tap, but none of the modern amenities of Reynolda Village residents. Instead, Five Row residents made do with outhouses and lanterns. Each spring and fall, the farm superintendent plowed up plots for residents and provided seeds. Five Row families used their plots to grow vegetables. They also raised their own livestock, poultry, hogs, and the occasional milk cow, although the superintendent supplied milk and vegetables at wholesale cost to residents.[138]

By the Depression era, former Five Row residents recalled Katharine's interest in them with apparent fondness, not least because residents hoped that the impending arrival of Katharine and R.J.R.'s daughter Mary and her husband, Charles Babcock, would augur better times for them. In a curious document titled "The Negro and Reynolda: A Pictorial Survey of the Negroes, Their Community Activity and Their Daily Work on the Reynolda Estate," the anonymous author(s) noted that Katharine had increased their wages with some regularity and always gave generous Christmas presents: knives for the men, baskets of fruit, and in some years, cash. The author(s) also noted, "Married women were bountifully rewarded for every child born to the family. This we know tended to recruit the building force on the estate."[139]

Five Row was its own community village to its residents, to Katharine, and beyond. Former residents like Rosalie Miller and Flora Pledger recalled that everyone in the Winston community knew Five Row.[140] Five Row men worked hard at Reynolda. Their first jobs required the backbreaking toil of constructing the enormous man-made lake, then "the Big House" and the village buildings, the roads, and finally the white and black laborers' homes. Wives of Five Row workers took part-time jobs on the estate, usually work that did not necessitate specific sets of skills, but mostly they raised their children and ran their households. Teenage sons took a succession of odd jobs around the estate, from washing cars to hauling wood to babysitting to caddying for golfers. Harvey Miller learned how to play golf by caddying for R.J.R. and family guests. He was eventually hired by Mary Babcock, Katharine and R.J.R.'s daughter, after their deaths, to work as a butler in the bungalow.[141]

In 1918, Katharine opened two schools on the Reynolda Estate, one for white children and one for black children. The Five Row School, as it was called, was situated in the Five Row chapel. It had two classrooms. The Reynolda School for the white children was in the village. Katharine supplied both schools with the same desks, same supplies, and same books on history, geography, spelling, grammar, and math. Both sets of students took classes in art and music. The Five Row School had a piano and an organ. All the students were expected to memorize Lincoln's Gettysburg Address, and they read Washington Irving's *Rip Van Winkle*.[142] The Five Row School held classes for eight months out of the year and operated for twenty years, much longer than the white school, because Katharine committed in 1919 to supporting a new, state-of-the-art public high school for white children in town. The black children's school yard held an outhouse, a volleyball net, horseshoe pitching targets, and basketball and croquet courts, and was bordered all around by hedges.[143] The Five Row School shared the same janitor with the white school, and the children all played together "because there wasn't nobody else to play with," according to Five Row student Harvey Miller. On cold, rainy days, Katharine sent hot soup to all the children, black and white.[144]

Physical space on the Reynolda Estate was usually segregated by race, work assignment, or both. Residents at Five Row were black wage workers who lived in family groups in the northwest quadrant of the property, their homes and community literally out of sight of the bungalow and the village. This arrangement was reminiscent of the Low Country plantations of the eighteenth and nineteenth centuries, where slave quarters were purposely put some distance from the master's house. Employees housed in the cottages in the village were usually but not always male and white, often lived with their families too, and were in charge of the many different operations of the estate. Not only was the village physically evocative of an English country parish; its social structure was too. Here middling white men and their families represented multiple skilled trades and occupations—horticultural, engineering, landscaping, farming, breeding, blacksmithing, electrician. In exchange for managing their respective duties, they and their families had the run of the estate; their children recalled bucolic days riding horses, canoeing on the lake, swimming in the pool, and playing tennis. Five Row children, while appreciative of the relative comfort in which they lived and the opportunities they gained, remember their access to the estate beyond Five Row as one shaped by the odd jobs they were asked to perform in unfamiliar locations, rather than the physical freedom they were given to explore the wonders of Reynolda. Young Harvey Miller, for example, dated the undertaker's daughter and liked to take her boating on Silas Creek, not on Lake Katharine, and well beyond the gaze of the bungalow and village residents.[145] While the gardens of Reynolda were open to public viewing, it was understood in the unwritten racial etiquette of the time that touring the grounds was for whites only.[146]

Families that lived in Five Row had little contact with the African American servants who worked in the bungalow and sometimes lived in the village. While Five Row residents had formal contact with their employers, they had little informal contact with the white families in either the bungalow or the village. Once the Reynolda School was opened in 1918, single white teachers lived in the village as well, but all together in one place—the

Manse—on the west side of the street. Like the male employees and their families in the village, they too had open access to the Reynolda grounds and even the bungalow, for Katharine invited them to dinner and rolled up the carpets and held dances for them in her enormous living room. Katharine was generous to all her employees whatever their color and station, and their living conditions were exceptional by the standards of the day, but she rigidly observed conventional boundaries of race and class. At Reynolda, just as in the larger society, one's skin color, gender, and social rank, and not just aptitude and ambition, were the chief determinants of occupation and status.

This reality was as true in Katharine's bungalow as it was on the farm. Her new home was impressive. Guests entered the nearly two-hundred-feet-long home through a tiled porte-cochere at its center and passed through French doors directly into the two-story reception hall, the centerpiece of the house. Surrounded by a cantilevered gallery, with a large marble fireplace as focal point flanked by curving staircases on either side, the huge room invited music and dancing. To ensure that music was an integral component of life at Reynolda, Katharine made the lavish purchase of an Aeolian organ for thirty thousand dollars. In making this purchase, she was signaling not only a desire for plentiful music in her home but her family's wealth too. Aeolian owners overwhelmingly included the newly affluent business families across the United States, such as the Carnegies, the Rockefellers, the Du Ponts, the Pulitzers, the Fricks, the Woolworths, and the Fords.[147]

Katharine filled her new home with fashionable furniture, lighting, and draperies. W. & J. Sloane of New York sent her an estimate for new furnishings for virtually the entire forty-room house totaling over forty-five thousand dollars.[148] Such a home needed great care and attention and was designed with the assumption that a staff of servants would assist the lady of the house in maintaining it.

But like many college-educated women of her generation, Katharine preferred bigger challenges than handling domestic duties.[149] Although she took social expectations about her responsibility for housekeeping seriously, she hired plentiful servants, directed their efforts, and purchased the latest appliances and technologies to make housekeeping more efficient, all of which freed her to pursue the larger work of the estate, the tobacco company, and social reform.

Everyone knew Katharine made the busy world of Reynolda work by being a tough taskmaster. People understood that she was a strong woman, very much in command, with a clear head for work. Aurelia Spaugh, a friend of the Reynolds children, captured Katharine's character well: "She was attractive, and there was a warmth to her. But if you were told something, like don't pick the daffodils—I mean, there were rules, and you abided by them, because we knew she wouldn't like [anything otherwise]. She was smart. You had the feeling she was very knowledgeable, had a keen mind. She was a good business person." Domestic servant Elizabeth Wade expressed similar thoughts: "She was stern, and if she wanted something she'd get it . . . and she did her [own] hiring and firing."[150] Her nurse Henrietta Van Den Berg tellingly wrote Katharine during one of her prolonged absences from the estate: "It seems to me there are too many bosses around here at present; nothing to worry about, however, and you can easily straighten things out when you come home."[151]

Katharine employed African American servants in her home at a time when many in the North and the South publicly conveyed their dissatisfaction with black domestics. Too many "New Negroes," complained these white critics, had willingly migrated to the biggest cities to take up industrial work, and those men and women who remained not only proved unreliable but acted with impudence. Casting such aspersions on the character of all black workers was an easy way to justify white anger and racism. Blacks' alleged failings became the subject of an impassioned diatribe by Robert Watson Winston, president of the Durham, North Carolina, chamber of commerce, who sought to explain why "the average Southern negro ha[d] lost to a certain extent his Southern white friend." The southern "white friend" most hurt by and least forgiving of this behavior, Winston insisted, was the white woman who employed black servants in her home. "The inefficiency of the negro makes the burden of the Southern white woman a thousand fold heavier than that of her husband. The servant question is the nightmare of the Southern home, and you will never begin to settle the negro problem until you settle this question of farm labor and domestic service."[152]

Katharine never expressed any such dissatisfaction with her servants. Stern and demanding with all her employees, regardless of skin color, she had clear expectations about what constituted excellent work. She assumed all her employees would meet them, whether they were well-educated professionals like her architect, her white and black domestic servants, or her poor black farmhands. Katharine did not necessarily mimic the social, gendered, and racial hierarchy of work that wealthy whites in the North and the South observed in this era. She respected education enormously, preferring to hire professional white men, ideally with college educations, to help her design, build, and maintain her estate and gardens. She also appointed well-qualified white men, some with higher education, as farm managers, livestock breeders, and engineers to ensure the smooth running of her farm, village, and household. She could be tough with these men, especially when making arrangements for their hiring. Although she was keen on employing W. P. Mahan, who had extensive experience in general farming and worked at R. W. Johnson's Greenhouses at Belleview Farm in New Brunswick, New Jersey, she struck a hard bargain, letting him know, "It is not customary here [in North Carolina] to furnish fuel, light, milk and vegetables, as mentioned in your letter; however, we will agree to furnish you with milk and vegetables, that you may grow on the farm and have on hand, for your own use. We will furnish a heater for the cottage, but you will have to provide your own fuel."[153]

She almost always employed white women as her children's nurses and governesses. Although male domestic help was always black, her female domestic help was black and white. The African American domestics she hired in the house were often educated and light skinned. She reserved farm work and manual labor in general for white and black male hands, but especially for the latter. She employed black women in her laundry in the village and part-time at dirty jobs, such as rendering lard after hog killings. Some of the house servants lived in a servant cottage, but most traveled from the city to Reynolda and back, taking a streetcar for a nickel to the downtown post office, and then a jitney that Katharine provided to the post office at Reynolda, and vice versa at day's end.[154]

For the Reynolds family members and the many relatives who visited them, the home was an open and welcoming place (although Katharine did consider her bedroom and her study sacrosanct places and therefore off-limits without her invitation). White staff members, like nurse Lizzie Thompson and governess Henrietta Van Den Burg, had almost the same access as the family members, filling in especially for Katharine, whose business, social, and estate-related duties were time consuming and never ending.[155] Katharine was clear about the nature of her relationship with her employees, even those closest to her own beloved family members, as she explained in a straightforward letter to a prospective domestic employee. "We pay high wages, and of course, expect first-class help." Katharine gave raises to her employees for "doing the work," though both staff members and estate employees, white and black, were known to ask Katharine for a raise in person or in writing.[156] Katharine and R.J.R. also gave their top staff, white and black, generous cash gifts of one hundred dollars at Christmas, the same amount they gave Katharine's siblings and R.J.R.'s nieces and nephews.[157]

The experience of working for the Reynoldses as a domestic servant was a unique one in Winston-Salem. Moreover, Katharine's domestic servants did not fit the general profile of local servants. Although she had not grown up with a staff of servants, Katharine quickly mastered her new role as head of an extended household of employees. She read Ellen Richards and S. Maria Elliot's *Chemistry of Cooking and Cleaning* and Lucy Maynard Salmon's *Domestic Service* and applied their advice religiously. She wrote elaborate notes delineating the specific duties of each servant, as well as role-plays for proper exchanges with guests, whether in person or over the phone. She could get angry, though infrequently. "But you better look out when she did," her servant Elizabeth Wade asserted. "When things were going wrong, you'd better look out."[158]

Though Katharine's domestic duties were enormous, she relied heavily on her servants to do the actual work. The spaces that the domestic staff could claim as their own included the pantry, the electric kitchen, the maid's lounge, the laundry room, the boiler rooms, the attic, the upstairs maid's closets, the butler's quarters, the telephone switchboard, and the janitorial closets. The most important positions of the African American domestic staff included the head butler, the head cook, the upstairs maid, and the switchboard operator. The top positions for the white domestic staff included Katharine's personal secretary, the children's nurse, and the children's governess. Each post was assigned a specific list of duties carefully crafted by Katharine. For example, the head butler was to keep the entire first floor cleaned and dusted; keep the silver, cut glass, and china polished; wash all dining-room china; set and wait on table; make all the fires; act as valet to R.J.R. and any visiting male guests; answer the doorbell, telephone (until Katharine hired a switchboard operator), and room bells; and even milk and attend the cows.[159]

Domestic service changed dramatically in Winston-Salem over the years that Katharine and R.J.R. were running their household and raising their family. In 1900, domestics represented 7 percent of the working population in the city, and 8 percent in 1910, but that number dropped precipitously to 2 percent in 1920, in the wake of wartime jobs and the growing demand for workers in the tobacco factory. Women represented 90 percent of domestic servants in 1900; that figure dropped to 76 percent in 1910 and 72 percent in 1920, signaling the rise in male domestic roles as butlers and chauffeurs at a time when the number of families acquiring new wealth was growing. In 1900, nine out of ten local domestics were born in North Carolina. By 1920, 20 percent had been born in South Carolina and 7 percent in Virginia. Throughout this twenty-year period, the majority of domestics were single and in their teens or twenties.[160]

Katharine employed slightly more women than men as servants, and the majority of her servants were African American. Her servants' experiences were unique in other ways too. Because she hired as many as a dozen staff members at any one time, job duties were not only carefully delineated but specialized by post. This situation contrasted sharply even with professional families, like the Wombles who lived in the West End section of town and employed Addie Siewers, a married African American woman who lived in Happy Hill. Siewers was expected to care for the six Womble children, while doing all the laundry and pressing all the clothes with a flatiron heated in the basement on a pot-bellied stove.[161]

But the servants in the Reynolds household had a much different experience. They were charged with keeping all aspects of life in the bungalow running with the smoothest of efficiencies and the most gracious of hospitalities. It was their responsibility to keep the house clean, make the meals, order the laundry, answer the phone, and so on. Because these employees surrounded Katharine on a daily basis, she had particularly high expectations for the work they performed depending on their position. Working in the Reynolds home carried a certain cachet; it was relatively well paying and prestigious. Therefore, these domestic service jobs seem to have been meted out only to those African American men and women whom Katharine perceived to be the hardest working, most loyal, finest educated, and best mannered.

Katharine trained her help herself. Elizabeth Wade recalled, "When they went in, I think Miss Katharine took that time and trained them, because they didn't even have such a thing as a school for this, like they do now.

And I think, when they went in, she taught them. They were very observant."[162] John Carter, the head butler, had begun his working career in the tobacco factory before R.J.R. hired him as his part-time butler. At first, John would come to the Fifth Street house after working in the factory all day and valet for R.J.R., pressing his clothes and polishing his shoes. He eventually became a full-time valet with some special training. "He knew how to clean up," Wade affirmed. "But he had to learn the finer things of life, which I think [Katharine] taught."[163] Carter, who allegedly could not read or write, learned those finer things so well that he worked as head butler until his death. He was a handsome man with bearing. "You would have thought he was a bishop or a Philadelphia lawyer, anything. . . . He was a really distinguished-looking person," recalled Harvey Miller, who was trained by Carter and replaced him after his death.[164] John Carter married Marjorie Goins, a young woman who had attended college for two years. She worked in the Reynolds household too, as an upstairs maid and a cook. The Carters presided over the running of the family household for two full generations and into the third before passing away.[165]

Once her staff learned their posts, Katharine gave them considerable responsibility and autonomy. For example, she authorized her house servants to purchase the tools they needed, like brushes and mops, in her absence or make purchases on credit downtown.[166] While these employees had uncharacteristic freedoms as well as a unique insider's view of Reynolds family life, which carried a certain standing in their broader black community, their workloads were heavy, and their emotional responsibilities were too. During the fall of 1917 through the spring of 1918, when R.J.R. grew very ill and was hospitalized in Baltimore and Philadelphia with Katharine traveling back and forth to attend to him, Miss Henrietta Van Den Berg wrote Katharine religiously about managing the Reynolds household in her absence. The challenges were many, not the least of which was securing enough good domestic help. "Aunt Fanny has broken down and says she will have to give up work indefinitely," Henrietta reported. She was frantically trying to find a replacement, and though John Carter had stated that his wife might help out from time to time, she was "not stout enough" to replace Aunt Fanny, while "Chaney [was] quite incapable of taking charge." Meanwhile, Van Den Berg complained, "All the good women in town are going into the factories, they make big wages and like it better." Aunt Fanny herself advised Katharine to send someone from Philadelphia or Baltimore; "Of course I know that will not be possible," Van Den Berg concluded despondently.[167]

Katharine based payment of house employees more on their skills than on their color. Johns Hopkins–educated nurse Henrietta Van Den Berg received one hundred dollars a month, while head butler John Carter received fifty dollars. Nannie Withers, the cook, received forty dollars. White nurse Lizzie Thompson and black head maid Pluma Walker each received thirty-five dollars a month, while black seamstress Savannah Webster received thirty-one dollars.[168]

Service in the house began in some cases before daylight and could last well into the evening and even overnight, leaving little time for mothers and fathers in domestic service to care for their own families. House butler Harvey Miller recalled, "I was here all the time. I'd come here in the morning at eight o'clock, seven thirty or eight o'clock, and would stay until everything was finished. I didn't work by the hour. You'd start and stop. I mean, you had a starting point but not too much of a getting off point."[169] Elizabeth Wade's aunt technically had Sundays off but was expected to return to the house to serve a cold Sunday-night supper.[170] The cook had especially demanding hours. Katharine expected breakfast served at 6:45 a.m., dinner at 12:40 p.m., and supper at 6:00 p.m. every day of the week except Sundays, when breakfast was served late, dinner after church, and a cold supper at 6:30 p.m. The housemaid, like the cook, needed to be at the Reynolds home early in the morning. She was expected in a single hour's time to wake Katharine and R.J.R., count and deliver all soiled linens to the laundry, and set the table for the servants' breakfast by 7:15 a.m. She could not leave for the day until the dishes had been washed and put up after the evening meal.[171] Elizabeth Wade, who like Miller worked at Reynolda for two generations of family members, described her work schedule as a domestic. "I just lived with them. I stayed night and day. I had Wednesdays off, and one Sunday off a month. . . . It wasn't hard; it was just confining." She felt strong guilt about leaving her children for long periods, especially because of the successive overnights. She would leave a week's menu with the woman who cared for them, and she would call her family daily. Her husband was also a big help.[172] Servants who were tired and wanted to sleep on the premises at the end of a long day were housed in the servants' cottage at the northern edge of the village. If the family needed to get up early in the morning to travel and expected a particular servant to attend to them, the servant would sleep overnight in the cottage to be ready early the next day. But the majority of servants preferred to live in their own homes in the city.[173] The powerful tug of family was not the only challenge domestic servants faced. They also felt the pull of the Reynolds Tobacco factory, where the hours were growing shorter and the wages better with the passing of each wartime year.[174]

Not surprisingly, Katharine taught her children to treat the staff with respect. Her daughter Mary Reynolds Babcock repeated that lesson with her own children.[175] Elizabeth Wade recalled young Nancy Reynolds's helpfulness when she was a new employee on the estate. Wade had gotten lost between the house and the laundry, prompting Nancy to hop off her bike and lead Wade to her destination. "It's funny how some things—kindness—just sticks in your mind," Wade recalled about the incident.[176] Harvey Miller, the son of Five Row residents Henry and Mamie Miller, and a lifelong employee of the Reynolds-Babcock family across three generations, described the relationship between servant and employer as a complex dance. When he was forced to do work he did not want to do, he learned how to sabotage the act of doing it somehow, such as "hollering during window washing" and tearing away enough of the decorative ivy around the window edges to frighten his employers. His employers might induce guilt by sweetening his wages, paying his YMCA dues, and giving donations to his church in his name. Elizabeth Wade noted that the Reynoldses paid for her children's graduate-school education at Columbia and the University of Wisconsin.[177] Katharine also provided meals for her staff. She instructed the cook to make "enough soups, meats, fish, vegetables and breads, pies, etc. for servants giving them such as we have on our table with exception of expensive fresh fruits, pickles, olives, oysters, and cakes. On Sundays give servants just such as we have including pickles, oysters, cakes and desserts and fruits for breakfast and so on." Harvey Miller recalled eating all the cake and ice cream he could ever want and being asked by the cook each morning, "How do you want your eggs?" He considered these sumptuous meals a real perk of the position.[178]

Katharine provided other benefits too. She gave Pluma and John the authority to divide her old china among the help because she had replaced it with "real china."[179] Harvey later observed that being the employee of such an established Winston family "softened race relations" because white store owners were far more willing to extend him credit than other black men.[180] He contrasted these realities with his experiences in the North, where he found racial discrimination rampant. He and his wife were refused service at restaurants, and he witnessed a white man throwing a black man out of a bus seat. Likewise Reynolda servants John and Marjorie Carter recalled finishing their meal at a restaurant in Philadelphia only to have the management break their finished dirty dishes in front of them.[181] Faithful service to the Reynolds family was rewarded with paternalistic protection across the generations by comparison.

In January 1919, when Katharine and the children were traveling over the Christmas season and mourning the death of R.J.R., Pluma Walker wrote her employer an extraordinary letter. She offered snippets of information about the household in the family's absence and then conveyed her gratitude to Katharine for her vacation and much more. "I had a real good rest which I am so thankful to you for you have been so nice to me I cant ever forget all the good things you have done I feel like I cant ever do enough work for you when I look back and think what a blessing you have been to me I cant express my self like some of the others can but deep down in my heart I am just as thankful as they are." To what extent Walker feared the family might relocate in the wake of R.J.R.'s death, and she might thus be out of employment, we cannot know, or whether her vacation was a paid or a forced unpaid one.[182]

Still, negotiating these relationships could be trying. Harvey Miller knew of employers, including his own, who hid money under the rug to test the thoroughness of their servants' cleaning. Employers could not "steal" a domestic servant from another household without extreme social disapproval. Domestics had to quietly line up a position with a new employer, formally quit with the current one, wait several weeks, and then "get hired" by the new employer. Even then, the new employer had to check with the former employer to make sure this new arrangement was acceptable.[183] If wealthy families like the Reynoldses wanted to prevent their domestics from switching jobs, Harvey observed, they could and they did.[184]

Despite these cold realities, Harvey Miller stated unequivocally about his lifelong experience as a servant, "Everybody respected everybody. I won't say it was love, but it was respect." He also liked the work he was doing. "Serving the meals was . . . really something nice. . . . You had the best of everything. And there was something artistic about the work, it was beautiful—the setting up and arranging the table the way it was carried out, it was absolutely a pleasure to do it."[185] Miller suggests a striking reality about the relationship between the wealthy and their domestic servants. The employers were utterly dependent on their employees, and the absence of their domestics created considerable unease. In fact, Katharine, R.J.R., and their children did not really know how to live alone.

Years later, Katharine's daughter Mary, now a grown woman, wrote her sister Nancy that she had held a house party at Roaring Gap. She reported she had pulled the event off "with not a 'nig' from Sunday noon to Monday breakfast, and no nurse and the mothers having a gay time until day break."[186] In fact, it would take the challenge of "making do" without enough servants during World War II to compel Mary to conclude, "I've got to look for a maid, at least. The war has taught me so much that I don't fear the servant problem as much as I should."[187]

"The servant problem" had long been an acknowledged challenge for wealthy Americans across the country, not just in the South. German-born Harvard psychologist Hugo Munsterberg had been fascinated by social conceptions of work in America in the early twentieth century. He argued that Americans considered any form of work serving industry and civilization, even in the shops and factories, honorable. The sole exception was domestic work, declined even by first-generation immigrants whenever possible, because it took away personal independence. "The servant appears to have no other end than complying with the will of another person," explained the professor. "The servant sells a part of his free-will and therefore his social equality, to another man." Munsterberg noted that Americans would have had significantly greater "servant problems" without "the several million negroes in the country and the heavy immigration from Southern Europe."[188]

Though there may have been some prestige in working in the personal home of the Reynolds, for many of Katharine's servants were quite light skinned and had some education or were able to provide an education for their families, and while she paid the highest wages around, she incentivized even more by incorporating the latest technologies to ease housekeeping duties, installing such conveniences as an electric range, a central vacuum system, and elevator lifts. The very design of her bungalow, like most new country homes throughout the United States, incorporated new efficiencies such as the placement of the kitchen next to the dining room and second-floor janitorial closets piped with hot water.[189] Katharine had an interhouse phone as well as a bell system to ensure easy access and smooth communication with her staff across the sprawling household at all times. Still, it was a well-known fact that most African Americans in Winston preferred factory wage work, posing a challenge to Katharine to find suitable people for her household staff. She located potential staff members at the recommendation of her current help, through letters of inquiry from prospective employees, and with the assistance of agents. Katharine's "excellent upstairs maid," Pluma Walker, whose husband worked as a chauffeur for Will Reynolds, recommended her stepniece, Elizabeth Wade, for laundry work.[190] Elizabeth, born in Winston in 1901, had attended the Allen School in Asheville, funded by white northerners and run by white northern teachers to train young women in the industrial arts, including sewing and cooking. She had then enrolled at Bennett College in Greensboro and began working in the Reynolda laundry during summers. Katharine was so impressed with her ability that she soon had Wade iron all her own clothes. Elizabeth left the position to marry, but after her second child she returned to Reynolda as the switchboard operator.[191] Prospective employees also wrote Katharine directly in search of a household position, such as Jennie McClellan from Statesville, a white woman who sought work caring for children or sewing. Katharine sent her a polite reply. Although she did not need someone at the moment, she explained, she was glad to have her name and suggested she might contact her in the future.[192] Katharine also worked with agents like Mrs. Knudsen in other cities to locate help. "I have now an experienced maid a refined German with a first class home," reported Mrs. Knudsen. She subsequently recommended a young woman whom Katharine refused to hire upon discovering from others she was "a most unsatisfactory person." But she expressed strong interest in another housemaid whom Mrs. Knudsen had identified and hoped Mrs. Knudsen would have the young woman write her terms directly to Katharine. "I believe that she must be the kind of girl I am seeking," especially since she would be able to check with her last employer, known to Katharine's nurse, in Baltimore. Meanwhile, Katharine added, she was "continuing to put up with a very unsatisfactory cook." Would Mrs. Knudsen be able to recommend someone else soon?[193] Whether they were white or black, Katharine expected her staff to be able to read and write; to be able to hold light, appropriate conversations with guests; and to entertain a certain level of social decorum and understanding.

Uniforms were critically important to Katharine and were being used increasingly throughout America as a means of social differentiation.[194] Her domestic staff were assigned specific outfits deemed appropriate to their work. The switchboard operator wore a white uniform. Maids wore blue striped uniforms purchased from department stores in the North like B. Altman and Company. The chauffeur was decked out in an Oxford-style summer-weight suit, a summer-weight coat, gloves, and a cap, all purchased from Rogers Peet in Manhattan and in colors that complemented the family's maroon automobile.[195]

The relationship of mistress and staff was one of mutual dependence. The staff knew Katharine kept detailed household records. She totaled up her expenses and compared them with her budget. She counted the number of people served in the dining room and in the kitchen per meal in planning her budget and then reconciled her budget with actual losses. There was little room for any borrowings or thefts on the part of her help.[196] This represented one of the many manifestations of a relationship in which employer and employee walked a tightrope of emotion far more complex than the exchange of money for work performed, and in which the relationships were inherently and unequivocally unequal. In the end, these relationships were fraught with fear, tension, responsibilities, and intimacies. Yet new scholarship also shows that within this fractious world of the white household, black servants defined themselves by their familial relationships, not by their roles as workers, and worked assiduously to preserve their familial bonds. This same important scholarship also illuminates the ways in which household servants employed a wide variety of resistance tactics and measures that let them retain their own agency.[197]

The black women servants who stayed with Katharine the longest, and even worked for the next generation, were all married. Both the black and the white communities in Winston have long held that Irene Hairston, an African American domestic who worked for R.J.R.'s brother Will and his wife, Kate Reynolds, had given birth to a son fathered by either Will or R.J.R., who have become increasingly tangled in the public mind now that several generations have passed since Will's death in 1954. The importance of hiring married women in strong positions of authority within the household as role models of decorum and to act as vigilant eyes attuned to even the beginnings of illicit relationships between the master and the help cannot be overlooked. Likewise, Katharine's personal chauffeur, Cleve Williams, was a light-skinned African American man who lived in a cottage in the village with his wife, two sons, and sister-in law, Alameda, "a very beautiful, sweet person" who sewed for Katharine. Cleve was a personal favorite of Katharine's. She put up with his tardiness much to the other servants' surprise and paid off his delinquent account at the local men's fine-clothes store.[198]

There can be little doubt that Katharine sought out African American men and women she considered to be exceptional as her servants. In fact, her employees were often from middle-class black families themselves. They were frequently light skinned in appearance and educated, especially the women, gracious and self-confident in their bearing, and wise in the ways of placating rich whites. Perhaps the most intriguing servant whom Katharine employed was Savannah Webster Jones. A beautiful young single woman whose Aunt Anna had worked for Katharine, she had been employed at both the Fifth Street house and the Reynolda Estate, mostly at sewing, but on occasion she operated the telephone too. She may have been particularly special to Katharine, for in an uncharacteristic move Katharine paid for ten weeks of Savannah's room rent as well as her wages in 1918.[199] Savannah married C. H. Jones, a black real-estate entrepreneur, who was quite wealthy, and they moved into a lovely home. But Savannah apparently grew "bored to death" with her newfound domesticity and elected to work at Reynolda now and then, but clearly on her own terms. She was an extremely talented seamstress who made beautiful clothes for Katharine and her daughter Nancy, who described Savannah with superlative after superlative.[200] After her husband's death, Savannah married again, to African Methodist Episcopal Zion Church bishop Hampton Thomas Medford, an accomplished pastor in North Carolina and in Africa, former secretary of foreign missions, author, and businessman, "regarded as one of the most wealthy men in the church."[201]

These servants and their complex relationships with Katharine were clearly an integral component of her life on her estate. But what should we think of Katharine's garden, for clearly the Reynolda Estate was her "garden." Unlike generations before her, she could not set out into the wilderness to cultivate nature into a middle landscape. Frederick Jackson Turner had long declared the American frontier dead. But Reynolda let Katharine create a brand-new middle landscape that offered not only a rural reform critique of men's impact on the urban environment but also a woman's corrective vision of her own. Katharine's Reynolda stood as a sharp rebuke to the artificial and chaotic city her husband had wrought and to the local farmers who had ruined the land with their backward methods. She borrowed from the American tradition of reifying rural life and the egalitarianism it symbolized, but unlike the American literary tradition that fought against the intrusion of "the machine in the garden," Katharine embraced technology too as a means to make a new "past." The idealized Reynolda Estate, with its state-of-the-art livestock and facilities, with its beautiful gardens and landscapes, epitomized not just what new money could create but the order and contentment that could be generated for a whole community of people, white and black, educated and illiterate, by a benevolent matriarch with an encompassing social plan based on rich rewards for the outstanding performance of clearly delineated duties, jobs, and responsibilities, better known as wage work. The actual relationships between employer and employee across color, class, and gender remained far more complex and far less egalitarian than Katharine ever acknowledged. But in the end she had in fact created her own estate upon a hill.[202]

7 A Woman for a New Day

As the United States prepared to enter World War I, Katharine and R.J.R. began the most difficult period of their lives. Although the Reynolds Tobacco Company had never been more profitable and their children healthier, and while their Reynolda bungalow was nearing completion after years of planning and construction, R.J.R. not only grew ill but took a serious turn for the worse. In the two years preceding his death, R.J.R. had never needed Katharine's understanding of social benevolence and reform more to foil the new labor and wartime challenges his company faced, even as his own health deteriorated.

Rapid urbanization and industrialization had long prompted city boosters to brag that Winston-Salem was a place of plenty. Katharine herself was proud of Winston-Salem's growth, writing her husband in 1917 that the federal government had just declared their hometown "the largest city in N.C. with a population of over 5,000 people."[1] The city boasted that it had the largest weekly payroll between Richmond and Atlanta.[2] Claimed one promoter, the city had become so bountiful with its expansion that "roast pigs were running around the streets with a knife and fork sticking in their backs, and a placard attached, inviting the hungry to come and eat."[3] Despite ample claims that Winston-Salem was not only prosperous but increasingly modern, it did not appear so to everyone who visited. English folk musicologist Cecil Sharp, traveling to Winston, had looked forward to his pending visit, until his train from Mount Airy drew near. "We *smelt* Winston Salem about 8 miles away—tobacco and molasses!—It is one of the largest tobacco manufacturing places in U.S.A." Yet as soon as he disembarked, he suffered an asthma attack from the toxins in the air and was shocked by what he saw. "Winston Salem is a dull, ugly sort of a place with a square in the middle of which stands the Town Hall, quite the ugliest building I have ever seen."

Nor could he get over the significant numbers of African Americans living and working in the downtown. "The place is stuffed full with negroes—I presume they work in the factories." Disappointed all around he concluded, "This is a noisy place and the air impregnated with tobacco, molasses and nigger!"[4] Other commentators were no more judicious. Winston, whispered some, was "the city with all those Negroes and white trash."[5]

The R. J. Reynolds Tobacco Company employed a significant portion of the city's working people. R.J.R., who had always worked hard to balance public perceptions, understood that his company's growing success and his own escalating wealth rested on the arduous labor of his workforce. Katharine understood that the social conditions her women's clubs and benevolent societies sought to improve stemmed from families making their living in factories, including the R. J. Reynolds Tobacco Company. At the same time, she grasped that the transition from rural to urban work was an enormous one, and that management's expectations about work ethics and attitudes were often at odds with those of the workers themselves.

Long active in the YWCA, she pressed her husband in 1914 to pledge five thousand dollars for a much-needed newer, larger YWCA building estimated to cost thirty-five thousand dollars. He promised an additional five thousand dollars if the leaders of the effort would raise the remaining funds themselves.[6] Although the leaders raised close to $20,000, they failed to secure the full amount by 1917, when the R. J. Reynolds Tobacco Company board of directors voted to contribute the ten-thousand-dollar difference.[7] But the company had every reason to do so. Katharine and her fellow YWCA officers had been formulating a new plan to help transform young, rural white women wage earners into a more ideal workforce. In 1916, the current YWCA officers Nathalie Lyons Gray (wife of Reynolds executive Bowman Gray Sr. and one of Katharine's best friends), Eleanor Taft, and Margaret Anderson announced their intention to organize YWCA clubs in all the local factories.[8] Katharine was subsequently elected YWCA president, and over two years a total of six YWCA clubs were organized in the R. J. Reynolds Tobacco Company factories alone. The club names, including "Ever Ready," "Willing Workers," and "Wide-a-Wake," spoke to their mission, as did their charter, which included statements like "give the employer a full day's service; exercise economy on behalf of the company; use good, clean language; use no gum in public places; wear a neat business dress; neither originate nor repeat slander about any girl; and make the new girl in the factory welcome." By 1917, the Reynolds Tobacco Company was hiring a secretary charged with "the industrial work" required to support the R. J. Reynolds Tobacco Company's YWCA clubs.[9] That same year, thirty of "the R.J.R. girls" attended the YMCA Blue Ridge Assembly in Black Mountain, N.C., one of the few social institutions in the South where race relations and their improvement could be discussed openly. Meanwhile, Katharine and the other local leaders addressed how best to institute a local Colored YWCA Association, and listened to reports from Miss Ruffin, an African American national staff member, on the viability of implementing a weekly study session for young black women on the Bible, health, and hygiene.[10] Under Katharine's leadership, the YWCA invested in building a dedicated workforce of responsible as well as progressive-minded young white and black working-class women, many of whom worked for the biggest employer in town.[11]

Meanwhile, the YWCA had not forgotten its mission to support individual women in their moral uplift. The local YWCA continued to create appealing places for young women to congregate and attend wholesome social events, self-improvement classes, and athletic activities. Katharine herself continued to finance physical improvements, including a number of renovations and additions to the YWCA headquarters, as chair of the Building Committee. She arranged and paid for her own contractor from Philadelphia to tile the Domestic Science Room, managed the grounds, and bought a stove for the kitchen. She sent Miss Van Den Berg to the new building with a donation of thirty "volumes of modern fiction" for the YWCA library. As dedicated as she was to the YWCA mission, she could be a tough taskmaster on money issues; she raised the price of board and the cost of lunch at the YWCA to ensure a balanced budget. By 1920, however, with the YWCA serving close to ten thousand lunches a year and experiencing exponential need to provide room and board for more and more young women, Katharine pressed the council in her role as executive chairman to assume a loan to cover the needed expenses.[12] She took her leadership of this local institution seriously. She used her work with the YWCA to improve young working women's lives, increasingly black as well as white, through skill training and education, as well as lessons in developing a strong moral compass and a progressive outlook. She was an avid manager of facilities and finances. At the same time, all her investments in the YWCA and by extension in working-class women helped curb the labor-related problems manifesting themselves in the family business.[13]

As the United States geared up its factories to support its allies in Europe, demand for labor increased nationwide. Not only was the company often simply short of hands, but this current climate meant protesting workers and labor unions gained some traction with their employers. Reynolds Tobacco felt the impact of an increasingly politicized workforce demanding higher wages at a time when the company wanted to increase production levels to meet soaring demand and needed plentiful and reliable labor.

Labor problems had challenged R. J. Reynolds since the turn of the century. In the early 1900s, black response to segregation and labor unrest across the state had led him to adopt once and for all a dualistic policy of personalism and paternalism. He made himself available to all his employees, and he avoided layoffs and work stoppages. But too many larger structural challenges prevailed to convince all his workers that Reynolds Tobacco made looking out for its employees its number one priority. When socialist Eugene Debs came to town in 1911, working people in Winston paid attention. During 1916, national socialist speakers and local Socialist Party candidates drew large crowds, and local Republicans accused R. J. Reynolds and key city leaders of using their money and their control of the Democratic Party to run competitors out of town, directing the news relayed in the *Winston-Salem Journal*, legislating against labor agents from other states entering the city, and paying the lowest daily wage for tobacco workers in the state. Accusations flew back and forth across the partisan divide over the entire summer and to some simply reflected the nature of politics in a presidential election year.[14]

At this same time, the company was struggling with its continued reliance on child labor in the face of national criticism against children under sixteen working eight-hour days. The proposed Keating child-labor law, with its expectation of implementation on January 1, 1917, generated some backpedaling at the Reynolds offices. R.J.R. himself spoke against legislation in general, arguing that many black and even some white children came to the factories before and after school to supplement their family's income. Still, Reynolds never received the depth of sustained criticism that southern progressives aimed at textile industries, where white child labor predominated.[15]

But R.J.R. recognized that with growing demand for his products and the company's rapid expansion to meet it, he needed to provide his workers with better wages and more incentives too, especially in light of a protean labor movement. In 1916, the same year in which his local leadership had come under attack by the Republicans and he was defending his child-labor practices, he implemented his first-ever 10 percent increase in the basic wage rate and an attendance bonus and a top-performer bonus too. He also made it significantly easier for wage workers to purchase stocks by creating a loan program. He then inaugurated a neighborhood home-rental program that provided his black employees with cheap housing well below the rates of local slumlords, and he developed a similar program for whites.[16]

Katharine had been working closely with key local and state social-reform groups throughout this period. Her knowledge and connections were especially useful given the new challenges that her husband and the company faced. She persuaded R.J.R. to open a lunchroom that served hot meals to its white employees. Three months later, Reynolds Tobacco opened a lunchroom for black employees too, apparently at her insistence.[17] Katharine then convinced her husband to build a hotel for the young white women from the mountains newly recruited to the factories to meet the rising labor needs. She encouraged him to let black women workers with children arrive late, so they could accommodate their family's needs, and she created a day nursery for the children of white women employees for one dollar a week. She also insisted that all mothers be allowed to leave work and nurse their children every three hours without loss of time.[18] She did not initiate these changes in a vacuum. The company as a whole had had to take an increasing interest in labor relations and by 1919 had established a series of committees to examine ways to improve workers' lot at the plants. The company began to employ a full-time doctor; a 1920 social services report states, "All employees are urged to come for medical advice, which is always free." But in effect, Katharine's on-the-ground efforts paved the way for more systemic and protracted labor management in the years that followed.[19]

Although most of these reforms did not bring about significant structural change, the material lives of Reynolds wage earners did experience some improvement at a time when the company needed its workers more than ever. On July 26, 1917, D. Rich wrote R.J.R. that 120 white workers alone had just been drafted.[20] Katharine did not limit her increasingly benevolent outreach to the company, however. The same year Katharine served as president of the YWCA, she was elected president of the Winston-Salem Civic Federation.[21] A national organization founded in 1900, the Civic Federation was comprised of leaders in business and labor, social scientists, and politicians, all of whom came together to work toward broad-based social and policy reforms. The federation used its collective conscience to press the federal government for model legislation that strengthened the economy and served its most vulnerable citizens. That Katharine presided over a local chapter of this organization speaks volumes about her commitment to finding new ways to build bridges between industry and labor, and her willingness to step outside the boundaries of women's reform to do so for the Civic Federation was a decidedly coed effort.[22]

Meanwhile, the realities of a United States at war loomed closer. Katharine quickly joined forces with other elite women in the city in April 1917 to meet expected wartime exigencies. One of her first efforts was to form a local chapter of the American Red Cross. The organization quickly developed into a powerful venue for orchestrating local support for servicemen, from Christmas parcels filled with cakes and tobacco, to clothing for needy families of soldiers overseas, to blankets and bandages for hospitals.[23]

World War I prompted Katharine and R.J.R. not only to engage in more progressive reforms but to adopt more overtly patriotic actions as well. Although Katharine's sister-in-law had actively participated in the local Daughters of the American Revolution and Daughters of the Confederacy clubs for many years, and although her father led Civil War veterans events, Katharine herself spent little time looking backward or invoking the past to serve her agendas in the present. While many conservative southerners like her sister-in-law and her father used these organizations to promote a particular brand of patriotism that sanctioned their political outlook, neither Katharine nor R.J.R. had much interest in grappling with the question of what national loyalty meant to conservative southerners.[24]

The advent of World War I marked a turning point in their lives as R.J.R. grew weaker and Katharine assumed a feminized version of his industrialist-citizen-leader mantle. Her record of participation in social-reform efforts led to numerous new invitations to take on war-related leadership positions in civic nationalism, giving her a bigger stage and a larger purpose in the process. Yet despite all her new opportunities to influence the world around her at not only the local but also the state and national levels, Katharine found herself also confronting the realities of her husband's declining health.

Now in his sixties, R.J.R. had long complained of intermittent stomach pains. He seemed to know that he would not recover from this illness. Never a religious man, despite his parents' and wife's entreaties to the contrary, he had refused to join the First Presbyterian Church in town or even Katharine's own church in Reynolda Village. In sharp contrast, R.J.R.'s oldest brother, A.D., had become a teetotaling, born-again Methodist, admittedly only after some regretted years of profligacy.[25] Throughout his own adulthood, R.J.R., who had no reservations whatsoever about cards or imbibing, had avoided organized religion altogether.[26]

But as the pains intensified over the summer of 1917, and at his oldest son's encouragement, one sultry Sunday he walked up to the front of Reynolda Church with eleven-year-old Dick Jr. when the minister was inviting sinners to be saved. Katharine was so thrilled that she sent out dozens of telegrams to family and friends across the country to share this news, not realizing that her husband's decision signaled his acceptance of his looming death.[27]

After a vacation in Atlantic City intended to bring R.J.R. relief as well as consultation time with some specialists, he had not recovered from his ailment, so he checked into the Jefferson Hospital in Philadelphia in late July 1917. He left the hospital in August only to go back to Atlantic City in hopes that the sea air would prove restorative, but to no avail. After another visit to the Jefferson Hospital, he returned home to Reynolda, only to check into Johns Hopkins Hospital in Baltimore in late September for extensive tests that revealed nothing. By October, R.J.R. had moved back to Baltimore, where he remained hospitalized that entire autumn. Katharine stayed with him for days and weeks at a time, trying to run the household and meet her growing wartime public obligations from afar. Miss Van Den Berg stayed with the children, in Atlantic City and at the Reynolda Estate.[28]

R.J.R., always a big man, had lost his appetite along with a considerable amount of weight, although Katharine made sure he had the freshest, most tempting foods always available to him. His stomach pains worsened, although he had days when he seemed on the mend, giving hope to his family and his company officers alike. The children visited him in October, including Smith, who was only six. "I know it is a good tonic to Mr. Reynolds to have [Smith] about," Van Den Berg observed.[29] Katharine, despite her onerous public duties, often nursed him herself, attentive to his every need and whim, even as her own health declined with the strain of his illness and the scale of the demands she juggled. When she could not be with him, she engaged round-the-clock private-duty nurses. Company officers and business colleagues traveled to Baltimore to consult with R.J.R. and Katharine personally, but as R.J.R. became increasingly fragile, Katharine took on more and more responsibility for conveying his wishes to his officers.[30]

Then in late November, R.J.R.'s doctor forbade even Katharine to visit him. Dr. Brown expressed concern that R.J.R.'s "regard for his business was so debilitating [that it was] inhibiting his recovery." He ordered "complete mental rest" and no visitors. He wrote Katharine that he believed R.J.R. understood that he could see her in charge of the company "with [her] great knowledge of his business and his supreme confidence in [her] judgement" during this imposed period of isolation.

Ten days later, Dr. Brown wrote Katharine that R.J.R. was improving and she might be able to see him in another week. The bungalow at Reynolda was now complete, and the family planned to spend Christmas there. Miss Van Den Berg, the children, and the staff made excited preparations for R.J.R.'s return. Having suffered months of separation from their father and intermittent weeks of separation from their mother, the children "were wild with delight to think you and father will be home on Sunday," Miss Van Den Berg wrote Katharine. The two agreed, however, that though the children wanted to greet their long-absent father at the train, it was best to keep them at home. "I too, am afraid it will make him nervous," Van Den Berg concurred.[31]

The doctor sanctioned a visit to Hot Springs, Virginia, first, with Katharine in attendance, so that R.J.R. could partake of the healing mineral waters. The couple then returned to Winston, where the family had their first and sadly their last Christmas together in their brand-new Reynolda home.[32]

Despite her husband's serious illness, Katharine's public duties were growing exponentially, creating greater responsibilities for her in the process. The national board of the YWCA requested her leadership, and presumably her financial resources too.[33] North Carolina governor Bickett appointed Katharine a member of the North Carolina Library War Council, charged with raising one million dollars to provide books for U.S. soldiers and sailors.[34] She was quickly becoming part of a burgeoning world in which women's civic leadership had significant impact during wartime when the state was increasingly bowing to federal authority. In 1917, former *News and Observer* editor turned secretary of the navy Josephus Daniels, a longtime Reynolds family friend, appointed Katharine chairwoman of the North Carolina Liberty Loan drive.[35]

This appointment had grown out of her membership on the state's Women's Committee and its representation on the newly organized Council of National Defense. Katharine accepted leadership of the second Liberty Loan drive in July 1917 and attended the meeting of the North Carolina Executive Committee of the Council of National Defense in Raleigh the same week she was to join the Women's Liberty Loan Conference in New York.[36]

Intent upon making the drive a tremendous success, she began her efforts by demanding that those around her help set the bar high. At Katharine's request, Reynolds Tobacco gave the largest single subscription of any institution in the state at one hundred thousand dollars.[37] But that commitment was not enough. She persuaded everyone at Reynolda Estate to purchase War Savings Stamps.[38] At Christmas time, Katharine gave Liberty Loan Bonds and War Certificates as gifts to all the children's teachers as well as to other employees and friends.[39] She expected her entire household and all her Reynolda employees to commit to the Red Cross drive too, and almost all did; all her black employees made donations, along with all but two of her white employees.[40] Her oldest son, Dick, a dedicated member of the Boy Scouts of America, had traded in scrap to collect sixty-four dollars to contribute. While his father was lying ill in a hospital and his mother with him, he wrote them both that he had attended a parade, marching with his fellow Boy Scouts, along with four hundred Red Cross nurses, campaign organizers, and volunteers in their uniforms, and six soldiers carrying the R. J. Reynolds Tobacco service flag, with so many stars representing employees at war that Dick could not count them all.[41] Miss Van Den Berg told Katharine that she had put so much money into Liberty Bonds she could not afford a vacation.[42]

The drive demanded that Katharine make numerous public appearances and employ a persuasive writing campaign behind the scenes. As R.J.R. grew weaker that fall, Katharine was forced to give some of this work to Miss Van Den Berg. "There has been a good deal of Liberty Bond matter, but it is all up to date, Mrs. Latham tells me she has written you of the enthusiastic meeting they had in Elkin," Miss Van Den Berg reported while Katharine was with R.J.R. in Baltimore.[43]

By January 1918, R.J.R. was not improving, despite the joyous holiday reunion with his family in their splendid new home. Katharine was exhausted, reporting to friends that she had been taking care of him at night by herself. Given her husband's deteriorating health, she felt compelled to resign her chairmanship of the Liberty Bond campaign. Later that year, Governor Thomas W. Bickett administered the oath of allegiance to 202 Federation Club delegates attending the annual meeting at Raleigh and celebrated Katharine's leadership of the drive. The group observed that women from their ranks had been recruited to take on leadership positions across the state during World War I. Their considerable skills, from being thoroughly versed in public speaking to organizing people to conducting meetings, had not only distinguished them as leaders but made an important contribution to the welfare of the country as a whole. They celebrated the exceptional contributions of white clubwomen to wartime activities and patriotic pursuits, especially the buying and selling of Liberty Bonds under the state chairmanship of Katharine Reynolds. The group then passed a resolution in favor of woman suffrage amid rousing cheers and applause and followed up the resolution by telegraphing Senator F. M. Simmons and Senator Lee S. Overman endorsing the suffrage amendment under debate in the Senate.[44] Katharine's war work, like that of North Carolina's club women in general, transcended old-school female benevolence and philanthropy. She was increasingly being recognized as an important state leader.

Beginning in 1915, she had accepted several high-profile public roles. Her first was as state president of the Memorial Committee for Mrs. Ellen Axson Wilson, President Wilson's recently deceased wife. Then came her Liberty Loan and Council of Defense work. But R.J.R.'s declining health had put this public work on hold. With R.J.R. now at home, Katharine lacked the support systems that his hospitalization had provided. She had turned her husband's Reynolda House study on the first floor—a heavily paneled room with a huge desk and deep shelves befitting the head of the R. J. Reynolds Tobacco Company—into a convalescent quarter, complete with a crankable hospital bed. She had a bell pull installed so that R.J.R. could easily rouse her from her own bed upstairs if he was in need. Katharine had hoped Miss Van Den Berg would help her by taking on R.J.R.'s nursing duties, but she had declined, citing not only R.J.R.'s "personal indisposition" against her but also her fears that she was not skilled enough at handling "a nervous case [and] stomach complications."[45] The nervousness and agitation that had plagued him all autumn returned unabated. Despite the beautiful new bungalow, R.J.R. was anxious for the old and familiar, prompting Katharine to ask her sister Irene to return two old rattan rockers he had always loved in a desperate effort to make him more comfortable.[46]

Unfortunately R.J.R. remained gravely ill and had to be hospitalized once again, this time in Philadelphia, in early spring. By late May, Katharine was not only exhausted but deeply discouraged. R.J.R. disliked his latest nurse, and Katharine was working double time to make up the difference. Miss Van Den Berg, home with the children at Reynolda, wrote a cheery letter encouraging Katharine to get more rest but to no avail. She also urged Katharine to avoid letting R.J.R. discuss business matters with his colleagues and associates. "He is not strong enough to stand the strain. I think that has been proved more than once, a little does him good, but when he gets with those that have their interests and not his at stake, there is always trouble, and it is almost impossible to draw the line."[47] Katharine recognized at this stage that her husband was not going to recover and spent several weeks trying to persuade his doctors to let him return home to die.

Katharine began letting adult family members know that her husband was on his deathbed. His illegitimate son, John Neal, who distributed R. J. Reynolds Tobacco products in Omaha, Nebraska, made the trip east to Philadelphia to see his father one last time. Katharine received him warmly, and Neal was grateful to her for encouraging him to visit. Over the last nine months, R.J.R. had grown increasingly agitated by guests. Neal must have been forewarned that his visit might upset his father. Katharine had written John reassuringly, "He enjoyed your visit so much. . . . You have my kindest regards and very best wishes." On returning to Omaha, he wrote Katharine that he hoped the visit had "had no evil effects upon Mr. Reynolds' condition, as [he] honestly tried to make everything as pleasant as possible for him."[48]

When the doctors finally agreed that they could do no more for R.J.R. and that he could go home, Katharine wrote Neal, "I wish you could have seen him when they told him that he might go home. He had never said a word about it before, but it made him so happy that big tears stood in his eyes and he had the biggest smile on his face that I have ever seen since he has been ill." She wrote her secretary, Evie Crim, "We are all so happy over the doctor's decision to permit Mr. Reynolds to come home and altho he is hardly strong enough to stand the trip, I do think it will be much better for him at home." She was equally frank in a letter to Rev. Neal Anderson: "My time for the past six weeks has been taken up in assisting in the care of Mr. Reynolds and in trying to keep him happy, cheerful, and contented. I have been on duty each night until 1 o'clock and frequently until 3. . . . He is very thin and very weak and is making the journey on a cot." To friends and acquaintances, she feigned only good things, as when she responded to Mrs. Jones's inquiry, "He is so happy over the thought of being home."[49]

Katharine arranged for a private Pullman car to transport R.J.R. from Philadelphia to Winston Salem for the arduous two-day trip. He lay prone on a cot in the car, attended by a physician and two nurses as well as Katharine. The car was coupled at the rear of the train to avoid noise and interruption and was dropped at a siding north of town on July 18, 1918. An ambulance took him the short distance to the estate.[50]

R.J.R., now extremely weak, added an important codicil to his will just days after coming home. In a final act of philanthropy, the ailing head of Reynolds Tobacco set aside a $120,000 bequest to build a black hospital and another $120,000 bequest for a new white hospital. This joint gift would mark the biggest donation of any kind that the city had received.[51] In the last years of his life, R.J.R. had broadened his reform and philanthropic interests. He had accepted appointment on the board of the Appalachian Park Association, whose mission focused on setting aside parts of the southern Appalachians for healthful pleasure and recreation.[52] As the chief subscriber to Winston-Salem's Liberty Bond, YMCA, and War Savings Stamp campaigns, he was credited with single-handedly enabling the city to exceed its quotas in each of those campaigns. But it was this final gift that was perhaps the most telling in regard to his crafting of his legacy. His commitment did honor Jim Crow segregation by creating a separate new hospital for each race. But it was an equitable bequest, one that signaled his commitment to black as well as white welfare in Winston.[53]

R.J.R. died a week later on July 30, 1918, probably from pancreatic cancer. Symptomless for long periods of time, the disease generally manifests itself only when the tumor has grown large enough to impede the functioning of the pancreas, and by then, the disease is always fatal. Only at this last stage do symptoms appear: stomach pain, weight loss, and lethargy.

As news of R.J.R.'s passing reached the public, outpourings of respect from across the nation followed. Secretary of the Navy Josephus Daniels wired Katharine, "I regarded your husband's friendship as one of my most valued possessions and sorrow with you in the great affliction which darkens your home and saddens the whole state."[54] She received so many telegrams and notes that she had them put together by a special agency that collected the dozens of national newspaper obituaries and editorials about her husband as well. The resultant effort was an "In Memoriam" book filled with hundreds of pages offering testament after testament to R.J.R.'s tremendous influence on the city, the region, American business, and scores of individuals.

Sectors of the black community mourned as publicly as the city's business leaders. Stating "Big Dad Is Dead," the local black newspaper, the *Winston-Salem Advertiser*, offered an explanation for why it gave R.J.R. this title:

> This was not an expression of the familiar kind. We meant nothing shallow. We meant from the depths of our hearts that he never allowed the Negro of Winston-Salem to suffer. He was with us first and last. And when we had to, we did it; that is to go to him and tell him all our troubles. This is what all good children do to their parents. This raises the question, did he so feel to us as our "Big Dad." In his will this question is fully answered with a $120,000 gift for a hospital. Mr. Reynolds can never die. He could not have ever died if he had not given the hospital, for every church, orphanage and all of these splendid homes we live in are the immediate products of "Big Dad." . . . It is the desire of all the colored people that Goodness and Mercy shall ever rest upon his grand widow and her four children.[55]

The Congregation of Reynolds Temple passed a series of resolutions in R.J.R.'s honor, grateful to him for providing five thousand dollars in matching funds to build their church, "and who [had] in other ways assisted in forwarding the work of the church among the colored people of the city." These resolutions extolled R.J.R.'s character, his commitment to the welfare of black and white, and his development of industrial enterprises that "employed more people than any other man in the state."[56]

Similar avowals of affection and respect for the man had been proffered by those residents of the city who believed R.J.R.s' economic leadership had made Winston prosperous. On the evening of his death, the aldermen had called a special session to pay R.J.R. tribute. R.J.R.'s funeral the next day began with a private ceremony at Reynolda House, the coffin born aloft by oldest son, Dick, and his fellow Boy Scouts. R.J.R.'s closest friends and associates were all present, including Governor Bickett and leading black educator Simon Atkins, with whom R.J.R. and Katharine had remained associated in their role as paternalists and benefactors long after R.J.R. had helped fund Slater Academy. The funeral turned into a public affair. Hundreds lined the streets en route to Salem Cemetery to witness R.J.R.'s hearse pass by, and hundreds more attended the graveside service. City offices, banks, and businesses were closed. All knew Katharine was devastated, although she held up her end, performing the requisite duties of new widowhood while comforting her children.[57]

In the wake of the funeral, Katharine continued to meet all her responsibilities, dressed in one of her two modest mourning costumes. She performed simple acts like telegraphing distant friends and acquaintances and sending acknowledgment cards on stationery from Tiffany's. She reviewed her financial circumstances and followed through on the probation of the will. The city leaders continued to honor R.J.R. through the month of August. The Wachovia Bank passed a resolution in tribute, while the *Winston-Salem Journal* ran articles and editorials about R.J.R.'s bequest for two new hospitals as the news reached the public. Despite her sadness, Katharine embraced a new project close to her heart. She had resolved to open her own public school on the Reynolda Estate that fall, having made arrangements with the superintendent the previous spring to do so. Parents had already begun signing up their children the previous May, and she had hired several teachers. The pupils would include her own children, their friends, children from the village, and the rural children in the neighborhood. (In time, Katharine would launch a smaller second school for the black children from Five Row.) Because Katharine's original school was registered as a county school, farm children from the neighborhood attended for free, while family friends from outside the district paid tuition. To make this work, the county had closed the local school and paid Katharine an allowance per local pupil to run hers in its stead. As her daughter pointed out many years later, Katharine in effect had gone into the business of managing a public school. She hired Charles Barton Keen to design and build the white school building and hired top teachers and paid them well, so she never broke even despite the financial collaboration with the school system. The children, white and black, received an exemplary education, unparalleled in the traditional public schools.[58]

The Reynolda School opened for the first time in October 1918 with three grades and three teachers. Within days, however, the city was stricken with the flu epidemic. The disease hit close to home. When Katharine's daughter Nancy became ill, she sent for Jessie Hill, R.J.R.'s nurse in Philadelphia. Miss Hill arrived by train, eager to take on her new position, but fell fatally ill almost immediately, a victim of the flu herself. Not only did Katharine have to console this young woman's family as well as her own, but she also had to quarantine her entire household, in hopes that no one else would suffer from the disease.[59]

R.J.R.'s death and the mourning period that followed changed Katharine. That Christmas she took the children by chauffeur-driven car to Pinehurst and then farther south through South Carolina, Georgia, and Florida, and back, staying at resorts all along the way to stave off her grief. But then she turned a corner, after which she pursued her own interests more, although she never truly gave up her multiple public and private responsibilities. It was also in this first year after R.J.R.'s death that Katharine hired a handsome young World War I veteran as superintendent of her Reynolda School.

J. Edward Johnston had grown up in South Carolina. After his father died in a train accident, his widowed mother had moved her children, Ed and his sister, to the town of Davidson, North Carolina, where Ed had eventually attended Davidson College and graduated in 1914. His college yearbook photo caption stated simply, "A handsome face is nature's best gift." He was a member of the Hebrew Club and the Eumenean Society who played guitar and football, and the college yearbook alleged, "[He] simply can't be held in when it comes to the girls."[60] After college, although he considered attending seminary, he worked instead as a principal in Davidson County, while his mother ran a boardinghouse for students on the edge of the campus to make ends meet. He then served with the First Division overseas in World War I, holding the rank of lieutenant. He was an officer of the Fifth Field Artillery Battalion and was sent first to England and then France. His post at the Reynolda School, on the recommendation of the Winston superintendent and with Katharine's final approval, marked his first job after the war.[61]

Reynolda cook Nannie Withers later claimed that Katharine and Ed Johnston fell in love at first sight when he came to the estate for an interview. Reynolda School teacher Ethel Brock, who accompanied Katharine as a chaperone on a tour of civic buildings in the Northeast with architect Charles Barton Keen; Mr. Latham, the Winston school superintendent; and Ed Johnston, claimed that sparks first flew on this trip months later.[62] There is truth to that observation. Ed Johnston wrote Katharine eight months after that February 1920 excursion, "Do you remember the blue sweater you gave me last February in Cleveland? Each time I put it on I am reminded of that school inspection trip and the events which followed that spring."[63] Three months later, Katharine wrote Edward that by February 1920, "[I knew] I loved you then Edward and I've been loving you ever since."[64] By the fall of 1920, Katharine and Edward were devoted to each other and planning their wedding, but committed to keeping their intentions secret from those around them. Edward had resigned from his post as superintendent at Reynolda and moved to Wilson, North Carolina, where he had taken on a management position in a tobacco manufactory owned by the Reynolds Tobacco Company. He expressed some trepidation about learning the business, but Katharine encouraged him. They wrote each other religiously, almost on a daily basis, exchanging heartfelt expressions of their love for each other, beautiful endearments, and deep longings.

But several other important aspects emerged in these letters as well. Both shared their mutual concern about what others would make of their relationship. Katharine was thirteen years older than Ed, at least ten million dollars wealthier, and had four children ranging in age from nine to sixteen. She was a businesswoman and a social-reform leader. Ed was a virtually penniless man by comparison. They reassured each other that their love was so strong they could withstand disapproval, be it from their family members, their friends and associates, or society at large. One by one, they began to tell their nearest kin and closest advisors about their love for each other and their plan to marry the following year. They quickly discovered that their affection had long been evident and their engagement therefore no surprise to those closest to them. Not everyone supported their relationship. Edward wrote Katharine, "I am so distressed that you are coming in for so much criticism." Katharine's sister Maxie and brother-in-law James Dunn disapproved of their romance and told Katharine so. Edward and Katharine feared Will Reynolds's reaction, although it proved milder than they had expected. Katharine did not even broach the subject with her own parents until the following January and did not tell her three youngest children of their wedding plans until shortly before the June 1921 wedding.[65]

The letter exchanges also reveal Katharine's special role in their relationship as Edward's mentor. Just as R.J.R. had trained Katharine in the tobacco business and helped her learn how to invest money in the stock market, Katharine now helped Edward in his pursuit of the tobacco business and making money on Wall Street. It was Katharine who secured the position for Edward in the company, and it was she who loaned him some fifty thousand dollars and helped him invest in Reynolds stock. "I can't thank you enough Katharine for all that you've done to secure such a huge block of

'A' stock for me and the check you so kindly included in your last letter," he wrote her in November 1920.[66] Edward reciprocated, much as Katharine had done for R.J.R., by looking out for her personal welfare. He worried constantly about her health and urged her to get more rest, eat better, and drink less. He recognized that she constantly pushed herself into an exhausted state by meeting the needs of everyone around her, from her children to her sisters to her farm managers to the Reynolds Tobacco Company officers to the political dignitaries who liked to be entertained at Reynolda at the drop of a hat. Only to Edward did Katharine complain that she had greeted fifty callers one Sunday afternoon and evening and had been unable to go to bed until she ushered the last one out close to midnight. This series of exchanges between the two—Katharine's knowledge of business and finance and Edward's attention and care—only seemed to deepen their love for each other.[67]

During this period in what would be late in her unexpectedly short life, Katharine stepped back and forth between respectable southern ladyhood and more modern pursuer of sensual experiences. She embraced entertainment and leisure more, holding dances in her living room that people still talk about today and traveling to greater numbers of resorts.[68] Falling in love with J. Edward Johnston marked her biggest leap forward in her search for a more self-serving life. Though Johnston was thirteen years her junior and lacked any financial wherewithal, Katharine adored him, and their relationship was a passionate one.[69] She made her new commitment to herself apparent to her parents when she finally told them about her engagement. She explained to Edward: "I told them how I'd worked and planned for the happiness of others, but now I was working and planning day and night for my own—of how I loved you. . . . Then I told them what a wonderful and splendid man you were. . . . Finally, I asked for their blessing for me and for you."[70]

On June 8, 1921, Katharine held a garden party for five hundred at her estate. She had even hired Mario Archer Chamblee, soloist at the Metropolitan Opera, to perform. At a much smaller dinner gathering of her closest friends and family later that evening, she announced her wedding date, set three days later. Family friend and Presbyterian minister D. Clay Lilly, who had married R.J.R. and Katharine sixteen years earlier, performed the ceremony.[71] Daughter Mary wrote in her diary about the event: "At about 7:15 Mother was married to Mr. Johnston. The affair was very quiet. Smith was ring bearer and Nancy and myself were flower girls."[72] The newlyweds spent the summer honeymooning in postwar Europe, touring historic buildings, popular gardens, and French battlegrounds, and sending the children frequent postcards bearing their love.

They returned to Winston-Salem in mid-August, and following a spate of parties welcoming them back as a newly married couple, Edward left for New York City to learn the banking business in early September. There he poured over dense books on accounting and finance, not unlike F. Scott Fitzgerald's young protagonist in *The Great Gatsby*. Meanwhile, Katharine told the company officers that Edward was resigning from his Reynolds position. Edward replied to her report about this conversation: "I was much amused over your description of Mr. Lasater's ill concealed joy and relief over our decision—not so much our being in New York but my not remaining with the company." He added that he thought he would enjoy his new work at the Guarantee Trust and was going to receive instruction in the Personal Trust and the Bond Departments immediately.[73]

While Edward trained as a banker in New York, writing lonely letters to Katharine about missing her, Katharine found herself caught up yet again in innumerable business and social demands, from her sister Ruth's marriage to Charles Lucas and her brother Eugene's marriage to Katie Spaugh to managing the farm and her money in preparation for moving to New York with the three youngest children, Miss Van Den Berg, and Elizabeth Thompson. (Katharine's oldest son, Dick, was enrolled at the Tome Boarding School in Baltimore.) Edward had been charged with finding the children good schools and had rented a spacious apartment at a tony address on East Sixtieth Street.

Meanwhile, Katharine was pregnant, despite her doctors' warnings against having another child after her heart attack and abortion in 1914. The family moved to New York that winter, which meant Katharine could be close to the best doctors in the country. Later that spring, Lola Katharine Johnston was born in the Plaza Hotel with Miss Van Den Berg attending, but the infant girl died the next day. The family traveled to Atlantic City, where Katharine wrote a friend, "I am here convalescing after a long illness," and one of the girls told her governess, "Bum, I am so happy. It is wonderful to have a father again."[74] By late June, the Johnstons were back in New York, where Katharine entertained Edith Vanderbilt and her daughter Cornelia, who was good friends with Nancy. The children enjoyed their time in New York City together, with four adults (Katharine, Ed, Miss Thompson, and

Miss Van Den Berg) and four children, crowded even in their large apartment and surrounded by canaries, turtles, love birds, and even a monkey.[75] Over the summer, Katharine vacationed at Thousand Islands with Edward, while the children attended camp. Katharine and Edward returned to Reynolda, and Edward started working at Wachovia Bank. Six months later, he was named assistant trust officer and appointed to Wachovia's board of directors.

Katharine had closed the Reynolda School, although the school for the black children on the estate continued in operation. She remained interested in progressive social reforms, although she had limited time to commit to them. Now in her early forties, her health was often precarious. Her pregnancy and recovery had been followed by another pregnancy, all of which seriously limited her energy between 1921 and 1924.

In the wake of women's critical World War I contributions, the nature of reform work and its demands for elite women's leadership had changed. The old-style Associated Charities, the predominant aid society in Winston, had long lacked real resources to meet growing need. In 1923, the city of Winston-Salem established a Community Chest to fill this social gap, collecting thirty-eight thousand dollars from the five agencies under its new umbrella—the Boy Scouts, the Salvation Army, the YWCA, the YMCA, and the Associated Charities—to do so. This consolidation also signaled that leadership in these organizations came no longer from voluntary benevolent locals but from salary-earning social-service professionals.[76] Meanwhile, the State Board of Charities and Public Welfare had established County Boards of Charities and Public Welfare across the state. The county committee's duties included administration of poor relief; oversight of the discharged insane, probationed prisoners, and delinquent children; assistance for the unemployed; and the provision of "wholesome recreation." With the institutionalization of aid through local and state government, Katharine could turn her attention elsewhere.[77]

Despite R.J.R.'s death, Katharine had remained a popular public figure in North Carolina's social world. During her nearly three years of widowhood, a number of businessmen and politicians, including at least one future governor, had courted her devotedly.[78] Everyone knew she was incredibly wealthy, having inherited a fifth of her husband's estate and been appointed guardian for the children's four-fifths share. They also knew that she still wielded considerable political clout as Josephus Daniels's longtime friend.

President Woodrow Wilson even appointed her to serve on the Annual Assay Committee, the first woman charged with examining the weight and fineness of newly minted U.S. coins. Her formal visit in February 1921 to the U.S. Mint in Philadelphia as a member of this committee created headline news. "Woman Handles and Counts Vast Sums at the Mint," proclaimed the front page of the *Philadelphia Public Ledger*. She had also been appointed to the executive committee of the North Carolina State Fair, a fitting honor given her sustained interests in agricultural reform.[79] In 1923, Katharine invited forty friends to Reynolda, where she asked them to form an auxiliary to the Juvenile Relief Association. They acquiesced, and that group soon morphed into the Winston-Salem Junior League. She hosted the NCFWC members once again during their state convention in Winston, providing a special tea for the delegates on the Reynolda porches. She continued to support Normal Women's College, even holding a special event for sixty alumnae at her home.

Katharine also upheld suffrage for women, an issue that had percolated through virtually all the reform efforts in which she had engaged over the previous decade. She had always been interested in politics. Hugh Chatham, a local politician, asked Katharine's father if his famous daughter would give him money to support the Democratic ticket in Surry County. Zach Smith told Chatham to ask her himself. When Hugh screwed up his courage and did so, she gave him double his request with the proviso that he had better win.[80] The NCFWC, with which Katharine had been long affiliated, was supporting suffrage by 1915. National organizer Mary Gertrude Fendall of the National Woman's Party had asked Katharine in 1917 to help arrange a woman-suffrage meeting in Winston.[81] Although Miss Van Den Berg had written Katharine that she had been disappointed after attending a speech by Congresswoman Jeannette Rankin because "she spoke most of the time for womans suffrage, rather than on some of the most vital questions," Katharine felt otherwise.[82] On Election Day in 1920, Katharine made sure she got to the polls to vote, publicly demonstrating her commitment to the Nineteenth Amendment at a time when many North Carolina women remained exceedingly reluctant to do so.[83]

All told, Katharine's reform interests in this later period were more scattered and eclectic than sustained perhaps, but her personal life had taken on a new primacy. By January 1924, Katharine was pregnant and expecting a child in May. Edward had settled into his appointment at Wachovia and had taken up competitive polo with a vengeance, a sport that allowed well-heeled people "to be rich together," as F. Scott Fitzgerald once famously observed.[84] Her oldest son, Dick, was proving difficult as an adolescent. He had dropped out of boarding school and out of college, wrecked his motorcycle, disappeared for days at a time, and expressed his dislike for Edward, who had become a scoutmaster early on in their relationship in an effort to win over the reluctant youth. Katharine and Dick remained in close touch, only because Katharine wrote him every day about the news from Reynolda and inquired about his health. These last years were curious ones for Katharine and her family.[85] Their lives could be surprisingly conventional for all their wealth and influence. The family was in the throes of reformulating itself as Dick Jr. came of age, Edward joined them as the new father of the family, and Katharine anticipated a new baby.

Katharine had been playing at the edges of a modernist sensibility throughout her marriage to R. J. Reynolds, if measured by her mercurial attraction to consumerism and leisure, and by her insistence on her own competence as a public reformer, a businesswoman, and a builder of a model world in Reynolda. Still, she never really escaped her belief in nineteenth-century moral absolutes, for she remained unwilling to forgo the language, aesthetics, and values of the Victorian era. R.J.R.'s death forced her to look at her life anew. Then she lost her heart to J. Edward Johnston. Although she would not have been able to articulate it as such, her relationship with Edward drew her into a more modernist landscape of sensuality and the subconscious, where a man's and a woman's role in this novel relationship were less clear and, in some aspects, turned upside down. Katharine, just entering her forties, remade herself at this time, dressing in the latest flapper fashions, with bared arms and cleavage, unleashing a newly sexual self.

Her great ambition had compelled Katharine to seek out some aspects of modernity and test the limits of southern womanhood throughout her life, and R.J.R.'s wealth had given her the independence to do it. What she discovered with his death is that she wanted to love again and in a different kind of partnership. Katharine's marriage to R.J.R. had burdened her with traditional as well as weighty responsibilities, even as that same marriage freed her to challenge some conventional expectations. R.J.R. had come of age in the rough-hewn rural world of postwar tobacco cultivation, manufacture, and selling. He had turned himself into a first-class industrialist by the turn of the century and remained an innovator for the rest of his life, eagerly investing in the latest machinery, marketing techniques, labor strategies, management advice. and business approaches, all of which brought him great fortune. Because Winston-Salem residents for the most part, white and black, believed they owed the city's relative prosperity to R.J.R., even if his company had also brought attendant urban problems hitherto unknown in North Carolina and much of the South, R.J.R. had had tremendous influence in shaping the political economy of the people and this place.

Katharine, although she constantly sought autonomy for herself and was a prominent public reform figure in North Carolina in her own right, never achieved the kind of power R.J.R. commanded. She certainly had the financial and intellectual wherewithal to incorporate modern ideas about technology, science, finance, domesticity, and social reform into her spaces, and she did: in her family and her home, her schools and her estate, her clubs and associations, and even the family business. But she never secured R.J.R.'s command of the company, or the town, or the region, even after he was dead and she owned or managed all his assets and property, including a disproportionate share of R. J. Reynolds Tobacco Company stock.

The company experienced a significant setback with R.J.R.'s death. As Reynolds Tobacco Company historian Nannie Tilley has written, "There is no way to estimate the decline in morale that undoubtedly followed the death of R. J. Reynolds."[86] There is every indication that this dampened morale was generated by bona fide changes in policy and action. The sustained efforts to improve the working lives of Reynolds workers came to a screeching halt and were not restored until workers launched a series of labor protests in 1919. No wonder then that within just a few months of R. J. Reynolds's passing, in light of these changes, the city experienced a race riot six days after Armistice, and three innocent people were killed. A disappointed gang of young white would-be lynchers turned their anger into a downtown looting spree and then headed to the black section of town, beating up and shooting at African Americans all along the way. But black Winstonites, much to the gang's surprise, fought back, and the handful of law enforcement officers on the scene simply fled. Law and order returned to the city the next day, and the white hoodlums were eventually tried and convicted to the black community's relief, but not before the incident made national news. Then, only four months later, national organizers from the Tobacco Workers International Union of the American Federation of Labor arrived in Winston to support worker disgruntlement. Throughout these incidents, the leadership that R.J.R. and Katharine had once provided was sorely missed.[87]

Despite her stature and wealth, for she was executor of R. J. Reynolds's estate, valued conservatively at ten million dollars, Katharine found herself vulnerable in her widowhood. The senior leadership at the company, led by her brother-in-law Will Reynolds, had squeezed her out of any decision-making role by racing against her to buy up class A stock holdings and trump even her behind-the-scenes authority. When she asked Will Reynolds to find a prominent place in the company for Johnston, he had allegedly balked. Then, after her marriage to Edward, and while they were on their honeymoon in Europe, she discovered to her great embarrassment that her New York bank had revealed her personal financial information to several Reynolds Tobacco Company officers. Katharine wound up sending one angry telegram after another from the Grand Hotel Beau-Rivage in Geneva to the National Park Bank in New York. Two of her one-hundred-thousand-dollar notes had come due while she was out of the country, and though she had requested an extension, the bank had written to James A. Gray, vice president of Reynolds Tobacco and head of the local Wachovia Bank. Incensed, Katharine wrote, "[This inquiry into my] private affairs, a private matter of mine which under no circumstances should be taken up with anyone but me, was entirely unwarranted and entirely uncalled for, and as I had always heretofore believed, opposed to the business principles and policy of your institution. . . . Your knowledge of my ample ability to protect these loans make me doubly regret this inexcusable action on your part."[88] Katharine resented not only the unnecessary doubts cast upon her financial situation but also the bank's reliance on Gray's opinion of her fiscal circumstances, as well as the loss of face it represented. As wealthy as she was, she could not secure herself a place at the Reynolds board table or receive respect from the banking establishment.[89]

That Katharine received this succession of snubs offers insight into the world of white southern women in the early twentieth-century South because it suggests that even the most privileged of women, and in this case a woman who had spent so much of her life deliberately seizing the freedoms of men, could press gendered boundaries only so far. In the end, she had to accept her reduced stature following her first husband's death, even as her wealth escalated. Still, she did have the freedom and the wherewithal to seek her happiness through an unconventional marriage.

Katharine discovered that when she could not escape the confines of southern womanhood, which she came to see as a series of unending duties on behalf of others, and as the new leadership at R. J. Reynolds Tobacco Company increasingly disregarded her authority after R.J.R.'s death, she looked to cultural expressions of modernity as a means through which to find pleasure. In this stage of her life, her pursuit of happiness turned less on cultivating family relations and contributing to society, and more on embracing consumerism, leisure, sport, and popular culture in general. She delighted in the latest jewelry and fashions. Her home and estate continued to model the most recent technologies and conveniences. She relished spending time at resorts where she could play golf and go riding. She enjoyed big cities, traveling frequently to Baltimore and New York to dine, attend parties, shop, tour, and conduct business. Facilitated by R.J.R.'s wealth, Katharine used these pursuits to conceive of herself as a thoroughly modern American woman, even as she continued negotiating the public and private expectations placed on her as one of the wealthiest and most powerful women in the South.

Katharine did not give up her commitment to reform work completely after R.J.R.'s death.[90] She was on the executive committee organizing the Southern Sociological Congress in Winston-Salem in 1919, for example. She fostered the organization of the Winston-Salem Junior League in 1923.[91] But she no longer showed the same enthusiasm for building on the bigger profile she had been developing earlier through her state service and reform work during the war years. Her pursuit of more personal satisfaction, signaling a new, modern sensibility, proved more important to her. Yet part of that pursuit centered on having more children, a decision she herself had made. Edward supported this choice but expressed concern for her health and feared for her safety. On May 20, 1924, she gave birth to her last child, J. Edward Johnston Jr. She had been ill through much of the pregnancy and had spent the last several months in New York City on bed rest and under hospital care. Edward immediately telegraphed the children that Katharine and the baby were doing well, but three days later Katharine died of an embolism.[92]

On May 26, 1924, the city of Winston-Salem, North Carolina, mourned Katharine's untimely death, hailing her as "a new woman for a new day." The members of the Retail Merchants' Association closed their stores to express their respect. The school board ordered exercises commemorating

Katharine in every public school. The board of aldermen organized a late-afternoon service at the brand-new Richard J. Reynolds Memorial Auditorium attended by more than a thousand "sorrowful" men, women, and children. Crowds lined the city streets after the ceremony, standing in silence as the funeral cortege passed by. At the Reynolds family grave site in the Salem cemetery, "an immense multitude" gathered in "reverent quiet."[93]

Public mourning of a woman on this grand a scale is an infrequent occurrence in the South, past or present. But Katharine Smith Reynolds Johnston deserved this recognition. During her relatively short life, she had negotiated the changing confines of white southern womanhood with aplomb. She had dedicated much of her adulthood to working hard for the well-being of others, starting with her own family and radiating outward. She had brought a new dynamic to her role as wife and mother in the domestic sphere, proved a skillful practitioner of the domestic arts with the aid of her domestic staff, and often applied her gracious hospitality to larger social and political purposes. She improved the working conditions of white and black tobacco workers, white women wage earners, and poor white rural men and women, even if her actions on behalf of working people remained circumscribed by her limiting beliefs about class and race and her desire to support the R. J. Reynolds Tobacco Company's interests. She had a gift for understanding moneymaking and accounting and evolved into an exceptional manager of her household and her estate. As a young woman, she had become an avid investor at a time when very few women (or men for that matter) understood Wall Street, and she bought and sold stocks with skill for the rest of her life.[94] She proved an adroit businesswoman, demonstrated by her influence on the R. J. Reynolds Tobacco Company, although she never held a formal office or a position on the board. Katharine oversaw the building of her own country home and landscape gardens, began a model farm village at least in part to train rural families in the latest scientific and technological practices, established her own public schools for white and black children, and funded her own Presbyterian church for family, friends, and neighbors, all the while maintaining a strong interest in missionary efforts at home and abroad. She was a well-known public person, not only in the North Carolina Piedmont but also in the governor's mansion in Raleigh, North Carolina, and the halls of Washington, D.C.[95] Her actions were followed closely by the press, and her philanthropic gifts were widely celebrated.[96]

Her death earned her an obituary in the *New York Times* because she had been the wife of tobacco magnate R. J. Reynolds. The *Times* observed that she had recently given the city of Winston-Salem a memorial auditorium valued at $750,000 in honor of her first husband, as well as the land for a new, state-of-the-art public high school. City fathers hailed these gifts as symbols of her commitment to providing an outstanding education for the children (understood to be the *white* children) of the Winston-Salem community to ensure its superiority in the South, if not the nation.[97]

By all reports, the public mourning over Katharine's death that late May day was unlike anything the city had ever witnessed. While Winston boasted its fair share of important people, including the Hanes and the Fries families, who had made their fortunes in textiles, as well as the Grays, who headed Reynolds Tobacco and Wachovia Bank and Trust, no public leader's death, including that of R. J. Reynolds himself, had ever received such a prominent display of public bereavement.[98]

Although Katharine's family held a private funeral service at her Reynolda Estate, presided over by four Presbyterian ministers, the large public service held at the brand-new R. J. Reynolds Auditorium she had built was ecumenical. Several ministers spoke to the assembled mourners, including Rev. J. Kenneth Pfohl of Home Moravian, the oldest, most respected church in the city. Reverend Pfohl reminded his audience of the controlling nature of gender as destiny at her eulogy: "On the altar of her motherhood she [had] sacrificed her own life." Katharine's existence, Pfohl told his audience, was meant to show that "the gentle spirit of womanliness may still be maintained and the loving service of the home continued and yet the wider demands of the new day not be neglected." Despite the freedoms that marriage to R.J.R. had given her, and despite the complex ways she had pursued those freedoms, in the end Katharine was heralded in death for being his wife and for her maternal commitment to the well-being of her community. Notably, in his eulogy Reverend Pfohl identified Katharine not as "Mrs. Johnston" but as "Mrs. Reynolds Johnston." Even her second husband, J. Edward Johnston, succumbed to popular opinion and his oldest stepson's insistence that Katharine be buried not in the plot he intended to occupy alongside her one day but in R.J.R.'s grave site.[99]

Reverend Pfohl had been quick to underscore Katharine's special role in the community. "She was a woman of wide vision . . . a dreamer of dreams. . . . She was a Christian wife, a Christian mother, a Christian friend, and a Christian citizen, working for a Christian city."[100] Pfohl articulated what the city leaders valued most in her contributions and feared least: Katharine's efforts to mold the image of Winston-Salem as a peaceful, promising, cultivated New South city. Her public roles, he suggested, conveyed the best of human capability, for hers was a charitable maternalism carried out before a benevolent God.[101]

By calling her "a woman for the new day," Reverend Pfohl also valued Katharine for her embrace of modernization, which he defined as her maternal commitment to the public welfare. Although he paid tribute to the community's foremothers for their dedication to their children and households, he commended Katharine for having the courage to care for not only her family but the wider public too. "We have trembled sometimes for the womanhood of the new day lest they might suffer from its too wide demands upon their thought and sympathy and effort." Indeed, Pfohl expressed concern that these new social expectations might undermine the very virtues of southern womanhood. He asked his listeners, "Will not this new day with its demands for attention to the public welfare, its calls for public service, the responsibilities of woman's suffrage, cause women to lose something of their womanliness, neglect the claims of home and family, and refuse the call of motherhood?"

He answered his provocative question by citing Katharine's sterling example. "To a degree unequalled by few others, Mrs. Reynolds Johnston gave of her time and thought to the public good," he explained, "and yet who has not admired her devotion to her home, the care with which she provided for the comforts and happiness of her loved ones."[102]

Katharine, because she had embraced "modernity" so strenuously and so publicly, even as she had upheld gendered convention so dutifully, had to be "refitted" into the southern-lady box upon her death, at the very least to salvage R.J.R.'s patriarchal reputation and that of the city's leadership and the tobacco company's dominance as well. In that light, the good reverend and all the city fathers could read Katharine's life and legacy simply as an extension of R.J.R.'s paternalism. The outpouring of townspeople, in all their variety, who lined the streets as her hearse passed by, who waited at the cemetery, and who attended her public service, undoubtedly mourned Katharine's passing for the same reasons too.

We will never know if Katharine, had she lived well into old age, would have pursued multiple reforms leading to significant social and political transformations that would have helped rock the region out of its intransigence. After R.J.R.'s death, she pursued a grand philanthropic venture that hints at what she might have accomplished with a longer life. In June 1919, she offered the mayor what she called "a proposition." She would give the city fifty thousand dollars for a new school site and build a beautiful state-of-the-art auditorium as the central building, to be flanked by a new high school and a new technical school, the latter paid for by the city, as a memorial to her husband. The public auditorium was intended to have a sweeping cultural impact on the region by hosting national figures from the performing arts.

There were problems with her proposal that few citizens felt they could raise. Some wondered if the gift of the land was not as selfless as the proposal suggested. Because the Reynolds estate owned the land being proffered and more lots in the vicinity, it stood to gain from the development that would surely follow the establishment of the school plant. The future school, even more importantly, was approximately two to six miles distant from the majority of the city's population and closest to the city's wealthiest families.[103] These issues notwithstanding, Mayor Gorrell and Superintendent Latham accepted Katharine's proposal, and she promptly hired Charles Barton Keen to design all three edifices. It was her hope, she explained to city residents, that Winston-Salem would now provide its best and brightest students with an exemplary education, indeed, the best in the South.[104]

Four years later, Katharine with Edward's help built another legacy. She had persuaded her old minister and family friend, Rev. D. Clay Lilly, to leave his large urban church in Lexington, Kentucky, to lead her tiny Reynolda Chapel with its twenty-five families. She assured him that she and the elders and deacons in her church wanted his help to "start missions in the counties back of [them]" and use "the fine influence of a man like [him]" to make their school even better.[105] She also wanted to start a "rural school" that would prepare up to 220 students from the first grade through high school to gain admission into the university, with the intention of turning it over to the Presbyterian Church.[106] She sweetened the invitation by financing a yearly conference that Lilly could organize on the most pressing religious issues of the day.

As an accomplished leader of the Southern Presbyterian Church, Lilly was a well-known minister, frequent author, and tireless organizer. Dedicated to promoting a religious education that took the intellect into account and a strong advocate for women's leadership in the Presbyterian Church, he greatly wished to see the Reynolda Church become an important conference center. He intended to gather together "a group of representative scholars from colleges, universities, theological seminaries and the pastorate who [would] concertedly study present-day problems of Christianity. . . . They would have as their purpose and spirit an honest and courageous approach."[107]

These meetings, which became known as the Reynolda Conferences, for they were held in Katharine's expansive living room, were open to the public and brought prominent conservative religious leaders and educators from around the country to discuss secular challenges to Protestantism in constructive ways on an annual basis between 1924 and 1927.[108] Beginning with the first conference, held only a month after Katharine's death, on evolution and the church, a topic Katharine Reynolds herself had approved, participants and the national press alike heralded the timeliness and the quality of the discussions invoked.[109]

Her commitment to public education and the arts, and to mission work, schools, and the Reynolda Conferences, intentions all cut short by her death, suggests that Katharine Smith Reynolds Johnston might very well have been "a new woman for a new day" had she lived longer. Together the lives of R.J.R. and Katharine complicate our reading of the early twentieth-century southern ruling elite. Neither villains nor heroes, they pursued ambitious goals that left them stranded more times than not between old worlds and new. Theirs was always an uneasy alliance between their wealth and power and the people who worked around them and for them, and whose lives, for good and bad, were fundamentally reshaped by Katharine and R.J.R.'s great fortune.

Epilogue

Over the course of their lifetimes, Richard Joshua Reynolds and Katharine Smith Reynolds shaped the experiences and opportunities of thousands of North Carolinians, black and white, rich and poor. R.J.R. left behind a complicated legacy for understanding the responsibility of business leaders to the communities that made their success possible. Katharine left behind a complicated legacy for understanding the motives shaping elite southern white women's commitment to a changing society. Together Katharine and R.J.R. worked hard to make their wealth, and they used most of it to their own benefit. But they also gave some of their money to their community and state. In fact, their acts of giving tacitly acknowledged that their company's success was rooted in the commitment of the working people around them as well as to the city they called home. For good or bad, theirs was the last generation in which that measure of personalism and paternalism prevailed.

The R. J. Reynolds Tobacco Company assumed a new life of its own after R.J.R.'s death. As a widow, Katharine had little authority despite her earlier influence. Under new leadership culled from the ranks of senior management, the company flourished. Despite protracted battles with organized labor that had long-term implications for foiling African Americans' quest for equality in the 1940s, and despite public acknowledgment of the proven links between cancer and smoking in the 1950s, the R. J. Reynolds Tobacco Company had evolved into a top international corporation by the 1960s. Today, even after the stiff penalties imposed by the Tobacco Master Settlement, Reynolds American continues its profit making by marketing its tobacco products around the globe.

While the city of Winston-Salem mourned Katharine and R.J.R.'s passing almost a century ago, their children suffered the most. Orphaned in the harsh world of adolescence, Katharine and R.J.R.'s sons never really outgrew that stage of their bereavement. Although their stepfather, Edward Johnston, and their uncle Will Reynolds had been named in Katharine's will as co-guardians for all four children, Dick Jr. had been living independently from his family for several years by the time of Katharine's death, and Smith soon joined him to pursue a fast-paced lifestyle of aviation, alcohol, and womanizing on both sides of the Atlantic. Mary and Nancy finished their schooling, spent time in Europe, and ran with a fast crowd of wealthy young people too, but their excesses paled next to their brothers, and they settled down to marry within a month of each other in 1929.

The Reynolda Estate had ceased being a working farm with Katharine's death and by the 1930s had become a lavish setting for wild parties during Prohibition. Winston-Salem residents of a certain social class and age still wax nostalgic about the music and booze they shared there. At the last of those parties, Smith Reynolds, newly married to the nightclub vocalist Libby Holman, died of a bullet wound to his head. The cause of his death was never determined, although speculation remains plentiful. Some accused Libby Holman of shooting her young husband; others blamed Smith's best friend, Abe Walker, who was allegedly having an affair with Libby at the time. Still others argue that the three young people, made foolish by too much drink, dared each other to a game of Russian roulette, and Smith lost.

The truth remains locked away in the minds and hearts of a generation of partygoers, servants, and relatives long ago sworn to secrecy. Smith's untimely death and the ensuing investigation made national news for months on end. The newspapers were filled with sordid stories about the endless supply of free-flowing alcohol available during Prohibition at Reynolda. Journalists examined every inch of Smith's short life, making public his bouts of depression at boarding school as well as his overly zealous pursuit of love interests. In one celebrated incident, gossipmongers learned that he had paved Libby Holman's private walk along the beach with rose petals he hand-dropped while piloting his low-flying airplane. Smith's death was so well known around the country that it grew into a cautionary tale about the excesses of the rich and famous in a time of scarcity and vulnerability for most Americans during the Depression. Not one but two movies and a host of books would later offer their own versions of the entire incident. No wonder that the surviving Reynolds family members ultimately elected not to press charges against Holman or Walker.[1]

Smith's death left his brother and sisters devastated. He had been the baby of the family, the darling little boy who had loved to go barefoot in the woods. His parents' passing had cultivated his growing daredevil inclinations. He had acquired his pilot's license at sixteen, signed by none other than Orville Wright. At nineteen, he had piloted his eighty-horsepower Savoia-Marchetti alone from London to China in an extraordinary seventeen-thousand-mile journey.[2] He had married textile heiress Anne Cannon and fathered their daughter, only to divorce Anne and marry the notorious torch singer Libby Holman, all before he had turned twenty years of age. His sudden death left his brother and sisters heirs to his fortune in the wake of their settling out of court with Libby Holman.

In their sadness and with the help of their Uncle Will, Dick, Mary, and Nancy used their inheritance from Smith's estate to create the Z. Smith Reynolds Foundation as a memorial to their youngest brother in 1936.[3] The foundation's mission focused on pursuing "charitable works in the state of North Carolina." Its first major commitment was a nationally heralded program to control venereal disease. In 1946, the foundation supported moving Wake Forest College in Wake County to Winston-Salem, bringing what was then a top regional institution of higher learning to the northwestern sector of the state, where colleges and universities were scarce. The foundation has continued to support Wake Forest University, now a leading national university, to this day through generous scholarships, endowed professorships, and other gifts. But it has also been an important benefactor to hundreds of educational programs and nonprofit initiatives across the state, providing grants to organizations in all one hundred of North Carolina's counties. Over the last nine decades, the foundation has committed support to rural health clinics, public school reform and advocacy groups, kindergartens, domestic violence programs, campaign-finance reform efforts, programs for the elderly, capacity building, environmental advocacy, and community economic development programs. The Z. Smith Reynolds Foundation has put doctors in rural emergency rooms, preserved Bluff Mountain in West Jefferson, North Carolina, and the Nags Head Woods on the Outer Banks, funded a wing in the state museum of art, and helped finance Martin Luther King Jr.'s trip to India to study nonviolence. Today, the foundation is a vibrant organization with an endowment that peaked in 2007 at $470 million. Its mission has matured over the years but retains the Reynolds siblings' original good intentions as captured in the foundation's current mission: to improve the lives of the people of North Carolina. Smith's death, however tragic, has had a significant impact on the state of North

Carolina through the foundation his sisters, brother, and uncle created in his name.[4]

Smith was not the only playboy in the family. R.J.R.'s oldest son and namesake, Dick Jr., acted out that role throughout his life. His drinking problems, which had begun in the 1920s, became legendary, culminating in a drunk-driving accident in England that killed a man in 1929. Unfortunately, Dick never mastered his alcoholism. But like all the Reynoldses, he not only played hard; he worked hard too. With his first wife, Blitz, he built his own country estate, Devotion, in the Blue Ridge Mountains near Roaring Gap, North Carolina, during the Depression, employing several hundred men in desperate need of paid work. He and Blitz had four sons.

He pursued a number of innovative and important ventures: purchasing Curtiss Air Field (later Roosevelt Air Field) on Long Island, facilitating local aviation development in Winston-Salem, establishing an early lab for producing color motion-picture film, buying a shipping company, and rescuing Delta Airlines with a big stock purchase. In 1940, he was elected mayor of Winston-Salem, and he was especially influential on the national political scene. When Franklin Delano Roosevelt ran for office in 1940, Dick chaired the finance committee for the Democratic Party, probably doing more than any other person to secure Roosevelt his third-term victory. He joined the U.S. Navy, served as chief navigator on the USS *Makin Island*, and was awarded the Bronze Star.

A competitive yachtsman, Dick relished nature and the sea far more than business and politics. He created a forty-four-thousand-acre estate on Sapelo Island off the coast of Georgia and founded the Sapelo Island Research Foundation at the University of Georgia in 1949. His second marriage to an actress produced two more sons. His third marriage, a childless one, failed too. His fourth marriage ended with his death in 1964 and produced his only daughter. Though a major stockholder in R. J. Reynolds Tobacco, he never worked for the company, nor did his brother and sisters.[5]

Oldest sister Mary Reynolds married Charles Henry Babcock, an investment banker from Philadelphia, and had four children. Charles Babcock was an influential businessman and a public-minded citizen whose influence continues to be felt throughout the state of North Carolina and especially the Piedmont in the twenty-first century. In 1936, Mary inherited her share of her father's fortune, roughly thirty million dollars, and found herself in the public spotlight, where she was labeled "one of the richest women in the world." She and her husband bought the Reynolda Estate from her siblings and renovated the house. They later gave three hundred acres of the estate to Wake Forest College for its relocation.

Unfortunately, Mary grew ill in the prime of her life and died of cancer in 1953. Her generous will provided twelve million dollars for a charitable trust established as the Mary Reynolds Babcock Foundation. The foundation has a long history of helping people in need. Today it is committed to getting people out of poverty in the southeastern U.S. by building "just and caring communities that nurture people, spur enterprise, bridge differences and foster fairness" across racial, ethnic, economic, and political differences.[6]

Youngest daughter Nancy Susan Reynolds married Henry Walker Bagley. The couple had four children before they divorced in 1953. She later married Gilbert Verney, whom she also divorced. Nancy, who made her home in Connecticut but visited Winston-Salem frequently, was a woman of energy and vision who understood the impact her parents had made on the region. She committed herself to the renovation of the Reynolds family homestead in Critz, Virginia, turning it into a state landmark. She supported scholar Nannie M. Tilley's research and writing of the history of the R. J. Reynolds Tobacco Company, even after the company backed out of the project. Nancy's persistence ensured Tilley's publication of her comprehensive business history, which had been stymied by the company for some two decades. A benefactor of many North Carolina institutions, including Wake Forest University, Nancy and her first husband also donated one hundred thousand dollars to the Harriet Lane Home for the Study of Children's Diseases at Johns Hopkins University in the name of her family's beloved childhood nurse, Henrietta Van Den Berg. This 1948 gift may have marked the first time a private-duty nurse anywhere in the country was publicly honored in this way. Though Miss Van Den Berg had returned to Baltimore once Katharine had remarried, the Reynolds children's adored governess remained close to her charges, attending the births of their own children years later until her death in 1952. Perhaps because Nancy Reynolds outlived her three siblings, she maintained her commitment to preserving the history of her family's past to the end of her life. In addition to supporting Nanny Tilley's research and ensuring the preservation of the Reynolds homestead, she was instrumental in setting up oral histories with living family members and servants associated with the Reynolda Estate before her own death in 1985.[7]

Katharine and Edward's infant son, J. Edward Johnston Jr., was cared for by Edward and Edward's mother, Lola, until Edward remarried. Edward Sr. had inherited a sixth of the Reynolds fortune and was executor for his son's sixth of the estate. He continued to make Winston his home through at least 1927.[8] Shortly thereafter, he relocated to Baltimore and several years later married and had two daughters with his new wife. He was no longer a happy man despite his wealth and second marriage, and according to Edward Jr. succumbed to long depressions and bouts of drinking that played havoc on the emotional lives of his family and especially his son, who feared his father's quick temper and the beatings that could ensue. In 1932, his father sent eight-year-old Edward Jr. alone on a three-day train trip across the country to boarding school in Arizona.

Edward Sr. continued to battle alcoholism through a distinguished World War II career, serving as a colonel in military intelligence and receiving the Legion of Merit badge and the Order of the British Empire for his service.[9] Edward Jr., whose worn face resembled that of his handsome father's even in his old age, had his mother's mathematical proclivities. A sweet, gentle man near the end of his life, he had married, divorced, and remarried happily, raised a big family, secured a PhD late in life, and created a financial advising company that applied physics formulas to investments. Known locally as "the Bird Man of Baltimore," he kept his exotic pets in floor-to-ceiling cages in his living room, taking them out on his front lawn once a year to give workshops about their care to local children. He seldom visited his Reynolds relatives over the course of his lifetime, but he bore them no ill will. He described the mother he never knew as "a strong businesswoman." His brutal treatment by his alcoholic father still haunted him in his last years.[10]

R.J.R.'s illegitimate son, John Neal, had been hired by his father's company as a young man. Like all the Reynolds relatives, he had often received $1,000 gifts of stock from his father and uncle. He was awarded $25,000 from his father's estate in 1918 (a hefty sum but substantially less than the estates R.J.R.'s legitimate children received). John had headed up Reynolds Tobacco's western marketing division as an adult and was headquartered in Omaha, Nebraska, before dying prematurely of pneumonia in 1920. His estate at his death totaled $750,000, nearly all of it in Reynolds stocks. He bequeathed over half a million dollars to the Methodist Children's Home in Winston-Salem and the Oxford orphanage where he had been raised, doing so, he told a close friend, because he wanted to ensure that orphaned children always had enough to eat, a sad commentary on his own childhood experience. Neal's bequest marked the single largest gift made by an individual in Winston-Salem's history up to that time, more than double his own father's bequest for the two hospitals made two years earlier. Neal was buried at Salem Cemetery but not in the R. J. Reynolds family plot. Many years later, Kate and Will Reynolds would be buried next to Neal, their adopted son.[11]

Former executive director of the Z. Smith Reynolds Foundation Tom Lambeth has noted that the wealth and philanthropic interests of Katharine and R. J. Reynolds have undergirded at least seven foundations over the course of the twentieth century and into the twenty-first. These include the Z. Smith Reynolds Foundation; the Mary Reynolds Babcock Foundation; the Josh and Marie Reynolds Foundation; the Kate B. Reynolds Foundation; the Sapelo Island Foundation; the Araca Foundation; and the Christopher Smith Reynolds Foundation. Their collective endowments topped $1.3 billion in 2007 and have bestowed more than $1 billion since their founding, 90 percent of it in North Carolina.[12]

Katharine and R. J. Reynolds believed that their commitment to their city as industrialists and philanthropists was a conscious moral response to the rapid industrialization and urbanization that the R. J. Reynolds Tobacco Company had generated over the last fifty years.[13] Their legacy lives on through their progeny, whose bequests and foundations still wield a social impact on twenty-first-century North Carolina and are now supported by third- and fourth-generation Reynolds family members. It is embodied in the national reputation for academic excellence that Wake Forest University has earned a half century after its relocation to Winston-Salem, thanks to the support of the Babcocks and the Z. Smith Reynolds Foundation. It lives on in the establishment of Reynolda House as an exceptional historic house and private museum of American art thanks to the ambition and energy of Mary Babcock's husband, Charlie, and especially his and Mary's daughter, Barbara Babcock Millhouse, who made the commitment to establish a permanent collection of American art. It lives on in Winston-Salem's embrace of culture and the arts as antidote to the rough-and-tumble world of tobacco. The city launched the first locally established arts council in the United States in 1949 and the first U.S. public arts conservatory (now the University of North Carolina School of the Arts) in 1963.

Katharine and R.J.R.'s legacy also lives on in the city's sustained efforts to build social capital in the twenty-first century. In 2000, Robert Putnam's Social Capital Evaluation of Winston-Salem revealed that while the city could take pride in its long history of charitable giving, much work remained. Relationships among residents across socioeconomic differences remained distrustful, leadership remained concentrated in traditional circles, too few public spaces for informal socializing existed, and volunteerism was minimal and rarely involved interaction with those being helped. In the decade or so since this report, local nonprofits and communities still struggle to generate long-lasting relationships among diverse groups of people to improve the overall health of residents; produce stronger local economies; create wider access to educational opportunities; fight class, race, ethnic and other biases; and make local and state government more responsive. R.J.R. and Katharine Reynolds's legacy remains complex. Their actions helped shape these current realities and challenges. Their philanthropic legacy continues to seek to make amends some one hundred years later.

Notes

Introduction

1. Rev. Dr. D. Clay Lilly, "Many Beautiful Expressions for Mr. R. J. Reynolds," *Winston Salem Journal* (hereafter cited as *WSJ*), July 30, 1918.

2. *Winston-Salem Twin City Sentinel*, July 30, 1918.

3. *Raleigh News and Observer*, July 30, 1918.

4. In "The Yankee of the South," John Gilmer Speed argued in 1901 that the one fail-safe pursuit for ambitious poor southern white men to pursue after the Civil War had been business. He claimed that the majority of all southern presidents of banks and manufactories had their origins in poverty, and the end of slavery created new equalities of opportunity that had not existed earlier. That R.J.R. painted himself as a poor boy made good speaks as much to this notion as to the American self-made man one. John Gilmer Speed, "The Yankee of the South," *Harper's Weekly*, March 4, 1901, 371–72.

5. Blair, "Richard Joshua Reynolds," in *Biographical History of North Carolina*, 334–40; H.E.C.B., "R. J. Reynolds," *Mount Airy News*, December 9, 1909; "The Junior Observer's Tribute to R. J. R.," *Winston-Salem Twin City Sentinel*, August 8, 1918; "Tobacco King Is Dead," *Baltimore Star*, July 29, 1918; obituary, *Raleigh News and Observer*, July 30, 1918; and "R. J. Reynolds, Advertiser of Prince Albert and Camel Brands," *Printers Ink* (New York), August 18, 1918.

6. "Funeral Service of Mr. Reynolds Held Yesterday," *WSJ*, August 1, 1918.

7. "A Tribute from Reynolds Temple," *Winston Salem Sentinel*, August 12, 1918.

8. Friend and Glover, *Southern Manhood*, vii–xiv.

9. "Funeral Service of Mr. Reynolds Held Yesterday."

10. Woodward, *Origins of the New South*, 130. For the best recent overview of the Woodward school and subsequent scholarship on the Woodward thesis, see Boles and Johnson, *Origins of the New South*.

11. Cash, *Mind of the South*, 200.

12. Billings, *Planters and the Making of a "New South"*; Escott, *Many Excellent People*.

13. Carlton, "Revolution from Above," 464–67.

14. Ibid., 465.

15. Brandt, *Cigarette Century*, 14.

Chapter One. Making a Business of It

1. Siegel, *Roots of Southern Distinctiveness*, 9, 48–49; Clement, *History of Pittsylvania County*, 32–48; Crawford, "Rock Spring Plantation," 5.

2. Crawford, "Rock Spring Plantation," 6.

3. Blair, "Richard Joshua Reynolds," 334.

4. Pedigo and Pedigo, *History of Patrick and Henry Counties*, 17–18; Tilley, *Reynolds Homestead*, 3–5.

5. Tilley, *Reynolds Homestead*, 2–5; Pedigo and Pedigo, *History of Henry and Patrick Counties*, 26.

6. Tilley, *Reynolds Homestead*, 5, 8–11.

7. Shanks, *Secession Movement in Virginia*, 1–17; Noe, *Southwest Virginia's Railroad*, 4–9; Tripp, *Yankee Town, Southern Town*, 6–12; Majewski, *House Dividing*, 12–14.

8. Tilley, *Reynolds Homestead*, 15, 17, 19.

9. Pedigo and Pedigo, *History of Patrick and Henry Counties*, 11.

10. Siegel, *Roots of Southern Distinctiveness*, 3–4, 124–25, 162–65, argues forcibly that the hinterlands surrounding Danville, including Patrick County, may have been blessed with men of strong entrepreneurial inclination, but they could not overcome their material conditions and the technical peculiarities of tobacco to bring widespread economic development to their region, making the successes of Hardin Reynolds the exception, not the rule.

11. Kulikoff, "Transition to Capitalism," 120–44.

12. Ibid.; Affidavits, 1865–83, box 2, file 262, Reynolds Family Papers (hereafter RFP), Archives, Reynolda House Museum of American Art (hereafter RHMAA), Winston-Salem, N.C.; twelve attendance certificates to witnesses for Hardin Reynolds in cases heard before the Patrick County Circuit Court between 1871 and 1876, file 264; Court Papers, Decrees, 1860–95, file 265; sixteen Patrick County summonses, 1854–82, file 266; all in box 4, RFP, RHMAA.

13. Tilley, *Reynolds Homestead*, 14–15; Connor, Boyd, and Hamilton, *History of North Carolina*, 4:1; Blair, "Reynolds, Richard Joshua," Barbara Millhouse private collection of family papers (hereafter BMFP).

14. Interviews with Reynolds Homestead docent Susannah Netherland and historic preservation consultant Elizabeth King, August 10, 2009, Reynolds Homestead, Critz, Va.

15. Pedigo and Pedigo, *History of Patrick and Henry Counties*, 18–19; Reynolds Homestead, Rock Spring Plantation, National Register of Historic Places Inventory-Nomination, 2.

16. Approximately sixty gravesites have been identified by Virginia Polytechnic Institute and State University (hereafter VT) researchers and students in recent years. Only three actual headstones remain, including the grave of Will Lee Reynolds (1851–1936), born a year after R.J.R.

17. Tilley, *Reynolds Homestead*, x; the bed, piano, seashells, etc. are all on exhibit at the restored Reynolds Homestead, a state and national historic landmark in Critz, Virginia, owned and operated by VT. Pedigo and Pedigo, *History of Patrick and Henry Counties*, 18, indicates that wealthy families in this region typically gave each of their daughters their "own particular maid."

18. On the inherent profit motives of slaveholders, see such formative books as Oakes, *Ruling Race*, and W. Johnson, *Soul by Soul*.

19. Tilley, *R. J. Reynolds Tobacco Company*, 16–17.

20. Tilley, *Reynolds Homestead*, 202. Catherine Cox (1818–93) married Madison Tyler Smith (1808–96) in 1837. The couple had four children and lived first in Patrick County and then in nearby Stokes County.

21. Fogel and Engerman, *Time on the Cross*, 200. Note that this Virginia figure pales when compared to the heaviest cotton-producing states in the Gulf South, where the average slaveholder owned 125 bondspeople.

22. Financial (Hardin William Reynolds)—Account Book, ca. 1877, file 185, box 3, RFP, RHMAA; Nancy Susan Reynolds, Oral History Archives, June 17, 1980, OH.01.004.2, RHMAA.

23. Financial (Hardin William Reynolds)—Account Book, ca. 1877, box 3, file 185; and Financial (H. W. Reynolds)—Accounts Payable, store, 1855–83, box 3, file 19, both in RFP.

24. Financial (H. W. Reynolds)—Receipts, 1840–78, box 3, file 206; and receipt for $5.00, cost of business license tax "for the privilege of selling goods near Rock Springs," May 1, 1875, box 4, file 262, both in RFP.

25. Robert, *Story of Tobacco in America*, vii, 128.

26. Financial (Hardin William Reynolds)—Accounts, box 3, folders 187, 191, 192, 204, RFP.

27. Tilley, *Reynolds Homestead*, 18–19.

28. Pedigo and Pedigo, *History of Henry and Patrick Counties*, 300. This story was related in a chapter titled "Our Faithful Colored People."

29. Brockenbrough, *New and Comprehensive Gazetteer of Virginia*, 258, quoted in Robert, *Tobacco Kingdom*, 175.

30. Robert, *Tobacco Kingdom*, 176; Pedigo and Pedigo, *History of Patrick and Henry Counties*, 20.

31. Robert, *Tobacco Kingdom*, 181.

32. S. P. Adams, *Old Dominion, Industrial Commonwealth*; Majewski, *Modernizing a Slave Economy*; Oakes, *Slavery and Freedom*; Link, *Roots of Secession*.

33. Robert, *Tobacco Kingdom*, 179.

34. Ibid., 210–15.

35. Robert, *Story of Tobacco*, 128, 157.

36. Legal Documents [Hardin Reynolds], box 4, folders 274, 287, RFP.

37. Ford, "Reconfiguring the Old South," 95–122; Majewski, *Modernizing a Slave Economy*; Carmichael, *Last Generation*; Eelman, *Entrepreneurs in the Southern Upcountry*; Delfino and Gillespie, *Technology, Innovation, and Southern Industrialization*.

38. "No Ordinary Hireling: A. D. Reynolds Declares R. J. Reynolds Worked in Father's Factory," 1915, newspaper clipping, box 1, file 47, RFP. R.J.R.'s obituary in the *Danville Register*, July 31, 1918, reported Reynolds had been put to work "plowing the hardest and meanest old rocky bottom of the plantation" by his father in an effort to encourage him to go back to school. This same article also reported that Hardin told his wife the young R.J.R. would "never make a salesman."

39. Robert, *Story of Tobacco*, 128.

40. Iannarelli, "Cognitive Development in Children of Business Owners" and "Family Business Essentials."

41. Red Buck Bryan, "R.J.R.," *Mount Airy News*, December 9, 1909; "No Ordinary Hireling: A. D. Reynolds Declares R. J. Reynolds Worked in Father's Factory," 1915, newspaper clipping, box 1, file 47, RFP.

42. His wife, Katharine Reynolds, gave these measurements to a tailor in a letter to H. Jaeckel and Sons, New York City, December 10, 1912, box 1, file 106, RFP.

43. Blair, "Sketch no. 1," 2, BMFP.

44. U.S. Census Records, Manuscript Returns, Patrick County, Va., 1850, 1860, Manufacturing Schedules; see also Tilley, *R. J. Reynolds Tobacco Company*, chap. 1. The extant record offers no explanation for why Reynolds switched to a mixed labor force between 1850 and 1860, but the expansion of market demand suggests a willingness to employ all available hands, disregarding any residual notions of gender differences. His decision may also have been influenced by the growing practice of using women slaves in the new urban manufactories.

45. Robert, *Tobacco Kingdom*, 216.

46. Flannagan, *Story of Lucky Strike*, 14–19, masterfully conveys the suspense of growing tobacco in the early twentieth century.

47. Pedigo and Pedigo, *History of Patrick and Henry Counties*, 22–24; Robert, *Tobacco Kingdom*, 222.

48. Gately, *Tobacco*, 164–75; Kluger, *Ashes to Ashes*, 12–18; "Why Men Smoke," *Tobacco* 1, no. 9 (June 11, 1886): 1.

49. Robert, *Tobacco Kingdom*, 222; Robert, "Tobacco Industry," 128–29. James A. Thomas's father, a North Carolinian, met his future wife while peddling tobacco through Florida and married her in 1855. See Thomas, *Pioneer Tobacco Merchant*, 3.

50. Blair, "Richard Joshua Reynolds," 335.

51. For example, he subscribed to the *Richmond Whig* and the *Winston Sentinel*; see Financial Records (H. W. Reynolds)—Tax in Kind, 1864, box 3, file 205, RFP.

52. Tilley, *Reynolds Homestead*, 37.

53. Financial (H. W. Reynolds)—Bills of Exchange, 1855–82, box 3, RFP.

54. Perry, *Free State of Patrick*, 2–5.

55. It did not help that Virginia troops, claiming they were looking for deserters, swept across the state border into North Carolina, where they demanded provisions and forage and, according to one account, "insult[ed] our women." Quoted in Porter, "'Defying the Destructives,'" 59, 69–70; Blair, *Virginia's Private War*, 56, 70–72.

56. Receipt, November 28, 1863, box 1, file 2, Critz—Correspondence, 1882–83, RFP.

57. A. D. Reynolds, *Recollections*, 1–4.

58. F. J. Byrne, *Becoming Bourgeois*, 159–61.

59. A. D. Reynolds, *Recollections*, 4–6; Perry, *Free State of Patrick*, 7.

60. Blair, "Richard Joshua Reynolds," 335; "No Ordinary Hireling"; Perry, *Free State of Patrick*, 9.

61. In 1906 close friend W. A. Blair wrote about R.J.R.'s growing up during the Civil War after his brother joined the Confederacy. "The responsibility of affairs at home naturally fell upon the shoulders of the next male member of the family, so early in life he assumed these responsibilities." Blair, "Richard Joshua Reynolds," 335. On R.J.R. as the favorite child, see Nancy Susan Reynolds, Oral History.

62. Patrick County Order Books, 8, 9, Patrick County Courthouse, Stuart, Va.; Financial Records (H. W. Reynolds)—Tax in Kind, 1864, box 3, file 205, RFP.

63. No one knows who named No Business Mountain. Several theories all turn on the notion that it was a place to be avoided, whether because of the large population of rattlesnakes that inhabited it, because the roads and paths up it were so dangerous, or as a warning to revenue agents because so many moonshiners cultivated their stills atop it, according to Reynolds Homestead docent Susannah Netherland.

64. Quoted from Robert Hine's Daughter's Letter to Another Daughter, reprinted in

Jackson, *Surry County Soldiers*; Perry, *Free State of Patrick*, 161, 164; Porter, "'Defying the Destructives,'" 100; A. D. Reynolds, *Recollections*, 12–13; Nancy Susan Reynolds, Oral History.

65. A. D. Reynolds, *Recollections*, 12–13.

66. "No Ordinary Hireling."

67. Nancy Susan Reynolds [to Nannie Tilley], February 4, 1970, box 1, file 1, RFP.

68. Appleby, *Relentless Revolution*, 168, 178.

69. "No Ordinary Hireling."

70. Sallie E. Critz to Robert Critz, February 29, 1876, box 1, file 2, Correspondence, 1882–83, RFP.

71. Blair, "Richard Joshua Reynolds," 335; Connor, Boyd, and Hamilton, *History of North Carolina*, 4:1; Tilley, *Reynolds Homestead*, 38–39; receipts dated August 29, 1859, March 22, 1860, October 16, 1860, April 7, 1867, box 3, file 205, RFP; receipt made to Nannie Walker for five months' tuition for Lucy and eighty-five days' tuition for Harbor, no date, box 4, file 282a, RFP.

72. H. E. C. "Red Buck" Bryant, "The Three Reynolds Brothers," *Charlotte Observer*, March 12, 1967.

73. "No Ordinary Hireling." Assessment of handwriting, spelling, grammar, and style is based on comparison of letters, notes, and account books of father and son in RFP.

74. Financial (H. W. Reynolds)—Receipts, 1840–78, box 3, file 206, RFP, RHMAA. For example, see receipt dated August 29, 1859 for seventy—five dollars "paid in advance by H. W. Reynolds for the board and tuition of his two daughters in D[anville] F[emale] College, James Jameson."

75. Tilley, *Reynolds Homestead*, chap. 3. Emory and Henry College opened in southwest Virginia as a manual-labor school; students initially worked in return for their tuition and board.

76. Stevenson, *Increase in Excellence*; Wells, *Origins of the Southern Middle Class*; Green, *Military Education*, finds that very few southern college graduates in the late antebellum era went into business careers, which begs the question why the Reynoldses were so insistent on sending their sons, who seemed destined to become tobacco manufacturers, to college.

77. A. D. Reynolds, "Origin of One of the Greatest Tobacco Manufacturing Enterprises in the World," in Pedigo and Pedigo, *History of Henry and Patrick Counties*, 26–27.

78. As late as 1881 and 1882, his personal property was valued at $3,000 and $2,000 respectively. Nancy Reynolds, Hardin Harbour Reynolds, Mrs. Mary Reynolds Lybrook, R. J. Reynolds, and Walter Reynolds were each assessed land taxes in 1884 as heirs of Hardin Reynolds. Those taxes totaled $334. Hardin Reynolds's estate paid $74.55 to the treasurer of Patrick County for 1885 taxes on 2,226 acres valued at $3,823. Tax Receipts, box 3, file 259, RFP.

79. Declaration, 1865, box 4, file 269, RFP.

80. A. D. Reynolds, "Recollections," 15–17.

81. Ibid., 18.

82. Robert, *Story of Tobacco*, 129.

83. Siegel, *Roots of Southern Distinctiveness*, 162–63; Daniel, "Crossroads of Change," 432; Daniel, *Breaking the Land*, 24; L. J. Morgan, *Emancipation in Virginia's Tobacco Belt*.

84. Financial Documents (Hardin William Reynolds), contract with Abe Reynolds, January 15, 1866, box 4, files 263, RFP.

85. Financial Documents (Hardin William Reynolds), Accounts Receivable, 1843–80, box 3, folder 189; box 4, folder 283A-3, RFP; Auditor of Public Accounts, Personal Property Tax Records, Patrick County, 1860–63, 1865–66, reel number 682, Library of Virginia, Richmond; Financial Documents (Hardin William Reynolds), Receipts, 1840–78, box 3, folder 206, RFP.

86. U.S. Census, 1880, Mayo River, Patrick County, Va., roll T9_1383, p. 73.2, Enumeration District 159.

87. Tilley, *Reynolds Homestead*, 17.

88. Financial Documents (Hardin William Reynolds), Accounts Receivable, 1843–80, Accounts for Lucy and A.D., box 3, file 189, RFP.

89. Tilley, "R. J. Reynolds Tobacco," manuscript draft, chaps. 1, 7, box 11, file 695, RFP.

90. *Virginia*, vol. 16, p. 536 I, R. G. Dun and Co. Collection, Baker Library Historical Collection, Harvard Business School.

91. Hardin's involvement in a case that began in 1872, which turned on whether he had received too much land to pay off a debt, was tried in Superior Court in Stokes, Forsyth, and Davidson Counties, North Carolina, before going to the State Supreme Court four times and was not resolved until 1884, two years after his death. That Hardin Reynolds had hired the best lawyers in the state for a piece of land worth far less than the expense of their hire drew great public interest in Virginia and North Carolina alike. See Tilley, *R. J. Reynolds Tobacco*, 15–16.

92. A. D. Reynolds noted this closeness with his brother in a letter to his sister-in-law Katharine Smith Reynolds about his brother's poor health. A.D. Reynolds to Katharine Smith Reynolds (hereafter KSR in correspondence), July 9, 1917, Correspondence "R", 1908–21, box 2, file 142, RFP.

93. Carmichael, *Last Generation*, 2–3.

94. R. J. Reynolds does not fit the generational patterns identified by important scholars of the period and region. He did not have a significant break with his father or express disappointment in his failings as Gilmore, in *Gender and Jim Crow*, has characterized white male leaders in North Carolina during his lifetime. He is too young to fit into Don Doyle's cohort of New South men born largely in the 1830s. See Doyle, *New Men, New Cities*. Reynolds was born in 1850, the decade that Paul Gaston argues spawned the key generation of New South spokesmen. See Gaston, *New South Creed*, 87–88. On Thomas Dixon, see Gillespie and Hall, *Thomas Dixon Jr.*

95. Lumpkin, *Making of a Southerner*, 111–121.

96. Peter Critz to Billy, September 28, 1867, Critz Correspondence, 1882–83 (note: this letter is misfiled), box 1, file 2, RFP.

97. Carmichael, *Last Generation*, 244–45n3.

98. "No Ordinary Hireling." There is every indication that Nancy raised her daughters to embrace their gendered roles as southern daughter. The preservation of Nancy's darning egg, big sewing chest, and weasel attest to her valuing of women's cloth- and needle-based skills. On the importance of using contemporary language to analyze social relationships in the nineteenth century, see Laird, *Pull*, 24.

99. Blair, "Reynolds, Richard Joshua," 1, BMFP.

100. Connor, Boyd, and Hamilton, *History of North Carolina*, 4:2; "Tobacco Industry

Loses an Honored Leader," *Tobacco* 66, no. 16:3–4; on white manhood's construction in the antebellum South, see Friend and Glover, *Southern Manhood*, vii–xiv.

101. Blair, "Richard Joshua Reynolds," 336; Obituary, *Danville Register*, July 31, 1918.

102. Interview with Zachary Smith, July 7, 2004, Reynolda Village, Winston-Salem, N.C.

103. Andrew L. Demling, "Advertising Transforms Depression into 'Biggest Year in History': Instead of Retrenching, R. J. Reynolds Increased Advertising Investment to Overcome Effects of European War on Business," *Cincinnati Enquirer*, March 20, 1915, newspaper clipping, BMFP.

104. In comparison to many other southern schools, Emory and Henry College had not been hard hit by the war. Little physical damage had occurred, although wounded Union officers, white and black, had been kept as prisoners in Wiley Hall, and several black soldiers had been murdered by marauding guerillas. Enrollment returned relatively quickly. By R.J.R.'s matriculation, 178 students were enrolled, although this number did not reach prewar levels and the endowment was minimal. See Stevenson, *Increase in Excellence*, 94–95.

105. Ibid., 148–49, 151, 155, 204.

106. Lach, "Richard Joshua Reynolds, Sr.," 384–85.

107. "No Ordinary Hireling"; the 1913 edition of *The Sphinx*, the Emory and Henry College Yearbook, contains a brief biographical profile of R.J.R. that recognizes his time at the college as a student, claiming he did not graduate because "other duties called him, and he was forced to drop his school work for a while, to enter into active business life," Reynolds Family, Biographical/Genealogical File, Reynolds, Richard Joshua, 1887–1991, box 1, file 53, RFP. The Reynolds Family Chronology (RHMAA), p. 3, states that Reynolds stayed at Fulton House while at college in 1868 and at Byres House while at college in 1869.

108. Pedigo and Pedigo, *History of Henry and Patrick Counties*, 233.

109. Ibid., 234.

110. *The Sphinx*, Dedication to Richard Joshua Reynolds; Blair, "Richard Joshua Reynolds," 336; Demling, "Advertising Transforms Depression"; Reynolds Family Chronology, July 1, 1873, p. 4.

111. Blair, "Richard Joshua Reynolds," 336; Blair, "Reynolds, Richard Joshua," 1, BMFP; Tilley, "Richard Joshua Reynolds," 203–4.

112. Blair, "Richard Joshua Reynolds," 336.

113. Tilley, "Richard Joshua Reynolds." 203–4.

114. Only those with cash and manufactured tobacco on hand after the war could survive these challenges. Although tobacco was first taxed in 1862, it would take another ten years for the imposition of an efficient system to catch up with the many country producers who had managed to evade tax collection for some time. But with a better system finally in place by 1872, the heavy tax forced men with limited means out of the business. Even Hardin, always able to juggle his finances, was struggling, delinquent on his merchant's license fees in 1871 and 1872. Receipt for $30 license, Isaac N. Atkins, Treasurer, Financial Records (H. W. Reynolds)—Promissory Notes, 1837–87, box 3, file 204, RFP.

115. Arnold, *History of the Tobacco Industry*, 58–63.

116. Robert, *Story of Tobacco*, 131–32; Biles, "Tobacco Towns," 156–90.

117. Siegel, *Roots of Southern Distinctiveness*, 162–65; Arnold, *History of the Tobacco Industry*, 63–65.

118. U.S. Manuscript Census, 1860, South District, Patrick, Va., roll M653_1369, 999; on Lybrook's academic interests and youthful interest in haberdashery, see Tilley, *Reynolds Homestead*, 114; on Lybrook's interest in land speculation through the Stuart development, see Lybrook—General Correspondence, A–Z, 1872–98, box 1, file 25, esp. Berryman Green's letter to Lybrook, dated July 23, 1880; on Lybrook's interest in pomology, see his frequent correspondence in same file on the topic with the U.S. Department of Agriculture, all in RFP.

119. "Receipt of Capt HW Reynolds, Two hundred thirty five dollars and 40 cents," Financial (H. W. Reynolds)—Receipts, 1840–78, box 3, file 206, RFP.

120. Reynolds Family Chronology, 1870–72, p. 3.

121. In 1870, twenty-five-year-old Mary and thirty-nine-year-old Andrew had two young sons, a black cook and her three young children, and two white male boarders, one a schoolteacher and the other a tinsmith, in their household. Andrew and Hardin meanwhile had a formal partnership in their Reynolds and Lybrook Tobacco Manufacturing Firm based on a capital investment of nine thousand dollars and twenty-two employees. Lybrook's personal estate totaled two thousand dollars while in a surprising twist, Mary counted two thousand dollars' worth of personal estate and one thousand dollars' worth of property. Whether Mary Reynolds's property came from her father or the Lybrooks kept these holdings in Mary's name to protect them while Andrew speculated in business is unclear. The couple certainly depended on the Reynolds family. Andrew's father-in-law was paying his taxes and advancing him cash for furniture in 1873. Mary's mother was still paying her grown daughter's medical bills ten years later. U.S., Ninth Census, 1870, Washington, D.C. National Archives and Records Administration, M593_1670, p. 529; Financial (H. W. Reynolds)—Receipts, 1840–78, box 3, file 206; Lybrook Family—General Correspondence, A–Z, 1872–98, box 1, file 25; Lybrook—Bible Records, box 1, file 16; the latter three all in RFP. Tilley, *Reynolds Homestead*, 172; Tilley, *R. J. Reynolds Tobacco Company*, 17.

122. Election certificate of A. M. Lybrook to the Virginia Senate, 1881, box 1, file 41, RFP; Tilley, *Reynolds Homestead*, 114–16; J. Dailey, *Before Jim Crow*, 32–42. A portrait of the "Big Four," the four Readjusters who challenged Mahone, including Andrew Lybrook, was painted by David Silvette at the bequest of the Art Commission of Virginia in 1930 and hung in the old Senate Chamber of the Virginia State Capital in 1932. The painting remains on that wall, although the chamber has been renamed Senate Meeting Room 1. The portrait lacked any attribution as of January 2012. See "The 'Big Four' and John E. Massey," in *Report of the "Big Four" Commission.*

123. Despite Lybrook's popular critique, the Readjusters pressed harder for racial change in the years that ensued, receiving heavy pushback from their opposition. By 1883, they had managed to elect the governor, both U.S. senators, and six of ten U.S. congressman. They dominated the state assembly and the courts and struck at the heart of white elite privilege and power. But at election time in late 1883, white Democrats used a violent dispute between whites and blacks over street etiquette in Danville, incidentally the town most heavily frequented by the Reynolds family, to take over the city and claim systemic black insurrection across the state. See Dailey, "Deference and Violence."

124. Lybrook, *Mahoneism Unveiled!*; Ruffin, *Colonel Frank G. Ruffin's Letter*; Massey, *Autobiography of John E. Massey*, 210–36.

125. Ex parte Virginia, 100 U.S. 339 (1880), in K. L. Hall, *Oxford Companion to the Supreme Court*, 844; Perry, *Free State of Patrick*, 4; Melton, "*Thirty-Nine Lashes—Well Laid On*," 183–208; Melton, *Pittsylvania County's Historic Courthouse*, 61–73.

126. Election certificate of A. M. Lybrook to the Virginia Senate, 1881, box 1, file 41; Critz Estate Papers: Raymond Critz, 1884, 1892, box 1, file 13; Lybrook—General Correspondence, box 1, file 25, all in RFP.

127. A. D. Reynolds to Andrew Lybrook, August 16, 1895, box 1, file 26, Lybrook/A. D. Reynolds Correspondence, Letters 1894–95; Nancy Susan Reynolds, Oral History Archives, May 5, 1980, OH.01.004.1, all in RFP. R.J.R.'s daughter Nancy recalled, "Daddy, my father, was the one they loved," although her Uncle Will and Aunt Kate looked after the Lybrook orphans as well. The nephews were hired to work for the company by their uncles, and the nieces received ample allowances and educations. R.J.R. was so close to his namesake nephew, George Richard "R.J.R." Lybrook (1874–1902) that he groomed him to be his successor over his own younger brothers. Lybrook's premature death in 1902 saddened R.J.R. greatly. Plentiful examples of the ongoing costs of R.J.R.'s support for the Lybrook children are listed throughout the R. J. Reynolds, Journal Day Book, 1894–98 and the R. J. Reynolds Ledger Individual no. 2, 1895–98.

128. Always an entrepreneur, Hardin was buying a millpond, a geared mill, and twenty-nine more acres as late as 1875. Long recognized as an innovator and risk taker, he had bought the first thresher in the region, considered "the wonder of the day," years before the Civil War. Blair, "Richard Joshua Reynolds," 335; personal communication from Jim Crawford, Roanoke, Va., February 21, 2008.

129. Bob Phillips, "Tobacco Processing Begins in City," *Bristol Herald-Courier*, August 20, 2006.

130. "Tobacco Industry Loses an Honored Leader," 4.

131. Accounts of Hardin Reynolds for R. J. Reynolds, 1879, 1880, box 3, file 188, RFP.

132. For outstanding analysis of this topic, see the masterful 2010 PhD dissertation by Drew Swanson, "Land of the Bright Leaf."

133. Tilley, *R. J. Reynolds Tobacco Company*, 30–31.

134. Appleby, *Relentless Revolution*, 194–95.

135. "Newspapers the Standard Form of Advertising: R.J.R. Says They Are the Right Mediums to Reach the People with a Good Article," newspaper clipping (1915), BMFP.

136. Reynolds Family Chronology, pp. 2–3.

137. "A Tremendous Increase," *Tobacco* 52, no. 3: 8; "Tobacco Industry Loses an Honored Leader," 4.

138. Gillespie and Beachy, *Pious Pursuits*; Wellman and Tise, *City's Culture*, 3–29.

139. Shirley, *From Congregation Town to Industrial City*, traces the rise of individual enterprise and its challenge to the authority of the centralized church over the course of the nineteenth century as a response to larger market forces reshaping the South and the nation; also see Tise, *Government*, 26–33.

140. *Winston Western Sentinel*, April 26, 1877.

141. Julian Ralph, "The Very Old and Very New Winston-Salem," *Harper's Weekly*, July 20, 1895.

142. Tursi, *Winston-Salem*, 160.

143. Anderson, "Eulogy," 1, BMFP; Appleby, *Relentless Revolution*, 197.

Chapter Two. A Hardworking, Painstaking Student

1. U.S. Federal Census, 1850, Reeds Shore, Stokes County, N.C., roll M432_645, p. 89, Madison T. Smith household.

2. North Carolina State Board of Health, Bureau of Vital Statistics, North Carolina Death Certificates, microfilm S.123, rolls 19–242, 280, 313–682, 1040–1297, North Carolina State Archives, Raleigh.

3. North Carolina State Board of Health, Bureau of Vital Statistics, North Carolina Death Certificates, vol. 12, p. 294, Surry County Courthouse, Dobson, N.C.

4. Shulman, *Fathers and Adolescents*, chap. 5.

5. Obituary of Mary Susan Jackson Smith, *Mount Airy News*, April 22, 1926, p. 7.

6. Interview with Zachary Smith, July 7, 2004, Reynolda Village, Winston-Salem, N.C.

7. *The Heritage of Stokes County*, vol. 1, *North Carolina* (Germanton, N.C.: Stokes County Historical Society, 1981), 82–83.

8. Justus, *Fetching the Old Southwest*, 53–55.

9. Robert, "Tobacco Industry in Ante-Bellum North Carolina," 119–30.

10. Davis and Goldston, *United States Department of Agriculture Soil Survey*, 1–3, 7–10, 30–31.

11. Oral tradition holds that Zachary Smith was born in Patrick County, which is confirmed by his death certificate, but census records from 1900 to 1930 list his birthplace as Stokes County, North Carolina.

12. The family also relied on at least two white hired hands in 1850. Their personal and real estate totaled an impressive thirty thousand dollars. See 1850 Slave Schedules, Quaker Gap District, p. 259, 1850 U.S. Federal Census, Reeds Shore, Stokes, N.C., roll M432_645, p. 89; and 1860 U.S. Federal Census, Stokes, N.C., roll M653_914, p. 119.

13. Interview with Zachary Smith, July 7, 2004.

14. A young man named Joshua Smith, from Stokes County, enlisted as a private in Company A, Second Infantry Regiment, North Carolina, on May 4, 1861, at the age of twenty-three and surrendered on April 9, 1865, but Joshua Cox Smith would have been twenty years old. Joshua Cox is not listed as a member of his father's household in the 1860 U.S. Census, perhaps because he was away at Trinity College.

15. Obituary of Zachary T. Smith, *Mount Airy News*, June 16, 1938, pp. 1, 8; Reynolds Family Chronology, p. 166.

16. His real-estate value dropped from $5,000 in 1860 to $370, 1870 U.S. Federal Census, Quaker Gap, Stokes County, N.C., roll M593_1160, p. 194; though family history suggests Zachary went west to escape his father's creditors, the twenty-four-year-old was listed as a member of his father's household in 1870, indicating he either headed west right after the Civil War or did not leave his parents until the 1870s.

17. Interview with Zachary Smith, July 15, 2004, Reynolda Village, Winston-Salem, N.C.

18. Nancy Susan Reynolds to Nannie Tilley, February 14, 1970, box 1, file 1, Critz—Biographical Information, RFP; "Katharine Smith Wed R. J. Reynolds in 1905," *Mount Airy News*, June 14, 1998. Although both Lucy and Mary attended Salem College, they did not do so during the same years; family history contends they had become friends while in school in Mount Airy.

19. Surry County Record of Deeds, book 25, pp. 120–21. That this property formed a significant portion of the Smith farm is corroborated by the 1926 deed referencing Z. T.

Smith's "original tract," Surry County Book of Deeds, book 104, p. 238; and the J. M. Fulton Farm Plat, surveyed in 1915, Plat Book 1, p. 205, Surry County, N.C., both in the Surry County Courthouse, Dobson, N.C.

20. Interview with Zachary Smith, July 7, 2004.

21. J. Edwin Carter and A. Kyle Sydnor, comps., *A General Directory of Mt. Airy, N.C., Rural Routes and Suburbs, 1913–1914*, n.d., p. 5.

22. White Sulphur Springs Resort, for example, opened in the 1880s just north of Mount Airy and had its heyday in the early 1900s. "Luxury Homes to Be Built on Site of 1880s Resort, *Winston-Salem Journal*, May 1, 2005.

23. Carter and Carter, "Footprints in the Hollow," 110–11.

24. Hollingsworth, *History of Surry County*, 158–59, 162.

25. Carter and Carter, "Footprints in the Hollow," 118.

26. State v. Sarah Anthony and Susan A. Lord, Indictment: Keeping a Bawdy House, January 1, 1906; and State v. Minnie Malone, January 1, 1906, Surry County, Criminal Action Papers, Superior Court, 1905–6 file, North Carolina State Archives, Raleigh. My thanks to Ken Badgett for sharing these cases with me.

27. "His Impressions," *Mount Airy News*, November 4, 1897, p. 2.

28. Porter, "Defying the Destructives," 99–100.

29. Carter and Carter, "Footprints in the Hollows," 108.

30. Porter, "Defying the Destructives," 100–101.

31. Ibid., 102–5.

32. Surry County Deed Book 25, Surry County Courthouse, Dobson, N.C., p. 120 (1886).

33. Surry County Deed Book 25, Surry County Courthouse, Dobson, N.C., p. 498 (1891).

34. "A Colored Minister Sees the Necessity of a Graded School," *Yadkin Valley News* (Mount Airy, N.C.), January 24, 1895, Schools clipping file, Mount Airy Museum of Regional History (hereafter MAMRH), Mount Airy, N.C.; Surry County Deed Book, Surry County Courthouse, Dobson, N.C., book 28, p. 375.

35. "And Still Another Church," April 23, 1896, *Mount Airy News*, p. 3; Editor's Column, April 2, 1902, *Mount Airy News*, p. 3.

36. Surry County Deed Books, Surry County Courthouse, Dobson, N.C., book 25, pp. 120, 257, 284, 498; book 27, pp. 30, 420, 440; book 28, pp. 254, 272, 375, 377; book 29, p. 396; book 30, p. 321; book 31, pp. 102, 376; book 32, p. 112; book 33, p. 144, 191; book 34, p. 559; book 35, pp. 18, 157; book 37, p. 537; book 38, pp. 101, 109, 111; book 42, pp. 369, 371; book 43, pp. 403, 421; book 44, pp. 381, 382, 487, 488, 587; book 45, p. 97; book 46, pp. 17, 19, 515; book 48, p. 89; book 50, p. 366; book 51, p. 161; book 56, p. 303; book 57, pp. 560, 562; book 58, p. 497; book 59, pp. 282, 283, 284, 291, 503; book 61, pp. 167, 409; book 62, pp. 360, 364; book 64, pp. 262, 263, 566; book 65, p. 375; book 66, pp. 50, 51, 102, 328, 470; book 68, pp. 124, 271; book 69, pp. 6, 392, 393, 572. This list covers deed transactions of Z. T. Smith and/or Mary S. Smith in Surry County from 1886 to 1916. Interview with Zachary Smith, September 15, 2004, Reynolda Village, Winston-Salem, N.C.

37. Nancy Susan Reynolds, Oral History Archives, May 5, 1980, OH.01.004.1, RHMAA.

38. *Yadkin Valley News*, Thursday, February 22, 1894; humorous notice, quoted in Agnes M. Wells, Virginia G. Phillips, and Carol J. Leonard, "Abstracts of Births, Deaths, Marriages and Other Items of Interest from Mount Airy, N.C. Newspapers, 1872–1895,"

p. 159, unpublished compilation, 1990 [?], Mount Airy Public Library; interview with Zachary Smith, July 15, 2004; Nancy Susan Reynolds, Oral History Archives.

39. Announcements, *Yadkin Valley News*, February 22, 1894, col. 1, p. 3.

40. Interview with Zachary Smith, July 15, 2004; Nancy Susan Reynolds, Oral History Archives.

41. Obituary of Zachary T. Smith, *Mount Airy News*, June 16, 1938, pp. 1, 8; he served as quartermaster general of the United Confederate Veterans of North Carolina and as lieutenant colonel of the Surry County Camp. This description of Zachary Smith was provided in an interview with his namesake grandson conducted by the author on July 7, 2004. Zachary Smith stated that his father, Eugene Gray Smith, used to take his father "to all the Confederate reunions."

42. Interview with Zachary Smith, July 15, 2004.

43. *Yadkin Valley News*, Thursday, June 22, 1893, obituary for Mrs. Matt Smith (mother of Z. T. Smith); Thursday, December 23, 1893, obituary of Mrs. S. E. Claffee, sister of Z. T. Smith; Thursday, September 13, 1894, report of Mrs. Lou Sarles's visit to brother Z. T. Smith, all quoted from "Abstracts of Births, Deaths, Marriages and Other Items of Interest from Mt. Airy Newspapers, 1872–1895," pp. 116, 150, 193.

44. Interview with Zachary Smith, November 21, 2005, Reynolda Village, Winston-Salem, N.C. This relative also remembered that his grandfather kept a barrel of whiskey at each location and gave drinks only to his fellow Democrats.

45. Interview with Zachary Smith, July 15, 2004.

46. Ruth Smith Lucas, Oral History Archives, July 26, 1980, OH.02.021.1, RHMAA.

47. For transactions listing Mary S. Smith only, see Surry County Deed Books, Surry County Courthouse, Dobson, N.C., book 31, p. 376 (1896); book 33, p. 191 (1898); book 42, p. 371 (1903); book 85, p. 190 (1920).

48. Surry County Deed Books, Surry County Courthouse, Dobson, N.C., book 33, p. 144.

49. Copy of contract entered into 1st of August 1898 giving M. S. Smith free-trader status in BMFP; offices reported in *Mount Airy News*, November 11, 1901, p. 3. On July 30, 1898, "M. S. Smith of the age of twenty-one years or upwards, wife of Z. T. Smith of Surry County with his consent, testified by his signature hereto, enters herself as a free trader from the date of the registration here of." Two days later on August 1, 1898, the Smiths entered into an agreement giving Mary Susan one share of stock of the par value of $100.00, "she having been duly constituted a free-trader," quoted in Reynolds Family Chronology, p. 166.

50. Sketch by Memory F. Mitchell in *Dictionary of North Carolina Biography*, vol. 3 (1988); *Raleigh Observer*, January 10, 1878; *Greensborough Patriot*, January 16, 1878; K. Harris, "Tabitha Anne Holton."

51. William B. Johnson, "Reverend Lottie M. Robertson Celebrates 80th Birthday," August 29, 1947, *Mount Airy News*, p. 1.

52. Hollingsworth, *History of Surry County*, 205.

53. Sparger, "Memoirs," p. 6. Twelve years younger than Katharine, Alma Sparger recalled growing up in Mount Airy with "plenty of colored help, and a white housekeeper." H. O. Woltz Sr. describes the preponderance of homes with black women housekeepers and "Mammies" in his "Never a Dull Moment," 20–21.

54. On the middle-class lifestyle of the Smith family, consider that the Reynolds

homestead contains artifacts and decorative art objects from the Smith household suggesting expensive Victorian tastes. For example, the Smith household draperies hanging in the Reynolds parlor are made of costly fabric. Their style was appropriate to a more formal decor and an upper-class sensibility. Frances Pateat was listed as a twenty-five-year-old black servant, born in North Carolina, who could not read or write, living in the Smith household according to the 1900 U.S. Federal Census, Mount Airy, Surry, N.C., roll T623_1219, p. 21B, Enumeration District 111.

55. Nancy Susan Reynolds, in Oral History Archives, stated that her grandmother had tuberculosis, adding, "And in those days if you had TB you were ashamed of it, you whispered it, and I'm sure that's what she did. Very thin, skin, and bones. And she must have been ill, that's my recollection of her. . . . Mother [Katharine] must have really been the head of the household. She brought up her younger brothers and sisters."

56. *Yadkin Valley News*, Thursday, June 22, 1893, obituary for Mrs. Matt Smith (mother of Z. T. Smith); Thursday, December 23, 1893, obituary of Mrs. S. E. Claffee, sister of Z. T. Smith, quoted from "Abstracts of Births, Deaths, Marriages and Other Items of Interest from Mt. Airy Newspapers, 1872–1895," pp. 116, 150; unpublished interview with Mary Madison Smith Cox by Rudy B. Lambert, n.d., p. 2. Many Smith family members were buried in the only large private family plot at Salem Methodist Church, just north of Mount Airy.

57. The descriptions of Katharine's siblings come from Zachary Smith in an interview with the author, July 23, 2004, Reynolda Village, Winston-Salem, N.C.

58. Family story shared with author, November 9, 2010, by Phil Archer and Sherry Hollingsworth, Winston-Salem, N.C.

59. Interview with Zachary Smith, September 15, 2004.

60. North Carolina State Board of Health, Bureau of Vital Statistics, North Carolina Death Certificates, vol. 12, p. 294, Surry County Courthouse, Dobson, N.C.

61. Ibid.

62. Leloudis, *Schooling in the New South*.

63. Editorial, *Yadkin Valley News*, January 18, 1894, 3.

64. "Graded School," *Yadkin Valley News*, January 10, 1895, Miss Graves School clipping file, MAMRH.

65. Leloudis, *Schooling in the New South*, 23–25.

66. Editorial, *Yadkin Valley News*, January 18, 1894, 3.

67. *Yadkin Valley News*, June 2, 1892, June 1, 1893, both in Miss Graves School clipping file, MAMRH. On the proliferation of schools in the area, see Schools clipping file, including Miss Bessie Harris's school at Lovell's Creek, *Yadkin Valley News*, February 28, 1895; Miss Alice Greenwood's School at Paul's Creek, *Yadkin Valley News*, March 7, 1895; and Miss Alice Booker of Round Peak, in South Street Chapel, *Mount Airy News*, August 4, 1895. Kate Smith is listed in two performances at the annual school concert that ended the 1892 school year, in a piano trio rendition of "Lehigh Polka" and a recitation with two school mates titled "Good Temper," "Miss Grave's School," *Yadkin Valley News*, June 2, 1892, Miss Graves School clipping file, MAMRH. "Miss Grave's School," *Yadkin Valley News*, September 22, 1892, Miss Graves School clipping file, MAMRH.

68. Ibid.

69. Undated Report Card, Miss Graves' School, Miss Graves School clipping file, MAMRH.

70. "Closing of Miss Graves' School," *Yadkin Valley News*, May 30, 1896, Miss Graves School clipping file, MAMRH.

71. *Mount Airy News*, February 20, 1896, Miss Graves School clipping file, MAMRH.

72. Announcement of Craven Appointment, *Mount Airy News*, January 2, 1896; "Mount Airy Male Academy," *Mount Airy News*, May 21, 1896, both in Miss Graves School clipping file," MAMRH.

73. Announcement, *Mount Airy News*, July 16, 1896, Miss Graves School clipping file, MAMRH.

74. *Mount Airy News*, August 13, 1896, Miss Graves School clipping file, MAMRH.

75. The officers were listed in the *Mount Airy News*, August 27, 1896, October 22, 1896, both in Miss Graves School clipping file, MAMRH.

76. Academy Honor Roll, *Mount Airy News*, November 19, 1896, December 10, 1896, both in Miss Graves School clipping file, MAMRH. On the development of graded schools in Mount Airy at this time see "An Act in Relation to the Public School in the Town of Mt. Airy, and providing for the levying of a tax to support the same," chapter 267, Public Laws of North Carolina 1899, North Carolina State Archives, Raleigh, N.C., pp. 397–400; and "Mount Airy Graded Schools," *Mount Airy News*, June 15, 1899, p. 1, cols. 2–4.

77. Hunter, *How Young Ladies Became Girls*, 2–3.

78. Sparger, "Memoirs of Alma Mitchell Sparger"; the Digital Sanborn map, Mount Airy, Surry County, N.C., June 1896, allows viewers to envision the physical landscape Katharine walked through several times each school day; Hunter, *How Young Ladies Became Girls*, 4–5.

79. "Old Rockford Street School: Recollections of Mozelle Owens Monson," in *Collections and Recollections: A Collection of Memories, Recipes and Recollections That Reflect Our Early Beginnings* (Mount Airy, N.C.: Mount Airy Restoration Foundation, 1985), 85, 108.

80. Woltz, "Never a Dull Moment," 20–23.

81. *Yadkin Valley News*, August 18, 1892.

82. Advertisement for White Sulphur Springs Resort, *Mount Airy News*, February 1891, Blue Ridge Inn clipping file, MAMRH.

83. "Fine Hotels Once Flourished," *Mount Airy News*, March 29, 1992; "The Great Fire!," *Yadkin Valley News*, January 8, 1892, both in Blue Ridge Inn clipping file, MAMRH.

84. *Yadkin Valley News*, March 17, 1892.

85. "New Blue Ridge Inn," *Yadkin Valley News*, February 12, 1892, Blue Ridge Inn clipping file, MAMRH; interview with Zachary Smith, July 7, 2004.

86. "For more than a half century, this [the Mount Airy area] was one of the most popular summer resorts in the state, losing its patrons at last to the lure of automobile travel along the newly paved roads of the twentieth century." Carter and Carter, "Footprints in the Hollow," 96.

87. *Yadkin Valley News*, February 22, 1894, p. 3.

88. Ruth Minnick, "Max Weber Visit," *Mount Airy News*, November 19 and 26, 1995; Kolko, "Max Weber on America," 245; Schweiger, "Max Weber in Mt. Airy."

89. "New Blue Ridge Inn," *Yadkin Valley News*, February 12, 1892, Blue Ridge Inn clipping file, MAMRH; digital Sanborn map, Mount Airy, Surry County, N.C., June 1896.

90. For example, see "The Blue Ridge Inn," *Mount Airy News*, August 15, 1895, and April 15, 1897, Blue Ridge Inn clipping file, MAMRH. Meals at the Blue Ridge on special

nights might include Chesapeake Bay oysters, deep-sea bass, smoked buffalo tongue, mountain gobbler, young pig, prime rib, quail on toast, opossum and potatoes, all varieties of vegetables laced with cream, and a half dozen pie and cake choices. See copy of the Blue Ridge Inn Thanksgiving Dinner Menu, 1897, Blue Ridge Inn clipping file, MAMRH.

91. "Stockholders Meeting," *Mount Airy News*, November 11, 1901, p. 3.

92. The hotel was the hub of the town. It was the place where city leaders shared information and made deals over cigars, coffee, and dessert; where church ladies held fund-raising events; even where debtors sold their property to raise money. Notice of Sale, *Mount Airy News*, April, 15, 1897, Blue Ridge Inn clipping file, MAMRH; *Yadkin Valley News*, August 18, 1892.

93. "Society Dance at Blue Ridge Inn," *Blue Ridge Daily*, December 7, 1908; "Account of Italians at Blue Ridge Inn," *Mount Airy News*, July 13, 1899; "A Beautiful Ball," *Yadkin Valley News*, June 6, 1893; "A Brilliant Banquet," *Yadkin Valley News*, January 5, 1893; Announcement of a Dance, *Mount Airy News*, July 7, 1895; Announcement of Ball, *Yadkin Valley News*, June 29, 1893, all in Blue Ridge Inn clipping file, MAMRH.

94. Advertisement, *Yadkin Valley News*, July 23, 1896, Blue Ridge Inn clipping file, MAMRH.

95. Announcement, *Yadkin Valley News*, August 8, 1894, Blue Ridge Inn clipping file, MAMRH. Emma Praither recalls the early years of her marriage when her husband took a position as clerk at the White Sulphur Springs resort. "That summer we had a wonderful time," she recalled. "I had nothing to do but visit with the guests, and I was supposed to help entertain them. I was soon good at pool and billiards and games of all kinds. Then the season was over, all too soon," she remembered regretfully, suggesting that Katharine's experience might have been quite similar at the Blue Ridge. Emma Praither Gilmer, *The Memoirs of Emma Prather Gilmer, Written in Her 90th Year for Her Children, Grandchildren, and Great-Grandchildren* (Philadelphia: Cherry, 1954), 17–18.

96. "Once a Victorian Resort, Now a Modern Take on History," *Latitude: Portraits of Carolina Culture* 2, no. 19 (July 2007): 20.

97. Young, *Study of the Curricula*, 197–98.

98. Gordon, *Gender and Higher Education*, 187, 189.

99. Ibid., 189–90.

100. McCandless, *Past in the Present*, 318.

101. F. H. Gaines, *The Story of Agnes Scott College, 1889–1921* (n.p., n.d.), 56.

102. It is surprising then that Kate did not attend Salem Female Academy in Salem, North Carolina, the oldest and most prestigious women's college in the region. Katharine's father had attended Salem Boys Academy. The Reynolds family had sent several daughters there. If she had attended Salem College, Kate would have had the protective presence of her cousins in nearby Winston. R.J.R's brother A.D. was even encouraging brother-in-law Captain Lybrook to send his children there. "Salem is the place for your children—they are safe and well cared for—a fine school." A. D. Reynolds to Andrew Lybrook, n.d., Lybrook/A. D. Reynolds Correspondence—Letters, 1894–95, box 1, file 1, RFP.

Salem was conferring a bachelor of arts degree on select students by 1890, thereby providing the first scholastic program leading to graduation for women in the North Carolina Piedmont. It was also adding courses in music, art, and elocution; an industrial course; and even a business department during this period, testament to changing and even contradictory expectations for white southern women of means by the end of the century. Young, *Study of the Curricula*, 20–21; McCandless, "Progressivism," 317.

103. McCandless, "Progressivism," 316–17.

104. Jane Turner Censer, *The Reconstruction of White Southern Womanhood, 1865–1895* (Baton Rouge: Louisiana State University Press, 2003).

105. McCandless, "Progressivism," 305–6.

106. Kousser, "Progressivism—For Middle-Class Whites Only"; McCandless, "Progressivism," 304–5.

107. At least several students ahead of Katharine at the Mount Airy Graded School had matriculated to State Normal and Industrial School according to R. C. Craven, principal, Mount Airy Graded School, in his letter to Charles D. McIver, Normal College, dated July 10, 1897, University of North Carolina at Greensboro (hereafter UNCG) Archives and Manuscripts.

108. Craven to McIver, July 10, 1897.

109. Trelease, *Making North Carolina Literate*, 30–31.

110. McCandless, "Progressivism," 302–25; Grantham, *Southern Progressivism*.

111. Graves, *Girls' Schooling during the Progressive Era*, xvii–xix, xxviii.

112. Ibid., xxviii, 280.

113. Eschbach, *Higher Education of Women*, 145.

114. Young, *Study of the Curricula*, 16–17.

115. Censer, "Changing World of Work," 54–55.

116. Ibid., 55; Wright, "'Grown-Up Daughter.'"

117. "Dr. Curry's Recent Visit," *State Normal Magazine* 1, no. 2 (June 15, 1897): 205.

118. Lathrop, *Educate a Woman*, 10; Page, "Forgotten Man"; McCandless, "Progressivism," 302–4; Link, *Hard Country and a Lonely Place*, 94–96; Dean, "Learning to Be New Women," 292–94.

119. Craven to McIver, July 10, 1897.

120. Trelease, *Making North Carolina Literate*, 8–9, 39.

121. Dean, "Learning to Be New Women," 288–89.

122. Daniels, *Tar Heel Editor*, 458–59.

123. Trelease, *Making North Carolina Literate*, 3–53. KSR to Dr. Anna M. Gove, May 17, 1912, box 2, file 184, Telegrams, ca. 1912, RFP; Dean, "Learning to Be New Women," 289–91.

124. Katharine Smith, Transcript, 1898; course catalog, 1897–98, Office of the Registrar, UNCG. Although the family later created a scholarship in chemistry at North Carolina Woman's College (formerly State Normal and Industrial College) in Katharine's honor, under the impression that she had majored in chemistry, that is not in fact the case according to the transcripts. Nephew Zachary Smith agreed with the author's conclusion in an interview on July 7, 2004.

125. Katharine pursued the language track in her new course of study. War between Spain and the United States had broken out in April 1898, but hostilities had ceased that August, and a treaty had been signed that December. Could Katharine's desire to add Spanish been awakened by the outbreak of war and the deep interest southerners had in the conflict and its influence on ideas about nationalism and citizenship? Yet how many southerners pursued the study of Spanish as a result of this conflict? Did Katharine develop a deeper desire to study the history of Spain and Latin America and Spanish

culture and politics from this larger political focus? Was she being encouraged to do so by the well-educated and deeply committed teachers she encountered at Normal? Grace Turlington Little to KSR, June 6, 1913, box 2, file 122, KSR Correspondence—L, 1905–22, RFP.

126. Ida Wharton Grimes ('01) to Julius Isaac Foust, April 10, 1935, Julius Isaac Foust Papers, College History—Alumnae Letters, Chronologically, by Class, box 100.

127. Speight stopped teaching after her marriage in 1906 but remained committed to education for the rest of her life, establishing a public library in Salisbury and leading local and state efforts to halt illiteracy. Betty Anne Ragland Starbuck, "Dr. McIver and State Normal," (interview of Emma Lewis Speight Morris), *Alumni News* 55 (Fall 1966).

128. Trelease, *Making North Carolina Literate*, 38; McCandless, "Progressivism," 312.

129. Charles Duncan McIver to Mattie E. Sessons, August 27, 1901, General Correspondence, August 1894–September 1901, box 130, p. 286; see also McIver to Stella Meredith, August 30, 1901, informing her that there were no free tuition places left, necessitating that she board with a private family if she wanted to attend Normal, General Correspondence, August 1894–September 1901, box 130, p. 339.

130. Marjorie Craig, ed., "Home-Life in Rockingham County in the 'Eighties and 'Nineties," *North Carolina Historical Review* 32, no. 4 (October 1956): 524.

131. Dean, "Learning to Be New Women," 291.

132. Trelease, *Making North Carolina Literate*, 42–43; Bowles, *Good Beginning*, 134.

133. She also, along with eight other students, created The Surry County Club. Its intention was to write monthly letters to the hometown paper to tell about the work of Normal. Kate was president of the organization. See *State Normal Magazine* 5, no. 2 (October 1900): 86–87.

134. Grimes to Foust, April 10, 1935.

135. Katharine Smith is listed as "ill malaria" in the 1899 Chapel Attendance Record Book, Typhoid Epidemic, Vertical File Folder, UNCG Archives and Manuscripts, and writes Charles McIver in a letter dated October 4, 1899, that her doctor has stated she could return to school the following week. A second letter, dated December 11, 1899, requests a place in the dormitories for second semester. KSR to Charles McIver, October 4, 1899, and December 11, 1899, Charles Duncan McIver General Correspondence and applications, Sm–Sq, 1899, UNCG Archives and Manuscripts; Grimes to Foust, April 10, 1935.

136. Trelease, *Making North Carolina Literate*, 50–51.

137. Stanback, "Kate Smith Reynolds," 3.

138. Unlike Katharine, Maxie did not graduate from Sullins. Instead Maxie flitted from school to school thereafter. "Misses Kate and Maxie Smith," September 12, 1901, *Mount Airy News*, p. 3; Maxie was at Greensboro Female College three years later, "Miss Maxie Smith," February 24, 1904, *Mount Airy News*, p. 3.

139. Reynolds Family Chronology, p. 166.

140. Reynolds Land Company Brochure, no date, box 2, file 146, RFP.

141. Katharine had observed in her application letter to President McIver that she had benefited from the advantage of being educated in both the public and the private schools of Mount Airy. Craven to McIver, July 10, 1897.

142. *The Omega* (Sullins College yearbook), 1902, 73.

143. Ibid.

144. Ibid., 74.

145. Ibid., 75.

146. Author's conversation with Susan Murdoch, Winston-Salem, N.C., June 6, 2004, about her grandmother, who attended Sullins with Katharine Smith.

147. *The Omega*, 16, 9, 115, 116, 132, 140, 141, 152–53.

148. On Katharine's happy school days that she shared with one pursuer, see Old Admirer to KSR, August 5, 1911, box 2, file 177, KSR Correspondence—unidentified, 1912–21; M. B. Bushong to KSR, July 30, 1918, RJR In Memoriam Book (hereafter IM), vol. 1, RFP. But there is next to nothing documenting anything about Katharine's beaux; we only know that she had them.

149. Lathrop, *Educate a Woman*, 20.

150. Ibid., *Educate a Woman*, 14, 25; Charles Duncan McIver to George Peabody, March 13, 1902, Chancellor Letterbooks, book 3, February 5– May 15, 1902, 148–49; Wright, "'Grown-Up Daughter.'"

151. Wright, "'Grown-Up Daughter.'"

152. Family history attests to Katharine's return to Mount Airy and pursuit of china painting, but an undated letter from Cara Hollingsworth seeking financial support to buy a kiln actually references Katharine's pursuit of a kiln "to do [her] firing" some years earlier. Cara Hollingsworth to KSR, box 1, file 106, KSR Correspondence—H, 1906–21, RFP; Mullen, *Paris Gowns*, 2.

153. Pastel of Winter Landscape, signed M.K.S., Temporary Deposit 67, Collections, RHMAA.

154. Stanback, "Kate Smith Reynolds," 3.

Chapter Three. Making Money

1. "The Golden Belt District," *Tobacco* 21, no. 10 (July 12, 1895): 3.

2. *Salem People's Press*, April 29, 1880; *Winston Union Republican*, August 5, 1880; *Winston Leader*, September 7, 1880.

3. *Winston Leader*, September 28, 1880; the number of tobacco establishments in Forsyth County had grown to thirty-one by 1885, according to *The Tobacco Journal Directory, 1884–1885*.

4. R. J. Reynolds obituary, *Newport News (Va.) Daily Press*, July 30, 1918, clipping, IM.

5. Biles, "Tobacco Towns," 156–59.

6. Ibid., 157.

7. Laird, *Pull*, 35–36.

8. Blair, "Richard Joshua Reynolds," 336–37; Tilley, "Richard Joshua Reynolds"; calculation of wealth based on an inflation calculator adjustable by date available at http://www.westegg.com/inflation/infl.cgi, accessed March 2, 2008.

9. Reynolds Family Chronology, 1875, p. 4.

10. *North Carolina*, vol. 10, p. 547, R. G. Dun and Co. Collection.

11. "Newspapers the Standard Form of Advertising: R.J.R. Says They Are the Right Mediums to Reach the People with a Good Article," newspaper clipping (1915), BMFP.

12. Phone interview with Mr. T. Davis, August 2, 2006, Winston-Salem, N.C.

13. Reynolds Family Chronology, p. 5.

14. *Winston Western Sentinel*, May 8, 1879; October 24, 1878; June 28, 1883; *Winston*

Union Republican, December 2, 1880; March 3 and 10, 1881; December 8, 1881; July 27, 1882; November 30, 1882; Tilley, *R. J. Reynolds Tobacco Company*, 44.

15. Speech given to the New England Club in New York, 1886, in J. C. Harris, *Life of Henry W. Grady*, 83–93.

16. *WSJ*, June 13, 2005, B1.

17. *Salem People's Press*, September 4, 1890.

18. Cindy H. Casey, *Images of America: Forsyth County, 1849–1999* (Dover, N.H.: Arcadia, 1998), 83, with photo of Thomas A. Edison at the streetcar inauguration event. Edison was intrigued by investment opportunities in the South and traveled the seaboard region in 1906 with his sons and a "travelling laboratory" in search of sources for cobalt and other minerals essential to the commercial use of electricity. "Edison's Quest and His Travelling Laboratory," *Harper's Weekly*, June 9, 1906, p. 809.

19. *Salem People's Press*, April 2, 1891.

20. *Winston-Salem Twin City Sentinel*, April 1, 1896; *WSJ* and *Sentinel*, April 10, 1966.

21. W[ill] N. Reynolds, letter to the editor, *WSJ*, October 14, 1940, clipping, box 1, file 58, RFP.

22. Quote in Tursi, *Winston-Salem*, 110.

23. *Condensation of Board of Commissioner's Minutes*, 430, 442–43, Forsyth County Government Center, Winston-Salem.

24. Between 1884 and 1899, R. J. Reynolds's name appeared eighty-nine times in Forsyth County public records as the grantee in real-estate transactions. It appeared fifty-seven more times between 1900 and his death in 1918. *General Index of Real Estate Conveyances, Forsyth County, N.C., Grantee "R,"* microfilm reel 1849/1965. He purchased all manner of properties, lots and houses, residential and commercial, as did his brother Will.

25. Tilley, *R. J. Reynolds Tobacco Company*, 50, 52; R. J. Reynolds Journal Day Book, 1894–98; R. J. Reynolds Ledger Individual no. 2, 1895–98.

26. See accounts listed throughout the R. J. Reynolds Journal Day Book, 1894–98, and R. J. Reynolds Ledger Individual no. 2, 1895–98. The Virginia and North Carolina Construction Company Record Book, 1888–96, conveys Reynolds's long-standing commitment to building this rail line between Roanoke and Winston, along with Winstonites Colonel Francis Henry Fries and Theodore Bahnson as well as prominent Martinsville residents. I am grateful to Randal Hall for sharing this reference with me.

27. Entry dated October 15, 1901, R. J. Reynolds Journal Day Book, October 10, 1901–December 31, 1903, 2.

28. See Appleby, *Relentless Revolution*, 162.

29. R.J.R. applied and was granted membership in the Masons in 1885 according to the Reynolds Family Chronology, 1885, p. 6; R. J. Reynolds, Trustee, and Member Committee on Elks' Home and Auditorium, Benevolent and Protective Order of Elks, Winston Lodge no. 449, Organized 1899, 254½ Main Street, *Walsh's Directory*, 1902–3, 31.

30. See receipts and expenses listed under "farm account" throughout the R. J. Reynolds, Journal Day Book, 1894–1898 and the R. J. Reynolds Ledger Individual no. 2, 1895–98. In 1895–96, the farm cost a little over twenty thousand dollars a year to maintain. Ledger no. 2, pp. 66–69.

31. Tilley, *R. J. Reynolds Tobacco Company*, 52; Reynolds Family Chronology, 1884, p. 6; *Condensation of Board of Commissioner's Minutes*.

32. G. G. Johnson, "Southern Paternalism"; Miller, "Blacks in Winston-Salem," 11.

33. Tise, *Government*, 34–39.

34. G. G. Johnson, "Southern Paternalism"; Miller, "Blacks in Winston-Salem," 11.

35. Wellman and Tise, *Education*, 32–37. Quote from Fries et al., *Forsyth*, 87. Other magazines like *Harper's Weekly* also applauded southerners for their new interest in a North-South reconciliation based on southern adoption of northern institutions. "North Carolina Sketches," *Harper's Weekly*, December 6, 1873, 1085; and "Waifs and Strays," *Harper's Weekly*, September 1, 1883, 1055.

36. Miller, "Blacks in Winston-Salem," 14.

37. Wellman and Tise, *Education*, 35–37; Lundeen, "Accommodation Strategies," 14; Korstad, *Civil Rights Unionism*, 44; Miller, "Blacks in Winston-Salem," 263–65; Newbold, *Five North Carolina Educators*, 7.

38. Miller, "Blacks in Winston-Salem," 15–16.

39. Quoted in Miller, "Blacks in Winston-Salem," 16.

40. *Salem People's Press*, January 22, 1891.

41. Lundeen, "Accommodation Strategies," 14; Korstad, *Civil Rights Unionism*, 44; Miller, "Blacks in Winston-Salem," 263–65.

42. It would be the second generation of Reynolds family members who would fund Wake Forest College's move from Wake County to Winston-Salem in 1956 and put the little Baptist school on a fast-paced trajectory to an elite national university.

43. Cohen, *Making a New Deal*, 181–206.

44. R.J.R. to Mr. D. Rich, May 13, 1905, R.J.R. Correspondence—M–R incoming, 1907–17 (note incorrect date on file folder), box 1, file 64, RFP.

45. *Salem People's Press*, May 4, 1882; January 30, 1890; *Winston Union Republican*, April 15 and 22, 1886; William P. Hairston told Nannie M. Tilley that he walked from Henry County to Winston in 1889, when he was eight years old. Tilley, *R. J. Reynolds Tobacco Company*, 38n42.

46. 1894, Condensation of Board of Commissioner's Minutes.

47. Data taken from table 2.1, Indications of R. J. Reynolds's Business during 1875–1887, in Tilley, *R. J. Tobacco Reynolds Company*, 35.

48. Winkler, *Souvenir of Twin-Cities of North Carolina*, 7.

49. Miller, "Blacks in Winston-Salem," 9–10; Logan, *Negro in North Carolina*, 91–94.

50. Miller, "Blacks in Winston-Salem," 10; Tilley, *Bright Tobacco Industry*, 515–18.

51. *WSJ*, February 10, 1929.

52. Julian Ralph, "The Very Old and Very New Winston-Salem," *Harper's Weekly*, July 20, 1895.

53. Korstad, *Civil Rights Unionism*, chap. 1.

54. Tilley, *R. J. Reynolds Tobacco Company*, 38; *Winston Western Sentinel*, April 4, 1889; April 11, 1889; *Western Tobacco Journal*, April 29, 1889.

55. Tilley, *R. J. Reynolds Tobacco Company*, 54.

56. Roberts and Knapp, "Paving the Way," 273.

57. Miller, "Blacks in Winston-Salem," 6.

58. *Salem People's Press*, April 29, 1886.

59. Logan, *Negro in North Carolina*, 182–83.

60. Ibid., 184.

61. Tilley, *R. J. Reynolds Tobacco Company*, 39.

62. Torain, "Development of the Liberty-Patterson Community," 1–4.

63. Miller, "Blacks in Winston-Salem," 12–14, 264–66.

64. Ibid., 18–19, 21–22; Tise, *Government*, 37–39.

65. Miller, "Blacks in Winston-Salem," 23–25; Tilley, *R. J. Reynolds Tobacco Company*, 52.

66. *Salem People's Press*, September 4, 1890.

67. *Salem People's Press*, April 19, 1888.

68. Logan, *Negro in North Carolina*, 174–80, shows how African Americans fought for their right to be seated in restaurants, at railroad stations, and on public transportation and the criticism they received from whites, but underlines the absence of any enactment of Jim Crow laws in North Carolina between 1876 and 1894. The author suggests that economic exigency more than humanitarian concern explains this "lapse."

69. Miller, "Blacks in Winston-Salem," 29–34.

70. Ibid., 33–35.

71. Ibid., 35–43.

72. Lundeen, "Accommodation Strategies," 17.

73. Miller, "Blacks in Winston-Salem," 42–43.

74. Ibid., 45–50.

75. "The Riot," *Winston Union Republican*, August 15, 1895, 2–3.

76. Miller, "Blacks in Winston-Salem," 51.

77. *WSJ*, November 4, 1898.

78. *WSJ*, November 7, 1898.

79. Miller, "Blacks in Winston-Salem," 61–66.

80. *Winston Union Republican*, December 15, 1898.

81. R.J.R. voted in favor of the Republican Party in the 1896 presidential election presumably because it was the party of big businessmen. Many prosperous businessmen in North Carolina shared his views. Brother Will also expressed his discomfort with the "silver Democrats" to Josephus Daniels shortly before the election. Daniels, *Editor in Politics*, 247–48. Many years later, Will Reynolds sent a letter to the editors of the *Charlotte News and Observer* and the *WSJ* dated October 14, 1940, stating that his brother felt national policies adopted by the Democrats in 1896 threatened the well-being of the United States. According to Will, not only did R.J.R. repeatedly state, "If Bryan is elected president he'll ruin this country," but he contributed heavily to McKinley as well as voted for him and aligned himself with Teddy Roosevelt in 1900. R.J.R. later supported Woodrow Wilson with special enthusiasm.

82. Gilmore, *Gender and Jim Crow*, chaps. 1–2.

83. Appleby, *Relentless Revolution*, 178, 216–17, 227.

84. Cell, *Highest Stage of White Supremacy*, 169–70.

85. Tilley, *R. J. Reynolds Tobacco Company*, 37.

86. Cell, *Highest Stage of White Supremacy*, 167–85.

87. Ibid., 190–91.

88. Schaffer, "Industrious Generation."

89. "Married," *Salem People's Press*, March 14, 1889.

90. Arnold, *History of the Tobacco Industry*, 65–72, masterfully describes the impact of the trust on small manufacturers in Virginia, characterizing competition as so "cutthroat" that profits were virtually nil and squeezed all but the most capitalized out of business or into American Tobacco.

91. Roberts and Knapp, "Paving the Way," 257, 283.

92. *Winston-Salem Twin City Sentinel*, October 21, 1951, quoting *Sentinel* editor in 1875.

93. R. J. Reynolds Tobacco Company. *Golden Leaves: R. J. Reynolds Tobacco Company and the Art of Advertising* [Winston-Salem, N.C.]: R. J. Reynolds Tobacco Company, 1986, 3–13. R.J.R. was not without hubris. An undated ad bears a likeness of R.J.R. himself. Advertisement, R. J. Reynolds Tobacco Company, n.d., http://www.tobaccodocuments.org.

94. *Articles of Incorporation of the "R. J. Reynolds Tobacco Company,"* February 11, 1890, Legacy Tobacco Documents Library, University of California, San Francisco, http://legacy.library.ucsf.edu/, accessed June 6, 2008.

95. Appleby, *Relentless Revolution*, 191–92.

96. Tilley, *R. J. Reynolds Tobacco Company*, chap. 2.

97. Interview with Zachary Smith, July 7, 2004, Reynolda Village, Winston-Salem, N.C.

98. Chandler, *Visible Hand*, 350; extant correspondence between R.J.R. and J. B. Duke, the American Tobacco Company, or the Consolidated Tobacco Company is virtually nil. The best sources on their dealings come from congressional testimony hearings from 1909 to 1911. Three letters from James B. Duke to R.J.R. exist in the James Buchanan Duke Papers, 1770–1990. One letter dated June 10, 1901, encloses a copy of an agreement for R.J.R. to sign ensuring he will not sell his Consolidated stocks for five years. Another, dated October 17, 1903, requests that all dividends paid by R. J. Reynolds Tobacco Company bear Duke's company's name, the Continental Tobacco Company. One other letter, dated November 6, 1911, is a personal one, congratulating R.J.R. and Katharine on the birth of their fourth child, Zachary Smith Reynolds. J. B. Duke to R. J. Reynolds Tobacco Co., October 17, 1903, box 2; J. B. Duke to R. J. Reynolds, November 6, 1911, box 3: April 12, 1909–December 18, 1911; and J. B. Duke to Mr. R. J. Reynolds, June 10, 1901, box 5: Correspondence, Letterbooks, July 31, 1894–October 10, 1904, all in the James Buchanan Duke Papers, Duke University Library, Durham, N.C.

99. Chandler, *Visible Hand*, 381.

100. Editor, *Tobacco*, May 6, 1887.

101. Brooks, *Green Leaf and Gold*, 15–28; Roberts and Knapp, "Paving the Way," 279–80.

102. Chandler, *Visible Hand*, 250, 292, 382–87; Durden, *Bold Entrepreneur*, 39–66.

103. *Report of the Commissioner of Corporations on the Tobacco Industry, Part I*, 350.

104. Chandler, *Visible Hand*, 286, 388.

105. Tilley, *R. J. Reynolds Tobacco Company*, 57, 64, 68–69.

106. For example, R.J.R. signed a petition on April 30, 1880, calling for an election to decide on a forty-thousand-dollar subscription to support an extension of the Danville line. Reynolds Family Chronology, April 30, 1880, p. 5; *Condensation of Board of Commissioner's Minutes*, 373–75.

107. Wellman, *Transportation and Communication*, 20; Connor, Boyd, and Hamilton, *History of North Carolina*, 6:2; Tilley, *R. J. Reynolds Tobacco Company*, 56–60.

108. Fries et al. *Forsyth*, 188; Tilley, *R. J. Reynolds Tobacco Company*, 60–61.

109. Tilley, *R. J. Reynolds Tobacco Company*, 61.

110. Ibid., 62.

111. Randal Hall makes this point in his forthcoming book *Mountains on the Market*; Rondthaler, *Memorabilia of Fifty Years*, 103; Tilley, *R. J. Reynolds Tobacco Company*, 59–61.

112. Strouse, *Morgan*, 321–22, quotation on p. 322.

113. Across the South, but especially in Alabama, Georgia, and North Carolina, Populist sympathies against state legislators in the pockets of the railroads was mounting. As late as 1908, a *Harper's Weekly* editorial applauded the South's decade-long new interest in the relationship between local affairs and national politics, and the democratic voices it represented. *Harper's Weekly*, December 5, 1908.

114. Daniels, *Editor in Politics*, 212–18, 468–79; Tilley, *R. J. Reynolds Tobacco Company*, 63; *Raleigh News and Observer*, February 6, 1897; February 7, 1897; February 13, 1897.

115. Daniels, *Tar Heel Editor*, 473.

116. H.E.B.C., "R. J. Reynolds," *Mount Airy News*, December 9, 1909.

117. Tilley, "Agitation against the American Tobacco Company," 217–20; Daniels, *Tar Heel Editor*, 151–53, 343, 473–79; Durden, *Bold Entrepreneur*, 3, 58, 160.

118. Reynolds had borrowed from his father and A. M. Lybrook especially, but also from the Parlett and Floyd families in Baltimore. Tilley, *R. J. Reynolds Tobacco Company*, 48–49, 51–53.

119. Ibid., 68–69.

120. Ibid., 70.

121. Roberts and Knapp, "Paving the Way," 263.

122. Tilley, *R. J. Reynolds Tobacco Company*, 75–81.

123. Ibid., 72.

124. Cost for Billboard Ads, October 1, 1895, R. J. Reynolds, Journal Day Book, 1894–98, p. 123; Tilley, *R. J. Reynolds Tobacco Company*, 74–75.

125. Tilley, *R. J. Reynolds Tobacco Company*, 88.

126. Patent no. 862,115, Treating Tobacco, July 30, 1907, Legacy Tobacco Documents. Reynolds later claimed that a brilliant German scientist discovered the special formula for Prince Albert tobacco. He may have been referring to Schweinitz, who had trained in German universities and at the University of Virginia and the University of North Carolina. See Tilley, *R. J. Reynolds Tobacco Company*, 161–62.

127. Wellman and Tise, *Industry and Commerce*, 28; Fries, *Records of the Moravians*, 6:28–58.

128. Arnold, *History of the Tobacco Industry*, 71–72.

129. Tilley, *R. J. Reynolds Tobacco Company*, 90–91.

130. Charles C. Hay III, "William Neal Reynolds," *Dictionary of American Biography*, ed. John A. Garraty, supp. 5 (New York: Charles Scribner's Sons, 1977) 565; Tilley, *R. J. Reynolds Tobacco Company*, 37, 44, 65, 78.

131. Tilley, *R. J. Reynolds Tobacco Company*, 88–89.

132. Ibid., 90.

133. Orthodox Creed Strictler, interview by Essie Wade Smith, Orthodox Creed Strictler life history [1939], Transcription, p. 4, WPA/VWP Life Histories, box 179, folder 9, Library of Virginia, Richmond, Virginia.

134. Tilley, *R. J. Reynolds Tobacco Company*, 90.

135. Daniels, *Editor in Politics*, 598–99.

136. Carlton, "Revolution from Above," 466; R. J. Reynolds bought out the smaller companies throughout the next decade. As late as 1900, he was purchasing the Brown Brothers Company, one of the original tobacco manufacturers in the city years ago. "A Big Tobacco Deal," *WSJ*, November 24, 1900, p. 2.

137. Because the tobacco industry had become so reliant on paying out promotions all along the marketing chain, from jobbers to salesmen to customers, farmers suffered increasingly lower prices as manufacturers sought to reduce their costs. Increased competition due to greater access to growers from around the world also hurt local tobacco farmers. See Arnold, *History of the Tobacco Industry*, 66–74; Tilley, *R. J. Reynolds Tobacco Company*, 96. On competition from overseas growers, see Trade Catalog, A. Hussey and Company Leaf Tobacco, 1898, Hagley Museum and Library, Wilmington, Del., in which Hussey advertises itself as "the pioneer house" for supplying Sumatran tobacco at prices "absolutely the lowest.

138. Tilley, *R. J. Reynolds Tobacco Company*, 97.

139. Obituary, July 31, 1918, *Wall Street Journal*, IM.

140. Tilley, *R. J. Reynolds Tobacco Company*, 97–100.

141. Obituary, August 1, 1918, *Tobacco Leaf*, IM.

142. Tilley, *R. J. Reynolds Tobacco Company*, 99.

143. Ibid., 101.

144. Ibid., 102.

145. Carlton, "Revolution from Above," 467–68.

146. Appleby, *Relentless Revolution*, 201–2.

147. Carlton, "Revolution from Above," 464–67.

148. Durden, *Bold Entrepreneur*, 16–21.

149. Appleby, *Relentless Revolution*, 205.

150. McGrath and McMillan, *Entrepreneurial Mindset*, 1–8.

151. One cannot underestimate the degree to which the political and economic elite of Winston-Salem across the twentieth century shaped the nature of how R.J.R. has been remembered and consciously and unconsciously constructed a self-serving narrative of this elite community's past. See Trouillot, *Silencing the Past*, for a broader, more theoretical discussion of how groups in power use story and narrative to affirm their version of events.

152. "Reynolds, Richard Joshua," p. 5, in Typescripts of Period Biographical Sketches, R. J. Reynolds's Biographical Sketches File, Mary Babcock Reynolds Correspondence, RHMAA.

153. R.J.R. at Roaring Gap Resort, Photograph Collection, North Carolina Room, Central Library, Forsyth County Public Library.

154. H. E. C. "Red Buck" Bryant, "R. J. Reynolds," *Mount Airy News*, December 9, 1909, p. 1, states he knew all three brothers when they boarded at the less-than-posh Jones establishment. The Winston City directories between 1884 and 1895 list R.J.R. boarding at the Central Hotel, the Hotel Fountain, in a house at 123 Chestnut, in a room at the corner of Third and Liberty, and in a room at 119 Chestnut.

155. *Winston-Salem Twin City Sentinel*, July 30, 1918.

156. Dr. John Howard Monroe, Oral History, RHMAA.

157. Blair, "Sketch no. 1," 335.

158. H. E. C. "Red Buck" Bryant, "R. J. Reynolds," *Mount Airy News*, December 9,

1909, p. 1; Tursi, *Winston-Salem*, 132; R. J. Reynolds Journal Day Book D, February 12, 1894–March 2, 1898, p. 141; $20.00 dues paid to Moses Point Gunning Club, February 1, 1903, R. J. Reynolds Journal Day Book, October 10, 1901–December 31, 1903, p. 99.

159. Cartoon, City Boy in the Country, *WSJ*, January 8, 1905, p. 1, cols. 3–4.

160. Reynolds Family Chronology, p. 5; *Winston Journal and Sentinel*, May 7, 1950.

161. Ibid. Although this story comes from a newspaper article on R. J. Reynolds in 1950, page after page of R. J. Reynolds's Journal Day Book D, February 12, 1894–March 2, 1898, reference payments for horse purchases and sales and maintenance of his extensive racing barn.

162. H. E. C. "Red Buck" Bryant, "The Three Reynolds Brothers," *Raleigh News and Observer*, March 12, 1967, p. 2C; *Winston Union Republican*, January 13, 1887.

163. Reynolds Family Chronology, p. 6; Mary Reynolds Babcock papers, undated column, RHMAA.

164. *Winston Union Republican*, January 13, 1887.

165. Laird, *Pull*, 41.

166. Tilley, *R. J. Reynolds Tobacco Company*, 108.

167. Quoted in Jo White Linn, *The Gray Family and Allied Lines* (Salisbury, N.C.: privately printed, 1976), 123–25; Parke, "Gordon Gray," 9.

168. Tilley, *R. J. Reynolds Tobacco Company*, 54.

169. *Winston-Salem: A Cooperative Spirit*, 32.

170. Carter Cue to author, June 19, 2006, references "a reputed relationship" between brother Will Reynolds and his African American housekeeper that resulted in the birth of an illegitimate son, Rufus Hairston, who graduated from Slater Academy and Normal Institute in 1914, was one of the first African American pharmacists in Winston-Salem, attended professional conferences around the country, and grew quite wealthy. He was named the first alumni trustee at Winston Salem State University. Rufus Hairston's wife, Mary McGee Hairston, told a reporter when she was ninety-five years old in 1991, that her husband himself did not know if the rumors about one of the Reynolds brothers being his father were true or not. His mother had never told her son the name of his father. One time, however, when Rufus and Mary were walking past the Reynolds factory, one of the brothers had waved hello, and Rufus told her, "They say that man is my father." Since R.J.R. died in 1918, and Rufus and Mary were wed in 1919, it corroborates Carter Cue's understanding that Will Reynolds was probably Rufus Hairston's father. Phoebe Zerwick, "Prosperity on 14th Street," *WSJ*, January 6, 1991. A letter from independent researcher Ken Badgett to the author, December 18, 2003, conveyed a story told by a former R. J. Reynolds employee about rumors of a special room in R. J. Reynolds Tobacco factory no. 5 where R.J.R. "used to take his black lady friends." Since R.J.R. had died in 1918 and Will lived until 1951, and because people today often confuse R.J.R. and Will with each other, it is hard to determine whether Will or R.J.R. was the perpetrator.

171. Dr. John Howard Monroe, Oral History, RHMAA.

172. Interview with Zachary Smith, September 15, 2004, Reynolda Village, Winston-Salem, N.C.; Dr. John Howard Monroe, Oral History Archives, September 23, 1996, OH.03.034.1, RHMAA. Such horrific local train accidents were not uncommon. See "Boy Loses Both Legs and Arms Playing with Train," *WSJ*, September 7, 1915. John Neal is buried at a large memorial also honoring William Neal Reynolds (1866–1951) and Kate

Bitting Reynolds (1867–1946) in Salem Cemetery, about an eighth of a mile from the R. J. Reynolds memorial and family gravesite. No birth or death certificates can be located for John Neal. His marker lists his birth date as April 28, 1887, and his death date as August 29, 1920. He is listed in the 1900 U.S. Census, Forsyth County, Winston Township, as the twelve-year-old adopted son of Will and Kate Reynolds. In this census record, his birth state is listed as North Carolina and his birth month as October 1887, different from the grave marker. The Family Bible Records (photocopy of R. J. Reynolds Bible), box 1, file 44, RFP, lists his year of birth (1887) and his year of death (1920). On cash outlays and rents collected, see R. J. Reynolds Journal Day Book D, February 12, 1894–March 2, 1898. On stock outlay (and multiple examples of continued financial support for John Neal), see R. J. Reynolds, Journal no. 9, 1904–5, esp. p. 106; also three quarterly payments for John Neal totaling $885.15 in Individual Ledger no. 7, 1916–18. For examples of tuition payment, clothing bills, and doctor's expenses for John Neal, see entries dated March 11, 1903, and November 30, 1903, R. J. Reynolds Journal Day Book, October 10, 1901–December 31, 1903, pp. 107, 204. For examples of John Neal's pasturage collections and commissions received, see entries dated July 2, 1903, and July 6, 1903, as well as a loan of $225 to John Neal by R. J. Reynolds, with interest totaling $248.87, dated July 22, 1903, R. J. Reynolds Journal Day Book, October 10, 1901–December 31, 1903, pp. 145, 147, 148, 153; Obituary, *WSJ*, September 12, 1920, pp. 1, 5.

173. Louis Menand, "Lives of Others: The Biography Business," *New Yorker*, August 6, 2007, 64–65.

Chapter Four. Dearest of All

1. Although Kate Smith, as the daughter of R.J.R.'s first cousin, was his first cousin once removed, it is interesting to note that many local histories have obscured this fact. See, for example, *Winston-Salem: A Cooperative Spirit*, 32, which states that R.J.R. "chose a distant cousin" to marry.

2. RJR to KSR, n.d., 1905, from the New Hoffman House, Madison Square, N.Y., box 1, file 65, RFP.

3. Stanback, "Kate Smith Reynolds," 3.

4. Nancy Susan Reynolds to Nannie Tilley, February 14, 1970, box 1, file 1: Critz—Biographical Information, RFP; Chudacoff, *Age of the Bachelor*, introduction.

5. RJR to KS(R), March 12, 1903, box 2, file 154 A, RFP.

6. Chudacoff, *Age of the Bachelor*, introduction; on Nancy Jane Cox Reynolds, see Notepaper, 6 sheets, Quarry Farm, Greenwich, Conn., written by Nancy Susan Reynolds, dated February 14, 1970, in box 1, file 1: Critz—Biographical Information, RFP; Nancy Jane Reynolds's death, recorded in the Reynolds Family Bible, copy, box 1, file 44: Bible Records, RFP.

7. KS(R), Mount Airy, N.C., to RJR, March 9, 1903, box 2, file 154 A, RFP.

8. RJR to KS(R), March 12 and March 19, 1903, box 2, file 154 A, RFP.

9. RJR to KS(R), March 19, 1903; KSR to RJR, March 8, 1913, box 1, file 63.02, RFP.

10. On a trip to Atlantic City, see entry dated August 22, 1903, p. 167; on tuition payments for John Neal, see entry dated January 30, 1904, p. 11, both in R. J. Reynolds Journal Day Book, October 10, 1901–December 31, 1903.

11. Some family members contend that Kate had joined her Lybrook cousins when

she was fourteen years old, but there is no extant evidence to prove it. Regardless, Katharine's reference to this trip ten years later suggests it was quite special and opened up the possibility for romance between the two cousins. Interview with Zachary Smith, July 7, 2004; KSR to RJR, March 8, 1913.

12. KSR to RJR, March 8, 1913.

13. Copy of Family Record from Reynolds Family Bible, box 1, file 16: Lybrook—Bible records, RFP.

14. Memorandum to the Files, February 29, 1960, Chancellor, Gordon Williams Blackwell, General Correspondence, 1960, E–M, box 20, University Archives, Special Collections Division, Walter C. Jackson Library, UNCG. Lewis Dull, "How We Went to Winston," *State Normal Magazine* 1, no. 2, June 15, 1897, 150–52.

15. *WSJ*, June 8, 1906; August 27, 1904.

16. For a thick description of the cultural world of early twentieth-century Winston-Salem, see Reines, "Cultural History," 202–30.

17. *WSJ*, April 24, 1905.

18. Anna Lula Dobson, "Our Family," p. 18, copy of unpublished typescript of family history dated 1956 in the author's possession.

19. Nancy Susan Reynolds, Oral History Archives, May 5, 1980, OH.01.004.1, RHMAA.

20. *Walsh's Winston-Salem, North Carolina City Directory for 1904–1905* (Charleston, S.C.: n.p., 1905).

21. Interview with Zachary Smith, July 15, 2004, Reynolda Village, Winston-Salem, N.C.; Tilley, *R. J. Reynolds Tobacco Company*, 37, 130–37.

22. R. J. Reynolds's Individual Ledger no. 4, 1898–1903, R. J. Reynolds Item no. 5725, p. 89. In an undated letter (probably 1887–92), prominent editor Josephus Daniels told his mother that his future wife, Addie, was working on her stenography courses, and it was proving "the hardest thing she ha[d] ever had to learn." Tackling business-assistant demands was not an easy set of skills to acquire on the fly, and there is no evidence that Katharine had pursued the business track at Normal Institute. Papers of Josephus C. Daniels (1862–1948), Special Correspondence, box 10, microfilm reel 1, Library of Congress, Washington, D.C.

23. Entry correcting mistake dated September 16, 1903, p. 179, R. J. Reynolds Journal Day Book, October 10, 1901–December 31, 1903. The last entry in Katharine Reynolds's handwriting appears to be the one dated February 8, 1905, in R. J. Reynolds Journal no. 9, 1904–5. Note that Katharine and R.J.R. were married on February 27, 1905.

24. Nancy Susan Reynolds, Oral History Archives. "The other story I recall was about when my father finally proposed to her. She had just entered a company contest."

25. Reynolds Family Chronology, p. 15, L. Blythe; entry dated April 26, 1904, p. 44, R. J. Reynolds Journal no. 9, 1904–5.

26. Katharine Smith's distinctive handwriting, consisting of small horizontal loops begins on May 1, 1903, in R. J. Reynolds's Individual Ledger no. 4, 1898–1903, R. J. Reynolds Item no. 5725.

27. R. J. Reynolds's Individual Ledger no. 4, 1898–1903, R. J. Reynolds Item no. 5725, entries dated April 26, May 16, June 18, July 16, July 31, September 1, September 15, October 28, and November 28, 1903.

28. Entries dated February 6, 1904, p. 17, and March 9, 1904, p. 62, R. J. Reynolds Journal no. 9, 1904–5.

29. R. J. Reynolds Journal Day Book, October 10, 1901–December 31, 1903, noted on p. 128 that Katharine Smith to be paid out of R.J.R.'s private account.

30. Entries dated March 1, 1904, p. 23, and March 26, 1904, p. 26, in R. J. Reynolds Journal Day Book, October 10, 1901–December 31, 1903.

31. Entry dated June 7, 1904, p. 61, R. J. Reynolds Journal no. 9, 1904–5.

32. Entry dated September 12, 1904, p. 109, R. J. Reynolds Journal No. 9, 1904–1905. R.J.R. continued to sell her shares of CFI he had bought himself. See entry dated October 21, 1904, p. 142, R. J. Reynolds Journal No. 9, 1904–1905.

33. Entry dated November 11, 1904, p. 139, R. J. Reynolds Journal no. 9, 1904–5.

34. Francis H. Pattisant to Miss Katharine Smith, Winston-Salem, N.C., April 14, 1904, box 2, file 167, RFP.

35. R.J.R. Personal Account Books, 1903–5.

36. Fraser, *Every Man a Speculator*, 389; Cohen, *Making a New Deal*, 344; Hochfelder, "'Where the Common People Could Speculate,'" 357. The enormous increase in investments by the middle class stemmed from Liberty Bond drives, the eradication of bucket shops, and participation in employee stock-ownership plans.

37. RJR to KSR, August 2, 1909, box 1, file 65, RFP.

38. Nancy Susan Reynolds, Oral History Archives.

39. Ibid.

40. The Church Register of the First Presbyterian Church, no. 3, Winston, N.C., from January 6, 1895, pp. 100–103, 108–9, 167, 180–81, First Presbyterian Church, Winston-Salem, N.C.

41. Entries dated May 25, 1903, p. 133, R. J. Reynolds Journal Day Book, October 10, 1901–December 31, 1903.

42. See, for example, entries dated March 31, 1904, p. 28, R. J. Reynolds Journal no. 9, 1904–5.

43. Letter to KSR dated May 19, 1903, acknowledging receipt of subscription, Charles McIver Letterbook, book no. 7, State Normal College, March 11, 1903–June 10, 1903; KSR to Dr. McIver, October 24, 1903, Charles Duncan McIver Papers, General Correspondence—Sh–Sm 1903, Applications, University Archives, Special Collections Division, Walter C. Jackson Library, UNCG.

44. Announcement that R.J.R. bought 555 Fifth Street house from brother Will, March 22, 1904, *WSJ*.

45. Entry dated December 7, 1904, p. 153, R. J. Reynolds Journal no. 9, 1904–5.

46. Entry dated February 8, 1905, p. 159, R. J. Reynolds Journal no. 9, 1904–5.

47. RJR to KSR, n.d., 1905, from the New Hoffman House.

48. *Mount Airy News*, March 2, 1905.

49. Mullen, *Paris Gowns*, 3.

50. Reverend D. Clay Lilly had begun his ministry at First Presbyterian on April 16, 1904, less than a year after Katharine Smith had become a member. Reverend Lilly would remain a close personal friend of the Reynoldses for the remainder of their lives.

51. *Mount Airy News*, March 2, 1905.

52. "Understated," *WSJ*, February 27, 2005, E1–2; Mullen, " *Paris Gowns*, 5.

53. "R.J.R. Buys Home," *WSJ*, March 22, 1904; William Neal Reynolds had purchased adjoining lots 287 and 288 on Fifth Street in 1899, Winston-Salem Register of Public Deeds, microfilm DB 57, pp. 308–9, 366–67.

54. Mullen, *Paris Gowns*, 4.

55. Passenger List, box 10, file 658, RFP. The ship sailed from New York City on March 1, 1905, and departed from Liverpool on June 16, 1905.

56. Janice Gaston, "Understated," *WSJ*, February 27, 2005, p. E1.

57. Fare Estimate, Thomas Cook and Son, no date, box 2, file 160, RFP.

58. Mullen, *Paris Gowns*, 7.

59. RJR, Hotel Bristol, to Mr. D. Rich, Winston, N.C., May 13, 1905, box 1, file 63: R.J.R. Correspondence—M–R Incoming, 1907 [note incorrect date; should be 1906] –17; L. Haag, Binder and Co., Sculptures Birenz (Suisse) Lucerne, November 6, 1905, shipping statement, box 1, file 64: R.J.R. Correspondence—S–Z Incoming, 1906–17; request by R. J. Reynolds to "pay Mr. Genova twenty-nine dollars $29 in receipt of four water colors pick up and charge to my account on April 4, 1905," on Grand Hotel-Venise stationery, no date, box 1, file 65, all in RFP.

60. Mullen, *Paris Gowns*, 7–18.

61. RJR to Mr. Rich, May 13, 1905.

62. Interview with Zachary Smith, July 15, 2004.

63. Dr. John Howard Monroe, Oral History Archives, September 23, 1996, OH.03.034.1, RHMAA.

64. Interview with Zachary Smith, July 7, 2004, Reynolda Village, Winston-Salem, N.C.

65. For example, see entries dated July 31, 1905, p. 210, and October 17, 1905, p. 235, R. J. Reynolds Journal no. 9, 1904–5.

66. Censer, "Changing World of Work," 53–55.

67. Nancy Susan Reynolds, Oral History Archives.

68. Hunt Wilkinson and Company Correspondence, 1908–13, box 2, file 122, RFP.

69. Elizabeth Wade, Oral History Archives, July 10, 1980, OH.01.006.1, RHMAA.

70. KSR to the Baltimore School of Art Needlework, June 21, 1912, box 1, file 77; KSR to Deans, [1912], box 1, file 90, both in RFP.

71. See receipts in KSR Correspondence—Annie Grogan [florist], 1909–12, box 1, file 105, RFP.

72. Nancy Susan Reynolds, Oral History Archives.

73. Ibid.

74. Mary Daniels to KSR, n.d., box 1, file 89, RFP.

75. Myra M. H. Ludlow to KSR, December 31, 1918, box 2, file 122, RFP.

76. In 1912, Katharine wrote her friend Emma Bernard Kaminer, "The town has been unusually gay during June; in fact there have been so many parties, teas, etc. that I have gotten out of the habit, to a great extent, of eating at regular times, and consequently have been gaining a pound or two a week." KSR to Emma Bernard Kaminer, July 1, 1912, box 2, file 319, RFP.

77. Invitation, June 14–20, 1912, box 2, file 165; invitation, November 23, n.d., box 1, file 79, both in RFP.

78. KSR to Louise, June 8, 1912, box 2, file 128, RFP.

79. Interview with J. Edward Johnston Jr., January 6, 2004, Baltimore, Md.

80. Hay, *Madeline McDowell Breckinridge*.

81. "James B. Duke Sues for Divorce," *New York Times* (hereafter *NYT*), September 3, 1905; less than two years after his divorce from Lillian McReady, Duke married another

widow, the Atlanta heiress and socialite Nanaline Holt Inman. "James B. Duke Weds Mrs. Inman," *NYT*, July 24, 1907; Durden, *Dukes of Durham*, 161–65.

82. Insurance Maps of Winston-Salem, N.C., Sanborn Map Company, 1900, 1907; *Walsh's Winston-Salem, North Carolina City Directory for 1904–1905*.

83. Nancy Susan Reynolds, Oral History Archives.

84. Party given by Mrs. Rich, *WSJ*, August 31, 1905; Whist Club Meeting, *WSJ*, September 5, 1905.

85. "Miss Senah Critz . . . with Mrs. Reynolds," *WSJ*, July 21, 1905; "Mr. William Lanier of West Point, Miss. and Messrs. J. W. Swann and P. A. Rhodes of Boston . . . to visit Mr. R. J. Reynolds of Winston," *WSJ*, August 3, 1905; "Mr. and Mrs. Zachary Taylor Smith . . . to spend some time with Mr. and Mrs. Reynolds, *WSJ*, August 17, 1905; "Seven Course Dinner Party at Mr. and Mrs. Reynolds," *WSJ*, August 25, 1905. On September 14, 1905, the *WSJ* reported that "one of the most delightful affairs of the season's many social functions, was the hay ride and supper given by Mrs. R. J. Reynolds last evening in honor of her sister, Miss Maxie Smith," and then described the event fully.

86. "Minutes of the Meeting of the Stockholders of the R. J. Reynolds Tobacco Company," April 3, 1917, Legacy Tobacco Documents. Incidentally, Will's shareholdings had not increased much at all, and Walter's by only about one hundred shares since 1906. "Resolution of the Board of Directors," February 16, 1906, Tobacco Legacy Documents. On Will's magnetism, see McQuilkin, White, and Tursi, *Lost Empire*, 17.

87. E. J. Brown to KSR, July 30, 1918, IM.

88. For example, see telegram from C. K. Faucette and George W. Coan to RJR, April 4, 1906, box 1, file 79; telegram from Bowman Gray to RJR, April 4, 1906, box 1, file 102; Governor R. B. Glenn to Mr. and Mrs. R. J. Reynolds, n.d., box 1, file 102, all in RFP.

89. Telegram from W. E. Brock to RJR, April 4, 1906, box 1, file 75, KSR Correspondence—Bl–By, 1905–21, RFP.

90. Telegram from J. B. Duke to RJR, November 6, 1911, box 1, file 88; James L. Boyd to RJR, August 28, 1908, box 1, file 75, both in RFP.

91. "Henrietta Van Den Berg," Obituary, *Baltimore Sun*, April 28, 1952, clipping in Henrietta Van Den Berg alumnae file, Johns Hopkins Archives, Baltimore; "Henrietta van Den Berg," *Johns Hopkins Nurses Alumnae Magazine* 51, no. 3 (July 1952), Johns Hopkins Archives (I am indebted to Sherry Hollingsworth for sharing her research in the Hopkins Archives with me); Nancy Susan Reynolds, Oral History Archives. Hiring Henrietta Van Den Berg did not alleviate all the worry about Katharine's subsequent pregnancies, however. By the time she was six months pregnant with Smith, she was having enough health problems that R.J.R. was consulting a Baltimore specialist. RJR to KSR, August 11, 1911, box 1, file 65, RFP. In addition to the above information, Nancy Crouch, Winston-Salem, N.C., provided the author with additional family history stories on October 22, 2006.

92. Nancy Susan Reynolds, Oral History Archives. Local historian Ken Badgett has suggested that John Kerr Pepper, who came to Winston-Salem in 1907, was recruited by Katharine in the same way. Born in Stokes County and a graduate of Guilford College, he had received his MD from the Medical College at the University of Maryland and was completing his internship at Johns Hopkins when he was persuaded to return to his home state and practice in Winston. Obituary, *Winston-Salem Twin City Sentinel*, October 31, 1944, p. 1; *WSJ*, November 1, 1944, p. 1.

93. Author's conversation with Barbara Millhouse, granddaughter of Katharine and R.J.R., August 10, 2010, Winston-Salem.

94. Invoice, California Fruit Company, June 30, 1912, box 3, file 210, RFP.

95. "Children's Parties Menace, Dr. Says," *WSJ*, January 3, 1913, p. 1, col. 1.

96. Nancy Susan Reynolds, Oral History Archives.

97. KSR to Irene Smith, June 7, 192, box 2, file 154, RFP.

98. KSR to Marie, August 13, 1913, box 2, file 179, RFP.

99. KSR to Lizzie, June 8, 1912, box 2, file 177, RFP.

100. Edith to Yette [Henrietta Van Den Berg], April 28, 1914, box 2, file 166, RFP.

101. Katharine's mother, presumably suffering from tuberculosis and essentially an invalid, rarely made the rough trip even by car from Mount Airy to Reynolda, and letters reference her poor health frequently. See, for example, Henrietta Van Den Berg to KSR, October 17, 1917, box 2, file 166, RFP. Irene "says your Mother is better, but still far from well."

102. Henrietta Van Den Berg to KSR, October 17, 1917, and December 18, 1917, box 2, file 166, RFP.

103. Ibid.

104. Ibid.

105. Nancy Susan Reynolds, Oral History Archives.

106. Ibid.

107. Ibid.; telegram from Henrietta Van Den Berg to Dr. Tom Brown, December 1, 1917, box 1, file 75, RFP.

108. Henrietta Van Den Berg to KSR, October 17, 1917, and December 18, 1917, box 2, file 166, RFP.

109. Nancy Susan Reynolds, Oral History Archives.

110. KSR to Senah Critz, June 10, 1912, box 2, file 148, RFP.

111. Mrs. Etta Mann to KSR, n.d., box 2, file 131; invitation from Governor of Virginia and Mrs. Mann to Mr. and Mrs. Reynolds to join them at the Executive Mansion on December 5, 1912, to meet "The Governors of Several States," box 2, file 131, both in RFP.

112. Nancy Susan Reynolds, Oral History Archives.

113. RJR to KSR, July 30, 1909, box 1, file 65, RFP.

114. RJR to KSR, November 5, 1909, box 1, file 65, RFP.

115. Nancy Susan Reynolds, Oral History Archives.

116. The only reference comparing R.J.R.'s treatment of John Neal with his legitimate children came from an oral history with the son of the dairyman at the Reynolda Estate. He stated that R.J.R. brought his "outside child," presumably John Neal, to the Reynolda Estate with some frequency. "He was particularly fond of him, and [Neal] was a very friendly fellow and was allowed more time out here [at Reynolda] than R.J.'s [legitimate] sons." Dr. John Howard Monroe, Oral History Archives. Given the number of references R.J.R. Jr. made about his experiences at Reynolda as well as the photographic evidencing of his time at Reynolda, this memory seems a bit suspicious. R.J.R. was fifteen years younger than John, who was working for his father collecting rents before he went to work at Reynolds Tobacco. In all likelihood, John probably did accompany his father to the Reynolda Estate during its building phase more than Dick Jr., who would have been a little boy in Miss Van Den Berg's and Katharine's charge. R.J.R. may also have avoided bringing Dick with him to the estate simply because of the hazards

present there, given John Neal's terrible accident at Tanglewood while in his father and uncle's care.

117. Nancy Susan Reynolds, Oral History Archives.

118. Ibid.

119. Ibid.

120. Ibid.

121. Ibid.

122. Dick Reynolds to Parents, n.d. [1917], box 2, file 183, RFP. Smith also reported "Dick's chickens are growing fine" to their parents, further testament to their importance to Katharine and R.J.R. as a responsible learning opportunity for their oldest son. Smith Reynolds to Parents, n.d. [probably 1917], typewritten [probably by Miss Van Den Berg for Smith], box 2, file 182, RFP.

123. Nancy Susan Reynolds, Oral History Archives.

124. KSR to Maryland Wagon Works, May 27, 1912, box 2, file 131, RFP. Did Katharine remember that in 1907 the *New York Times* observed that Buck Duke had bought his future ten-year-old stepson a pony and cart upon announcing his formal engagement to the boy's mother, Nanaline Holt Inman? "James B. Duke Weds Mrs. Inman," *NYT*, July 24, 1907.

125. Henrietta Van Den Berg to KSR, October 17, 1917, box 2, file 166, RFP.

126. Nancy Susan Reynolds, Oral History Archives.

127. Smith Reynolds to Parents, n.d. [probably 1917], typewritten [probably by Miss Van Den Berg for Smith], box 2, file 182; Henrietta Van Den Berg to KSR, October 17, 1917, box 2, file 166, both in RFP.

128. Nancy Susan Reynolds, Oral History Archives; ad for *The Birth of a Nation*, *WSJ*, March 13, 1916, p. 5; KSR to Louise, June 8, 1912, box 2, file 128, RFP.

129. "Possum Hunt Proves a Delightful Event," *Winston Western Sentinel*, November 13, 1913, p. 3, and November 15, 1912, p. 10. William Watson to KSR, July 30, 1911, box 2, file 167, RFP.

130. KSR to Senah Critz, June 10, 1912; *WSJ* announcement that R.J.R., Katharine, and their children traveled to Mount Airy to see the Smiths for the weekend "in a magnificent touring car," May 6, 1915, p. 7, col. 1.

131. Ralph Sloan, "R. J. Reynolds Early Customer," *Statesville Record and Landmark*, October 19, 1966, p. 3.

132. Nancy Susan Reynolds, Oral History Archives.

133. Mrs. Henry M. Noel, Mr. and Mrs. Jackson D. Wilson, comp., *Roaring Gap* (Winston-Salem: Bradford Printing Services, 1976), 11. I am grateful to J. D. Wilson for giving me a copy of this private publication.

134. Author's conversation about family memories of the hunting preserve with Barbara Millhouse, granddaughter of Katharine and R.J.R., and Sherry Hollingsworth, family researcher, August 10, 2010, Winston-Salem, N.C.

135. "Mr. and Mrs. R. J. Reynolds and Son Leave for Trip," *WSJ*, February 9, 1907; Adelaide Douglas to KSR, March 20, 1907, box 1, folder 88, RFP; "Mr. and Mrs. R. J. Reynolds leave for Philadelphia," *WSJ*, July 31, 1907.

136. KSR Correspondence—Ethel Reynolds [Mrs. H. W.], 1908, box 2, file 146, RFP.

137. Nancy Susan Reynolds, Oral History Archives.

138. KSR to Scottie [?], January 8, 1913, box 2, file 177, RFP.

139. RJR to H. D. Saxton, request for rooms at the Belleview Hotel, February 13, 1917, box 1, file 106; H. Martin to KSR, May 8, 1917, box 3, file 131; "Going and Coming," January 3, 1919, *Jacksonville (Fla.) Metropolis*, clipping, box 1, file 59, all in RFP.

140. KSR to Miss Mollie Bernard, February 18, 1913, box 1, file 74, RFP.

141. Nathalie Gray to KSR, n.d. [1919?], box 1, file 102, RFP.

142. Smith Reynolds [written by "Bum"] to RJR, n.d. [1917], box 2, file 182, RFP.

143. "Atlantic City, Playground of the Nation," permanent exhibit, Atlantic City Historical Museum, Atlantic City, N.J.

144. Oliver Zunz, *Making America Corporate*, 182–83.

145. KSR to RJR, March 8, 1913, box 1, file 63.02, RFP.

146. RJR to KSR, September 19, 1910, box 1, file 01–065–20–32, RFP.

147. KSR to RJR, December 24, 1915, box 1, file 63, RFP.

148. RJR to KSR, n.d., box 1, file 65, RFP.

149. RJR to KSR, April, 8, 1908, box 1, file 65, RFP.

150. RJR to KSR, n.d. [1905], box 1, file 65, RFP.

151. See RJR to KSR Correspondence, box 1, file 65, RFP.

152. RJR to KSR, September 20, 1919, box 1, file 65, RFP.

153. Ibid.

154. RJR to KSR, August, 11, 1909, box 1, file 65, RFP.

155. See RJR to KSR, RFP, box 1, file 65, esp. letters dated August 10 and August 14, 1909, RFP.

156. "For Apartment Houses in City," *WSJ*, January 22, 1909.

157. See Smith, "Reynolda"; Howett, *World of Her Own Making*.

158. Katherine Jellison, *Farm Women and Technology, 1913–1963*, Chapel Hill: University of North Carolina Press, 1996, chap. 1.

159. Katharine took a trip west with R. J. Reynolds and their first son, R.J.R. Jr., born ten months earlier, described in the *WSJ*, February 9, 1907. The trip through New England and Canada occurred the following summer; see *WSJ*, July 31, 1907. R.J.R. applied for passports for himself, Katharine, son Dick, and two others to go to China and Japan, but the family never actually traveled there; *WSJ*, January 28, 1908.

160. Her first documented trip alone was to New York City in June 1907; *WSJ*, June 3, 1907.

161. KSR to RJR, n.d., box 1, file 63.01, RFP.

162. KSR to Marie, August 13, 1913, box 2, file 177, RFP. As early as November 7, 1909, Katharine was staying in the New Willard Hotel in Washington, D.C., while R.J.R., Dick Jr., and infant Mary were home in Winston. Telegram from A. S. Gray to KSR, November 7, 1909, box 1, file 102, RFP.

163. Babcock, *Lady of Good Taste*, quote from dedication written by her husband, Charles H. Babcock, v.

164. For example, see subscriptions paid on R.J.R.'s private account in Individual Ledger no. 7, June 16, 1916, p. 235; KSR to W. H. Watkins, December 9, 1912; and W. H. Watkins, Winston-Salem, to KSR, Invoice, December 11, 1912, both in box 2, file 168; invoices, December 16, 1912, January 25, 1918, box 1, file 79, all in RFP.

165. Invoices, Putnam's Books, July 1 and September 1, 1911, box 3, file 233, RFP.

166. W. H. Watkins, Winston-Salem, to KSR, January 18, 1912, box 2, file 168; F. D. Lackey, Putnam's Books, to KSR, December 21, 1911, box 2, file 138, both in RFP.

167. Subscription Manager, Country Life Press, to KSR, June 12, 1912, box 1, file 88, RFP.

168. Miss Anna Jean Gash to H. M. Spring, Director, Drexel Institute, November 14, 1912, box 2, file 149.5; List of Publications on Domestic Science and Household Economics, December 1912, box 2, file 167; KSR to the Housekeeping Experiment Station, November 7, 1912, box 1, file 106, all in RFP.

169. For examples of each, see box 3, file 106, RFP.

170. See preface by Stella Standard in Babcock, *Lady of Good Taste*, vii.

171. The foods cited here were all made by Marjorie Carter, her cook, and included in the recipe book of Mary Reynolds Babcock, *Lady of Good Taste*, 5, 19, 25, 26, 29, 89, 96.

172. Household Inventory, 1922, RFP.

173. Ibid.

174. Aurelia Plumly Spaugh, Oral History Archives, August 6, 1980, OH.01.002.1, RHMAA.

175. Nancy Susan Reynolds, Oral History Archives.

176. Stephanie Cole, "White Woman, of Middle Age."

177. Henrietta Van Den Berg to KSR, October 17, 1917, box 2, file 166, RFP, describes some of Mrs. Lathem's duties for Katharine.

178. Henrietta Van Den Berg to KSR, December 18, 1917, box 2, file 166, RFP.

179. Charlotte Laundry postcard, December 17, 1912, box 3, file 210, RFP.

180. Frank K. Dunklee, Zinzendorf Laundry, to KSR, January 20, 1913, box 1, file 188, RFP.

181. Elizabeth Wade, Oral History Archives; KSR to Emil Fisher, Clothes Cleaner, Baltimore, box 1, file 98, RFP.

182. Senah Critz to KSR and RJR, n.d. [1918], box 1, file 87; Joe Carter to KSR, n.d. [1912], box 1, file 79, both in RFP.

183. KSR to Louise, January 14, 1913, box 2, file 128; KSR to Irene Smith, June 7 and July 1, 1912, box 2, file 154; invoice of S. J. Crowe, MD, Baltimore, for services for Miss Irene Smith, paid December 12, 1912, box 3, file 210, all in RFP. For example, Katharine's Baltimore dressmakers wrote Irene that they were shipping two gowns by Adams Express at Katharine's request; Houghton and Houghton to Miss Irene Smith, January 15, 1913, box 2, file 107, RFP.

184. Alumni Files for Maxie Smith, Archives, Converse College, Spartanburg, S.C.; H. J. Stockton, President, to KSR, September 18, 1909, box 2, file 138; Gunston Hall invoices for school bills and personal accounts for Irene Smith made out to KSR, dated May 2, May 8, and June 14, 1912, box 1, file 102, and box 3, file 216, all in RFP.

185. KSR to Irene Smith, June 7, 1912, box 2, file 154; KSR to Ruth Smith, February 13, 1918, box 2, file 154, both in RFP.

186. For example, Katharine paid a total of $208.75 to F. C. Brown Son's Company, Winston, for suits, shirts, collars, shoes, coats, and hats for her father and her brothers Matt and Eugene, according to an invoice made out to Mrs. R. J. Reynolds detailing the items purchased for each family member and dated February 2, 1913, box 3, file 215, RFP.

Katharine's relationship with her mother seems to have been somewhat complicated, perhaps because her mother was so ill and could not participate in Katharine's hectic life. But Katharine's affection for her parents was consistent. Although her parents were not members of Salem Methodist Church on the outskirts of Mount Airy, Katharine's mother had expressed support for its mission, and in 1924 Katharine gave money to the little church for a new building, allegedly designed by her architect, Charles Barton Keen, in honor of her parents, who were subsequently buried in a large walled plot at the crest of the hill above the rest of the church cemetery, along with other Smith family members. "Surry Church, 100 Years Old," *WSJ*, July 21, 1957; *A History of Surry County Churches*, comp. Surry County Genealogical Association (Dobson, N.C.: Surry County Genealogical Association, 2003), 308–9.

187. See, for example, invoice, E. W. O'Hanlon, September 1, 1918, box 3, file 213; and receipt, E. W. O'Hanlon, Druggist, August 9, 1918, box 3, file 213, both in RFP.

188. Z. M. (Matt) Smith to KSR, July 2, 1917, January 2, 1918, and February 4, 1918, box 2, file 156, RFP.

189. E. S. Gray, Assistant Cashier, Wachovia National Bank, to KSR, August 24, 1909, box 2, file 156, RFP.

190. "Beautiful Women and Fine Animals in Great Horse Show at Fair," *WSJ*, October 8, 1908, p. 1; *WSJ*, June 14, 1906, reported, "The Daughters of the American Revolution were entertained yesterday morning at the apartments of Mrs. R. J. Reynolds at Hotel Phoenix," but as Reynolds family scholar Sherry Hollowingsworth notes, the newspaper erred. Kate Bitting Reynolds [Mrs. W. N. Reynolds] was the local DAR regent and had an apartment at the Phoenix, not Katharine. In fact, the James B. Gordon Chapter no. 211, Forsyth County, N.C. (chartered March 30, 1898) of the United Daughters of the Confederacy does not list Katharine Reynolds as a member, although it does list Kate B. Reynolds; see http://www.forsythnchistory.com/udcmain.html, accessed November 15, 2010.

191. See, for example, KSR to Louise, January 14, 1913, box 2, file 128, RFP. Katharine had especially close friends like Nathalie Gray who shared significant personal information with Katharine in their correspondence. See KSR Correspondence—Nathalie F. Lyons Gray, 1912–19, box 1, file 102, RFP.

192. Nancy Susan Reynolds, Oral History Archives.

193. L. L. Miller to KSR, June 6, 1912, box 2, file 125; KSR to L. L. Miller, June 20, 1912, box 2, file 125; L. L. Miller to KSR, June 24, 1912, box 2, file 125; KSR to L. L. Miller, June 27, 1912, box 2, file 125, all in RFP.

194. RJR to KSR, September 16, 1910, box 1, file 65, RFP. He apologizes for not getting her pearls restrung in the same letter.

195. "So your dressmaking 'achieved a reputation,'" Gash wrote Katharine after her visit. "I am so glad." Gash later supervised the Domestic Science Department for Asheville public schools; Annie Jean Gash to KSR, September 16, 1912; November 28, 1912; December 14, 1912; May 31, 1913, box 1, file 102, RFP.

196. Doubleday, Page and Company Subscription Renewal Notice, January 9, 1913, box 1, file 88, RFP.

197. KSR to Miss A. M. Hall, Baltimore, February 18, 1913, box 1, file 106, RFP. A month later, she was purchasing leghorn hats from the Francois Shop in New York. Julia to KSR, March 19, 1913, box 2, file 122, RFP.

198. Invoice, Mrs. Farrar to KSR, n.d., work listed covered March 25 to April 25, no year, box 3, file 214, RFP.

199. Invoice, Hitchcock-Trotter, April 1912, box 3, file 220; invoice, Mrs. T. W. Hancock, July 30, 1918, box 3, file 219, both in RFP.

200. Invoice, Hitchcock-Trotter Company, The Woman's Store, June 1910, box 3, file 220, RFP.

201. KSR to Genie Guyn, Idlewilde Farm, Mount Airy, to KSR, February 25, 1918, box 1, file 102, RFP.

202. Ruth Mullen, "As Seen on Broadway," *Gallery Talk*, December 2, 2008, RHMAA; Weidensaul, *Of a Feather*, 156–57.

203. KSR to Henrietta Van Den Berg, May 17, 1912, box 2, file 184; Susanna Cocroft, Chicago, to KSR, December 28, 1912, box 1, file 84, both in RFP.

204. Invoice, Hitchcock-Trotter Company, The Woman's Store, June 1910, box 3, file 220, RFP.

205. Invoice for $50, Miss Corcoran, Baltimore, Ladies Shampooing, Manicuring and Facial Massage, May 8, 1912, box 3, file 210, RFP.

206. Invoice for $72.75 from R. F. C. Brown Son's Co., December 23, 1904, box 3, file 215, RFP.

207. For example, she paid $75.00 for a suit for R.J.R. by Fischer and Shafer, Tailors, Baltimore, on April 2, 1910, box 3, file 214, RFP, and $85.00 for another suit from the High Art Tailoring Company, on February 28, 1910, box 3, file 218, RFP.

208. Dr. John Howard Monroe, Oral History Archives.

209. Invoice, Carolina Cold Storage and Ice Company, April 26, 1912, box 3, file 210; KSR to H. Jaekel and Sons, N.Y.C., December 10, 1912, box 1, file 106, both in RFP.

210. Elizabeth Wade, Oral History Archives.

211. Ibid.

212. Pierre Bourdieu, *Distinction: A Social Critique of the Judgement of Taste*, trans. Richard Nice (Cambridge, Mass.: Harvard University Press, 1984).

213. For example, see balance of payment made to Penelope Lindgren for a portrait, R.J.R., Individual Ledger no. 7, May 19, 1917.

214. On Katharine's working relationship with Edward Belmont as her consultant, see correspondence and receipts in KSR Correspondence—John Wannamaker, 1917–18, box 2, file 117, RFP.

215. Ethel Reynolds to KSR, n.d. [1918], box 2, file 145, RFP.

Chapter Five. Brains and Backbone

1. Halttunen, *Confidence Men, Painted Women*, and especially her brilliant epilogue, "The Confidence Man in Corporate America."

2. Nannie Tilley to Nancy Reynolds, August 17, 1970, file PC 194, box 11, files 696–97, RFP.

3. In his chapter "The Foundation Cracks, 1880–1920," Huston (*Securing the Fruits of Their Labor*, 343–78) delineates beautifully the death of economic republicanism, the rise of corporatism, and an antithetical socialist ethos that these enormous economic and ideological changes generated.

4. Zunz, *Making America Corporate*, 202–3.

5. Ibid., 179–81.

6. Ibid., 195–97.

7. Eaton, "Winston-Salem," 1–3.

8. In 1902, a quarter-page ad in the *WSJ* provided fourteen reasons why the metropolis was rising in importance across the region, including "its enterprising people and diversification of industries," "the largest tobacco manufacturing center for the goods

in the world," "the best commercial rating of any town in the South," "the cheapest tax rate of any city in the State," and "the addition of four millions of taxable property in 20 years." See "Why Does Winston Lead?" *WSJ*, April 6, 1902, p. 4, cols. 4–5. Quote from *WSJ*, January 3, 1905, p. 3, col. 1.

9. Biles, "Tobacco Towns," 1–2.

10. *Winston-Salem: A Cooperative Spirit*, 27.

11. Ibid., 30.

12. "R. J. Reynolds for Consolidation," *WSJ*, January 23, 1913, p. 1, cols. 1–2; p. 5, col. 3.

13. *Winston-Salem: A Cooperative Spirit*, 24, 30.

14. The purchase was announced in the local paper, "Another Tobacco Deal," *WSJ*, December 5, 1900, p. 1, col. 3.

15. The Hanes brothers were quite successful in their new enterprises and apparently harbored no grudges against R.J.R. The Hanes family members owned some 2,500 shares of Reynolds stock by 1917. *Minutes of the Annual Meeting of the Stockholders of R. J. Reynolds Company*, Jersey City, N.J., April 3, 1917, Legacy Tobacco Documents; *Report of the Commissioner of Corporations on the Tobacco Industry, Part II*, 191.

16. "Big Knitting Mill Certain," *WSJ*, April 12, 1902, p. 1, col. 3; *Winston-Salem: A Cooperative Spirit*, 34; quote from Langdon Opperman, "Winston-Salem's African American Neighborhoods, 1870–1950," *Winston-Salem*, (*Winston-Salem, N.C.: Forsyth County Joint Historic Properties Commission, 1993*), p. 11. The Hanes hosiery and Hanes underwear enterprises did not merge until 1965, when they became Hanes Corporation.

17. "Manufacturing Industries," *WSJ*, September 17, 1900.

18. "The Future of the Leaf Market," *Statesville Landmark*, December 19, 1900.

19. "Growers of Tobacco," *Raleigh Morning Post*, January 18, 1900, Tobacco Digital Exhibit, http://digital.lib.ecu.edu/exhibits/tobacco/Newspapers.html, accessed February 2, 2012.

20. "Further Particulars," *WSJ*, November 28, 1900.

21. "Another Tobacco Deal," *WSJ*, December 5, 1900, p. 1, col. 3; *Report of the Commissioner of Corporations on the Tobacco Industry, Part I*, 106.

22. *Report of the Commissioner of Corporations on the Tobacco Industry, Part I*, 111, 139.

23. *Report of the Commissioner of Corporations on the Tobacco Industry, Part II*, 190.

24. "R. J. Reynolds Is Claimed by Death," *Lexington Leader*, July 29, 1918, clipping in box U49, IM.

25. *Report of the Commissioner of Corporations on the Tobacco Industry, Part I*, 41.

26. Ibid., 103–4.

27. "The Future of the Leaf Market," *WSJ*, December 19, 1900.

28. *Report of the Commissioner of Corporations on the Tobacco Industry, Part II*, 193–94.

29. "R. J. Reynolds Branch to Be Split Up," *Tobacco* 51, no. 14 (July 27, 1911): 4.

30. "Plan Campaign in North Carolina," *Tobacco* 45, no. 22 (September 24, 1908): 19.

31. "Industrial Diversification of Winston-Salem," *WSJ*, May 11, 1907.

32. "Machine Boys Strike," *WSJ*, February 12, 1900. The same week as the strike, R.J.R., ever the strategist, donated one thousand dollars to help with the construction of the Thomasville Mills Memorial Building, where a workshop for training orphan boys in the trades would be housed. "R. J. Reynolds Donates," *WSJ*, February 17, 1900.

33. "Acute Stage Reached," *WSJ*, March 15, 1900.

34. "Labor Looking Up," *WSJ*, January 10, 1902.

35. "Organized Labor," *WSJ*, January 10, 1902; "Don't Borrow Trouble," *WSJ*, January 24, 1902.

36. "Robert Ely," *WSJ*, February 8, 1902.

37. For example, see "The Child Labor Question," *WSJ*, December 19, 1900; and "The Child Labor Law," *WSJ*, August 7, 1907.

38. See Tilley, *R. J. Reynolds Tobacco Company*, 153, 613n45; *North Carolina Reports: Cases Argued and Determined in the Supreme Court of N.C.*, 141:248–60; *Winston Union Republican*, May 23, 1901; March 26 and April 2, 1903; and March 1, 1906.

39. *WSJ*, October 16, 2011, A2.

40. "Reynolds Tobacco Co. Is to Build a Large Addition," *WSJ*, February 6, 1902; "Trade Unions," *WSJ*, February 4, 1902; "Didn't Strike," *WSJ*, April 4, 1902, p. 1, col. 4; "Trade Unions," *WSJ*, February 6, 1902; "Robert Ely," *WSJ*, February 8, 1902; See, for example, *WSJ*, February 22, 1902, p. 3, col. 1; February 25, 1902, p. 3, col. 1. On welfare capitalism as an early twentieth-century industrial strategy, see Brody, "Rise and Decline of Welfare Capitalism," 147–78; Cohen, *Making a New Deal*, 160–71; Tone, *Business of Benevolence*, 246–49.

41. Shirley, *From Congregation Town to Industrial City*, 202.

42. Torain, "Development of the Liberty-Patterson Community," 1–3. The presence of two black physicians, three black attorneys, and a number of black teachers testify to a black middle class living with a larger black working class as early as 1896. See Branson, *Branson's North Carolina Business Directory*.

43. *Winston-Salem: A Cooperative Spirit*, 38.

44. "Colored Tough," *WSJ*, March 23, 1902, p. 1, col. 3.

45. "Murder in Salem," *WSJ*, February 21, 1904, p. 1, cols. 5–6.

46. "Quick Arrest, Speedy Trial," *WSJ*, March 19, 1904.

47. "They Will Quarrel," *WSJ*, July 25, 1902, p. 4, col. 4.

48. *Winston-Salem Twin City Sentinel*, January 11 and 21, 1913.

49. *WSJ*, June 5, 1913, p. 4; see extended coverage of a well-to-do citizen charged with "a crime against nature," in *WSJ*, July 18, 23, 26, 28, 29, 1912.

50. "Desperate Negro," *WSJ*, January 6, 1904, p. 3, col. 1.

51. Eaton, "Winston-Salem," 1–2.

52. *WSJ*, January 3, 1905, p. 5, cols. 3–5.

53. Miller, "Blacks in Winston-Salem," 116.

54. "1000 Houses Needed," *WSJ*, May 14, 1904, p. 1, col. 3.

55. Torain, "Development of the Liberty-Patterson Community," 15; *Winston-Salem Twin City Sentinel*, April 16, 1962, p. 7.

56. This situation existed despite efforts to the contrary by his father, Mayor Eaton, who "fought in vain against its take-over by the city government." Eaton, "Winston-Salem," 1.

57. *Winston Union Republican*, February 20 and April 10, 1902.

58. Winston, "Unconsidered Aspect of the Negro Question."

59. *WSJ*, June 23, 1912.

60. Quote from Eaton, "Winston-Salem," 3; Miller, "Blacks in Winston-Salem," 68–69, 71–72, 74–76.

61. Based on a 26 percent sample of the 1900 population records for Winston and

Salem drawn from the 1900 Forsyth County Federal Census Records, using frequency and cross tabulation analyses by race, sex, marital status, occupation, and nativity. Miller's statistics corroborate my findings, "Blacks in Winston-Salem," 75.

62. *WSJ*, January 9, 1902, p. 2, col. 2; *Columbia (S.C.) State*, August 1, 1901, p. 3; Tilley, *R. J. Reynolds Tobacco Company*, 144–45.

63. "Simon G. Atkins," *WSJ*, February 10, 1929.

64. U.S. Department of Commerce, Bureau of Census, *Eleventh Census: 1890* (Washington, D.C.: U.S. Census Office, 1892); U.S. Department of Commerce, Bureau of Census, *Thirteenth Census: 1910* (Washington, D.C.: U.S. Census Office, 1912).

65. Manning, *Hours and Earnings in Tobacco Stemmeries*, 1, 5–6, 10.

66. Quoted in Manning, *Hours and Earnings in Tobacco Stemmeries*, 11.

67. Miller, "Blacks in Winston-Sale," 79–80; Tilley, *Bright Tobacco Industry*, 583–91.

68. Simon G. Atkins to Rev. W. H. Goler, DD, Salisbury, N.C., January 31, 1899, Simon G. Atkins Letterbook, 1899–1902, Simon G. Atkins Papers, Winston-Salem State University.

69. Simon G. Atkins to Rev. Julius D. Dreher, Roanoke College, Salem, Va., March 23, 1899, Simon G. Atkins Letterbook, 1899–1902.

70. Ibid.

71. Feimster, *Southern Horrors*, 142; Somerville, *Rape and Race*, 241.

72. "Commencement of Slater School," *WSJ*, May 4, 1909, p. 2. col. 6.

73. Atkins to Dreher, March 23, 1899.

74. On the dignity of manual labor as an increasingly archaic conception in the United States by 1900, see Huston, *Securing the Fruits of Their Labor*, 364–65.

75. Simon G. Atkins to Alexander Furves, Hampton Institute, Hampton, Va., November 15, 1899, Simon G. Atkins Letterbook, 1899–1902.

76. Simon G. Atkins to Professor P. P. Claxton, Greensboro, N.C., November 20, 1899, Simon G. Atkins Letterbook, 1899–1902.

77. Simon G. Atkins to Rev. B. J. Burrell, 5th Ave., 29th St., N.Y., N.Y., November 17, 1899, Simon G. Atkins Letterbook, 1899–1902.

78. Simon G. Atkins to Rev. B. J. Burrell, 5th Ave., 29th St., New York, N.Y., November 17, 1899; Simon G. Atkins to S. E. Albert, DD, Germantown, Pa., October 17, 1900, both in Simon G. Atkins Letterbook, 1899–1902.

79. Simon G. Atkins to Hon. Curtis Guild Jr., Boston, Mass., October 9, 1901, Simon G. Atkins Letterbook, 1899–1902. Atkins references R.J.R. as a slaveholder in several other letters. For example, see Simon G. Atkins to Dr. E. Worcester, March 7, 1902, Simon G. Atkins Letterbook, 1899–1902. In doing so, Atkins was attempting to underline the possibilities for a liberal white South that embraced black education, for if a former planter could make such an apparently magnanimous gift, surely wealthy whites across the country could do likewise.

80. "The Board of Managers," *WSJ*, November 21, 1900.

81. Simon G. Atkins to Hon. J. K. Robinson, Goldsboro, N.C., January 16, 1901, Simon G. Atkins Letterbook, 1899–1902.

82. Ibid.

83. No address, letter fragment [August 1900?], handwritten, p. 267, Simon G. Atkins Letterbook, 1899–1902.

84. "White Men's Club," *WSJ*, July 3, 1900; and "Five Hundred Men," *WSJ*, July 5, 1900;

the officers elected did not have any formal affiliation with the R. J. Reynolds Tobacco Company at this time although President J. K. Norfleet, an active Mason, was partner in Liipfert, Scales and Company, a tobacco concern Reynolds would quietly acquire by 1904. Vice-President O. B. Eaton would be elected mayor. Tilley, *R. J. Reynolds Tobacco Company*, 113–14, 243.

85. "For Refusing to Register Negroes," *WSJ*, July 6, 1900; "Indignation Meeting," *WSJ*, July 7, 1900.

86. "Trial of Registrars," *WSJ*, July 7, 1900.

87. Editorial, *WSJ*, July 13, 1900.

88. "A Glorious Victory," *WSJ*, August 3, 1900.

89. "Repudiate the Man," *WSJ*, September 18, 1900.

90. "Investigate, Say the County Fathers," *WSJ*, June 1, 1907.

91. "Emancipation Day," *WSJ*, January 1, 1909.

92. Eaton, "Winston-Salem," 1.

93. Andrew L. Demling, "Advertising Transforms Depression into 'Biggest Year in History': Instead of Retrenching, R. J. Reynolds Increased Advertising Investment to Overcome Effects of European War on Business," *Cincinnati Enquirer*, March 20, 1915, newspaper clipping, BMFP.

94. John Gilmer Speed, "The Yankee of the South," *Harper's Weekly*, March 4, 1901, 371–72.

95. Samuel L. Schaffer, "Industrious Generation."

96. *Minutes of the Annual Meeting of the Stockholders of R. J. Reynolds Tobacco Company*, April 3, 1917, motion 8, p. 19, Tobacco Legacy Documents.

97. G. G. Johnson, "Southern Paternalism toward Negroes," 483–509, here 486.

98. Ibid., 501.

99. Page, *Negro*, 250, 303.

100. Glenn had also been helped by Zachary Smith, R.J.R.'s father-in-law. He may even have been supported by Katharine herself, who was known to make her own contributions to candidates she liked. R. B. Glenn to KSR, August 1, 1918, IM; interview with Zachary Smith, July 15, 2004, Reynolda Village, Winston-Salem, N.C.

101. "Nominate Hon. Robt. B. Glenn for Governor," *WSJ*, April 24, 1904.

102. *WSJ*, January 3, 1905.

103. Ibid.

104. "Gov. Glenn Inaugurated," *WSJ*, January 12, 1905.

105. Haley, *Charles N. Hunter*, 164.

106. Daniels, *Editor in Politics*, 598–99.

107. Brandt, *Cigarette Century*, 30–31.

108. Brandt, *Cigarette Century*, 35–36; Chandler, *Visible Hand*; Zunz, *Making America Corporate*.

109. *Report of the Commissioner of Corporations on the Tobacco Industry, Part I*, 236.

110. *Minutes of the Annual Meeting of the Stockholders of the R. J. Reynolds Tobacco Company*, April 3, 1917, Legacy Tobacco Documents.

111. *Report of the Commissioner of Corporations on the Tobacco Industry, Part I*, 213.

112. Ibid., 236.

113. Ibid., 236–37.

114. Ibid., 256, 274; *Report of the Commissioner of Corporations on the Tobacco Industry, Part II*, 189.

115. *Report of the Commissioner of Corporations on the Tobacco Industry, Part I*, 378.

116. Ibid., 202.

117. R. J. Reynolds Individual Ledger no. 4, 1898–1903, R. J. Reynolds Company Item no. 5725, p. 71.

118. Beatty, *Our 100th Anniversary*, 6.

119. Prince Albert ad, *Harper's Weekly*, October 12, 1910, 23.

120. *Winston-Salem: A Cooperative Spirit*, 34.

121. KSR to RJR, Hotel Belvedere, March 8, 1913, box 1, file 63.02, RFP.

122. "Winston-Salem's Tobacco Industry," *Tobacco* 54, no. 7 (December 5, 1912): 25.

123. Prince Albert ad, *Harper's Weekly*, October 12, 1910, 23.

124. "Holiday Package of Prince Albert," *Tobacco* 52, no. 9 (December 17, 1914): 7.

125. Beatty, *Our 100th Anniversary*, 6.

126. Tilley, *R. J. Reynolds Tobacco Company*, 125–26.

127. Brandt, *Cigarette Century*, 38–39; the Supreme Court decree was formally filed with the justices of the U.S. Circuit Court for the Southern District of New York the following October. See "Re-Organization Plan," *Tobacco* 51, no. 26 (October 19, 1911): 3.

128. Quote from Tilley, *R. J. Reynolds Tobacco Company*, 122.

129. Obituary, August 1, 1918, *Tobacco Leaf* (New York), IM.

130. RJR to KSR, New Hoffman House, Madison Square Garden, New York, April 8, 1908, box 1, file 65, RFP.

131. RJR to KSR, Plaza Hotel, August 11, 1909, box 1, file 65, RFP.

132. RJR to KSR, September 26, 1910; June 28, 1911, box 1, file 65, RFP.

133. RJR to KSR, September 22, 1910, box 1, file 65, RFP.

134. RJR to KSR, September 20, 1910, box 1, file 65, RFP.

135. Obituary, August 1, 1918, *Tobacco Leaf*, IM.

136. Brandt, *Cigarette Century*, 41–42.

137. "R. J. Reynolds Is Optimistic," *WSJ*, May 30, 1911.

138. RJR to KSR, July 10, 1911, box 1, file 65; RJR to KSR, n.d. [probably July or August 1911], box 1, file 65, both in RFP.

139. RJR to KSR, September 27, 1910, box 1, file 65; RJR to KSR, June 28, 1911, box 1, file 65; RJR to KSR, August 11, 1911, box 1, file 65, all in RFP.

140. RJR to KSR, August 12, 1911, box 1, file 65, RFP.

141. Ibid.; Tilley, *R. J. Reynolds Tobacco Company*, 191–92.

142. James B. Duke to R.J.R., November 6, 1911, box 3, James B. Duke Papers, Duke University, Durham, N.C.

143. Brandt, *Cigarette Century*, 42–43, 45–67.

144. Anonymous interview, September 20, 2010.

145. Telegrams from RJR to KSR, June 26 and June 27, box 1, file 65, RFP.

146. Jeffrey S. Gurock, *American Jewish History: The Colonial and Early National Periods, 1654–1840* (New York: Routledge, 1998), 71; Jerry W. Markham, *A Financial History of the United States: From the Age of Derivatives to the New Millennium, 1970–2000* (New York: M. E. Sharpe, 2002), 141.

147. R. J. Reynolds Individual Ledger no. 4, 1898–1903, R. J. Reynolds Company Item no. 5725, entry dated July 25, 1902, p. 53. By 1916, R. J. Reynolds had established a stock

syndicate for his employees. On September 30, 1916, he purchased $168,000 worth of shares; on December 2, 1916 $47,700; and on January 27, 1917, $117,000, R. J. Reynolds Individual Ledger, no. 7, p. 348.

148. Interview with Zachary Smith, July 15, 2004; R. J. Reynolds Individual Ledger no. 4, 1898–1903, R.J.R. Archives Item no. 5725, 136–39, 172, 279, 287.

149. "To the Stockholders of R. J. Reynolds Company," August 12, 1912, box 2, file 122, RFP. On the value of creating profit sharing for workers in industry, see Adams, *History of Cooperation*, 523.

150. Essie Wade Smith, interviewer, Orthodox Creed Strictler Life History [1939], transcription, WPA/VWP Life Histories, p. 4, box 179, folder 9, Library of Virginia, Richmond, Va.

151. Ethel Brock Sloan, Oral History Archives, July 9, 1980, OH.01.001.1, RHMAA.

152. Tilley, *R. J. Reynolds Tobacco Company*, 194–95.

153. Nancy Susan Reynolds, Oral History Archives, OH.01.004.3, June 18, 1980, RHMAA.

154. Daniels, *Editor in Politics*, 599.

155. McQuilkin, White, and Tursi, *Lost Empire*, 18.

156. Ibid., 18–19.

157. Obituary, August 1, 1918, *Tobacco Leaf*, IM.

158. *Report of the Commissioner of Corporations on the Tobacco Industry, Part I*, 104–5.

159. R. Simon G. Atkins to Hon. J. K. Robinson, Goldsboro, N.C., January 16, 1901, Simon G. Atkins Letterbook, 1899–1902; R. J. Reynolds Individual Ledger no. 4, 1898–1903, R. J. Reynolds Company Item no. 5725, pp. 257, 292, 310, 314, 294, 255, 309, 242, 305, 299, 302, 153, 302, 206–7, 301, 147, 309.

160. RJR to KSR, September 19, 1910, box 1, file 01–065–20–32, RFP.

161. Obituary, *Raleigh News and Observer*, July 31, 1918, IM.

162. For examples, see R. E. Horn to KSR, n.d. [probably 1918]; W. M. Armistead, Greensboro, N.C., to KSR, July 31, 1918; J. Moore, Moore-Shenkberg Grocery Company, Sioux City, Iowa, to KSR, September 6, 1918; Thomas Settle, Attorney and Counselor-at-Law, Asheville, N.C., to KSR, July [probably August], 2, 1918; C. A. Worley, Denver, Colo., to KSR, August 2, 1918; Winston Tobacco Association Resolution, August 1, 1918, all in IM.

163. These reports are plentiful. C. A. Worley, an R. J. Reynolds Tobacco Company salesman in Denver, Colorado, recalled, "I loved Mr. Reynolds as I loved my own Father." William S. Clough wrote Katharine, "Next to my own father Mr. Reynolds did more to help me along in life than any other man—He put his hand on my shoulder and told me to 'go ahead.'" Tobacco seller and wholesaler David Chalmers, writing from Kansas City, Missouri, believed that R.J.R.'s most important leadership quality lay in his "ability to surround himself with able and loyal helpers." Junius Whitaker to KSR, August 22, 1918; William S. Clough to KSR, n.d. [but probably August 1918]; David Chalmers to KSR, July 29, 1918, all in IM.

164. RJR to KSR, August 5, 1909, box 1, file 65 RFP.

165. RJR to KSR, July 10, 1911, box 1, file 65, RFP.

166. Nancy Susan Reynolds, Oral History Archives.

167. RJR to KSR, WS, N.C., November 5, 1909, box 1, file 65, RJR to KSR, 1905–, RFP.

168. Sales Department, R. J. Reynolds Tobacco Company, to Salesmen working the State of Florida, July 20, 1907, Legacy Tobacco Documents.

169. "R. J. Reynolds Company to Our Division Managers," September 2, 1915, Winston-Salem, N.C., Legacy Tobacco Documents.

170. Parke, "Gordon Gray," 3, 6, 9; "Bowman Gray Is Buried in North Atlantic; Tributes Paid to City," *WSJ*, July 9, 1935, 1.

171. Parke, "Gordon Gray," 9.

172. Quoted in Jo White Linn, *The Gray Family and Allied Lines*, (Salisbury, N.C.: privately printed, 1976), 123–25; Parke, "Gordon Gray," 9.

173. On World War I challenges on procurement, see Tilley, *R. J. Reynolds Tobacco Company*, 314–18.

174. Southern Railway Law Department to Clement Manly, on behalf of H. T. Crook, May 19, 1913; copy of receipt for $25.00 paid to Adam Ziegler on September 25, 1914, discharging R. J. Reynolds Tobacco Company of any further claims associated with any injury; W. R. Harding v. R J. Reynolds Tobacco Company, February 14, 1916, Fulton County, Ga., received $100.00 settlement; declaration, H. L. Dykes v. R. J. Reynolds Tobacco Company, Marion County, Mississippi Circuit Court, November 1920; stenographers notes, A. L. Sullivan v. R. J. Reynolds Tobacco Company, Davidson County, N.C. Superior Court, May Term, 1915; W. M. Miller v. R. J. Reynolds Tobacco Company, Forrest County, Mississippi Circuit Court, November 1914, all in Legacy Tobacco Documents Library.

175. "Tobacco Man Believes in Printer's Ink," *Tobacco* 59, no. 3 (May 6, 1915): 9.

176. Brandt, *Cigarette Century*, 19–20.

177. Gately, *Tobacco*, 205–7.

178. *WSJ*, January 1, 1905, p. 6, cols. 5–6.

179. Gately, *Tobacco*, 209–11.

180. McQuilkin, White, and Tursi, *Lost Empire*, 20–21; "A Turkish Tobacco Factory," *Tobacco* 11, no. 15 (August 14, 1891): 9; "Turkish Tobacco Cigarettes," *Tobacco* 16, no. 17 (February 23, 1894): 1; and 16, no. 18 (March 2, 1894): 1.

181. Beatty, *Our 100th Anniversary*, 8.

182. "Cigar Smoking Dromedaries," *Tobacco* 23, no. 12 (July 23, 1897): 12.

183. *Winston-Salem: A Cooperative Spirit*, 39.

184. Ibid., 35.

185. McQuilkin, White, and Tursi, *Lost Empire*, 20–21.

186. *Winston-Salem: A Cooperative Spirit*, 35.

187. Beatty, *Our 100th Anniversary*, 10.

188. "A Bequest, A Memorial, and a Promise," *Alumnae News* 5 (1962–63), 13.

189. *Printers' Ink: Fifty Years, 1888–1938*, (New York: Garland, 1986), 278.

190. "The Camels Have Come," *Tobacco Leaf*, December 3, 1914, p. 4, Legacy Tobacco Documents.

191. At least eleven different Camel ads appeared in the *Saturday Evening Post* in 1915 (January 2, 30; February 27; April 24; July 17; August 31; September 11; October 2; December 19, 23, 25). Five different Camel ads appeared in six months in both *Collier's Weekly* (January 15; February 26; April 8; May 20; June 17) and *Leslie's Weekly* (January 20; March 30; April 13; June 8, 29) in 1916. See Legacy Tobacco Documents.

192. Legacy Tobacco Documents contains hundreds of Camel ads for this period. For examples, see *Town and Country*, June 1914; *Life*, January 20, 1916; *Puck*, January 29, 1916; *Smoke*, January 1915; *Tobacco Leaf*, March 18, 1915; *Tobacco*, January 6, 1916; *U.S.*

Tobacco Journal, January 29, 1916; *Retail Tobacconist*, January 6, 1916; *Western Tobacco Journal*, January 24, 1916; *Army and Navy Journal*, May 6, 1916; *Army and Navy Register*, April 29, 1916.

193. "To the Jobbers of America," ad copy, 1913, Legacy Tobacco Documents.

194. Camel Cigarette Window Display no. 162, Specifications and Instructions for Installation, n.d., Legacy Tobacco Documents.

195. "Prelude to a Most Bitter War," *Tobacco* 50, no. 9 (December 16, 1915): 1, 4; "Presentation . . . of Their Case," *Tobacco* 50, no. 11 (December 30, 1915): 3.

196. Tilley, *R. J. Reynolds Tobacco Company*, 222–23; *Meeting of the Stockholders of the R. J. Reynolds Tobacco Company*, April 3, 1917, Legacy Tobacco Documents; Ad Copy Book, pp. 62–68, 1917, Legacy Tobacco Documents.

197. "Reynolds New Factory," *Tobacco* 51, no. 9 (June 15, 1916): 3; "New Reynolds Plant About Completed," *Tobacco* 51, no. 25 (October 5, 1916): 29.

198. "A Tremendous Increase," *Tobacco* 52, no. 3 (November 2, 1916): 8.

199. "North Carolina's Great Progress," *Tobacco* 52, no. 4 (November 9, 1916): 13.

200. Ibid.; Beatty, *Our 100th Anniversary*, 8.

201. Announcement, *Tobacco* 52, no. 16 (February 1, 1917): 25.

202. "Soldiers and Tobacco," *Tobacco* 59, no. 3 (May 6, 1915): 9; Beatty, *Our 100th Anniversary*, 10.

203. R. R. Haberkorn to RJR, box 1, file 1: RJR Correspondence, A–F incoming, 1906–17, RHMAA.

204. "Preferred Stock Increased," *Tobacco* 52, no. 21 (March 8, 1917): 11.

205. "Reynolds Raises Wages," *Tobacco* 53, no. 3 (May 3, 1917): 27.

206. "A Tremendous Increase," *Tobacco* 52, no. 3 (November 2, 1916): 8.

207. Becker, "Human Capital"; Hamermesh and Biddle, "Beauty and the Labor Market"; Hersche and Stratton, "Household Specialization."

Chapter Six. A Thousand Cattle on a Hill

1. Quote in Betty Ann Ragland, "Kate Smith Reynolds," [North Carolina College for Women] *Alumnae News* 52, no. 3 (April 1964): 3, 41.

2. Ella McGee Geer, Easley, S.C., to KSR, June 15, n.d., Correspondence—G, 1906–21, box 1, file 102, RFP.

3. "Reynolda Farm, Splendid Country Estate of Mrs. R. J. Reynolds: Its Origins and Development, and the Aims of Its Owner," *Twin-City Sentinel*, July 7, 1917.

4. Bell Lee, "A Tourist's View of Twin-City," *Twin-City Sentinel*, June 21, 1919, clipping, box 1, file 59, RFP.

5. Bowers, *Country Life Movement*, 120.

6. On the dedication, see *WSJ*, November 28, 1915.

7. Bowers, *Country Life Movement*, 128–29.

8. W. E. B. Du Bois to Liberty Hyde Bailey, November 23, 1908, Commission on Country Life Collection, Rare Books and Manuscripts Library, Cornell University, Ithaca, N.Y.

9. Bowers, *Country Life Movement*, 130–35.

10. Ibid., 3–5, 130–34.

11. Katharine sends money to Danbury, January 3, 1912, Reynolds Family Chronol-

ogy, p. 33; Superintendent R. K. Rothwell to KSR, December 8, 1909, p. 101, both in RFP; *WSJ*, December 20, 1912.

12. Southard, "History of a Pioneering Agency," 1, 18–28; Dowdy, "Development of the Social Welfare Movement," 45–47; Winston-Salem Family Services Inc., brochure, 1995, 30, 45–50.

13. Receipt, Alumnae Association Dues, State Normal and Industrial College, December 9, 1909, RFP.

14. *WSJ*, October 6, 1906.

15. *WSJ*, December 27, 1906; Katharine made the first contribution of one hundred dollars according to the *WSJ*, March 12, 1910.

16. Mrs. Percy Garner, President, Business Women's Association, to KSR, n.d., box 1, file 102, RFP.

17. Carraway, *Carolina Crusaders*, 13.

18. Wilkerson-Freeman, "From Clubs to Parties"; Wilkerson-Freeman, "Stealth in the Political Arsenal"; Sims, *Power of Femininity*, introduction and chap. 1.

19. Sims, *Power of Femininity*, 80–127.

20. "Lucy Bramlette Patterson," in *Dictionary of North Carolina Biography*, ed. William S. Powell, vol. 5 (Chapel Hill: University of North Carolina Press, 1994); *WSJ*, October 4, 1906.

21. Carraway, *Carolina Crusaders*, 13–15.

22. Cotten, *History of the North Carolina Federation of Women's Clubs*, 41–42; Carraway, *Carolina Crusaders*, 32–33, 113–15.

23. Sims, *Power of Femininity*, 194–96.

24. Cotten, *History of the North Carolina Federation of Women's Clubs*, 49–50.

25. Ibid., 54.

26. Photograph 006-396-01, Archives, RHMAA.

27. Carraway, *Carolina Crusaders*, 50–51.

28. Robertson, *Christian Sisterhood*, 1–44.

29. *WSJ*, November 24, 1906.

30. *WSJ*, February 27, 1909; March 9, 1909; December 29, 1910; August 14, 1912.

31. Mrs. D. Rich and Sara Shaw to KSR, August 10, 1912, box 2, file 176, RFP.

32. See, for example, the lengthy letter of December 5, 1912, from Anna D. Casler, executive secretary of the Provisional South Atlantic Territorial Committee, trying to persuade Katharine to serve on the field committee as the Winston-Salem representative. Miss Casler and Katharine maintained a lengthy correspondence over several years as the former worked to build and connect more local YWCA chapters across the Southeast. See the Casler-KSR correspondence in box 1, file 82, RFP.

33. "Splendid Annual Banquet," *WSJ*, February 25, 1916.

34. Booker T. Washington to Walter Hines Page, November 9, 1910, *The Booker T. Washington Papers*, vol. 10, *1909–1911*, edited by Louis R. Harlan, Raymond W. Smock, Geraldine McTigue, and Nan E. Woodruff (Urbana: University of Illinois Press, 1981), 449–50; Miller, "Blacks in Winston-Salem," 12. On Washington's tragic "civilizing mission" approach, see Sehat, "Civilizing Mission of Booker T. Washington," 322–62.

35. M. Brown Lathem to KSR, December 3, [1912], box 3, file 122, RFP; "Constitution and By-Laws," *Winston-Salem Twin City Sentinel*, January 13, 1913. Katharine was one of three members charged with establishing the constitution.

36. "Women Plan Great Work," *WSJ*, February 12, 1913. Katharine was one of nine women leading the organization, and one of three in charge of the building improvement work.

37. KSR to Miss Casler, box 1, folder 79: KSR Correspondence—C, 1905–1921, RFP; *WSJ*, March 12, 1913.

38. See Blight, *Race and Reunion*, 9, for the governor's speech in 1913 referencing that event at the reunion of Union and Confederate veterans.

39. Poe's ideas were detailed in the local Winston paper in "Segregation of the Races," *WSJ*, September 5, 1913.

40. Crow, "Apartheid for the South"; Kirby, "Clarence Poe's Vision."

41. Gulledge, *North Carolina Conference for Social Services*, 10, 15, 16; Swift, *Child Labor Welfare in North Carolina.*

42. Nancy Susan Reynolds, Oral History Archives, May 5, 1980, OH.01.004.1, RHMAA.

43. For example, see RJR to KSR, August 7, 1911, box 1, file 65, RFP.

44. For example, she corresponded with C. M. Morgan, in Washington, D.C., on the best dairy management practices. KSR to C. M. Morgan, August 20, 1912, box 2, file 132, RFP; Mr. Rabild wrote from his position in charge of dairy farming investigations at the U.S. Department of Agriculture that he would send Katharine a series of government circulars on dairy buildings and was requesting that Mr. W. H. Eaton, their North Carolina agent, be in touch with her to assist her in her planning, Rabild to KSR, August 20, 1912, box 2, file 164, RFP.

45. R.J.R., Individual Ledger no. 7, June 29, 1916, and December 26, 1916. Between June 1 and July 27, 1918, the ledger shows expenses for the bungalow at Reynolda totaling $229,369.00, with the total amount marked "Gifts to Mrs. Katharine Smith Reynolds."

46. R.J.R. Individual ledger no. 7, in entries dated June 16, 1916, and July 27, 1918, shows that R.J.R. was still paying out fairly large sums and had a thirty-thousand-dollar budget for his Skyland Farm. Katharine's nephew Zachary T. Smith III described the friendly rivalry between the two farm owners in an interview with the author on July 7, 2004; each farm had its own accounting, and suppliers were urged to keep the accounts separate too. See, for example, a monthly statement from Forsyth Roller Mills dated June 1910 on which Katharine has jotted this request, box 1, file 100, RFP. The name Maplewood is listed on 1910 invoices from Brown-Rogers Co., Farming Implements and Hardware, box 3, file 209; Farmers' Trade House Co., May 28, 1910, box 3, file 214, both in RFP. An invoice dated May 9 and marked paid on June 1, 1910, is made out specifically to Mrs. R. J. Reynolds, Maplewood Farm, box 3, file 218, RFP.

47. Ethel Reynolds to KSR, n.d. [1908], box 2, file 146, RFP.

48. Mayer, *Reynolda*, 11.

49. Katharine purchased her first piece of property from the Eatons in "Old Town" in her own name in 1906; she purchased seventeen more in her own name between 1907 and 1911. General Index of Real Estate Conveyances, Forsyth County, N.C., Grantee "R," microfilm reel 1849–1965, pp. 77–80; interview with Zachary T. Smith July 15, 2004.

50. RJR to KSR, September 22, 1910; RJR to Dick Jr., September 24, 1910, box 1, file 65, both in RFP.

51. RJR to KSR, May 26, 1908, box 1, file 64, RFP.

52. RJR to KSR, July 30, 1909, box 1, file 65, RFP.

53. RJR to KSR, August 5, 1909, box 1, file 65, RFP.

54. The vice president of Merchants-Mechanics Bank in Baltimore wrote R.J.R. on January 27, 1913, "We have yours of the 24th inst, covering check for $41,003.28 for the credit of Mrs. Reynolds. I assume that under the circumstances you do not care for us to give Mrs. Reynolds direct advance," suggesting that R.J.R. did keep a watchful eye on Katharine's expenditures and dug her out of trouble when her expenses mounted precipitously, box 2, file 134, RFP; Winston Township Taxes, 1911–15, box 3, file 259, RFP.

55. See KSR Correspondence: Dominick and Dominick, N.Y., 1906–18, box 1, file 2, RFP. For an example of dividend checks, see Woodside Cotton Mills Company Dividend to KSR, July 1, 1912, for $18,440.50, box 2, file 167, RFP. For examples of investments, see box 2, file 167, RFP; Wachovia Bank and Trust Company wrote her on July 12, 1917, that she had overdrawn her account by $321.03, for example, (box 2, file 170, RFP), and she made regular interest payments on her loans with the same local bank; see Wachovia Bank to KSR, June 30 and July 16, 1917, box 2, file 170, RFP.

56. D. Clay Lilly, sermon in clipping dated July 31, 1918, from "Thousands Pay Tribute to Mr. R. J. Reynolds," *Winston-Salem Twin City Sentinel*, box U49, IM; Neal Anderson, sermon, clipping dated August 1, 1918, from "Funeral Service of Mr. Reynolds Held Today," *WSJ*.

57. Camilla Wilcox, "Horatio Buckenham in Winston-Salem," *Gardener's Journal*, Reynolda Gardens at Wake Forest University newsletter, Spring 2010:1, 5–7.

58. M. S. Smith, "Reynolda," 301.

59. R.J.R. in fact told Katharine he was seeking terms for someone "to plow in the pease." RJR to KSR, September 20, 1910, box 1, file 65, RFP.

60. Mayer, *Reynolda*, 36.

61. Ibid., 52.

62. Margaret Supplee Smith, "Charles Barton Keen: Main Line to Tobacco Road," MS, 1–2.

63. "American Country House," *Architectural Record* 44, no. 4 (October 1918): 285–86.

64. Cindy Hodnett, "One of a Kind," HomePlace, *WSJ*, December 28, 2008, H1, H35.

65. McQuilkin, White, and Tursi, *Lost Empire*, 23.

66. Camilla Wilcox, "Thomas Sears and the Trees of Reynolda," *Gardener's Journal*, Reynolda Gardens at Wake Forest University newsletter, Winter 2006:8–10.

67. Camilla Wilcox, "The Water System at Reynolda, Part I: Pure Water," *Gardener's Journal*, Winter 2009, 12–14; KSR to Messrs. Wiley and Wilson, December 3, 1917, box 2, file 172, RFP.

68. Contract, July 23, 1912, box 2, file 127, RFP.

69. Mayer, *Reynolda*, 63.

70. Ibid., 64; Clipping, "Chrysanthemum Show a Pronounced Success," October 31, 1913, *Twin City Daily Sentinel*, in YWCA Scrapbook, 1908–14, YWCA of Winston-Salem, 1201 Glade Street, Winston-Salem, N.C.

71. Interview with Earline King, May 22, 2003, Winston-Salem, N.C.; Mayer, *Reynolda*, 75.

72. Wiley and East, *Book of Remembrance*, 62.

73. Bill East, "Do You Remember?," *Winston-Salem Sentinel*, January 17, 1963, North Carolina Room Vertical Files, Central Branch, Forsyth County Public Library, Winston-Salem, N.C.

74. Junia A. Graves, 529 Longwood Avenue, Bedford, Va., to KSR, October 9 and November 26, 1918, box 1, file 102, KSR Correspondence—G, 1906–21, RFP.

75. For example, see Robert R. King, Mutete, to KSR, September 8, 1917; Marguerite King, Little Rock, Ark., to KSR, November 24, 1918, box 2, file 118, KSR Correspondence—K, 1909–19; Charles H. Pratt, Executive Committee of Foreign Missions, Presbyterian Church in the U.S., to KSR, May 15, 1912, box 2, file 138, all in RFP.

76. Millhouse, *Reynolda*, 99, 102, 103.

77. M. S. Smith, "Reynolda," 300; Lane, "Period House in the Nineteen-Twenties."

78. M. S. Smith, "Reynolda," 300.

79. *WSJ*, July 7, 1917.

80. Millhouse, *Reynolda*, 38.

81. *WSJ*, September 22, 1915, p. 1; Ella McGee Geer to KSR, June 15 [no year], box 1, file 102, RFP; Helen H. Kerney to KSR, January 4, 1918, box 2, file 132, RFP.

82. For a wonderful look at the village in imagination and history, see Aslet, *Villages of Britain*.

83. KSR to Charles Barton Keene, April 16 and June 20, 1912, box 2, file 121, RFP.

84. Wiley and Wilson to Charles Barton Keen, October 31, 1913, copy of letter, box 2, file 172, RFP.

85. Millhouse, *Reynolda*, 34.

86. Ibid., 34.

87. Quoted in Millhouse, *Reynolda*, 29.

88. Peyton F. Russ, "Design History of Reynolda Gardens, 1910–1920, Garden for the Estate of Mr. and Mrs. R. J. Reynolds, Winston-Salem, N.C.," [s.n., 19—?], 45, extant copy in North Carolina Room, Central Branch, Forsyth County Public Library, Winston-Salem, N.C. This passing of trade skills from a set of experienced contractors from more-established communities to unskilled men in more-rural places reflected a two-centuries-old pattern of trade acquisition in America. See Gillespie, *Free Labor in an Unfree World*, chap. 1.

89. Millhouse, *Reynolda*, 30.

90. KSR to L. D. Wilkinson, December 10, 1912, box 2, file 124; KSR to Messrs. P. D. Schmidt and Company, box 2, file 138, both in RFP.

91. KSR to Southern Bell Telephone and Telegraph Company, September 19, 1917, box 2, file 149.4, RFP. The problem was still not resolved a year later, compelling Katharine to write, "I shall expect better service in the future or I shall consider that you are breaking your part of the contract and are not due the contract price for service," KSR to Southern Bell Telephone and Telegraph Company, September 10, 1918, ibid.

92. KSR to Louise, June 8, 1912, box 2, file 128; KSR to Senah Critz, June 10, 1912, box 2, file 148, both in RFP.

93. Alex Lichtenstein, *Twice the Work of Free Labor*, 152–85; Millhouse, *Reynolda*, 32.

94. Elizabeth Wade, Oral History Archives, July 10, 1980, OH.01006.1, RHMAA.

95. Millhouse, *Reynolda*, 33.

96. Ibid., 54, 55.

97. M. S. Smith, "Reynolda," 288.

98. Branson, *Farm Prosperity in Forsyth*, 1–26.

99. Mrs. Richard Anderson, Denton, N.C., to KSR, October 30, 1916, box 1, file 68, RFP.

100. Mrs. Mary B. Harrell to KSR, November 6, 1916, box 1, file 106, RFP.

101. Mrs. Lola James to KSR, October 2, 1916, box 2, file 114, RFP.

102. Mrs. Wille Sugg to KSR, July 22, 1918, box 2, file 149.7, RFP.

103. Lula Boyette to KSR, August 11, 1918, box 2, file 167, RFP.

104. List of Subscriptions, box 2, folder 168; invoices, December 16, 1912, January 25, 1918, box 1, file 79, all in RFP. Katharine's books are listed in the 1924 Household Inventory, RFP.

105. Millhouse, *Reynolda*, 48.

106. "Reynolda Farm: Splendid Country Estate of Mrs. R. J. Reynolds, Its Origins, Development, and the Aims of Its Owner," *Winston-Salem Twin City Sentinel*, July 7, 1917.

107. Commissioner of Fisheries to KSR, box 1, file 88, RFP.

108. Tax List of Reynolda Farm Co., May 1, 1917, box 3, file 259, RFP.

109. Harvey Miller, Oral History Archives, June 7, 1980, OH.01.02.023.1, RHMAA.

110. "Reynolda Farm," *Winston-Salem Twin City Sentinel*, July 7, 1917.

111. RJR to KSR, July 10, 1911, box 1, file 65, RFP.

112. Nancy Susan Reynolds, Oral History Archives; "Reynolda Farm," *Winston-Salem Twin City Sentinel*, July 7, 1917.

113. "R.J.R. Is Claimed by Death, July 29, 1918, *New York Evening Post*, clipping, box U49; KSR to F. W. Ayer, September 19, 1917, box 2, file 136; F. W. Ayer, Meridale Farms, to KSR, September 25, 1917, box 2, file 132, all in RFP; Tara Collins, "Meridale Farms: The End of a Dynasty," http://townofmeredith.com/about/meridale-farms.html, accessed November 20, 2010; indecipherable signature, Meridale Farms, to KSR, September 25, 1917, box 2, file 132, RFP.

114. "Chance Remark Credited for Tamworth Boom," *WSJ*, January 7, 1953, 4; Gabriella Hart Dula to KSR, November 13 [no year], box 1, file 88, RFP. A generation later, thanks to Reynolda's introduction of Tamworths to the region, Piedmont, North Carolina, was proclaimed "The Tamworth Capital of the South."

115. Millhouse, *Reynolda*, 92.

116. Ibid., 37.

117. RJR to KSR, August 12, 1911, box 1, file 65; Thomas Settle to KSR, February 22, 1918, box 2, file 149.1; KSR to Thomas Settle, February 25, 1918, box 2, file 149.1, all in RFP.

118. "Reynolda Farm," *Winston-Salem Twin City Sentinel*, July 7, 1917.

119. Dr. John Howard Monroe, Oral History Archives, September 23, 1980, OH.03.034.1, RHMAA.

120. KSR to R. E. Snowden, December 9, 1912, box 2, file 149.4; KSR to Annie Jean Gash, box 1, file 102, both in RFP.

121. M. S. Smith, "Reynolda," 204; RJR to KSR, August 12, 1911, box 1, file 65, RFP.

122. Mary Martha Lybrook Spitzmuller, Oral History Archives, July 14, 1980, OH.01.007.1, RHMAA.

123. Luncheon reported in the *WSJ*, October 4, 1906; "Clarence Hamilton Poe," in *Dictionary of North Carolina Biography*, ed. William S. Powell (Chapel Hill: University of North Carolina Press, 1976–96), 5:105–6.

124. M S. Smith, "Reynolda," 302.

125. "Reynolda Farm," *Winston-Salem Twin City Sentinel*, July 7, 1917.

126. Ibid. Katharine clearly was invested in the project. She had acquired literature on girls' demonstration work and canning clubs from the USDA; see materials in box 2, file 164, RFP.

127. Martha A. Nolan, *A Chronicle: The Woman's National Farm and Garden Association, Incorporated 1914–1984*, (Fremont, Ohio: Lesher, 1985); *Woman's National Farm and Garden Association Quarterly* 3, no. 1 (1916): 29–30; "Woman's National Farm and Garden Association," flyer, box 2, file 167, RFP.

128. *Bulletin of the Garden Club of America*, no. 23 (January 1918): 2–3.

129. Katharine L. McCauley to KSR, July 11, 1918, box 2, file 167, RFP.

130. *Woman's National Farm and Garden Association Home Acres* 7, no. 1:1.

131. Hilda Louies to KSR, February 19, 1919, box 2, file 122, RFP.

132. Ibid.

133. "A Peripatetic Pilgrimage: What the League to Enforce Peace Is Doing," *Outlook* 121 (January–April 1919): 229.

134. Harvey Miller, Oral History Archives, June 12, 1980, OH.01.02.023.2, RHMAA.

135. Millhouse, *Reynolda*, 93.

136. "The Spirit of Reynolda: African American Contributions, 1912–1962," exhibition at Reynolda House, 1993; Millhouse, *Reynolda*, 31; see also "A Place in the Heart," *WSJ*, March 21, 1993.

137. Millhouse, *Reynolda*, 112.

138. The superintendent plowed up garden plots in the spring and fall and provided seeds to all Reynolda residents; Harvey Miller, Oral History Archives, June 12, 1980; Millhouse, *Reynolda*, 116.

139. "Negro and Reynolda," 3–5.

140. Rosalie Miller, Oral History Archives, July 17, 1980, OH.02.016.2; Flora Pledger, Oral History Archives, June 26, 1980, OH.01.005.1, both in RHMAA.

141. Harvey Miller, Oral History Archives, June 7, 1980; Millhouse, *Reynolda*, 117.

142. Harvey Miller, Oral History, Archives, June 7, 1980; Millhouse, *Reynolda*, 114.

143. Harvey Miller, Oral History, Archives, June 7, 1980; Millhouse, *Reynolda*, 116.

144. Harvey Miller, Oral History, Archives, June 7, 1980.

145. Interview notes, Lu Ann Jones, from interview with Harvey Miller, June 12, 1980.

146. Russ, "Design History of Reynolda Gardens," 45.

147. The four-manual console sat in the expansive reception hall; its 2,566 pipes were hidden behind tapestries on the second floor. Aeolians were organs designed specifically for residences, not churches. Owners did not have to know how to play their organ, only how to insert the paper music rolls to initiate automatic playing. Rollin Smith, *The Aeolian Organ* (Winston-Salem, N.C.: Reynolda House Museum of American Art, 1997), 1–5; Kemp, *God's* Capitalist, 250–52.

148. Estimate from W & J. Sloane to KSR [1916], box 2, file 169, RFP.

149. Munsterberg, *Americans*, 580.

150. Elizabeth Wade, Oral History Archives.

151. Henrietta Van Den Berg to KSR, December 19, 1917, box 2, file 166, RFP.

152. Winston, "Unconsidered Aspect of the Negro Question."

153. KSR to W. P. Mahan, August 19, 1912, box 2, file 131, RFP.

154. Elizabeth Wade, Oral History Archives.

155. The racial hierarchy of employment inside a wealthy family's home was well understood across social class. Miss Jennie McClellan of Statesville, N.C., wrote Katharine Reynolds seeking a position as "a white girl to help with the work in your home." Jennie preferred working with the children most of all but would have been happy to

mend, sew, or wait on table. She did not want to do any cooking. Jennie McClellan to KSR, June 10, 1912, box 2, file 131, RFP.

156. KSR to Jennie McClellan, July 5, 1912, box 2, file 131, RFP; Elizabeth Wade, Oral History Archives; W. B. Harrison to KSR, May 29, 1912, box 1, file 106, RFP.

157. R.J.R., Ledger, December 23, 1916. Note that R.J.R.'s "outside child," John Neal, received a one-thousand-dollar stock option as his gift.

158. Elizabeth Wade, Oral History Archives.

159. List of Responsibilities for Domestic Servants, box 8, file 516a, RFP.

160. 1900, 1910, 1920 U.S. Census figures.

161. "Across the Creek from Salem: The Story of Happy Hill, 1816–1952," exhibition text, The Gallery at Old Salem, February 7–June 7, 1998, 14.

162. Elizabeth Wade, Oral History Archives.

163. Ibid.

164. Nancy Susan Reynolds, Oral History Archives; Harvey Miller, Oral History Archives, August 4, 1980, OH.01.02.023.4, both in RHMAA.

165. Nancy Susan Reynolds, Oral History Archives.

166. KSR to Mr. F. E. Johnson, December 9, 1912, box 2, file 114, RFP.

167. Henrietta Van Den Berg to KSR, May 27, 1918, box 2, file 166, RFP.

168. R.J.R. Individual Ledger no. 7, entries dated January 1, 1917; June 1, 1917; July 1, 1917; Savannah Webster to KSR, n.d. [1918], box 2, file 167, RFP.

169. Harvey Miller, Oral History Archives, June 7, 1980.

170. Elizabeth Wade, Oral History Archives.

171. Instructions for Domestic Servants, box 8, file 516a, RFP.

172. Elizabeth Wade, Oral History Archives; notes, Lu Ann Jones, from interview with Elizabeth Wade, July 18, 1980, in the author's possession.

173. Nancy Susan Reynolds, Oral History Archives.

174. Notes, Lu Ann Jones, from interview with Rosalie Miller, July 17, 1980, in the author's possession.

175. Author's conversation with Barbara Millhouse, August 10, 2010.

176. Elizabeth Wade, Oral History Archives.

177. Ibid.

178. Harvey Miller, Oral History Archives, August 4, 1980; Instructions for Domestic Servants, box 8, file 516a, RFP.

179. Elizabeth Wade, Oral History Archives.

180. Notes, Lu Ann Jones, from interview with Harvey Miller, August 4, 1980.

181. Notes, Lu Ann Jones, from interview with Harvey Miller, n.d.; Harvey Miller, Oral History Archives, August 4, 1980.

182. Pluma [Walker] to KSR, January 7, 1919, box 2, file 167, RFP.

183. Notes, Lu Ann Jones, from interview with Harvey Miller, August 4, 1980.

184. Notes, Lu Ann Jones, from interview with Harvey Miller, June 25, 1980.

185. Harvey Miller, Oral History Archives, June 7 and 12, 1980.

186. Mary Reynolds Babcock to Nancy Susan Reynolds, May 20, 1942, copy in author's possession.

187. Mary Babcock Reynolds to Nancy Susan Reynolds, December 22, 1955, copy in possession of author.

188. Munsterberg, *Americans*, 540–41.

189. Aslet, *American Country House*, 101–6.

190. Nancy Susan Reynolds, Oral History Archives.

191. Elizabeth Wade, Oral History Archives.

192. McClellan to KSR, June 10, 1912; KSR to McClellan, July 5, 1912.

193. Mrs. Knudsen to KSR, May 1, 1912, box 2, file 118; KSR to Mrs. Knudsen, May 4, 1912, box 2, file 118, both in RFP.

194. Munsterberg, *Americans*, 606.

195. KSR to B. Altman and Co., May 29, 1912, box 1, file 76, RFP; Elizabeth Wade, Oral History Archives; KSR to Rogers Peet and Company, New York City, May 27, 1912, box 2, file 142, RFP.

196. Budget Template, n.d., box 3, file 260, RFP. The budget template is in Katharine's own hand.

197. Three critical books that highlight the complexity and hierarchies within household relationships are Sharpless, *Cooking in Other Women's Kitchens*; Light, *Mrs. Woolf and the Servants*; and O'Leary, *From Morning to Night*.

198. Nancy Susan Reynolds, Oral History Archives; Mock-Bagby-Stockton Company to KSR, January 2, 1919, box 2, file 102, RFP.

199. Receipt marked paid from Belle Gibson for ten weeks of room rent for Savannah Webster, dated February 23, 1918, box 3, file 216, RFP.

200. Nancy Susan Reynolds, Oral History Archives.

201. Alexander Barnes, "Final Rites for Bishop Medford," *Star of Zion*, October 22, 1964, p. 1; editorial, *Star of Zion*, October 22, 1964, p. 4; William J. Walls, *The African Methodist Episcopal Zion Church: Reality of the Black Church* (Charlotte, N.C.: AME Zion Publishing House, 1974), 423, 607. I am grateful to Ken Badgett, who shared his research on Savannah Webster, C. H. Jones, and Hampton Thomas Medford with me. On Savannah's first husband, Charles Henry Jones, see especially Hall and Badgett, "Robinson Newcomb," 386–88.

202. See the wonderful book by Leo Marx, *Machine in the Garden*.

Chapter 7. A Woman for a New Day

1. KSR to RJR, July 12, 1917, box 1, file 63, RFP.

2. Weaver, *Winston-Salem*, 7.

3. Foltz, *Winston Fifty Years Ago*, 2.

4. Cecil Sharp Diaries, Journal Entry, August 30, 1918, 245–47, http://library.efdss.org/exhibitions/sharpdiaries/sharpdiaries.html, accessed November 14, 2010.

5. Marjorie Hunter, *WSJ*, March 27, 1960, clipping file, North Carolina Room, Central Branch, Forsyth County Public Library, Winston-Salem, N.C.

6. "[R. J. Reynolds] Is to Give $5,000 if Ladies Can Raise $5,000," *Winston-Salem Twin City Sentinel*, August 22, 1913, in YWCA Scrapbook, 1908–14, YWCA of Winston-Salem, 1201 Glade Street, Winston-Salem, N.C.

7. "Probably $20,000 Has Been Raised," *WSJ*, March 19, 1914, in YWCA Scrapbook, 1908–14, YWCA of Winston-Salem, 1201 Glade Street, Winston-Salem, N.C.

8. Book of Minutes of the YWCA, Winston-Salem, N.C., January 1917–1932, YWCA of Winston-Sale, 1201 Glade Street, Winston-Salem, N.C., 20, describes setting up programs for "the girls" in knitting, Bible, domestic science, and "Night School work" at the

R. J. Reynolds Tobacco Company and the P. H. Hanes Knitting Mill, Hosiery Mill, Arista Mill, and Moline Mill under an industrial secretary hired by the local YWCA by 1917.

9. "Industrial Work for Girls of the City," *WSJ*, September 5, 1917.

10. Book of Minutes of the YWCA, Winston-Salem, N.C., January 1917–32, YWCA of Winston-Sale, 1201 Glade Street, Winston-Salem, N.C., 11, 15, 17, 38–39, 44; Andrew McNeil Cannady, "The Limits to Improving Race Relations in the South: The YMCA Blue Ridge Assembly in Black Mountain, North Carolina, 1906–1930," *North Carolina Historical Review*, October 2009 86, no. 4:404.

11. *WSJ*, February 16, March 28, April 1, and September 10, 1916; November 16, 1919; Tilley, *R. J. Reynolds Tobacco Company*, 273–74.

12. Book of Minutes of the YWCA, Winston-Salem, N.C., January 1917–1932, YWCA of Winston-Sale, 1201 Glade Street, Winston-Salem, N.C., 3, 13; and Reynolds Family Chronology, RHMAA.

13. Katharine served on the board of directors through 1922. Book of Minutes of the YWCA, Winston-Salem, N.C., January 1917–1932, YWCA of Winston-Sale, 1201 Glade Street, Winston-Salem, N.C., 49, 100, 113, 115, 117.

14. *WSJ*, April 7, 1916; Tilley, *R. J. Reynolds Tobacco Company*, 243–44.

15. Harry H. Shelton, Attorney, to RJR, July 17, 1917, box 11, file 64, RFP; Tilley, *R. J. Reynolds Tobacco Company*, 276–77; Sallee, *Whiteness of Child Labor Reform*, 35, 116–23.

16. *Winston Union Republican*, October 19, 1916; Tilley, *R. J. Reynolds Tobacco Company*, 252.

17. "Lunch Room for Colored Hands," *WSJ*, July 30, 1915.

18. Tilley, *R. J. Reynolds Tobacco Company*, 267–70.

19. Survey of City, a study [of Winston-Salem], compiled by Florence D. McCarthy, January 16, 1920, 12, North Carolina Room, Central Branch, Forsyth County Public Library, Winston-Salem, N.C.; Tilley, *R. J. Reynolds Tobacco Company*, 260–67, 275. The committees included "safety and accident prevention," "adjustment of wages and working conditions," "investigation of complaints," "housing problems," "sanitation, health and restaurants," "education and publication," and "industrial relations."

20. D. Rich, Treasurer, to RJR, July 26, 1917, box 1, file 63, RFP.

21. *WSJ*, January 2, 1917.

22. Cyphers, *National Civic Federation.*

23. "Chrysanthemum Show," *Winston-Salem Twin City Sentinel*, October 29, 1917; A. H. Latimer to KSR, December 13, 1918, box 2, file 122, RFP; "Red Cross Parade," *WSJ*, May 19, 1918; "Splendid History of Work of the Local Red Cross," *WSJ*, December 18, 1919.

24. On this rich literature, see, for example, F. Morgan, *Women and Patriotism*; Cox, *Dixie's Daughters*; Neff, *Honoring the Civil War Dead*; and W. Blair, *Cities of the Dead.*

25. A. D. Reynolds, *Recollections*, 27–30.

26. Tilley, *Reynolds Homestead*, 37; Pedigo and Pedigo, *History of Henry and Patrick Counties*, 231–32; Blair, "Reynolds, Richard Joshua," 1.

27. William J. Martin, President, Davidson College, to KSR, July 10, 1917, box 2, file 131; Sue R. Staley, Bristol, to KSR, July 2, 1918, KSR Correspondence—Staley, Sue Reynolds (1875–1933), 1907–18, box 2, file 159; W. B. Taylor, Taylor Brothers, Tobacco Manufacturers, June 18, 1918, to Master R. J. Reynolds Jr., KSR Correspondence—T, 1906–18, box 2, file 160, all in RFP.

28. Business correspondence between R.J.R. and his attorney, Henry H. Shelton, through that late summer and into the early fall suggests that R.J.R. was deeply concerned about the politics of national excise taxes, while also seeking to get his affairs in order. See R.J.R. Correspondence in box 1, file 64, RFP; on a summary of R.J.R.'s health challenges to this point, see Henrietta Van Den Berg to KSR, October 4, 1917, box 2, file 166, RFP. The children, with Miss Van Den Berg's help, wrote sweet get-well cards to their father religiously; see Children's Correspondence, box 2, file 182, RFP.

29. Henrietta Van Den Berg to KSR, October 17, 1917, box 2, file 166, RFP.

30. For example, see correspondence from Harry H. Shelton, Attorney and Counselor at Law, Winston-Salem, N.C. to R. J. Reynolds, Johns Hopkins Hospital, November 8 and 9, 1917, box 2, file 149.2 and file 167, RFP.

31. Henrietta Van Den Berg to KSR, October 18, 1917, box 2, file 166; Henrietta Van Den Berg to KSR, December 19, 1917, box 2, file 166, both in RFP.

32. Henrietta Van Den Berg to KSR, December 18 and 19, 1917, box 2, file 166, RFP.

33. Emma Bailey Spere to KSR, August 30, 1917, box 2, file 176, RFP.

34. Mrs. Minnie Leatherman Blanton, Director for N.C., to KSR, September 13, 1917, box 2, file 167, RFP; "State Committee for Library Announced," *WSJ*, September 15, 1917.

35. Josephus Daniels to KSR, May 7, 1917, box 2, file 167, RFP.

36. Laura Holmes Reily to KSR, July 13, 1917, box 10, file 692; letter from the N.C. National Council of Defense to KSR, September 27, 1917, box 9, file 592, both in RFP. For a good overview of southern white women's wartime organizational work through the Women's Committee, see Breen, "Southern Women at War."

37. *WSJ*, October 24, 1917.

38. Evie Crim to KSR, June 25, 1918, box 1, file 86, RFP.

39. Henrietta Van Den Berg to KSR, October 18, 1917, box 2, file 166, RFP.

40. "Red Cross Campaign, Reynolda, This Week," *WSJ*, clipping, box 1, file 59, RFP.

41. Dick Jr. to KSR and RJR, n.d. [1917 or 1918], box 2, file 183, RFP. The campaign he referenced might well have been the Red Cross parade on May 19, 1918; "Great Parade on Tuesday," *WSJ*, May 19, 1918.

42. Henrietta Van Den Berg to KSR, May 27, 1918, box 2, file 166, RFP. A month later Katharine's secretary wrote her stating, "Everybody bought War Savings Stamps yesterday, the entire city being canvassed from house to house. I undertook $100 for Elsie and hope I can manage it." Evie Crim to KSR, June 25, 1918, box 1, file 86, RFP.

43. Van Den Berg to KSR, October 17, 1917.

44. Cotten, *History of the North Carolina Federation*, 21, 29–30, 49–51. Note that the council had met in Winston-Salem in preparation for this especially important Raleigh convention.

45. Henrietta Van Den Berg to KSR, October 18, 1917, box 2, file 166, RFP.

46. KSR to Irene Smith, February 25, 1918, box 2, file 154, RFP.

47. Henrietta Van Den Berg to KSR, May 27, 1918, box 2, file 166, RFP.

48. John Neal to KSR, July 20, 1918, box 2, file 136; KSR to John Neal, July 18, 1920, box 2, file 136, RFP.

49. KSR to John Neal, July 18, 1920, box 2, file 136; KSR to Dr. Neal Anderson, July 18, 1918, box 1, file 70; KSR to Mr. Armistead, box 1, file 68; KSR to Mrs. Jones, July 18, 1918, box 2, file 114, all in RFP.

50. KSR to John Neal, July 18, 1920, box 2, file 136; Itinerary, Private Car Trip, The Pennsylvania Railroad Company, July 17, 1918, box 2, file 138, both in RFP.

51. Despite his intentions, the money was used to update the 1914 hospital, and only a wing for black patients in 1922. An additional wing for whites was added two years later. Tursi, *Winston-Salem*, 220.

52. *Winston-Salem Sentinel*, April 2, 1914.

53. R.J.R. obituary, *Charlotte News and Observer*, July 29, 1918, and *Wilmington (N.C.) Dispatch*, July 29, 1918, clippings, IM; copy of Affidavit of Katharine S. Reynolds and W. N. Reynolds, Exhibit "B" in "Will of R. J. Reynolds, deceased," August 12, 1918, spelling out details of hospital bequests, copy in RFP.

54. See clippings, IM.

55. Editorial, *Winston-Salem Advertiser*, August 16, 1918, clipping in IM.

56. A tribute from Reynolds Temple, *Winston-Salem Sentinel*, August 12, 1918, IM.

57. "Thousands Pay Last Tribute to Mr. R. J. Reynolds," *Winston-Salem Twin City Sentinel*, July 31, 1918; "Tribute Paid by Citizens to Late Mr. R. J. Reynolds," *Winston-Salem Journal*, July 31, 1918.

58. Nancy Susan Reynolds, Oral History Archives, May 5, 1980, OH.01.004.1, RHMAA.

59. William Hill to KSR, October 25, 1918; and Mrs. Marion Hill to KSR, January 6, 1919, both in box 1, file 106; Frances I. Hartman to KSR [Fall 1918], box 1, file 106; Emma Kaminer to KSR [Fall 1918], box 2, file 119; Sophia B. Norfleet to KSR [Fall 1918], box 2, file 136; Matt [Zachary Madison] Smith to KSR [Fall 1918], box 2, file 156, all in RFP.

60. Davidson College Yearbook, 1914.

61. *Davidsonian*, Davidson College, February 21, 1917, p. 4; Beaty, *Davidson*, 77; "J. E. Johnston Passes, Leaves 5% Estate," *Davidsonian*, November 9, 1951, p. 1.

62. "Supt. Latham Talks of Schools of Various Cities," *Winston-Salem Twin City Sentinel*, March 8, 1920.

63. J. Edward Johnston (hereafter JEJ) to KSR, November, 8, 1920, RFP.

64. KSR to JEJ, February 1, 1921, RFP.

65. JEJ to KSR, October 1, 12, 13, November 8, 9, 12, 14, 20, 1920, RFP.

66. JEJ to KSR, November, 8, 1920, RFP.

67. JEJ to KSR, October 9, 13, November 9, 1920, RFP.

68. Aron, *Working at Play*, chaps. 3 and 4.

69. "Katharine Reynolds Weds J. Edward Johnston," *WSJ*, June 11, 1921.

70. KSR to JEJ, January 29, 1921, RFP.

71. "Johnston-Reynolds Marriage Last Night," *WSJ*, June 12, 1921.

72. Mary Reynolds Diary, BMFP.

73. JEJ to KSR, September 7, 1921, RFP.

74. KSR to Ellen Jones, June 6, 1922; Henrietta Van Den Berg to KSR, May 31, 1922, both in RFP.

75. Nancy Susan Reynolds, Oral History Archives.

76. Southard, "History of a Pioneering Agency," 1, 18–28; Dowdy, "Development of the Social Welfare Movement," 45–47.

77. Dowdy, "Development of the Social Welfare Movement," 45–50; Winston-Salem Family Services Inc., brochure, Family Services, Inc., 1200 S. Broad Street, Winston-Salem, N.C. 27101. In fact, Henrietta Van Den Berg, Katharine's nurse, attended the black ward of the hospital during the epidemic.

78. Ed Johnston constantly referenced beaux courting Katharine at Pinehurst Resort, the governor's mansion, and at other prominent social events and homes. See, for example, JEJ to KSR, October 22 and 23, 1920, RFP; interview with Zachary Smith, July 15, 2004, Reynolda Village, Winston-Salem, N.C.

79. *Philadelphia Public Ledger*, February 11, 1921.

80. Interview with Zachary Smith, July 7, 2004, Reynolda Village, Winston-Salem, N.C.

81. Mary Getrude Fendall, National Organizer, to KSR, September, 27, 1917, box 2, file 136, RFP.

82. Henrietta Van Den Berg to KSR, October 17, 1917, box 2, file 166, RFP. "We enjoyed hearing Miss Rankin very much, I was sorry that she spoke most of the time for womans suffrage, rather than on some of the most vital questions of the day, but she has a charming personality and a very quiet interesting way of speaking, she had to leave that night by train for Raleigh, as they wanted her there very early, Mrs. Will Reynolds, Mrs. Patterson and Senah went over in Mr. Will Reynolds' car, she insisted on using her own, they had a very good time, luncheon at the Governors mansion, etc. but things were badly managed and Mrs. Patterson did not get to make a speech. . . . Senah said she never saw such a mob of people, and that scarcely anyone could hear any of the speeches."

83. KSR to JEJ, November 3, 1920, RFP.

84. "Fort Bragg and Pinehurst Teams Combine against Local Polo Club," *Winston-Salem Twin City Sentinel*, August 29, 1923; "Local Club Organized," *WSJ*, September 9, 1923; for F. Scott Fitzgerald's quote, see *The Great Gatsby* (New York: Charles Scribners' Sons, 1925), 6, 19.

85. Based on reading personal correspondence between Dick Reynolds Jr. and his mother, Katharine Reynolds, graciously shared with the author from the personal collection of Noah Reynolds, Winston-Salem. N.C.

86. Tilley, R. J. Reynolds Tobacco Company, 242.

87. *WSJ*, November 17, 18, 19, 20, 21, 22, 23, 28, 30, 1918; *Winston-Salem Twin City Sentinel*, November 18, 1918; Tilley, *R. J. Reynolds Tobacco Company*, 260–61.

88. Draft of letter or telegram, KSR, Geneva, to National Bank, N.Y., no date [1921], KSR Correspondence—Wachovia Bank and Trust, box 2, file 168, RFP. Katharine's long-standing feud with the male board members of the company is borne out in the love letters she exchanged with J. Edward Johnston, 1920–24, RFP.

89. Tilley, *R. J. Reynolds Tobacco Company*, 288.

90. Cotten, *History of the North Carolina Federation*,172; incidentally Mrs. James Gray was a delegate in attendance (179).

91. "Committee of 100 for Sociological Congress in City," *WSJ*, July 20, 1919; "Winston-Salem Junior League 46th in Association of Jr. Leagues in America," *Winston-Salem Twin City Sentinel*, May 4, 1935.

92. For local newspaper coverage of Katharine's death, see "Mrs. Edward Johnston Dies in New York Hospital," *WSJ*, May 24, 1924; "Mrs. Johnston's Body Will Arrive in City Today," *WSJ*, May 25, 1924; "Mrs. J. Edward Johnston to Be Buried Here Today," *WSJ*, May 26, 1924; "Mrs. Johnston Buried as City Pays Her Honor," *WSJ*, May 27, 1924; "Mrs. Katharine Smith Johnston's Will Announced," *WSJ*, May 30, 1924.

93. "Mrs. J. Edward Johnston to Be Buried Here Today"; "Mrs. Johnston Buried as City Pays Her Honor."

94. For an example of her decision making about investments, see the exchanges between Katharine and F. C. Abbot and Company (stockbrokers) in the months preceding R.J.R's death, when she was clearly shifting investments to protect her own financial security and access to money in the likelihood that she would soon became a widow and have limited access to R.J.R.'s resources during the settling of his estate. KSR Correspondence to F. C. Abbot and Co., 1917–18, box 1, file 99, RFP.

95. Katharine began this role early in her marriage, receiving Governor Robert Glenn at the Twin City Club with her husband the week of October 2, 1906, according to the *WSJ*.

96. KSR Correspondence to F. C. Abbot and Co., 1917–18.

97. "Erection of the Greatest High School Plant in South in Winston-Salem Made Possible by Mrs. R. J. Reynolds' Offer," *WSJ*, June 7, 1919; "Winston-Salem's New High School under Construction," *WSJ*, August 30, 1922; "Mrs. Katharine Johnston," *New York Times*, May 25, 1924.

98. Fries et al., *Forsyth*, 67–78; on R. J. Reynolds's death and public mourning, see the *WSJ*, July 30, 31, August 1, 2, 13, 1918; *New York Times*, July 30, 1918.

99. "Mrs. J. Edward Johnston to Be Buried Here Today"; "Mrs. Johnston Buried as City Pays Her Honor."

100. "Mrs. Johnston Buried as City Pays Her Honor."

101. Ibid.; Singal, "Towards a Definition of American Modernism."

102. "Mrs. Johnston Buried as City Pays Her Honor."

103. Shields, *Just Plain Larnin'*, 13; "Shields' New Novel Will Go on Sale Today," *WSJ*, January 25, 1934; Shields, "Woes of a Southern Liberal," 78.

104. "Erection of the Greatest High School Plant"; "Winston-Salem People Generally Talking of High School Proposal," *WSJ*, June 8, 1919.

105. KSR to Dr. D. Clay Lilly, February 1, 1923, D. Clay Lilly Papers, Montreat Collection, Presbyterian Historical Society, Philadelphia, Penn.

106. KSR to Dr. J. Y. Joyner, February 13, 1919, James Yadkin Joyner Papers, 1873; 1902–19, Correspondence-1919; undated, North Carolina State Archives, Raleigh, N.C.

107. Undated newspaper clipping, "A Big Man with a Big Vision," Call to Dr. D. Clay Lilly, DD of the Synod of Kentucky by Reynolda Presbyterian Church, Synod of North Carolina, D. Clay Lilly Papers, Montreat Collection, Archives, Presbyterian Historical Society, Philadelphia, Penn. On Lilly's commitment to women's leadership, see his sermons titled "Woman's Work" and "Women at the Helm," also in the D. Clay Lilly Papers. For his better-known articles and books, see "The Attitude of the South to the Colored People, *Union Seminary Magazine* 16, no. 3:270–87; *A Partnership in Living: A Course of Four Bible Studies on Stewardship, Prepared Especially for Men* (Chattanooga: General Assembly's Stewardship Committee, Presbyterian Church U.S., 1924); *Some Teachings of Jesus* (Saint Louis: Woman's Auxiliary, Presbyterian Church U.S., 1926); *Faith of Our Fathers* (Richmond, Va.: Presbyterian Committee of Publication, 1935).

108. Lilly corresponded with ministers, theologians, educators, and religious leaders from around the country on the role of religion in education and science. His correspondents included the Department of Sociology at Dartmouth College; the Theological Seminary in New Brunswick, N.J.; the School of Education at New York University; the Presbyterian Theological Seminary of Kentucky; Henry Louis Smith, president of Washington and Lee University; Clarissa H. Spencer of the Council of the Churches of

Christ in America; Reverend D. P. McGeachy of First Presbyterian in Decatur, Georgia; President J. R. McCain of Agnes Scott College; Executive Secretary Robert L. Kelly of the Council of Church Boards of Education of New York; Bert Cunningham, professor of Zoology at Duke University; and Nolan R. Best, editor of the *Continent*. See "The Reynolda Conferences," D. Clay Lilly Papers, Montreat Collection, Presbyterian Historical Society, Philadelphia, Penn.

109. "I am still under the spell of the Reynolds Conference, and the inspiration it afforded me," wrote Jacob S. Roison of the Jewish Welfare Board of the U.S. Army and Navy on June 18, 1927, "Reynolda Conferences," D. Clay Lilly Papers, Montreat Collection, Presbyterian Historical Society, Philadelphia, Penn.; on an overview of the 1927 conference discussion on tax-supported public schools and moral values, as well as an assessment of the significance of the conferences as a whole, see D. Clay Lilly, "Training for Good Citizenship," *Christian Observer*, July 20, 1927, 5–6.

Epilogue

1. "Smith Reynolds Shot in the head," *WSJ*, July 6, 1932; "Coroner Says Reynolds Killed Self," *WSJ*, July 7, 1932; "Strange Story Reynolds Tragedy," *WSJ*, July 9, 1932; "Reynolds Killer Unknown," *WSJ*, July 12, 1932; "Forsyth Grand Jury Indicts Libby Holman," *WSJ*, August 5, 1932; "Reynolds Family Expresses Willingness for State to Drop Holman-Walker Case," *WSJ*, October 13, 1932; Hollywood films offering a fictionalized version of the tragedy include *Reckless*, directed by Victor Fleming, 1935, and *Written on the Wind*, directed by Douglas Sirk, 1956.

2. "Wings of Adventure: Smith Reynolds and the Flight of 898 Whiskey," Reynolda House Exhibit, 2007; Log of Aeroplane NR-898W: Experiences, Comments, Impressions of a Flight from England to China, 1931–32, 1932, original in archives, RHMAA.

3. Wilson, *For the People of North Carolina*.

4. The Z. Smith Reynolds Foundation uses its funds to support social, economic, and environmental justice; strengthen democracy; educate the populace; and implement progressive public policy and social change. See Haislip, *History*, xi–xiii, 18–26, 34–46; Z. Smith Reynolds Foundation website, "History," http://www.zsr.org/history.htm, accessed May 27, 2011; and Lambeth, speech on Reynolds family philanthropy.

5. "Private Lives," *Life*, November 23, 1936, 81; although based on the perspective of Dick's third wife, Schnakenberg's *Kid Carolina* conveys the broad outlines of Dick's remarkable adult life ably enough.

6. "Mission and Beliefs," Mary Reynolds Babcock Foundation website, http://www.mrbf.org/missionAndBeliefs.aspx, accessed May 27, 2011.

7. Nancy Susan Reynolds, *Dictionary of North Carolina Biography*, edited by William S. Powell, vol. 1 (Chapel Hill: University of North Carolina Press, 1979); obituary, Nancy Susan Reynolds, *New York Times*, January 12, 1985; obituary, Henrietta Van Den Berg, *Baltimore Sun*, April 28, 1952; Helen S. W. Althey, typewritten manuscript about Henrietta Van Den Berg, Archives, Johns Hopkins University, Baltimore; interview with Nick Bragg, former director of the Reynolda House Museum of American Art and friend and confidante of Nancy Reynolds, Winston-Salem, N.C.

8. Letterhead correspondence from the Winston-Salem Community Chest bears Edward Johnston's name as a YMCA representative for the years 1925, 1926, and 1927, but

not 1928, in Roy Milton Hinshaw Papers, files 1925–28, Raven Knob Boy Scout Museum, Old Hickory Council, Boy Scouts of America, Winston-Salem, N.C.

9. "Johnston Wins British Citation," *Baltimore Sun*, July 23, 1948.

10. Interview with J. Edward Johnston Jr., January 6, 2004, Baltimore, Md.

11. Interview with Zachary Smith, nephew of Katharine Smith Reynolds, September 15, 2004, Reynolda Village, Winston-Salem, N.C.; John Neal is buried at the large memorial in honor of William Neal Reynolds (1866–1951) and Kate Bitting Reynolds (1867–1946) in the Salem Cemetery. See also Tilley, *R. J. Reynolds Tobacco Company*, 527; obituary, *WSJ*, September 12, 1920, pp. 1, 5.

12. Lambeth, speech on Reynolds family philanthropy.

13. On the limits of elite philanthropy in the progressive South, see Kirkland, "Envisioning a Progressive City," esp. the introduction.

Bibliography

Primary Sources

Manuscript Sources

Duke University Library, Manuscripts and Archives, Durham, N.C.
James Buchanan Duke Papers.

First Presbyterian Church, Winston-Salem, N.C.
Church Register, no. 3, from January 6, 1895.

Hagley Museum and Library, Wilmington, Del.
Associated Factory Mutual Fire Insurance Company, Plans Division, R. J. Reynolds Company, 1912, 1924, reel 3, microfilm.
"The R. J. Reynolds Story: The Evolution of a Global Enterprise," address delivered by J. Paul Sticht at a national meeting of the Newcomen Society of the United States, Winston-Salem, April 13, 1983.
Wilmington Trust Co., Investment Analysis Files, R. J. Reynolds Company, 1926–54, accession no. 2118, box 35.

Harvard Business School, Cambridge, Mass.
R. G. Dun and Co. Collection, Baker Library Historical Collection.

Library of Congress, Washington, D.C.
Papers of Josephus C. Daniels (1862–1948), Special Correspondence, box 10, microfilm reel 1.

Library of Virginia, Richmond, Va.
Auditor of Public Accounts, Personal Property Tax Records, Patrick County, 1860–63, 1865–66, reel 682.

Millhouse, Barbara. Private Collection of Family Papers, Winston-Salem, N.C.
Anderson, Neal. "Eulogy," 1918, copy of typescript.
Blair, W. A. "Reynolds, Richard Joshua," draft, June 10, 1919, copy of typescript.
Blair, W. A. "Sketch no. 1 from Biographical History of North Carolina, vol. 3, pp. 334–35, Richard Joshua Reynolds," draft, no date, copy of typescript.

Mount Airy Museum of Regional History (cited as MAMRH), Mount Airy, N.C.
Blue Ridge Inn clippings file.
Miss Graves School clippings file.
Schools clipping file.

Patrick County Courthouse, Stuart, Va.
Order books 8, 9.

Reynolda House Museum of American Art (cited as RHMAA), Archives and Collections.
In Memoriam, Richard Joshua Reynolds, leather-bound book of newspaper clippings, gift of Katharine Smith Reynolds to Mary Katherine Reynolds, box U49 (cited as IM).
Reynolds Family Chronology, compiled by Sherry Hollingsworth.
Reynolds Family Papers, 1840s–1984 (cited as RFP).
Tilley, Nannie M. "R. J. Reynolds Tobacco." MS.

Surry County Courthouse, Dobson, N.C.
Record of deeds books and plat books.

University of North Carolina at Chapel Hill, Southern Historical Collection.
Eaton, Clement. "Winston-Salem in the First Quarter of the Twentieth Century: A Recollection," unpublished brief memoir, 1976.
Virginia and North Carolina Construction Company Record Book, 1888–96.

University of North Carolina at Greensboro.
University Archives, Special Collections Division, Walter C. Jackson Library.
Alumnae News 51 (1962); 52 (1964); 54 (1967).
"A Bequest, a Memorial, and a Promise," *Alumnae News* 51, no.1, 12–13.
Blackwell, Chancellor Gordon Williams. General Correspondence, 1960.
Board of Trustees, general correspondence, 1920–23.
Bulletin of the North Carolina College for Women, annual catalogs, 1897–1902; 1920–22.
The Carolinian, Women's College of the University of North Carolina at Greensboro 42, no. 13 (January 11, 1963): 1.
The Decennial, published by the Adelphian and Cornelian Literary Societies of the State Normal and Industrial College, Greensboro, N.C. Roanoke, Va.: Stone Printing and Manufacturing Co., 1902.
Foust, Chancellor Julius Isaac, Papers, General Correspondence, 19??-22(24?).
Foust, Julius Isaac, Papers, College History, Alumnae Letters, box 100.
Coit, Laura, to Julius Isaac Foust, Nov. 23, 1934.
Grimes, Ida Wharton, to Julius Isaac Foust, April 10, 1935.
Pasmore, Julia, to Julius Isaac Foust, May 21, 1935.
Rankin, Eunice K., to Julius Isaac Foust, May 27, 1935.
Saunders, Annie Hawkins, to Julius Isaac Foust, March 25, 1935.
Wray, Oeland Barnett, to Julius Isaac Foust, March 3, 1935.
"Katharine Smith Reynolds," *Alumni News*, University of North Carolina at Greensboro, 71, no. 1 (Fall 1982): 16–17.
Stanback, Betty Anne Ragland, "Kate Smith Reynolds," [North Carolina College for Women] *Alumnae News* 52, no. 3 (April 1964): 3, 41.
State Normal Magazine (published quarterly by the Board of Editors elected from the Adelphian and Cornelian Literary Societies at State Normal and Industrial College, Greensboro, N.C.), vols. 1–5.

Vice Chancellor for Development.
Alumnae Association Records, box 1.
Class Lists and Constitutions, 1893–1907 folder.
Vice Chancellor for Development and University Relations.
Office of Alumnae Affairs, 1899–1988, box 1.
Alumnae folder.
Austin, Emily Semple, 1901x.
"Emily Semple Austin," by Mary B. Collins, typescript.
Baugham, Phoebe Pegram, 1896x
"History of Phoebe Pegram," no author or date, typescript.
Dixon, Mary Dail, 1896x.
Typescript of letter.
McFadden, Mary, 1900.
Riddick, Elsie, 1894.
Wolf, Sudie Israel, 1894.
Wooten, Bayard Morgan, 1896x.
Yoder, Emily Asbury, 1896.
Office of Alumni Affairs, 1899–1988, box 2.
Alumni Correspondence, 1899–1987, folder.
Wyche, Pearl, to her mother, Greensboro, November 29, 1899.
Alumni Correspondence, 1926–88, folder.
President, Graduate Group, Inc., 230 Park Avenue, NYC to Miss Clara B. Byrd, Alumnae Secretary, North Carolina College for Women, June 14, 1931.
Alumnae Association, 1907–31, folder.
Correspondence, 1909–11, "R" folder, box 2.
Correspondence, 1913–14, "R" Folder, box 4.

U.S. Census Records.
Manuscript Census Returns, Forsyth County, N.C., 1850–1920.
Manuscript Census Returns, Patrick County, Va., 1850, 1860, Manufacturing Schedules.
Manuscript Census Returns, Patrick County, Va., 1850, 1860, Population Schedules.
Manuscript Census Returns, Stokes County, N.C., 1850, 1860, 1870.

Winston-Salem State University, Winston-Salem, N.C., Archives.
Simon G. Atkins Papers

YWCA of Winston-Salem, Winston-Salem, N.C.
Scrapbook, 1908–14
Book of Minutes, January 1917–32

Newspapers and Trade Journals

Jacksonville, Florida Metropolis
Mount Airy News
New York Times (cited as *NYT*)
Raleigh Morning Post

Raleigh News and Observer
Statesville Record and Landmark
Tobacco
Tobacco Journal
Winston Western Sentinel
Winston-Salem Journal (cited as *WSJ*)
Winston-Salem Sentinel
Winston-Salem Twin City Sentinel
Winston Union Republican
Yadkin Valley News (Mount Airy, N.C.)

Electronic Databases

Harper's Weekly, http://www.harpweek.com/.
Legacy Tobacco Documents Library, University of California, San Francisco, http://legacy.library.ucsf.edu/.

Printed Sources

Adams, Herbert B., ed. *History of Cooperation in the United States*. Vol. 6. Baltimore: Johns Hopkins University, 1888.
Arnold, B. W. *History of the Tobacco Industry in Virginia from 1860 to 1894*. Baltimore: Johns Hopkins University Press, 1897.
Beatty, Jerome. *Our 100th Anniversary*. Winston-Salem: R. J. Reynolds Industries, 1972.
Blair, W. A. "Richard Joshua Reynolds." In *Biographical History of North Carolina from Colonial Times to the Present*, edited by Samuel A. Ashe, vol. 3. Greensboro: Charles L. Van Noppen, 1906.
Branson, E. C. *Farm Prosperity in Forsyth: The City and the Country End of the Problem*. Winston-Salem: Winston-Salem Board of Trade, 1917.
Branson, Rev. Levi. *Branson's North Carolina Business Directory*. Raleigh: Levi Branson, 1896.
Brockenbrough, William Henry. A *New and Comprehensive Gazetteer of Virginia, and the District of Columbia. Wash., D.C.: J. Martin, 1835*.
Connor, Robert Diggs Wimberly, William Kenneth Boyd, and Joseph Gregoire de Roulhac Hamilton. *History of North Carolina*. Vols. 4, 6. New York: Lewis Publishing, 1919.
Cotten, Sallie Southall. *History of the North Carolina Federation of Women's Clubs, 1901–1925*. Raleigh: Edwards and Broughton, 1925.
Davis, W. A., and E. G. Goldston. *United States Department of Agriculture Soil Survey of Surry County, North Carolina, Series 1931*. no. 20, issued October 1937. Washington, D.C.: Bureau of Chemistry and Soils, 1937.
Flannagan, Roy C. *The Story of Lucky Strike*. N.p., 1938.
Foltz, Henry Wesley. *Winston Fifty Years Ago*. N.p., 1926.
Fries, Adelaide L., ed. *Records of the Moravians in North Carolina*. Raleigh: Edwards and Broughton, 1922–47.

Gulledge, Virginia Frances Wooten. *The North Carolina Conference for Social Service: A Study of Its Development and Methods*. Raleigh: North Carolina Conference for Social Services, 1942.

Harris, Joel Chandler. *Life of Henry W. Grady including Speeches and Writings*. Rahway, N.J.: Mershon, 1920.

Hussey, A. and Company. *Leaf Tobacco*. Trade catalog, 1898.

Lybrook, Andrew M. *Mahoneism Unveiled! The Plot against the People Exposed: Judge Lybrook, the Readjuster Senator from Patrick, Tears the Mask from Mahone. Other Interesting Campaign Facts—Shall Virginia Be Sold Out to the Arthur-Mahone Republican Party?* N.p., 1882(?).

Manning, Caroline. *Hours and Earnings in Tobacco Stemmeries*. Bulletin of the Women's Bureau 127, U.S. Department of Labor. Washington, D.C.: U.S. Government Printing Office, 1934.

Massey, John E. *Autobiography of John E. Massey*. Edited by Elizabeth H. Hancock. New York: Neale Publishing, 1909

Munsterberg, Hugo. *Americans*. Translated by Edwin B. Holt. New York: McClure, Phillips, 1904.

Page, Thomas Nelson. *The Negro: The Southerner's Problem*. New York: Charles Scribner's Sons, 1904.

Pedigo, Virginia G., and Lewis G. Pedigo. *History of Patrick and Henry Counties*. Roanoke: Stone Printing and Manufacturing, 1933.

Report of the "Big Four" Commission. Submitted to the General Assembly [Virginia], January 1932, Pursuant to a Joint Resolution Agreed to March 4, 1930. Richmond: Division of Purchase and Printing, 1932.

Report of the Commissioner of Corporations on the Tobacco Industry, Part I: Position of the Tobacco Combination in the Industry. February 25, 1909. Washington, D.C.: U.S. Government Printing Office, 1909.

Report of the Commissioner of Corporations on the Tobacco Industry, Part II: Capitalization, Investment and Earnings. September 25, 1911. Washington, D.C.: U.S. Government Printing Office, 1911.

Report of the Commissioner of Corporations on the Tobacco Industry, Part III: Prices, Costs, and Profits. March 15, 1915. Washington, D.C.: U.S. Government Printing Office, 1915.

Reynolds, A. D. *Recollections of Major A. D. Reynolds, 1847–1925*. Edited by Barbara Babcock Millhouse. Winston-Salem: Reynolda House, 1978.

Rondthaler, Edward. *The Memorabilia of Fifty Years, 1877–1927*. Raleigh: Edwards and Broughton, 1928.

Ruffin, Frank G. *Colonel Frank G. Ruffin's Letter: A Terrible Arraignment. Mahoneism Unveiled! The Great Plot to Sell Out Virginians to the Republican Party Exposed* . . . . N.p., 1882.

Shields, James M. *Just Plain Larnin'*. New York: Coward-McCann, 1934.

———. "Woes of a Southern Liberal." *American Mercury* 34 (January–April 1935): 73–79.

Swift, Wiley Hampton. *Child Labor Welfare in North Carolina*. New York: National Child Labor Committee, 1918.

Thomas, James A. *A Pioneer Tobacco Merchant in the Orient*. Durham, N.C.: Duke University Press, 1928.

Walsh's Winston-Salem, North Carolina City Directory for 1904–1905. Charleston, S.C., 1905.

Weaver, C. E. *Winston-Salem: City of Industry; Illustrated Historical, Biographical Facts and Figures*. Winston-Salem: Winston Printing, 1918.

Werner, Carl Avery. *Tobaccoland: A Book about Tobacco; Its History, Legends, Literature, Cultivation, Social and Hygienic Influences, Commercial Development, Industrial Processes and Governmental Regulation*. New York: Tobacco Leaf Publishing, 1922.

Winkler, A. V. *Souvenir of Twin-Cities of North Carolina, Winston-Salem, Forsyth County*. Salem, N.C.: Blums' Steam Power Press, 1890.

Winston, Robert Watson. "An Unconsidered Aspect of the Negro Question." *South Atlantic Quarterly* 1 (July 1902): 265–67.

Secondary Sources

Adams, Sean Patrick. *Old Dominion, Industrial Commonwealth: Coal, Politics, and Economy in Antebellum America*. Baltimore: Johns Hopkins University Press, 2004.

Appleby, Joyce. *The Relentless Revolution: A History of American Capitalism*. New York: W. W. Norton, 2010.

Aron, Cindy S. *Working at Play: A History of Vacations in the United States*. New York: Oxford University Press, 1999.

Aslet, Clive. *The American Country House*. New Haven, Conn.: Yale University Press, 1990.

———. *Villages of Britain: The Five Hundred Villages That Made the Countryside*. London: Bloomsbury, 2010.

Babcock, Mary Reynolds. *A Lady of Good Taste: Mary Reynolds Babcock, Her Recipe Notes*. Winston-Salem: privately printed by Charles H. Babcock, 1954.

Beaty, Mary D. *Davidson: A History of the Town from 1835 until 1937*. Davidson, N.C.: Briarpatch Press, 1979.

Becker, Gary. "Human Capital, Effort, and the Sexual Division of Labor." *Journal of Labor Economics* 3, no. 1 (January 1985): 33–58.

Biles, Roger. "Tobacco Towns: Urban Growth and Economic Development in Eastern North Carolina." *North Carolina Historical Review* 84, no. 2 (April 2007): 156–90.

Billings, Dwight B., Jr. *Planters and the Making of a "New South": Class, Politics, and Development in North Carolina, 1865–1900*. Chapel Hill: University of North Carolina Press, 1979.

Blair, William. *Cities of the Dead: Contesting the Memory of the Civil War in the South, 1865–1914*. Chapel Hill: University of North Carolina Press, 2004.

———. *Virginia's Private War: Feeding Body and Soul in the Confederacy, 1861–1865*. New York: Oxford University Press, 1998.

Blight, David W. *Race and Reunion: The Civil War in American Memory*. Cambridge, Mass.: Belknap Press, 2001.

Boles, John B., and Bethany L. Johnson, eds. *Origins of the New South: Fifty Years Later; The Continuing Influence of a Historical Classic*. Baton Rouge: Louisiana State University Press, 2003.

Bowers, William L. *The Country Life Movement in America, 1900–1920*. Port Washington, N.Y.: Kennikat Press, 1974.

Bowles, Elizabeth Anne. *A Good Beginning: The First Few Decades at the University of North Carolina at Greensboro*. Chapel Hill: University of North Carolina Press, 1967.
Brandt, Allan M. *The Cigarette Century: The Rise, Fall and Deadly Persistence of the Product That Defined America*. New York: Basic Books, 2009.
Breen, William J. "Southern Women at War: The North Carolina Woman's Committee, 1917–1919." *North Carolina Historical Review* 55, no. 3 (July 1978): 251–83.
Brody, David. "The Rise and Decline of Welfare Capitalism." In *Change and Continuity in Twentieth-Century America: The 1920s*, edited by John Braeman et al., 147–78. Columbus: Ohio State University Press, 1968.
Brooks, Jerome E. *Green Leaf and Gold: Tobacco in North Carolina*. Rev. ed. Raleigh: Division of Archives and History, N.C. Department of Cultural Resources, 1975.
Brownlee, Fambrough L. *Winston-Salem: A Pictorial History*. Norfolk, Va.: Downing, 1977.
Byrne, Frank J. *Becoming Bourgeois: Merchant Culture in the South, 1820–1865*. Lexington: University Press of Kentucky, 2006.
Carlton, David L. "The Revolution from Above: The National Market and the Beginnings of Industrialization in North Carolina." *Journal of American History* (September 1990): 464–67.
Carter, William Franklin, Jr., and Carrie Young Carter. "'Footprints in the Hollow,' Bicentennial Issue, Surry County, 1775–1975." 1976. Typescript. Mount Airy Pubic Library, Mount Airy, N.C.
Carmichael, Peter S. *The Last Generation: Young Virginians in Peace, War, and Reunion*. Chapel Hill: University of North Carolina Press, 2005.
Carraway, Getrude S. *Carolina Crusaders: History of North Carolina Federation of Women's Clubs*. Vol. 2 of *State Federation History*. New Bern, N.C.: Owen G. Dunn, 1941.
Cash, W. J. *The Mind of the South*. 1941. Reprint, New York: Vintage, 1969.
Cell, John Whitson. *The Highest Stage of White Supremacy: The Origins of Segregation in South Africa and the American South*. Cambridge: Cambridge University Press, 1982.
Censer, Jane Turner. "A Changing World of Work: North Carolina Elite Women, 1865–1895." *North Carolina Historical Review* 73, no. 1 (January 1996): 28–55.
Chandler, Alfred Dupont. *Visible Hand: The Managerial Revolution in American Business*. Cambridge, Mass.: Belknap Press, 1977.
Chudacoff, Howard P. *The Age of the Bachelor: Creating an American Subculture*. Princeton, N.J.: Princeton University Press, 1999.
Clement, Maud C. *The History of Pittsylvania County, Virginia*. Baltimore: Regional Publishing, 1976.
Cohen, Lizabeth. *Making a New Deal: Industrial Workers in Chicago, 1919–1939*. Cambridge: Cambridge University Press, 1990.
Cole, Stephanie. "A White Woman, of Middle Age, Would Be Preferred." In *Neither Lady nor Slave*, edited by Susanna Delfino and Michele Gillespie, 75–101. Chapel Hill: University of North Carolina Press, 2002.
Cox, Karen L. *Dixie's Daughters: The United Daughters of the Confederacy and the Preservation of Confederate Culture*. Gainesville: University Press of Florida, 2003.
Crawford, Jim. "Rock Spring Plantation: Incubator of Two American Industries." March 2007. MS.
Crow, Jeffrey J. "An Apartheid for the South: Clarence Poe's Crusade for Rural Segrega-

tion." In *Race, Class, and Politics in Southern History*, edited by Jeffrey J. Crow et al., 216–59. Baton Rouge: Louisiana State University Press, 1989.

Cyphers, Christopher J. *The National Civic Federation and the Making of a New Liberalism, 1900–1915*. New York: Praeger, 2002.

Dailey, Jane. *Before Jim Crow: The Politics of Race in Postemancipation Virginia*. Chapel Hill: University of North Carolina Press, 2000.

———. "Deference and Violence in the Postbellum Urban South: Manners and Massacres in Danville, Virginia." *Journal of Southern History* 63, no. 3 (August 1997): 553–90.

Daniel, Pete. *Breaking the Land: The Transformation of Cotton, Tobacco and Rice Cultures since 1880*. Urbana: University of Illinois Press, 1986.

———. "The Crossroads of Change: Cotton, Tobacco, and Rice Cultures in the Twentieth-Century South." *Journal of Southern History* 50, no. 3 (August 1984): 429–56.

Daniels, Josephus C. *Editor in Politics*. Chapel Hill: University of North Carolina Press, 1941.

———. *Tar Heel Editor*. Chapel Hill: University of North Carolina Press, 1939.

Dean, Pamela. "Learning to Be New Women: Campus Culture at the North Carolina Normal and Industrial College." *North Carolina Historical Review* 68, no. 3 (July 1991): 292–94.

Delfino, Susanna, and Michele Gillespie, eds. *Technology, Innovation, and Southern Industrialization*. New Directions in the History of Southern Economy and Society 2. Columbia: University of Missouri Press, 2008.

Dowdy, Clara M. "The Development of the Social Welfare Movement in Winston-Salem, N.C." MA thesis, College of William and Mary, 1939.

Doyle, Don. *New Men, New Cities, New South: Atlanta, Nashville, Charleston, Mobile, 1860–1910*. Chapel Hill: University of North Carolina Press, 1990.

Durden, Robert Franklin. *Bold Entrepreneur: A Life of James B. Duke*. Durham, N.C.: Carolina Academic Press, 2003.

———. *The Dukes of Durham, 1865–1929*. Durham, N.C.: Duke University Press, 1975.

Eelman, Bruce W. *Entrepreneurs in the Southern Upcountry: Commercial Culture in Spartanburg, South Carolina, 1845–1880*. Athens: University of Georgia Press, 2008.

Eschbach, Elizabeth Seymour. *The Higher Education of Women in England and America, 1865–1920*. New York: Garland, 1993.

Escott, Paul D. *Many Excellent People: Power and Privilege in North Carolina, 1850–1900*. Chapel Hill: University of North Carolina Press, 1985.

Feimster, Crystal Nicole. *Southern Horrors: Women and the Politics of Race and Lynching*. Cambridge, Mass.: Harvard University Press, 2009.

Fogel, Robert William, and Stanley L. Engerman. *Time on the Cross: The Economics of American Slavery*. New York: Little Brown, 1974.

Ford, Lacy. "Reconfiguring the Old South: 'Solving' the Slavery Problem, 1787–1838." *Journal of American History* 95 (June 2008): 95–122.

Fraser, Steve. *Every Man a Speculator: A History of Wall Street in American Life*. New York: Harper Collins, 2005.

Friend, Craig Thompson, and Lorri Glover, eds. *Southern Manhood: Perspectives on Masculinity in the Old South*. Athens: University of Georgia Press, 2004.

Fries, Adelaide, et al. *Forsyth: A County on the March*. Chapel Hill: University of North Carolina Press, 1949.

Gaston, Paul M. *The New South Creed: A Study in Southern Mythmaking*. Baton Rouge: Louisiana State University Press, 1976.
Gately, Iain. *Tobacco: A Cultural History of How an Exotic Plant Seduced Civilization*. New York: Grove Press, 2001.
Gillespie, Michele. *Free Labor in an Unfree World: White Artisans in Slaveholding Georgia, 1790–1860*. Athens: University of Georgia Press, 2000.
Gillespie, Michele, and Robert Beachy, eds. *Pious Pursuits: German Moravians in the Atlantic World*. New York: Berghahn Books, 2007.
Gillespie, Michele K., and Randal L. Hall, eds. *Thomas Dixon Jr. and the Birth of Modern America*. Baton Rouge: Louisiana State University Press, 2006.
Gilmore, Glenda. *Gender and Jim Crow: Women and the Politics of White Supremacy in North Carolina, 1896–1920*. Chapel Hill: University of North Carolina, 1996.
Gordon, Lynn D. *Gender and Higher Education in the Progressive Era*. New Haven, Conn.: Yale University Press, 1990.
Grantham, Dewey. *Southern Progressivism: The Reconciliation of Progress and Tradition*. Knoxville: University of Tennessee Press, 1981.
Graves, Karen. *Girls' Schooling during the Progressive Era: From Female Scholar to Domesticated Citizen*. New York: Garland, 1998.
Green, Jennifer R. *Military Education and the Emerging Middle Class in the Old South*. Cambridge: Cambridge University Press, 2008.
Haislip, Bryan. *A History of the Z. Smith Reynolds Foundation*. Winston-Salem: John F. Blair, 1967.
Haley, John H. *Charles N. Hunter and Race Relations in North Carolina*. Chapel Hill: University of North Carolina Press, 1987.
Hall, Kermit L., ed. *The Oxford Companion to the Supreme Court of the United States*. New York: Oxford University Press, 1992.
Hall, Randall. *Mountains on the Market: Industry, the Environment, and the South*. Lexington: University Press of Kentucky, 2012.
Hall, Randal L., and Ken Badgett. "Robinson Newcomb and the Limits of Liberalism at UNC: Two Case Studies of Black Businessmen in the 1920s South." *North Carolina Historical Review* 86, no. 4 (October 2009): 373–403.
Halttunen, Karen. *Confidence Men, Painted Women: A Study of Middle-Class Culture in America, 1830–1870*. New Haven, Conn.: Yale University Press, 1982.
Hamermesh, Daniel S., and Jeff E. Biddle. "Beauty and the Labor Market." *American Economic Review* 84, no. 5 (December 1994): 1174–94.
Harris, Kelly. "Tabitha Anne Holton: First in North Carolina, First in the South." Research paper, Women's Legal History, Stanford University, 2002.
Hay, Melba Porter. *Madeline McDowell Breckinridge and the Battle for a New South*. Lexington: University Press of Kentucky, 2009.
Hersche, Joni, and Leslie Stratton. "Household Specialization and the Male Marital Wage Premium." *Industrial and Labor Relations Review* 54, no. 1 (October 2000): 78–94.
Hochfelder, David. "'Where the Common People Could Speculate': The Ticker, Bucket Shops, and the Origins of Popular Participation in Financial Markets, 1880–1920." *Journal of American History* 93, no. 2 (September 2006): 335–58.
Hollingsworth, J. G. *History of Surry County or Annals of Northwest Carolina*. N.p., 1935.

Howett, Catherine M. *A World of Her Own Making: Katharine Smith Reynolds and the Landscape of Reynolda*. Amherst: University of Massachusetts Press, 2007.
Hunter, Jane H. *How Young Ladies Became Girls: The Victorian Origins of American Girlhood*. New Haven, Conn.: Yale University Press, 2002.
Huston, James L. *Securing the Fruits of Their Labor: The American Concept of Wealth Distribution, 1765–1900*. Baton Rouge: Louisiana State University Press, 1998.
Iannarelli, Cindy. "Cognitive Development in Children of Business Owners: An Entrepreneurial Learning Model." Bernelli research project. 2009.
———. "Family Business Essentials: Helping Kids Make Sense of Growing Up in a Family Business." Paper presented at the Wake Forest University Family Business Center, Winston-Salem, N.C., February 19–20, 2008.
Jackson, Hester Bartlett, ed. *Surry County Soldiers in the Civil War*. Charlotte, N.C.: Delmar Printing, 1992.
Johnson, Guion Griffis. "Southern Paternalism toward Negroes after Emancipation." *Journal of Southern History* 23, no. 4 (November 1957): 483–509.
Johnson, Walter. *Soul by Soul: Life inside the Antebellum Slave Market*. Cambridge, Mass.: Harvard University Press, 1999.
Justus, James H. *Fetching the Old Southwest: Humorous Writing from Longstreet to Twain*. Columbia: University of Missouri Press, 2004.
Kemp, Kathryn W. *God's Capitalist: Asa Candler of Coca Cola*. Macon, Ga.: Mercer University Press, 2002.
Kirby, Jack Temple. "Clarence Poe's Vision of a Segregated 'Great Rural Civilization.'" *South Atlantic Quarterly* 68 (1969): 27–38.
Kirkland, Kate Sayen. "Envisioning a Progressive City: Hogg Family Philanthropy and the Urban Ideal in Houston, Texas, 1910–1975." PhD diss., Rice University, 2004.
Kluger, Richard. *Ashes to Ashes: America's One-Hundred-Year Cigarette War, the Public Health, and the Unabashed Triumph of Philip Morris*. New York: Knopf, 1996.
Kolko, Gabriel. "Max Weber on America: Theory and Evidence." *History and Theory* 1, no. 3 (1961): 243–60.
Korstad, Robert. *Civil Rights Unionism: Tobacco Workers and the Struggle for Democracy in the Mid-Twentieth-Century South*. Chapel Hill: University of North Carolina, 2004.
Kousser, J. Morgan. "Progressivism—For Middle-Class Whites Only: North Carolina Education, 1880–1910." *Journal of Southern History* 46, no. 2 (May 1980): 169–94.
Kulikoff, Allan. "The Transition to Capitalism in Rural America." *William and Mary Quarterly*, 3rd ser., 46, no. 1 (January 1989): 120–44.
Lach, Edward L., Jr. "Richard Joshua Reynolds, Sr." In *American National Biography*, edited by John A. Garraty and Mark C. Carnes, vol. 18, 384–85. New York: Oxford University Press, 1999.
Laird, Pamela Walker. *Pull: Social Networking and Success since Benjamin Franklin*. Cambridge, Mass.: Harvard University Press, 2006.
Lambeth, Tom. Speech on Reynolds family philanthropy given at the Winston-Salem Rotary Club Meeting, Winston-Salem, N.C., July 10, 2007.
Lane, Jonathan. "The Period House in the Nineteen-Twenties." *Journal of the Society of Architectural Historians* 20, no. 4 (December 1961): 169–78.
Lathrop, Virginia Terrell. *Educate a Woman: Fifty Years of Life at the Woman's College of the University of North Carolina*. Chapel Hill: University of North Carolina Press, 1942.

Leloudis, James L. *Schooling the New South: Pedagogy, Self, and Society in North Carolina, 1880–1920*. Chapel Hill: University of North Carolina Press, 1996.
Lichtenstein, Alex. *Twice the Work of Free Labor: The Political Economy of Convict Labor in the New South*. New York: Verso, 1996.
Light, Alison. *Mrs. Woolf and the Servants: An Intimate History of Domestic Life in Bloomsbury*. London: Bloomsbury Press, 2009.
Link, William A. *A Hard Country and a Lonely Place: Schooling, Society and Reform in Rural Virginia, 1870–1920*. Chapel Hill: University of North Carolina Press, 1986.
———. *Roots of Secession: Slavery and Politics in Antebellum Virginia*. Chapel Hill: University of North Carolina Press, 2003.
Logan, Frenise Avedis. *The Negro in North Carolina, 1876–1894*. Chapel Hill: University of North Carolina Press, 1964.
Lumpkin, Katharine Du Pre. *The Making of a Southerner*. 1946. Reprint, Athens: University of Georgia Press, 1992.
Lundeen, Elizabeth Ann. "Accommodation Strategies of African American Educational Leaders in North Carolina, 1890–1930." MA thesis, University of Cambridge, June 2008.
Majewski, John. *A House Dividing: Economic Development in Pennsylvania and Virginia before the Civil War*. Cambridge: Cambridge University Press, 2000.
———. *Modernizing a Slave Economy: The Economic Vision of the Confederate Nation*. Chapel Hill: University of North Carolina Press, 2009.
Marx, Leo. *The Machine in the Garden: Technology and the Pastoral Ideal in America*. New York: Oxford University Press, 1964.
Mayer, Barbara. *Reynolda: The Creation of an American Country House and Its Survival into the Present*. Winston-Salem, N.C.: John F. Blair, 1997.
McCandless, Amy Thompson. *The Past in the Present: Women's Higher Education in the Twentieth-Century American South*. Tuscaloosa: University of Alabama Press, 1999.
———. "Progressivism and the Higher Education of Southern Women." *North Carolina Historical Review* 70, no. 3 (July 1993): 302–25.
McGrath, Rita Hunter, and Ian McMillan. *The Entrepreneurial Mindset: Strategies for Continually Creating Opportunity in an Age of Uncertainty*. Cambridge, Mass.: Harvard University Press, 2000.
McQuilkin, Steve, Susan White, and Frank Tursi. *Lost Empire: The Fall of R. J. Reynolds Tobacco Company*. Winston-Salem, N.C.: Winston-Salem Journal, 2000.
Melton, Herman. *"Thirty-Nine Lashes—Well Laid On:" Crime and Punishment in Southside Virginia, 1750–1950*. N.p., 2002.
———. *Pittsylvania County's Historic Courthouse: The Story Behind Ex part Virginia and the Making of a National Landmark*. Amherst, Va.: Central Virginia Publishing, 1999.
Miller, Bertha Hampton. "Blacks in Winston-Salem, North Carolina 1895–1920: Community Development in an Era of Benevolent Paternalism." PhD diss., Duke University, 1981.
Millhouse, Barbara. *Reynolda: 1906–1924*. Charleston, S.C.: Arcadia Press, 2011.
Morgan, Francesca. *Women and Patriotism in Jim Crow America*. Chapel Hill: University of North Carolina Press, 2005.
Morgan, Lynda J. *Emancipation in Virginia's Tobacco Belt, 1850–1870*. Athens: University of Georgia Press, 1992.

Mullen, Ruth. *The Paris Gowns in the Reynolda House Costume Collection.* Winston-Salem, N.C.: Reynolda House, Museum of American Art, 1995.
Neff, John. R. *Honoring the Civil War Dead: Commemoration and the Problem of Reconciliation.* Lawrence: University Press of Kansas, 2005.
"The Negro and Reynolda: A Pictorial Survey of the Negroes, Their Community Activity and Their Daily Work on the Reynolda Estate covering One Quarter Century; Presented to Mr. and Mrs. Charlie H. Babcock in Appreciation of Their Extensive Good Will throughout Our Community." 1940. Copy in archives, RHMAA.
Newbold, N. C. *Five North Carolina Educators.* Chapel Hill: University of North Carolina Press, 1939.
Noe, Kenneth W. *Southwest Virginia's Railroad: Modernization and the Sectional Crisis.* Urbana: University of Illinois Press, 1994.
Oakes, James. *Ruling Race: A History of American Slaveholders.* New York: Knopf, 1982.
———. *Slavery and Freedom: An Interpretation of the Old South.* New York: Knopf, 1990.
O'Leary, Elizabeth. *From Morning to Night: Domestic Service at Maymont and the Gilded-Age South.* Charlottesville: University Press of Virginia, 2003.
Page, Walter Hines. "The Forgotten Man." In *The Rebuilding of Old Commonwealths: Being Essays toward the Training of the Forgotten Man in the Southern States,* 20:1–47. New York: Doubleday, 1902.
Parke, Julia C. "Gordon Gray: A Public Servant in Historic Preservation." MA thesis, Wake Forest University, 1991.
Perry, Thomas David. *The Free State of Patrick: Patrick County, Virginia, in the Civil War.* Ararat, Va.: Laurel Hill, 2005.
Porter, Douglas, Jr. "'Defying the Destructives': Confederate Disaffection and Disloyalty in North Carolina's Northwestern Foothills, 1861–1865." PhD diss., North Carolina State University, 2007.
Reines, Phillip. "A Cultural History of the City of Winston-Salem, North Carolina: 1766–1966." PhD, University of Denver, 1970.
Robert, Joseph C. *The Story of Tobacco in America.* New York: Alfred A. Knopf, 1952.
———. "The Tobacco Industry in Ante-Bellum North Carolina." *North Carolina Historical Review* 15, no. 2 (April 1938): 128–29.
———. *The Tobacco Kingdom: Plantation, Market, and Factory in Virginia and North Carolina, 1800–1860.* Durham, N.C.: Duke University Press, 1938.
Roberts, B. W. C., and Richard E. Knapp. "Paving the Way for the Tobacco Trust: From Hand Rolling to Mechanized Cigarette Production by W. Duke, Sons and Company." *North Carolina Historical Review* 69, no. 3 (July 1992): 256–81.
Robertson, Nancy Marie. *Christian Sisterhood, Race Relations, and the YWCA, 1906–1946.* Urbana: University of Illinois Press, 2007.
Sallee, Shelley. *The Whiteness of Child Labor Reform in the New South.* Athens: University of Georgia Press, 2004.
Schaffer, Samuel L. "An Industrious Generation: The Watauga Club and Industrial Education, 1884–1913." Paper presented at the Southern Industrialization Project Conference, Kennesaw State University, June 14, 2008.

Schnakenberg, Heidi. *Kid Carolina: R. J. Reynolds Jr., a Tobacco Fortune, and the Mysterious Death of a Southern Icon*. New York: Center Street, 2010.
Schweiger, Beth. "Max Weber in Mt. Airy, or, Revivals and Social Theory in the Early South." In *Religion in the American South: Protestants and Others in History and Culture*, edited by Beth Schweiger and Donald Matthews, 31–66. Chapel Hill: University of North Carolina Press, 2004.
Sehat, David. "The Civilizing Mission of Booker T. Washington." *Journal of Southern History* 73, no. 2 (May 2007): 322–62.
Shanks, Henry T. *The Secession Movement in Virginia*. Richmond, Va.: Garrett and Massie, 1934.
Sharpless, Rebecca. *Cooking in Other Women's Kitchens: Domestic Workers in the South, 1865–1960*. Chapel Hill: University of North Carolina Press, 2010.
Shirley, Michael. *From Congregation Town to Industrial City: Culture and Social Change in a Southern Community*. New York: New York University Press, 1994.
Shulman, Shmuel. *Fathers and Adolescents: Developmental and Clinical Perspectives*. New York: Routledge, 1997.
Siegel, Frederick F. *The Roots of Southern Distinctiveness: Tobacco and Society in Danville, Virginia, 1780–1865*. Chapel Hill: University of North Carolina Press, 1987.
Sims, Anastatia. *The Power of Femininity in the New South: Women's Organizations and Politics in the New South, 1880–1930*. Columbia: University of South Carolina Press, 1997.
Singal, Daniel Joseph. "Towards a Definition of American Modernism." In "Modernist Culture in America," special issue, *American Quarterly* 39, no. 1 (Spring 1987): 7–26.
Smith, Margaret Supplee. "Reynolda: A Rural Vision in an Industrializing South." *North Carolina Historical Review* 65 (July 1988): 287–313.
Somerville, Diane. *Rape and Race in the Nineteenth-Century American South*. Chapel Hill: University of North Carolina Press, 2003.
Southard, Nancy H. "History of a Pioneering Agency, Family Services, Inc., Winston-Salem, N.C." MA thesis, Wake Forest University, 1984.
Sparger, Alma Mitchell. "Memoirs of Alma Mitchell Sparger." June 1982. Typescript. Mount Airy Public Library, Mount Airy, N.C.
Stevenson, George James. *Increase in Excellence: A History of Emory and Henry College*. New York: Appleton-Century-Crofts, 1963.
Strouse, Jean. *Morgan: American Financier*. New York: HarperCollins, 2000.
Swanson, Drew. "Land of the Bright Leaf: Yellow Tobacco, Environment, and Culture along the Border of Virginia and North Carolina." PhD diss., University of Georgia, 2010.
Tilley, Nannie M. "Agitation against the American Tobacco Company." *North Carolina Historical Review* 24 (1947): 207–23.
———. *The Bright Tobacco Industry, 1860–1929*. Chapel Hill: University of North Carolina Press, 1948.
———. *Reynolds Homestead, 1814–1970*. Introduction by Nancy Susan Reynolds. Richmond, Va.: Robert Kline, 1970.
———. "Richard Joshua Reynolds." In *Dictionary of North Carolina Biography*, edited by William S. Powell, 203–4. Chapel Hill: University of North Carolina Press, 1994.

———. *The R. J. Reynolds Tobacco Company*. Chapel Hill: University of North Carolina Press, 1985.

Tise, Larry Edward. *Government*. Winston-Salem in History 6. Winston-Salem, N.C.: Historic Winston, 1976.

Tone, Andrea. *The Business of Benevolence: Industrial Paternalism in Progressive America*. Ithaca, N.Y.: Cornell University Press, 1997.

Torain, Tammy Regina. "The Development of the Liberty-Patterson Community in Winston-Salem, North Carolina, 1900–1950." MA thesis, Wake Forest University, 1994.

Trelease, Allen W. *Making North Carolina Literate: The University of North Carolina at Greensboro, from Normal School to Metropolitan University*. Durham, N.C.: Carolina Academic Press, 2003.

Tripp, Stephen Elliott. *Yankee Town, Southern Town: Race and Class Relations in Civil War Lynchburg*. New York: New York University Press, 1997.

Trouillot, Michel-Rolph. *Silencing the Past: Power and the Production of History*. Boston: Beacon Press, 1995.

Tursi, Frank. *Winston-Salem: A History*. Winston-Salem, N.C.: John F. Blair, 1994.

Weidensaul, Scott. *Of a Feather: A Brief History of American Birding*. New York: Houghton Mifflin Harcourt, 2007.

Wellman, Manly Wade. *Transportation and Communication*. Vol. 4 of *Winston-Salem in History*. Winston-Salem, N.C.: Historic Winston, 1976.

Wellman, Manly Wade, and Larry Edward Tise. *A City's Culture: Painting, Music and Literature*. Vol. 5 of *Winston-Salem in History*. Winston-Salem, N.C.: Historic Winston, 1976.

———. *Education*. Vol. 3 of *Winston-Salem in History*. Winston-Salem, N.C.: Historic Winston, 1976.

———. *Industry and Commerce, 1766–1896*. Vol. 7 of *Winston-Salem in History*, Winston-Salem, N.C.: Historic Winston-Salem, 1976.

Wells, Jonathan Daniel. *The Origins of the Southern Middle Class, 1800–1861*. Chapel Hill: University of North Carolina Press, 2004.

Wiley, Mary Callum, and William E. East. *The Book of Remembrance, 1862–1962: First Presbyterian Church of Winston-Salem, North Carolina*. Winston-Salem, N.C.: Carmichael Printing, 1962.

Wilkerson-Freeman, Sarah. "From Clubs to Parties: North Carolina Women in the Advancement of the New Deal." *North Carolina Historical Review* 68, no. 3 (July 1991): 320–39.

———. "Stealth in the Political Arsenal of Southern Women: A Retrospective for the Millennium." In *Southern Women at the Millennium: A Historical Perspective*, edited by Melissa Walker, Jeannette R. Dunn, and Joe R. Dunn, 42–82. Columbia: University of Missouri Press, 2003.

Wilson, Emily Herring. *For the People of North Carolina: The Z. Smith Reynolds Foundation at Half-Century, 1936–1986*. Chapel Hill: University of North Carolina Press, 1988.

Woltz, H. O., Sr. "Never a Dull Moment: Memoirs of H. O. Woltz, Sr." Photocopy. Surry County Public Library, Mount Airy, N.C.

Woodward, C. Vann. *Origins of the New South, 1877–1913*. Vol. 9, *A History of the South*. Edited by E. Merton Coulter. Baton Rouge: Louisiana State University Press, 1951.

Wright, Annette C. "'The Grown-Up Daughter': The Case of North Carolina's Cornelia Phillips Spencer." *North Carolina Historical Review* 64, no. 3 (July 1997): 260–83.
Young, Elizabeth. *A Study of the Curricula of Seven Selected Women's Colleges of the Southern States*. New York: Teachers' College, Columbia University, 1932.
Zunz, Oliver. *Making America Corporate: 1870–1920*. Chicago: University of Chicago Press, 1992.

Index